Always an Updraft

MUNROE SCOTT

ALWAYS AN UPDRAFT

a writer remembers

Maybe some younger dreamers out there will read and take heart.
Throw off the yoke of corporate drudgery and strike out
into the creative unknown.

PENUMBRA PRESS

PENUMBRA
PRESS

ARCHIVES
of
CANADIAN ARTS
CULTURE & HERITAGE
www.penumbrapress.com

Copyright © Munroe Scott, 2005
Published by PENUMBRA PRESS.
Printed and bound in Canada.
Edited for Penumbra Press by Douglas Campbell.
Cover and page design by Mag Carson.

LIBRARY AND ARCHIVES CANADA CATALOGUING IN PUBLICATION

Scott, Munroe, 1927-
        Always an updraft : a writer remembers / Munroe Scott.
ISBN 1-894131-71-1
        1. Scott, Munroe, 1927-. 2. Authors, Canadian (English)--
20th century--Biography. 3. Television producers and directors--
Canada--Biography. I. Title.
PS8587.C634Z463 2005   C818'.5409   C2005-900713-3

Canada

Penumbra Press gratefully acknowledges the financial support of the
Government of Canada through the Book Publishing Industry Development
Program (BPIDP) for our publishing activities. We also acknowledge the
Government of Ontario through the Ontario Media Development
Corporation's Ontario Book Initiative

To my lassie from Lancashire, gone but never absent,
and our three sons, all of whose love, forbearance,
and co-operation made this story possible.

For Michael, Kendra, Caitlin, Ryland, and Donald.

CONTENTS

1   A Briefing / 13

2   The Background of a P.K. / 17

3   The Doctor's Horses / 23

4   The Teens / 26

5   Burning the Christmas Cross / 37

6   Water and Wilderness / 45

7   Choices / 61

8   Getting into Movies / 65

9   Crawley Films Limited / 74

10   Going Freelance / 85

11   Africa / 91

12   Holland, Ireland, and a Literary Man / 106

13   The Strange World of Rankin Inlet / 118

14   On the Rim of Tomorrow / 129

15   The Military Mind / 146

16   *Inquiry* / 151

17   From James Bond to Bell Island / 164

18   The Second Coming of Jacques Cartier / 173

19   Great Slave Lake Reflections / 184

20   Drama at the CBC / 190

21   Centennial Year / 205

22   *The Tenth Decade* / 217

23   The Resurrection of Governor Wu / 228

24   Making Up Diefenbaker / 254

25   Visions / 263

26   Hail and Farewell / 267

27   McClure in China / 270

28   Shylock / 278

29   Global Glimpses Along the McClure Trail / 285

30   The Third Coming of the Devil / 305

31   Do-It-Yourself / 309

32   Sound-and-Light / 315

33   Cavalier Treatment / 320

34   The Age of Aquarius / 334

35   The Final Decade: Part One / 341

36   The Final Decade: Part Two / 353

37   Into Exile / 358

38   Epilogue / 363

ACKNOWLEDGEMENTS

I BLAME MY SONS for encouraging me to tackle this project in the first place. "Dad, write it down," became a refrain that finally seduced me.

Several patient people read some or all of the manuscript at various stages and gave me the benefit of suggestions and, very important, encouragement. They are (alphabetically) Sheila Entwistle, Doris Etherington, Dr. Rae Fleming, Professor Orm Mitchell, Edward Smith, Ivy Szobonya, Professor John Wadland, and Professor (Emeritus) Vincent Vaitiekunas. I occasionally communicated with former associates in order to jog my memory and have relied more on memory than the paper trail. (They will know who they are and, indeed, will find themselves within these pages.) It is time I offered a heart felt thank-you to my computer guru, Ev Brooks, who for several years has helped me over the hurdles created by unruly bits and bytes. I appreciate the willingness of Penumbra Press to venture with me once again, and am impressed by designer Mag Carson's creative input. I owe a special debt of gratitude to my editor, Douglas Campbell, for his insight, tolerance, and unfailing good humour.

Munroe Scott
Peterborough, Ontario
November 2004

1

A BRIEFING

I FEEL LIKE A TOUR GUIDE who is preparing travellers for the journey ahead, not to build up their anticipation or to dampen their enthusiasm, but simply to give them some sense of their mode of travel and the terrain they'll be traversing.

These are my recollections of some of the people, places, and events I have encountered during the course of a generously long life. And because memory is an ever-present companion, I have chosen present tense narrative as our mode of travel. The fact that my career has been that of a freelance writer merely gives a rather unpredictable structure to much of the terrain travelled. Some is geographical, ranging from Canada's sub-Arctic to Africa, the Caribbean, Europe, Asia, and even southern Ontario. Other ground trod has been less physical; it includes the bizarre worlds of documentary film, television drama, television public affairs, stage drama, literature, and, alas, newspaper journalism.

But where does the journey begin? I cannot ignore family, parents, or even ancestors. Memory is ancestral. It reaches back beyond birth. Parental memories are handed down and absorbed, and become part of who we are. Family attitudes, too, shape our attitudes. Perhaps I can illustrate. Regress with me for a moment.

I'm just a youngster. It's a summer night at Stoney Lake, in central Ontario's cottage country, and an enormous thunderstorm is underway. Mother calls from the living room to my brothers and me.

"You must be awake. Come and join us."

Mother and Dad have the window drapes open and are sitting watching the spectacle. The thunder alone is awesome. It comes in great rolling waves, interspersed with nearby explosions that shake the cottage and assault the eardrums. The lightning is almost constant, and turbulent white-crested waves hurl themselves against the Precambrian rock of tree-studded islands that flicker in and out of ragged silhouette. The scene and the noise are apocalyptic. Armageddon is on tour.

"Come and sit with us," says Mother, calmly. "We wouldn't want you to miss anything so beautiful."

That moment, etched in memory, must surely have conditioned my reaction, years later, to a spectacularly turbulent night on the waters of Great Slave Lake in Canada's Northwest Territories, where I will, eventually, take you.

I don't intend to analyse further, except to say that life is an accumulation of experiences, and that each of them, however seemingly isolated, must play a part in shaping us. This means, paradoxically, that we are never fully formed. Each of us, no matter how old, is a work in progress. For that reason I will let this narrative flow more or less chronologically. I say "more or less" because the actual chaos of a freelance life must yield to the structural requirements of the writer's craft. Whether you as reader wish to grow with the flow or dip in at random is your choice.

You will recognize some of the people we encounter, such as John George Diefenbaker, mischievous former prime minister of Canada, and Ian Fleming, who turned a birdwatcher into Agent 007, and Dr. Robert McClure, who, according to Patrick Watson, was "the last of the Christians." You have probably never heard of Senhor Paulino Ngonga Liahuca, Angolan witchdoctor's apprentice turned pastor, or of Dr. Kin Ho Wang, who fought black foot disease with a bone saw in Taiwan, but they too inhabit real terrain in memory.

There are others who are vivid in memory but whose names elude me. One such is a lobsterman. I recall sitting beside him on a grassy hillside overlooking Northumberland Strait on the west side of Nova Scotia's beautiful Cape Breton Island.

It is late spring. The little port of Pleasant Bay is spread out before and below us. Far offshore, near the horizon but clearly visible, lies an icefield.

I am intrigued by the gentle inflection of my companion's Cape Breton accent. The word "ice" comes out as *oice*, somehow softer, less brittle. But that is misleading. At this time of year, in the lobster season, the presence of *oice* is a most menacing phenomenon. The *oice* appears to be receding, but a few days ago it came close inshore and cleaned out an entire season's set of lobster traps. The men are now repairing old traps and buying and building more, but for the time being they hesitate to put them out. If they do not, they will be financially ruined. If they do, and the *oice* returns, they will be even further in debt. These are the days before adequate social safety nets.

I ask my companion what he thinks of it all.

"Oh," comes the answer, quietly, softly, "we been burned out, flooded out, blowed out — now we be oiced out. We be all right."

His kind are worth recalling.

I don't have the same warm recollection of a certain bush pilot who tried to give me a heart attack. The scene is as clear now in memory as it was starkly vivid then.

I have been to Bella Bella on the coast of British Columbia and am flying inland across the Coastal Range of the Rocky Mountains. I'm up front with the pilot. The plane, a small float-equipped Cessna, is heading directly at the upper face of a great, bald mountain. The pilot appears to be unconcerned. I estimate the top of the approaching rock wall to be at least a hundred feet higher than we're now flying.

"What's our ceiling?" I ask, desperately trying to sound merely curious.

"We're at it," the pilot says, nonchalantly, as he glances away to one side, apparently intrigued by the view.

The Cessna is not a fast plane, but even so that towering rock impediment is approaching at a remarkable speed. I tell myself to have faith in the pilot. This is not a car, where I'm probably as adequate a driver as the next guy and might seize control. I decide the pilot is having me on and will peel away at the last minute. He does not.

Just before we fly into oblivion, a miracle happens. The pilot has not moved the stick or flexed a foot, but the little plane rises as though on a hoist and soars over the top of old baldy. I could lean out and strike a match on the bare rock.

The pilot chuckles. "There's always an updraft."

"Always?"

"So far."

Yeah. Well, maybe. But in a way my own life has been like that. Relying on the updraft. Often I have been absolutely broke — flat, with no way to pay the mortgage — waiting for the phone to ring, for a producer to offer a film assignment, or a director to say he likes a play, or a publisher to accept a manuscript. The phone has been my updraft.

And let's be honest. I'm not writing this, nor are you reading it, because either of us has any illusions about my being some icon of Can-Lit, or CanFilm, or any of the other Cans. I'm just a survivor. But I must admit it's been a good life. Happy, challenging, fulfilling. Sweetheart of a wife — pretty, supportive, loving, gentle, tough as nails. Great sons. Good friends. Travel. I've seldom regretted being freelance, and I recommend it, not so much as a way of making a living, but as a state of being. Maybe some younger dreamers out there will read and take heart. Throw off the yoke of corporate drudgery and strike out into the creative unknown. Of course, the unknown they will face is not the same as the one that faced me. So rapid is the pace of change that my account should be taken for what it is, not a guide book for the present but personal recollections of a bygone era.

If you're still with me, let's go journeying.

2

THE BACKGROUND
OF A P.K.

I AM ONE OF THAT FORTUNATE BREED who grew up as a "P.K."
— a preacher's kid. I say "fortunate," although during childhood and
youth it often felt almost like a curse, or at least a heavy responsibility.
The world is littered with P.K.s, and when we identify each other we
often bond, with a puzzling mixture of sympathy and high expectations.
There are sub-classifications of the species, and I fit into two: "son of the
manse" and "grandson of the parsonage."

I am not sure when Dad first got the call to the ministry. It hit him
sometime during his teens, when he was homesteading in
Saskatchewan, but I guess the seeds were planted when he was a kid, in
Beaverton, Ontario.

Beaverton was a dour sort of place. Very Presbyterian and Scottish in
those days. The earliest residents even built their homes out of faded
yellow brick, instead of the red clay that gives a town a look of flushed
cheerfulness. The Presbyterians had built a church, the "Auld Kirk," on
the edge of the village way back in the 1840s. Dad tells of going to services as a lad and sitting through an hour-long sermon in English, followed by another in Gaelic. I suspect the Gaelic session gave him lots of
time for introspection.

My Grandfather Scott was a jack of all trades and probably a master
of none. He had tried farming, as his father had done before him. Dad
talks very little about Grandfather. It is only in later years I discover he was
once the sheriff in Beaverton. According to records, a prisoner escaped
one day and, following some primordial urge, sought refuge up a tele-
graph pole. Sheriff Scott went into the general store and returned with a
dozen eggs, which he proceeded to hurl at the fugitive. Since Grandpa
was a large man, not tall but massive, weighing well over 200 pounds and
with hands like dinner plates, those eggs were the forerunners of rubber

bullets. They also greased the pole. The fugitive slid down into the arms of the law. A humane man, the sheriff.

He was also a convivial man, or so I conjecture. The only evidence I have for this comes one day, unannounced, from Mother, another P.K. We are washing the dishes together, as usual, and talking family, as usual, when she suddenly says, "Don't let anybody tell you your grandfather was an alcoholic."

Nobody has told me that, but I let her continue.

"He was just too sociable. He couldn't get his pay packet without taking friends to the beer parlour."

I gather that this "sociableness" also afflicted Dad's eldest brother, and I begin to get a glimmering of why Dad is a teetotal temperance man.

But if Grandpa helped direct Dad to teetotalism it was my two great-grandmothers who immersed him in the Faith.

Dad's paternal grandmother had come to Canada from southern Ireland as a young woman along with her father and several brothers. Two brothers died on the ship. She married in Canada but her husband soon died as well. Then she married Horatio Nelson Scott, my great-grandfather. He too had come from southern Ireland — in 1832, at the age of 26 — and had been married, and his first wife had also died. In those days, Death was a member of the family. One of Horatio's second family was a son, Alfred William.

Dad's maternal grandmother had arrived in Canada already married, with two children, and pregnant. Her husband died almost on arrival, and she raised her three children by means of much perseverance and hard work. A pioneer single mother. A daughter, Elizabeth Anne, grew up to marry Horatio's son, Alfred William, and she became Dad's mother. Horatio died in 1871, so Dad never knew either of his grandfathers, which I suppose was one good reason for not talking about them at all. But right from the start he had those widowed grandmothers on hand.

The two grandmothers, their faith apparently unshaken by the traumas of life, participated vigorously in the religious upbringing of their grandchildren, one with love and the other with rules.

Dad's Grandma Scott lived in a small house in Beaverton, and he and his three older brothers took turns staying with her. Dad claims she knew the whole Bible by heart and could quote from any part of it. She attempted to pass her knowledge on to her grandsons, subjecting them to rigorous catechizing. Even so, Dad remembers her for her "loving heart," and feels sorry his own inadequate memory caused her pain.

His Grandma Cooper, that pioneer single mother, was something else. She lived with her daughter's family much of the time, and, according to Dad, made Sundays something of a nightmare. All chores had to be completed by Saturday night, and on Sunday the kids had to go to Sunday school, and then to church, twice. The occasional sermon in Gaelic was simply one affliction on top of all the others. Sunday play was restricted to their own yard, and anything as frivolous as whistling was strictly forbidden. Singing was permitted, but it had to be a psalm, or at least a paraphrase of a psalm. Years later I ask Mother why my Grandfather and Grandmother Scott are buried in the Cooper plot at the Auld Kirk instead of in the Scott plot with Horatio and his wife, Margaret Louisa. "It was the old lady," says Mother. "She drew them into the grave after her."

I begin to wonder whether the old lady's son-in-law, the sheriff, might not have had good reason for his beer parlour sociability. As for Dad, at the age of fifteen he took off for Saskatchewan with the proverbial twenty-five cents in his pocket. He found work in a general outfitting store and was promoted rapidly from sales clerk to bookkeeper, and then to manager. But eventually he took up a quarter section of land as a homesteader.

I like listening to Dad's stories of homesteading near Dunblane, Saskatchewan — how he built his first sod hut and how he learned to bake bread. He says the first loaves were so heavy he used them to tether his horse. He broke land with a plough pulled by oxen, and tried to ride a Brahma bull. He eventually broke a wild bronco to the saddle so that he could use it when, still a teenager, he rode a multi-mile Sunday circuit as a saddlebag preacher for the Presbyterian Church. His first sermon, he says, was delivered in a settler's house to a congregation of assorted immigrants from Ontario, the United Kingdom, and central Europe. The homily lasted a full five minutes. Afterwards an elder came up to him and said, "Well, young man, I'll say this for you. You know when you're done." It was a compliment more preachers should attempt to earn.

My youthful imagination blends Dad's stories of homesteading into an ongoing saga of farming, horseback riding, hunting, preaching, escaping prairie fires, driving wagons across flooded fords on the South Saskatchewan River, and other adventures. It is not until he puts it into writing, in his eighties, that I'm able to work out the progression.

Homesteading was a seasonal means to an end. Dad figured he could farm during the summer, and then, when fall and winter shut everything down, he could continue with his education, which he had abruptly interrupted by leaving Beaverton. This was why, while still a teenager, he had become a homesteader. Saskatchewan had just become a province. Although not yet the prairie breadbasket, she would soon become so, with the railroad bringing immigrants from eastern Canada and from overseas. Now, every autumn, the same railroad took Dad back to Ontario.

He went to Beaverton's larger neighbour, Lindsay. Lindsay sported an institution of higher learning in the form of a Collegiate Institute. Dad enrolled as a mature student and took most of high school in one school year. This became a pattern. Saskatchewan farming and circuit riding put money in the bank for the trip to Ontario in the late autumn. He enrolled at Queen's University in Kingston, where a merciful registrar turned a blind eye to the young man's tendency to arrive after the fall deadline. At Queen's he fell in love with Mother. She was five years older than Dad but by now he was five years more mature than his age.

Mother was the eldest daughter of James Ford, a theologically liberal Methodist parson in southwestern Ontario whose own father, Joseph Ford, a weaver, had immigrated from England in 1832 and settled in Peterborough. Her mother was from Scottish stock, all of whom had come to Canada from the United States as staunch United Empire Loyalists. It is from these clan branches that my eldest brother inherits the name Douglass and I inherit the name Munroe.

Like Dad, Mother was working her way through university, and she, too, was using Saskatchewan as the key to higher education. Ferocious prairie winters dictated that rural schools could only function in the summer. Mother would take the train west in the spring and teach until autumn. It was lonely teaching in isolated schoolhouses on the prairies while boarding in the homes of equally isolated school trustees, but she viewed it all as a means to an end.

One summer she was a little late arriving in Saskatchewan, but she got a school anyway and was picked up at the station by a member of the school board. They drove in a buckboard across endless open prairie until she saw her school marooned in the middle of nowhere. "Well," said the trustee, "there it is and I wish you luck. You're the third teacher we've had already this summer."

Mother claims her heart stopped. "What ... what happened to the others?" she asked.

"Oh, wild bunch of kids." He seemed to eye mother rather doubtfully. She had visions of young teachers lying battered and bruised.

"Yep. Wild bunch, I'm afraid. Teachers couldn't keep discipline. Fired 'em."

"What ... what do the students do?"

"Well, the boys all go out the windows and take off home."

I ask Mother if she was scared and lonely, and how she managed.

"Oh, no problem."

I never do discover her secret. She must have made learning more fun than shooting gophers. And I do know that for some reason I tend to do whatever Mother wishes, and it has nothing to do with fear. It may have been this same secret that made her, before she married Dad, one of Ontario's earliest female high school principals.

Dad earned his Bachelor of Arts degree and enrolled in theology. By this time his three older brothers and even his father had followed him to Saskatchewan homesteads. Grandpa returned to Beaverton, but two of the brothers, Nelson and Walter, remained on the prairies. Taking an almost paternal interest in the efforts of their kid brother, they acquired land near his. The fourth brother, Charlie, became a travelling salesman, married, and fathered my artist cousin, Lloyd.

When the First World War unfurled its banners, Dad, the young theolog, went off to war as a buck private in the medical corps and Walter took over the homestead. Dad went to Egypt and never did return to farming. He was invalided home to Ontario in 1917, a year that saw him complete theology, marry Mother, and settle in Port McNicoll, Ontario. But at Queen's he had won a travelling scholarship for post-graduate studies, and so, just a few years later, Mother took their first child, my brother Doug, home to her parents in Goderich, Ontario, and Dad went off to New York to activate his scholarship and earn a master's degree from Union Theological Seminary. Since he was in New York anyway, and because he didn't wish to waste time, he simultaneously enrolled at Columbia University and earned an M.A. there in history. His S.T.M. degree from Union was awarded *magna cum laude* and carried with it another scholarship.

Ignoring the new scholarship, Dad returned to Canada and to Mother and Doug, and they moved to Wiarton, Ontario, where he became the Presbyterian minister and where my brother Don was born. The Wiarton Presbyterians, a stubborn breed, refused to join with the Methodists and Congregationalists in 1925 when the United Church of Canada was created. As a young saddlebag preacher Dad had cut his ecumenical teeth on the polyglot gatherings in the homestead shacks of the Saskatchewan prairies. Mother, the Methodist, had already united with a Presbyterian. The United Church was their natural church home. With his congregation opting to remain Presbyterian, Dad had to leave Wiarton. The text for his final sermon was Matthew 23:38 and Luke 13:35: "Behold, your house is left unto you desolate."

They moved to Owen Sound, where, shortly after one o'clock on a wintry February night in 1927, I was born, somewhat premature and rather delicate. Dad says I was about the size of a big potato. Mother was forty-three. By the standards of the time, I was the child of her old age. I am an adult before I discover she is not the usual year or two younger than Dad.

We move to Flesherton, Ontario, when I am two years old, and the rest is, if not history, memory.

3

THE DOCTOR'S HORSES

FOR ME, RECOLLECTIONS OF A HAPPY childhood are illustrated by a day plucked at random from memory.

It has been snowing for two days. What I really mean is that it has been snowing *again* for two days, because it is already the middle of February and I am sure the world has been white forever.

The first few flakes of this storm came along on Thursday in little scouting parties, but by yesterday afternoon they were coming in battalions, travelling level, riding on the back of the North Wind. I am eight years old, and I think of the North Wind with capital letters because of a book I have read. It has a picture of a ragged little boy who lives in a loft somewhere, and the Wind blows through the cracks between the boards and is his friend. There is a picture of the North Wind, and she is a silver-blue lady with long hair and a flowing dress and fine hands. The ragged little boy must live in another country because his North Wind is not my North Wind.

My North Wind howls and turns snow into bullets and a fellow has to walk backwards into it all the way across town to get to the school that sits on a hill at the north end of the village. It would be fun if they would close the school or let a fellow stay home, but no one ever thinks of that. You try to walk behind some big guy of ten or twelve and let him break trail and break the wind. I used to get behind my brothers, but now both Don and Doug go to the high school in another part of town and are no use as a windbreak.

Anyway, it snowed most of Thursday and all day Friday and then last night the wind dropped and the snow stopped. This morning, Saturday, the sun is out. The drifts are big beyond belief and packed hard. Every high drift is a potential igloo. Every long drift is a potential tunnel. Doug and Don and I have already dug a tunnel in the drift that runs the length of the stone wall along the outer edge of our front lawn. Today we may be able to add a few extensions. The house where we live is called "the parsonage" because it belongs to St. John's Church, which was Methodist before it became United.

Right now I am on an errand downtown to collect the mail. Dad gets a real stern look if his mail is not called for in good time. It doesn't matter whether or not there is any, as long as it's called for. To me, getting the mail is a ritual like adults taking communion, and is just as illogically and just as inevitably linked to whatever gears keep the universe turning.

So I am going for the mail, but I am taking my time about it. Later on I might take the toboggan up to McKinnon's Hill, just a block from home, and slide down old lady McKinnon's terrifyingly steep side yard. If we had had an ice storm instead of snow we would lug the bobsleigh up there and come back down the road. We have the fastest bobsleigh in town. Doug made it. It is eight feet long, a foot wide, and runs on two long, low, iron-runnered sleighs about four inches high. One day when it was real icy we loaded her up with passengers on top of McKinnon's and came belting down the road past MacDonald's barn, turned the corner at McCracken's house, went past our place and on down the hill to the highway, made a tight right and then another, and put the front runners right into Mr. McCracken's blacksmith shop.

But that was on ice. Today it is snow.

The main street is impassable for wheeled vehicles and will be that way until the big snowplough carves its way through, heading north toward Owen Sound. But already the farmers' teams are pushing their way in to town. I hear them coming, the slow sway of their harness bells like icicles breaking in the crisp air, followed by the impact of heavy hooves, the squeak of snow, and the slither of sleigh runners. The sounds of their coming are almost as exciting as the sight of their arrival. There are deep-chested Percherons, huge hairy-footed Clydes, and dapple grey Belgians with big round rumps, and all are steaming sweat as they haul great twin-sledded bobsleighs into town, with their masters standing, feet astride, just aft of the front stake-rail, looking like sea captains on the poop deck of snow-going galleons.

I stand aside, respectfully, to let a team of Clydes go by and then quick as a flash I am onto the tail end of one runner of the rear sleigh, which sticks out about a foot beyond the back edge of the sleigh box. I cling to the box and ride that runner across the white waves of a wilderness sea — until the Captain swings his ship into Mr. McCracken's blacksmith shop.

I am tempted to stay and watch the horses being shod. If I do I may get to pump the bellows at the forge while watching the red-hot iron being shaped on the anvil and learning the interesting words that seem to make horses pay attention. They are not words I ever hear at home, but some of them have a Biblical ring to them. And there is a funnel attached to the smithy wall. Its spout goes right through to the outside. That funnel is a kind of height gauge that separates the men from the boys. A chalk sign above it says "Piss Here." I am hoping to grow tall enough to use that.

But I am on my way for the mail, so I resist the temptation to loiter and instead catch another sleigh going the other way. I stay with it until it turns in to the flour mill. A short sprint and a long jump and I make it to the tail of another runner, and leave this one only when it is piloted into the hotel yard, where there is a place called a "beer parlour." We have a parlour at home where the piano sits and where parishioners get to talk to Dad and where a mad professor gives Don violin lessons. Doug and Don say the professor is not really mad but only slightly drunk. I am not sure what that means except that it is a word I hear Dad using when he talks about the parlour at this hotel. Anyway, the sleigh turns in to a part of the world that is none of my business. But the hotel is across from the Post Office and I am still duty bound on my errand.

There is the sound of more bells. Fast bells, bright bells, determined bells. I know these bells. I stand and wait, holding my breath. Around a corner comes another sleigh. No, not just another sleigh. A cutter. It is bright red with great slender runners curling up at the front and coiling back toward a gracefully curved dashboard. And this cutter, even though it is light — compared to the great farm sleighs almost weightless — it, too, is drawn by a team. What a team! It is a pair of long-legged, high-stepping, proud-necked, tail-arching drivers. Their flanks gleam chestnut-brown in the sunlight. The man in the cutter is sitting tall and holding the reins firmly but gently. He is fur-hatted and wrapped in a big fur coat. He is the village doctor and he is on an Errand of Mercy.

My friends and I know that Doctor Milne is always on an Errand of Mercy. He owns a car, but this time of year on an Errand of Mercy he relies on iron-shod horseflesh and the cutter.

I watch the doctor and his team go by the way other boys must have watched King Arthur through the streets of Camelot. Here, on the main street, the larger farm beasts have the drifts well broken and the doctor's bays are already moving fast. As he goes by he waves to me and then touches his chargers' flanks with a light flick of the long reins. The horses shake their heads, arch their necks, quicken their pace. They are farting in unison, one proud blast per stride. A boy's winter heaven is complete.

4

THE TEENS

DAD GETS THE CALL TO Stirling, Ontario, when I am nine years old and still in public school. Don and Doug are both in high school. The best thing about Stirling is that it is only fifty miles from Stoney Lake, where we have spent part of every summer since I was four years old. Four years later my brothers are both at Queen's University, I am ready for high school, and Dad gets the call again. This time it is to Almonte, in the Ottawa Valley.

Almonte is a picturesque town with a turbulent river, thundering waterfalls, decaying woollen mills, and old stone mansions. It is home to descendants of Englishmen, Irishmen, and Scotsmen, and also Orangemen, whom I think of as being somehow a race apart, like aliens. There are two United Churches in Almonte, one formerly Methodist, the other formerly Presbyterian. By uniting without uniting, they have managed the fine art of stubborn Canadian compromise. Dad is the minister in Bethany United Church. It was formerly Presbyterian, so the fine old Ontario Gothic stone house that we live in is known as the "manse." In Stirling we lived in the "parsonage." Almonte becomes my real hometown and I come to think of myself as a son of the manse. I also learn to think of myself as being "from the Valley" — the Ottawa Valley, a region that is more a state of mind than a geographical reality.

It is here, as a Valley boy, resident in Almonte, that I get my first indoctrination into the realities of politics; possibly significantly, it occurs on Parliament Hill, a location destined to play a considerable role in my life.

It is the spring of 1940, I am thirteen years old, and I am in Ottawa with an entire hour to spend by myself. Dad has business in the city and has brought me with him. He has dropped me on Wellington Street beside the statue of Sir Galahad. He will meet me here in one hour's time, which will be announced by the big bells behind the clock high in the Peace Tower on Parliament Hill.

I am not familiar with the city. My country has been at war with Germany since last year and gas rationing is in effect, so we seldom drive into Ottawa, even though it is only thirty-five miles from Almonte. I was here a year ago with Mother and Dad but didn't see much of the city. Too many people. We were all here to see King George the Sixth and Queen Elizabeth. I was wearing my boy scout uniform and the crowd eased me into the front line near the big war memorial where the bronze soldiers are hauling a field gun through a big arch and I got a real good view of the King and Queen as they went by in their open carriage. But they were nothing compared to the Royal Dragoons wearing gleaming breastplates and shiny helmets topped with plumed spikes and mounted on splendid horses with brass-studded harness, and even they were eclipsed by the scarlet-coated Royal Canadian Mounted Police carrying long javelins with pennants flying from the spearheads.

Anyway, that was a year ago, and today I am on my own and Dad has given me no particular instructions. I have a suspicion he hopes curiosity will draw me onto Parliament Hill instead of into city soda fountain fleshpots. He is correct.

I go up the long, wide walkway that cuts through the great expanse of lawn and leads to the wide steps that in turn lead to the paved terrace that fronts the Centre Block of the Gothic buildings. My eyes are fixed in awe on the soaring height of the Peace Tower with its leering gargoyles leaning out into space, its lookout balcony just under the huge clock face, and its tapered spire topped by the pole that flies the Red Ensign with the Dominion coat of arms in one corner.

When I reach the terrace I realize that the base of the tower is even more intriguing. Here the main entrance portal is flanked by a regal stone lion and an elegant stone unicorn, and standing on the steps beside the lion there is a real Mountie. He is wearing a wide-brimmed Stetson hat, a rich red jacket with a Sam Browne belt, dark breeches with yellow stripes down the sides, and riding boots of shining leather. I have to pinch myself to be certain I am awake and able to stand close to such a hero.

There are other men in uniform here on the Hill, but they are wanderers like myself. They wear the dark blue of the Navy, the light blue of the Air Force, and the brown of the Army. They are my heroes, too. I read about them on the front page of the newspaper, hear about them on Jim Hunter's radio news, which follows a trumpet fanfare and has something to do with Bee Hive Golden Corn Syrup, and we talk about them in school, because they are our brothers and our cousins and in some cases even our uncles and our fathers and they are making the world safe for Democracy.

I walk all the way around the Centre Block and look at the statues of great men, most of whom I have never heard of, but apparently they made Democracy safe for Canada by turning it into Federalism. I get the feeling that old politicians must automatically turn into bronze and that their laws turn into stone.

At the back of the building some sailors are taking pictures of their girlfriends, with the round stone library in the background, its arched buttresses making the stonework look elegant and ethereal. But my eyes lock onto the view from the cliff top that overlooks the Ottawa River. I am hardly aware of the city of Hull, or of Eddy's paper mill with its mountain of pulpwood, or of the purple hills of the Gatineau in the background. I do watch the tugboats jockeying their vast pulpwood rafts on the river below, but mostly I see the river itself and the foaming Chaudière Falls and the turbulent river beyond, flowing from the northwest. In my imagination, I see Champlain and his Huron guides making their way up that river. I also see ghostly Iroquois war canoes sliding downriver, their warrior occupants intending to destroy Montreal, little knowing that Dollard des Ormeaux and a handful of valiant friends are lying in ambush, about to give their lives to save the seeds of the country that will eventually spread from sea to sea. My country.

I inspect the old cracked bronze bell that sits in a cradle on the cliff top and I read the inscription that tells me that this bell hung in the old Centre Block tower and that way back during the First World War when the Parliament Buildings burned, the bell struck the final hour of midnight and then crashed through the flames to the ground. There is something heroic about that bell, as though it refused to concede defeat without first rounding out the day to the final stroke. I know about that fire because Mother's brother, my Uncle Art, who would later become the editor of *The London Free Press*, was in the press gallery and was lucky to escape.

As I come full circle around the building I find Queen Victoria standing on a high square pedestal. She appears to be waiting for a tall carriage to come along and rescue her. I know she is dead but I also know she is not dead, because we celebrate her birthday every 24th of May. She is part of a living chain that links my own King George to Elizabeth the First, to Richard the Lionheart, to Alfred the Great, to Arthur of Camelot, tying this Parliament Hill to something big and splendid and mystical and that now, in the Second Great War, is in danger.

I stand close to two soldiers who are talking to each other beside the low stone parapet near the top of the stairway from the lawn. I wish I were old enough to be in uniform, too. I watch them from the corners of my eyes, not wanting to be rude but wanting to observe real heroes. My ears strain to overhear their noble conversation.

A man comes out of the Centre Block, passing between the lion and the unicorn. He is not a large man. He is, in fact, rather short and somewhat round. He is wearing a dark suit and a dark homburg hat. I have seen his picture in the newspapers and recognize him instantly. My heart leaps. It is Mackenzie King, Prime Minister of Canada from Sea to Sea. The two soldiers also see him. They stop talking and turn to look. They, too, are overcome with awe.

I do not realize it but I am about to witness, up close, a high-level Political Act. It takes effect when the Prime Minister, seeing the two heroes in uniform, veers toward them. I am only ten feet away so he is coming toward me, too.

The Prime Minister and the soldiers shake hands. They smile at each other and speak, but I cannot hear the words for the awe that is in my heart.

Mackenzie King goes on his way. He has not seen me but I am privileged to have seen him. I move closer to hear what my heroes have to say. Again, I do not realize it but I am about to hear a Grassroots Political Reaction.

One of the soldiers is looking down at the hand that just shook the hand of the Prime Minister of Canada. "You know," he says to his friend, "I was raised on the farm but this is the first time I ever stuck my hand into bullshit."

I have just learned that one can be a patriot and still criticize one's leaders. It is liberating knowledge.

I like Almonte. These are happy years, even though the Second World War is underway. Paradoxically, perhaps *because* of the War, we teenagers have a sense of purpose. The high school boys are all in the Army Cadet Corps. We learn more about marching than about anything else, but if a war can be won by troops who are able to "form fours," or do a precise "about face," or "mark time" impeccably, or execute a flawless "in line, right wheel," then the Germans had better give up before we're old enough to enlist. We do get some hands-on instruction on the firing range with .303 rifles. In this farming community, ground hogs are a natural enemy and the .22 a common rifle, so we adapt with rather deadly ease to the .303.

To begin with, our uniforms are somewhat improvised. For some weird reason I eventually become the Commanding Officer, probably because I have a full uniform. It's Dad's First World War outfit from

Egypt and is a light-coloured, lightweight khaki complete with the leg wrappings called *puttees* and the breeks that we call "shit-catchers." Becoming the c.o. is more of an appointment than an achievement. It's a dubious honour, somewhat like making it to the Senate.

One summer we join a few thousand other would-be warriors at a cadet camp on the shores of Lake Ontario. The company of which we are a part is officered by guys from big Ottawa schools who have no respect for authority, and after breaking some regulation or other they, and we, get assigned to a couple of days of "kitchen patrol." K.P. consists mainly of peeling potatoes. I suspect that eventually everyone will be found to transgress, so that there will always be a reservoir of kitchen slaves. A real army officer comes to inspect us at our menial task, and, encouraged by our Ottawa mentors, we all sing heartily,

> Merrily we shovel shit, shovel shit, shovel shit,
> Merrily we shovel shit
> All the livelong day.

Later, on the firing range, I get to lie on my belly and fire a Bren gun over the waters of Lake Ontario. I consider it a reward for all the potato-peeling.

But even the cadet corps is centred on the high school, and the high school is the core of our daily existence.

The teachers are all distinct individuals and we have nicknames for most of them. It is essential for teenagers' sense of self to identify their teachers with nicknames or abbreviations. Even so, there is respect here. The principal, W.F. Thom, is "Frankie" when we are talking about him, but by God it is "Mister" or "Sir" when we are talking to him.

Frankie has full authority as principal, and it's best not to mess with him. He declares a "no-smoking zone" that extends for two blocks from the school in all four directions. Since two of those directions are open farmland it's a little difficult to know where the zone ends. Some of the fellows transgress, but discreetly. It never occurs to us to defy Frankie openly. Except once, when Sheldon lets his mouth go too far in class. Frankie teaches math and likes a disciplined mind and disciplined behaviour. This day I am sitting at the back of the room and I hear the command, "Scott! Open the door!" I do so and Sheldon exits, travelling horizontally. No one complains, not even Sheldon. The fact is, we love Frankie. He coaches both the junior and the senior basketball teams and

the football team. In these days we call football "rugby." If he accidentally gets in the way of a line rush we run him down and he gets up,
laughing. In football we are regularly beaten to a pulp by Carleton Place
and Smiths Falls, both much bigger schools with more choice of brawn.
In Almonte, if you can stand up, hear thunder, and see lightning, you are
on the football team. But Frankie makes us feel happy even in defeat.

In basketball it's another matter. This town is the home of James
Naismith, the inventor of basketball. When I get up in the morning I
look down from my bedroom window into a Naismith backyard. We are
all honour bound to be good at basketball. Our small school is blessed
with a state-of-the-art basketball court in a modern gym with a real
hardwood floor, not the asphalt horror that adorns one big Ottawa high
school. Frankie arranges exhibition games for us with teams from Glebe
and Lisgar Collegiates in Ottawa. With these guys we struggle for survival. He throws us into exhibition games with Air Force teams. These
players are older than us but we're in better shape. In one game, playing man on man rather than zone, I always know where my man is. I just
follow his cigar breath.

During the winter months, Frankie is with us in the gym after
school and most Saturday mornings. By the time we're into our own
Lanark County basketball playoffs we are ready to clean up the trophies,
and usually do. I eventually captain the football team, which is painful,
and the basketball team, which carries more prestige than being c.o. of
the cadet corps.

Another teacher, Howard Pammett, also helps out in the gym,
which is not his favourite place. "Howie" teaches history, and is a nervous, scholarly man. He must spend ages in the classroom before school
hours, because by the time we file in for history every map on two sides
of the room is pulled down to hide the underlying blackboards. Howie,
using the lecture technique, almost puts us to sleep, and then, with
about fifteen minutes of class time still to go, he rushes around raising
the maps to reveal copious notes laboriously chalked onto the blackboards. We're supposed to scurry these into our notebooks. He is such a
nervous type that we tend to give him a hard time, but we appreciate
the fact that in the winter he drives us to neighbouring towns for basketball games and in doing so not only endangers his car but consumes
much of his precious quota of rationed gasoline.

Mr. Norman Carruthers teaches French. He has a club foot and he
walks with a limp. Our nickname for him is "Croochy," though Lord
knows why. We seem to have inherited it from our predecessors. In

these days of wartime teacher shortages, Croochy finds himself teaching chemistry. He likes chemistry even less than I do. Neither of us learns a great deal about it. For me, Croochy comes into his own after hours, when he directs the school plays for Commencement and other occasions. "Commencement" is the paradoxical name given to a fall concert that begins the school year, a trifle late; it also embraces graduation, which seems more of an ending. One year I do an incredibly lugubrious job of acting, playing the father in *The Monkey's Paw*, a popular horror story. Another year, Howie Pammett drills us guys in a routine that is supposed to be a pirate dance. We wear rubber boots and red sashes and feel like idiots, a not inappropriate sensation. But it's Croochy who inspires in me a love for drama and the stage and, for better or worse, partially shapes my career.

Miss Isabel Firth, "Izzy," teaches English, both grammar and literature. Grammar is a real bind and I have difficulty comprehending the need for rules when all one has to do is to talk the way one has been taught to talk. I'm an adult before it dawns on me there is a certain advantage in having educated parents. Izzy, like Frankie, demonstrates that one can push a good teacher too far. One day I am whispering across the aisle, an activity that is strictly *verboten*, when she snaps at me to be quiet. I give her the innocent surely-you-don't-mean-me look and she screams like a banshee. It's humiliating for both of us. As a reading assignment I read Charles Kingsley's *Westward Ho!* and write a review of it. Writing the review is a lot of fun and Izzy seems to enjoy reading it. She gives it a very high grade and adds an enthusiastic comment that jolts me into the sudden realization that writing, like the stage, might offer some long-term possibilities.

The most senior teacher is Miss Jessie Mathews. To us she seems very elderly and motherly. Her initials are J.E.M. and she is indeed a gem. She teaches Latin patiently, and Art resignedly, and Ancient History with enthusiasm. She has travelled in both Greece and Italy. Even in Latin class she puts travel anecdotes to good use. Jessie makes the ancient Assyrians, Egyptians, Greeks, and Romans seem alive and vibrant. In later years when I read Mika Waltari's *The Egyptian*, or Mary Renaud's *The King Must Die*, or Robert Graves's *I, Claudius* my enjoyment is built on a foundation laid by Jessie Mathews.

Social Studies and Health are both taught by Miss Cowan. Her name is "Maizie" and we all call her that, but strictly behind her back. We have Maizie tagged as an old maid and torment her in health class by asking apparently naive and oblique questions that we hope will lure her into attempting to explain human reproductive techniques. She sidesteps us, but we may have hit a nerve. She eventually becomes a *femme fatale* and then a wife.

Under Maizie's guidance we all learn plane-spotting, which, in wartime, is apparently associated with maintaining good health. Maizie gets stuck with teaching this the way Croochy gets stuck with chemistry. We become quite expert at spotting silhouettes of Heinkels, Messerschmitts, Stukas, Dorniers, and other German machines, as well as Spits, Hurricanes, Mosquitoes, Typhoons, and all the rest of the good guys. Surely the authorities don't really believe we're ever going to put this knowledge to use here in the Ottawa Valley. If we ever do see an enemy machine that's not a black silhouette we'll be stymied. But at least it's more fun than studying "health."

When real warlike devastation is forced upon us one Christmas it comes not by air but by rail, in the shape of a troop train.

It is Christmas time in 1942, and our family is a very happy one, because my big brothers are home for Christmas. Doug is an engineer officer in the Royal Canadian Navy, the "wavy navy" to be exact,* and I am full of admiration for the gold braid on his cuffs. He is the first naval officer to have turned up on the streets of Almonte, and since he didn't go to high school here no one knows him; the word has gone around that we have a new town policeman.

Don is twenty years old and at medical school. He's in the accelerated course that's headed for the army. Don is five years my senior but is cursed with the appearance of youth. He looks as though he should be with me in our high school cadet corps. I guess Mother and Dad are worried about what the future holds for their sons, but I know it is almost inconceivable that anything bad could happen to my brothers.

I say "almost" because I remember Carl. I had been bullied in public school and when we moved to Almonte and I started high school I figured I wouldn't put up with it any more, so at noon the first day of school I picked a quarrel with the biggest guy I could find in First Form** and invited him outside to settle it, thinking a display of guts might dissuade any prospective bullies. The big fellow came along far too willingly and so did half the guys in the school. We were about to square off and I was

---

* The RCNVR (Royal Canadian Naval Volunteer Reserve), nicknamed the "wavy navy" because of the zig-zag design of the officers' gold braid.

** Today's Grade Nine.

pretty sure I'd goofed up big-time when Carl, a Fifth Former, waded in and broke us up. He joked a bit, made us shake hands, put his arms across both our shoulders, and walked us back into school. I never do have to fight in that school, and my hand-picked opponent turns out to be a really gentle guy, a friend, and a powerhouse on the football field. But Carl was one of the first young men from town to be reported "missing in action." It seems unfair that Carl, a peacemaker, should die fighting, and it also reminds me now that my brothers are not immortal.

Even though it's only December there's already lots of snow and it's promising to be a hard, cold winter. In the Valley anything else would be ridiculous. This evening the family is sitting in Dad's study, talking. We don't use the study much because the living room is larger, but the study has a fireplace, and tonight, with just the five of us, the coziness of the study and the fire seems to suit the family mood.

We hear a strange, heavy sound from outside. Conversation stops abruptly as we all listen. It could be a snow slide from the roof but it is harder, heavier, more prolonged. It could be a train shunting in the railway yard only a block away, but this sounds more like ten trains shunting.

I go onto the front verandah and look north to where our street runs into the station yard. There's something very peculiar going on up there but it's too dark to see clearly.

My brothers and I struggle into our heavy gear and leave the house. The walking is easy because the sidewalk snowplough has been along. It's a wooden "V" plough pulled by an old horse and it has already begun to pile the snow high on either side. The night must be cold because the snow squeaks a little as we walk. I like walking at night, when the streetlights make inviting pools of light in the semi-darkness.

We walk into the station yard and stop in horror.

The entire railway line for several hundred yards west from the station looks like a scene from the War. There is wreckage everywhere. There are wooden panels, metal strips, window frames, railway wheels, wreckage unbelievable. But the unbelievable has just happened. Other town folk are arriving, too, and the moment of monstrous first shock is only now coming to an end. Voices are beginning to cry out in the darkness. There are isolated screams from within the wreckage, but mostly there is almost silence, except for the shuddering of the great steam locomotive that is standing hip-high in the midst of the carnage, its own cars stretching behind it, westward, into the darkness.

We don't need a map to know what has happened. A passenger train has been standing at the station, heading east. An express has come along, also heading east, and has ploughed into the rear of the stationary local, which was already loaded. Three passenger cars have been demolished by a monster locomotive that went down their centre aisle. They have been split in two and tossed aside the way the snow-plough clears a walk. An entire coach roof, sliced off but intact, lies at a crazy angle on the ground.

Soon we realize that the express is a troop train, and later we hear that the engineer had an appalling decision to make. He saw the rear lights of the standing train as he came in from the west, rounding the bend just before the flour mill. Past the mill the tracks soar out across the river. The river is deep and the bridge is high and long, as I and my friends well know, for we have run the length of it pursued by the whistle of approaching trains. The engineer applied his brakes and then locked them. The cars behind him began to sway, building up a terrible rhythm of their own. The engineer knew if he left his brakes locked he would put his own trainload of soldiers into the chasm, onto the ice, to break through into the deep waters below. He held spark-screaming friction as long as he dared, and then released. Later he commits suicide and I don't think it's fair for a good man to assume such guilt.

But that is all later knowledge. Right now all I know is that the peace of the Christmas fireside has dissolved into a nightmare. My brothers disappear. Doug, the engineer, goes straight into the wreckage. Now and then throughout the remainder of the night I catch glimpses of his tall uniformed figure silhouetted against work lights as he and other men struggle to release trapped victims. I lose track of Don completely. I move into this nightmare world and begin carrying stretchers. Other teenagers have materialized. Our whole basketball team seems to be here and we are all carrying stretchers. Local tradesmen have brought their trucks. We carry the injured from the wreckage to the trucks and lift the stretchers aboard. Then we ride with the victims as they are taken to the town hall. The stately old stone Victorian building stands high above street level and a steep flight of steps leads up to the auditorium level, so it's a long carry and a steep lift and we have to be very careful on the snow and ice.

Soon the interior of the town hall begins to look like a scene from *Gone with the Wind*. At some time during the night I realize I am helping to carry a dead person. It's not so much the staring eyes that tell me as the grey colour. It's my first experience with undecorated death. I soon learn that the colour alone is misleading. People in deep shock also wear the colour of death.

First aid people are swarming in the town hall. Some are medical corpsmen from the troop train but many are just men and women from town. I am surprised to see how calm and efficient ordinary people can be. Dad is here now but of course he would be, having been in the medical corps in the First World War.

I go with a truckload of victims who are being dispatched to the hospital. The ambulance is the open back of a stake-body truck and we are worried as much about the patients freezing to death as dying of their wounds. We try to keep the blankets tucked snugly and make hopeful efforts to block the wind. A young woman on a stretcher is crying and saying she was going home for her birthday. I tell her not to worry and that she is going to be able to tell her grandchildren about this most memorable of all birthdays. I am trying to sound mature and reassuring but in my ears my voice breaks a little and sounds unnaturally high. Maybe she has not noticed. Maybe she thinks I am a man and not just a scared fifteen-year-old.

The little cottage hospital is very busy and some of the town mothers who used to be nurses have dug out old uniforms and are busily pitching in. I hear a registered nurse ask if any more doctors are on their way. I hear another one ask who the boy is. The answer is that nobody knows but that he sure knows his stuff so no one is asking any questions. I look around and see they are talking about my brother Don, gowned in white, and blood to the elbows.

Deep into the night a hospital train arrives from Ottawa and makes its way as far into the station yard as it can go. We begin ferrying patients out of the town hall and back to the station. We teenagers are still coping, but I wonder if the other fellows are getting as tired as I am. I hear some elders saying more than thirty people are already dead, but that is a mere statistic. I have seen the wounded we are shunting onward. The long-term suffering and the ensuing deaths can never be precisely tabulated.

It's almost morning when I go home. My brothers and Dad are not home yet but Mother is waiting. She pours hot chocolate into me and I hit the sack. I'm exhausted but I don't go to sleep. My mind is full of terrible images that have nothing to do with the world I have inhabited until now. Those images contain memory etchings of my brothers at work in the carnage, and since we have all been there this world must be real. And I have learned important things about myself. I can look upon wounds and blood and death without turning away and in the process can actually feel a physical ache in the heart for others who are in pain.

5

BURNING THE
CHRISTMAS CROSS

TIME FLIES. I am seventeen. It is another Christmas and the carol service is about to begin. The interior of old Bethany United Church is lit only by coloured tree lights and the congregation is expectantly in place. The vestibule inside the front door is in total darkness but is far from empty. It is jam-packed with members of the choir, all of us wearing long black gowns, and the women wearing flat mortarboard caps, each cap with a tassel dangling to one side. At the moment we are all catching our breath, because there is no interior passage from the choir room to the vestibule so we have all skittered here through the snow and the freezing cold, looking like great grounded crows. If there is a latecomer to the congregation he or she will have to wait, or use a side door, because the processional is about to begin.

A match flares in the darkness and then other small flares break away from it and multiply among themselves. Each of us is carrying a candle seated in a little wooden block, and as the tiny igniting flames spread among us the whole vestibule lights up. Now we look like members of the Inquisition preparing for an *auto-da-fé.*

A soprano opens the door to the nave and waves a candle up and down. Hector, the organist, must be watching in his rear-view mirror, because he changes gears in mid-chord, opens the throttles, and soars into the processional. We wait for our cue then carol forth. "O Come All Ye Faithful" is almost too big for the vestibule.

We enter the nave one at a time, our hymn books open in our left hands, our flickering candles in our right hands, and proceed in single file down the right-hand aisle. Our thrifty Scottish predecessors didn't build a centre aisle. The sopranos go first, followed by the altos, then the tenors, and we basses bring up the rear, trailed by Dad in his full clerical regalia — gown, dickie, tabs, dog collar, and the handsome white satin academic hood with the purple border.

As the sopranos enter the nave the volume in the vestibule drops off alarmingly, and subsides even more when the altos leave. By the time it's my turn there are only two members of the bass section behind me, and as I enter the nave I feel I am singing a solo. The candle is flickering too dimly to give me a clear view of the hymn book and without the printed notes I can't hold harmony in a bucket, but I know the words by heart, so I mouth them vigorously but almost silently, and pace my solemn way down the aisle in the wake of the flaming choir. I hear the two men behind me rumbling away as they enter the nave and my ears tell me they are proceeding toward Bethlehem with about the same confidence as myself. Then I hear Dad at the end of the procession and I listen for a moment. He has a better voice than all the rest of us put together but I never know whether he is going to sing tenor or bass. It all depends on his mood. If it's tenor I am lost in the cross-currents, but if he happens to boom in on the bass then I can catch the vibrations and tune in. This evening, thank God, it's bass. I wait for a bass D to go by. There are only two of them in the verse and two in the chorus, but I like them and they're worth waiting for. Launched from a D and with Dad behind, I sing the gauntlet of the aisle without disgrace.

The old church is austerely beautiful. Its Presbyterian roots go way back into the mid-1800s. At the front, the choir loft rises up behind the central pulpit and is in turn backed by the soaring pipe organ. Organist Hector Dalrymple has built great arches that tower over the front of the choir loft. He has clothed these arches in evergreen boughs and impregnated the boughs with Christmas tree lights. There is the scent of balsam, the twinkle of coloured lights, the flicker of candle flames, the singing of the choir and the congregation, and over it all the triumphant music from the big organ, whose pipes line the entire back wall of the choir loft. It is fitting that the keyboard is at the base of the pipes and the organist is not cowering in a pit but sits high on his bench for all to see, because this is his evening and he knows it. Hector pulls out a few more stops.

The processional passes across the front of the church, below the pulpit and past the communion table. At the table we each in turn dispose of our candles. I know that Dad has been labouring in the basement armed with saw, hammer, nails, two-by-fours, tin, and shears. Now the product of his labour is here for all to see. A great wooden cross stands four-square on the communion table. Its entire main stem and its outreaching arms are lined with holders made of tin. Dad also made the little wooden blocks that carry our candles, and we now find that those blocks fit neatly onto the holders. By the time we have all passed by on our way to the choir loft the plain wooden cross has been transformed by candle flames into a symbol of everlasting life and hope.

A few overhead lights are now turned on so that everybody, including members of the congregation, can see their hymn books. Dad voices the Call to Worship and Hector holds a gentle chord for a moment while we all strike our mental tuning forks. Then, softly, we sing "Again As Evening's Shadow Falls."

I love this hymn, with the deep dark and the quiet snow outside, the soft light and the warmth inside, just a little rustle from the congregation, and the big organ all muted down, its pipes fluting softly overhead. This evening, as soon as that one bit of ritual is completed, Dad throws away the regular Order of Service. We warm up the congregational voice with "Hark the Herald Angels Sing," then carol on into "The First Noel." The choir unleashes a couple of anthems. Some teenagers read portions of the Christmas story. I am happy to be marooned up in the back row of the choir loft where I can't get tagged for any of that. But I do hope the power stays on.

If there's a hydro break tonight, I'm in trouble. The power has been known to fail during a winter service, and when the break strikes in the middle of a hymn it is highly diverting. The big organ blows along until it exhausts all the air in its bellows, then dies with a great wailing moan that sinks down and down and out. The death of the organ makes for a memorable moment, because the choir and the congregation also wind down to a halt, usually with two or three voices bravely attempting to carry on before being overwhelmed by the embarrassment of isolation. When a hydro failure occurs it's my job to nip through a little door, panelled into the woodwork, that leads into the back of the organ where a long wooden handle protrudes from the bowels of the huge instrument. I seize that handle and laboriously pump it up and down. After about the third stroke the organ returns to life, and I keep it going. My willingness to perform this duty may be the reason I am tolerated in the bass section.

It occurs to me now that I had better offer a little private prayer on behalf of Ontario Hydro. A carol service could be a long hard pump.

I am thinking of that pump handle when I am distracted by the advent of the Long Prayer. This being a carol service, we are saved, for tonight, from the Sermon, but there is no rescue from the Long Prayer, which is a mini-sermon disguised as a prayer. I don't think this subterfuge is fair, but I can't blame it on Dad, because all his ministerial friends indulge in it. Even the bachelor clergyman from Carleton Place, who reminds me of Raymond Massey and who tells hilarious jokes at the dinner table, goes all solemn and long-winded when he launches into the Long Prayer. I have a problem, because I start listening for all the things the preacher is telling God that God already knows, or that He probably doesn't want to know. My mind then drops information into compartments — information for Him, for Us, for Him — weighing them up on imaginary scales. When the scales begin not only to tilt but to bend on the Us side I sometimes begin to laugh, and it's not a good idea for the minister's son, sitting high up on the exposed upper rank of the choir loft, to burst into laughter. So I smother it. Then I begin to smother me, and the damned suppressed laughter takes on unreasonable proportions. I'm sure I'm turning purple and am probably going to expire where I sit and Mother will never know I died of good manners. I laughed right out loud once in the middle of a sermon because I was daydreaming and had thought of something amusing. I managed to turn the laugh into a snort and then converted that into a bout of coughing until an alto sent back a cough drop.

Right now it's not the Long Prayer that has distracted me so much as the burning cross. I stare in fascination. The candles are burning, of course. That's the whole idea. But some of them have guttered very low. In fact, some of them have ignited the wooden blocks in which they are embedded. As the Long Prayer drones on I realize that the cross itself is igniting. Very interesting.

I nudge my companions awake and the bass section sits and ponders the implications of the scene below. I wonder that Dad can't see it. Perhaps he has his eyes closed, or fixed on the heavens. It's right under his nose, why can he not smell it! He has a nose like a beagle. If I were to light a cigarette within ten blocks of the house he would smell it instantly. I wonder if I could get him on the back of the head with a spitball, but figure I don't have a clear shot through Hector's decorative arches.

The flames are well established on the upright, and the bass section decides that if an elder doesn't come to the rescue by the time the arms catch fire we will have to take action. We are praying for an elder.

I have seen an elder step into the breach before now. One Sunday morning a lady of unsound mind came running down the aisle in the middle of Dad's sermon. She was loudly damning the preacher and all the other sinners and exhorting the saved to rally. An elder overtook her just as she reached the front and guided her off through a side exit without even breaking stride. Dad never dropped a metaphor. And one memorable morning an aged Pillar of the Church who always sat in a front pew went to sleep during the sermon. His hearing aid fell out of his ear and dropped down beside the large microphone that was clipped to his vest. The little machine cycled itself into instant feedback and shrieked and yowled at full volume while Dad tried to ignore both the sleeper and the sound. An elder came hotfooting down the aisle that time as well. I have thought of him ever after as a compassionate man. He did not awaken the sleeper, he merely switched off the hearing aid.

But now, alas, we are in the middle of the Long Prayer and the cross is burning and the elders are all being devout. Their heads are bowed and their eyes are shut. May the Dear Lord send us one heretical elder before the bass section shouts "Fire!" in unison and awakens an entire congregation.

An elder comes.

At the sound of his footsteps heads are raised cautiously and eyes crack open, but the prayer goes on. This elder walks with a slightly rolling gait that could be mistaken for a sailor's walk but comes from years of following a plough along the furrows. Trust a farmer to know when it's time to abandon the niceties and get on with the action. He picks that big cross up by its heavy wooden base and holds it out at arm's length as though it were made of balsa wood. He marches away along a transept aisle and the blood of my Scottish ancestors stirs within me. The fiery cross, sanctified at the altar, is now being carried out into the night! Soon the clansmen will pour from the hills. Gaelic war cries will make the welkin ring. "A Bellendaine!" yells a ghostly Scott somewhere in my bloodstream. "Castle Fulis na theine!" answers an ancient Munro, and down deep in my ancestral depths a towering black-haired border thane bellows, "A Douglas, a Douglas!" and rides off to war. A door is thrown open and the runner with the fiery cross exits into the night.

The atmosphere, the spectacle, my ancestral blood, and the incongruity have done me in. One carol service has just gone up in smoke.

As I leave the church I see the charred remains of the fiery cross upside down in a snowdrift about twenty feet from the nearest sign of footsteps. That muscular elder must have cupped his hands and given a mighty heave as though he were tossing the caber. Any passing Catholic will have gone home wondering what new heresy the Protestants were practising tonight.

The church, in the form of old Bethany United, is for me an important institution. Quite apart from carol services, cross burnings, and other celebratory occasions, it's the focus for a great deal of free time. The high school is on the other side of town but the solid limestone bulk of the church is just across the street. The Sunday school wing sports a badminton court that is easily and generously available during the week. The same wing has a stage where community concerts are held. The local jeweller, Mel, who suffered polio as a kid and lives in steel leg braces, and whose wife is one of the prettiest women in town, plays a real mean guitar and mouth organ, a combination that is a guaranteed hit at any concert. And here the Young Peoples Union puts on plays. I am Buddy in *Buddy Buys an Orchid*. It's a starring role and I learn that offstage logistics can be more demanding than onstage acting. Just before the final curtain Buddy has to do a fast offstage change into a tuxedo. My Buddy doesn't quite make it. When he answers his final cue he goes off to a formal dance wearing neither shoes nor a bow tie. Even so, there is something enticing about "play-acting."

Here, in the church hall, Dad gives lectures on Egypt and other esoteric subjects and I get to operate the magic lantern that projects the images from big glass slides. Dad likes to use a large wooden pointer, and when it's time for a slide change he simply pounds the end of it on the floor. There's no chance for either me or the audience to stay asleep. Here, too, visiting missionaries show slides of faraway exotic places like China. Such visitors usually stay with us for a day or two and are interesting guests.

When given the opportunity I leap at the volunteer job of bell-ringer. A half-hour before the morning service I find myself in the old church grasping the bottom end of the bell-ringer's rope and firmly but gently beginning the up and down sawing motion that gets the big bell swinging in the tower above. After the first sonorous chimes ring out over the town I keep the rhythm steady. Too much enthusiasm and the big bell can do a somersault, inextricably fouling the rope and spoiling my ringing career. I love the sound, particularly on a crisp winter morning. It seems to me it is not so much calling the faithful to prayer as asking everyone to pause wherever they are and count their myriad blessings. There is something organic about that bell, like a voice of Nature saying "Pause. Think. Listen. Look around you." In later years the memory of old Bethany's bell creates in me an almost visceral hatred of the ubiquitous automated electronic steeple blasphemies that mindlessly pollute the airwaves and defile the spirit.

Along one edge of the church's side yard there is a long low driving shed to shelter the horses that in winter bring the farm families to church in elegant cutters. Most cutters here are one-horse vehicles, but

Mr. Turner and his family arrive in their double cutter, drawn by a full team, and one heavy winter Sunday they arrive four-in-hand. A splendid sight.

Just next to the driving shed there is a large house owned by a Jewish family, the Smolkins. For all I know they're the only Jewish family in town. They own a men's clothing store on the main street and sometimes I work there part-time. The store is run by a son, "Mo," a big, friendly man who is very patient with me. His elderly mother usually keeps an eye on things from a chair in the back of the store. She, too, seems kind, but her English isn't very good. I've a feeling she could tell interesting stories about growing up in eastern Europe. Sometimes I work in the local hardware store, but that doesn't have the same cultural mystique.

When I remember my teens in Almonte I also remember former prime minister Mike Pearson telling CBC cameras years later about his youthful years in a Methodist parsonage. He says it was a "holy" upbringing, and then explains that "holy" means "healthy" in the fullest extent of the word. I listen to Mike speaking of a time a generation before me, but I know exactly what he means.

Years later I think fondly of old Bethany United. It lives in memory. Dad is a "liberal" theologian and by no means pietistic. He gives rather convoluted sermons, with academic references that go over my head and, I suspect, the heads of the congregation. But Dad is a New Testament man. He is a preacher who knows there was a philosophical revolution between the days of the Old and the New Testaments and he seldom mixes them up. And he makes me lastingly sensitive to blatant forms of evangelism.

Mother and I loyally go to church twice every Sunday. I prefer the evening service, particularly in the winter when darkness has fully fallen. The evening congregation is seldom large, and there is a quiet atmosphere that appeals to me. Here there is no strident amplification. The service always begins with a gentle rendition of the first verse of Longfellow's evening hymn, and even the pipe organ seems awestruck. In later years, I try to put a little of that ambience onto paper.

EVENING'S SHADOW
"Again as evening's shadow falls
We gather in these hallowed walls
And vesper hymn and vesper prayer
Rise mingling on the holy air."

Soft the organ, softly muted,
Pipes in shadows, soaring, fluted,
Singers adding sweet dimension,
Time and worry in suspension.

Father praying, heads are bending,
Asking God, His love extending,
Please forgive our worldly errors,
Lead us through our human terrors.

Books are opened, pages turning,
Words are found to answer yearning,
Ancient psalm in lovely phrase,
The alchemy of love is praise.

Offering given, sermon offered,
Homily from pulpit proffered,
Shorter, simpler, seldom searing,
Evening's not a time for fearing.

Mystic shadows, vaulted ceiling,
Shepherd figures in glass kneeling,
Warmth of oak in amber light,
All is safe within the night.

Final hymn and service ended,
Father standing, arms extended,
Go in peace, the Lord be with you.
Shaking hands at foyer door,
Bless you, keep you,
        and the shining of His face
            be upon you, now
                and forever
                    ever more,
                        amen.

6

WATER AND
WILDERNESS

THERE'S NEVER ANY DOUBT in my mind that university will follow high school. It's as inevitable as summer following spring, and with both parents and both brothers already graduates of venerable old Queen's at Kingston, I have no heretical thoughts of any alternative. But the experience will never occupy a great deal of space in my memory banks. The extracurricular Drama Guild makes a more lasting impact than do academic lectures and studies (and I'll get around to explaining that), but two summer jobs that are about as off-campus as one can get do leave an indelible impression.

In the summer of 1947 I luck into a job alternating as a waiter and a bellhop aboard the S.S. *Manitoulin*, an aging iron bucket of a tourist and cargo boat that sails out of Owen Sound and cruises the waters of Georgian Bay and of Lake Huron's beautiful, island-studded North Channel as far as Sault Ste. Marie and the east end of Lake Superior. In addition to a passenger list happily composed of a goodly number of maiden Michigan aunts taking pretty nieces on summer vacations, the ship also carries freight, and probes in and out of small harbours, serving isolated communities that will be reached by road only in the years to come. I begin to gain a sense of just how remote Canadian communities can be.

I and my fellow servants, all but one of us Queen's students, are happy to oblige when passengers request that the Chief Steward permit his boys to attend dances on the hurricane deck, but we also discover that some of the denizens of the freight deck and the engine room are every bit as interesting as the holidaying folk on the upper decks. We like to smuggle pretty tourists down to the freight deck for impromptu singalongs led by a guitar-playing chef.

On weekends the character of the tour tends to alter. The ship takes a shorter run, up to South Bay on the southeast corner of Manitoulin

Island, down to Tobermory, the "Tub," on the Bruce Peninsula, and then home again. These are somewhat chaotic voyages, a great deal of beer, whisky, and other lubricants having come aboard the unlicensed ship in passengers' luggage. And the passenger list is quite different from that of the week-long voyage. The maiden aunts and nieces have given way to couples, which may include somebody's aunt, but certainly not many maidens. Now, when the bellhop's call board bell rings, I never know whether the request will be for a bucket of ice or simply a bucket, and when I knock on the cabin door I cannot predict what educational scene will be unveiled.

By the end of the summer I verify, painfully, what I already know — I am a sailor but my stomach is not. It is mid-September. We are on the last tourist run for the year and my inner man feels secure and well seasoned. I suffered through rough weather at the beginning of the season, but I have forgotten that there is such a thing as the summer calm before the autumn storm. On this last trip I am a bellhop, and have drawn the lonely midnight to morning shift.

We leave the North Channel, strike south past Manitoulin Island, and head into Georgian Bay. For the steward's crew it's the home stretch of our final run. But when the old lady sails south across the edge of the gap that lies between Manitoulin Island and the Bruce Peninsula the wind rises and all hell breaks loose. She turns around and scurries for cover.

For a day and a night we hide behind a pile of rock the charts appropriately call "Lonely Island." We are due in Owen Sound Saturday morning, but it's going to be late Sunday at the earliest before we make it. Some of the passengers are enraged. They are bloody well nuts. I want to get back, too, to university, but my stomach is willing to stay here until freeze-up and then crawl home on the ice.

It is nighttime before we finally hoist anchor from behind Lonely Island and again dive off into the turmoil. My stomach is making dour comments about life in general, but my brain is wildly excited. I have never before been out of sight of land in a *real* storm.

For a while I stay down near the call board next to the passageway to the engine room and watch through a window as the dark seas foam by. There are a couple of calls from passengers, but tonight no one is after ice. They've had misfortunes en route to the bog and want their tracks covered. My stomach tells me such clean-ups are not a good exercise even for a seasoned sailor. I tell it to shut up.

About 0200 hours I desert my post and head for the bridge. This is a desperation move. My brain says there will be so much action on the bridge it will take my mind off my stomach. My brain is partly right. There is lots of action on the bridge — or, to be more precise, just outside. Great waves are coming right over the bow. They break and divide against the passenger lounge below, and the spray soars over the wheelhouse.

My stomach reports from my engine room that I have made a miscalculation. Down in the lobby, amidships and almost at the waterline, there was less movement. Here on the bridge, well forward and high up, both the forward pitch and the sideways roll are extreme. Probably the only place that is worse is that iron hellhole deep in the bow where the steward's crew burrow, and no power on earth will get me down into it.

Lance, the First Mate, is watching me with a silly look on his face. He thinks my bilges are about to overflow. He's right, damn him. I make it to the leeward rail of the hurricane deck and pray that no idiot below has a porthole open. Having pumped the bilges I then go through the recreation lounge, down onto the passenger deck, and down again into the lobby. I don't even look at the call board. If anyone is dying let them die. I'll see them in the sweet Hereafter. I unlock a little door that leads under a counter and into the canteen and I crawl through and close it behind me. I lie down on the floor of the canteen, pouring with sweat. I tear off the silly bow tie, open my shirt, loosen my jacket, and slip into oblivion.

When I come to, the pounding and the swaying and the plunging have all ceased. I lie with my eyes closed wondering if I am dead. Then I realize I can feel the vibration of the engines through the steel floor that is my bed. There are voices and they are right over me, only a few feet away. The voices belong to the First Mate and the Captain. I keep my eyes closed, hoping the officers will go away. This is no place for the duty bellhop to be performing his duties — a seasoned sailor, and a Queen's man to boot.

"Well, I don't know," says Lance, "I'd say there's not much left. Why don't we just put a stamp on him and mail him home?"

"Could do," says the Captain, "but I hate to pass up a chance for a burial at sea."

I know Captain Morrison has been waiting to get his hands on me. One of the steward's crew is always duty waiter at the Captain's table in Owen Sound harbour even when there are no passengers on board. There have been some devilish hot days this summer and at one point we took to serving in our shirt sleeves. The Captain issued strict written orders that the officers were always to be served by waiters wearing both jacket and tie. Or else! I had been the next one on the roster and the day had been hot enough to melt the hinges of Hell. I turned up at the Captain's side, napkin on arm, menu in hand, wearing my jacket and tie, as ordered, but no shirt. He hadn't said a word, but had stared at me, thoughtfully, for a full minute.

Now, here I am, helpless, laid out, my eyes firmly shut, and here is the Captain muttering about burial at sea.

Suddenly I utter a large shout and sit bolt upright. The Captain has just deposited a handful of ice on my bare chest.

"Congratulations," he says. "You made it. The whole summer. We figured you'd jump ship at the Soo on that first trip."

There is a smile on that dour face. If I had a picture of it I would frame it, like an award.

I complete my Queen's studies in the spring of 1948, but continue my off-campus, non-academic education during a long summer in which the Precambrian Shield, with its rivers, forests, granite, and lakes, becomes embedded in my Canadian psyche.

I am twenty-one years old and for the first time in my life I am in an airplane. Not just any airplane, but a Norseman, on floats, flying over the forests of the Thunder Bay Region in Northern Ontarios, heading for a forest fire.

According to the radio reports the whole of Northern Ontario must be on fire. Doesn't look like it from up here. For one thing, at least half of Northern Ontario seems to be water. I've never seen so many lakes, even in my dreams. Big lakes, small lakes, round lakes, long lakes, jagged lakes; clear water, deep water, sparkling water; swamps, rivers, creeks, waterfalls, and rapids — it all flows past a thousand feet below our wings. And around the water and under it and in it is rock. The forest itself appears to be rooted in rock. I've spent my entire life living on the fringe of the Canadian Shield but never until now did I really understand that when the geography books talk about the Precambrian rock, they mean ROCK.

I have the best seat in the house. The co-pilot's seat. The other fellows are on the benches behind. There are six of us in the team, all university students employed for the summer by Ontario Lands and Forests, later to become MNR, Ministry of Natural Resources. Our team leader, Ray Alexander, is studying engineering and three of the others are studying forestry. Alex Davidson and I are artsmen, both from Queen's. The other guys are from lesser institutions, like the U. of T. Alex's home is Fort William,* and he's the one who alerted me to this job.

We are supposed to be a fire prevention team, not a firefighting team, but Lands and Forests has its back to the wall. The rangers have already been recruiting in the beer parlours and flophouses of the Lakehead and the Soo. "Recruiting" is a euphemism. When the fires are burning, the forestry men have impressive authority. They can go through a flophouse like an old-time press gang impounding manpower for the Royal Navy. We students have not been shanghaied, but we tell ourselves that when the Department sends us into battle it has obviously reached the bottom of the barrel. We must be Ontario's last hope.

The fires are not fictitious. There is smoke on the horizon. Great clouds of it are rolling up from scattered locations. The pilot points to the smoke that marks our destination, Dog Lake. We fly into turbulence. Those big bonfires can disrupt the airflow over hundreds of square miles! The plane begins to bucket and thump around as though its floats are on a ploughed field. I am on my first flight and I'm en route to a forest fire and suddenly I can't get my mind off my stomach. My stomach doesn't seem to know this is an exciting day.

Our fire is almost beneath us. It stretches for miles, but one edge is close to the shores of a lake, our lake, Dog Lake. The pilot puts the stick forward and we come down at a ridiculous angle. He goes into a tight bank and we are supposed to peer down and get a good view of our destination. I look out and down and see the whole world revolving around the end of the wingtip and my stomach begins to whirl with it. I search the cockpit frantically, fruitlessly, hoping to find a box, a paper bag, an old boot. The only container I find is my hat. The pilot flies a circuit of the bay where he intends to land. He tells me he's checking for floating logs so we don't prang on touchdown. I couldn't care less. I'm thinking of taking a shortcut and jumping. I clench my teeth and pray for a fast touchdown. The pilot thinks he is a tour guide. He points out the cluster of tents on shore. That is our base camp. Who the hell cares? I am about to astonish him and disgrace myself. I decide that if necessary I will definitely use the hat.

Our floats touch down and suddenly we are a motorboat. There's more wave on the surface than I had realized and the pilot thinks he's running a carnival ride. He crosses the bay, cheerfully skipping his craft from wave crest to wave crest, until we move into more placid waters.

---

*   Also known as "The Lakehead"; today it is part of Thunder Bay, Ontario.

We are still on the go but I am already out on the starboard float. I don't recall getting here but by God the air feels good and I'm relieved to find I have stayed in one piece. The plane swings alongside a little rustic dock and I am the first ashore. If the other fellows think I must be gung-ho for action, that's okay by me.

It is late in the afternoon so we pitch our tent and take stock. The other valiant firefighters have been flown in within the last twenty-four hours, but we are surprised to find most of them still in camp. We soon discover that we are the only ones who have not arrived either drunk or hungover. Except for the Ranger.

He is a lean, slight, wiry man of Scandinavian ancestry. He has been given the impossible task of containing a rim segment of a forest fire with a handful of derelict troops. He wears no uniform and has no support staff — no officers, no sergeants. He doesn't need them.

The last sound we hear before we go to sleep is the Ranger's voice and the sound of breaking glass. He is raiding tents and smashing bottles of confiscated booze against a big rock. The first sound we hear in the morning is the Ranger's voice bawling for action. Some of his bleary-eyed troops are still carrying their heads, gently, under their arms, but all report for duty.

Our little team is broken into three pairs and each pair is assigned duty as nozzle men with a pump team of conscripts. We are told what the fire is doing and what our Ranger is hoping to accomplish and where there are other groups of men working out of other base camps. We go into the woods carrying rolls of fire hose. The pump men are carrying the portable gasoline pumps that we refer to by their trade name, Wajax. The pumps will draw from streams, springs, ponds, swamps, whatever we can find. Judging by what I saw from the air, it's not unreasonable to expect to find water close to wherever we need it.

Alex and I, the two artsmen, are together as a nozzle team. The pumps put out impressive pressure, but one man can handle a nozzle. He requires the other fellow with him, however, to haul the hose and keep it clear of snags. The two can trade duties to prevent exhaustion.

We come to the top of a narrow ridge and we're facing an inferno. The fire moves fastest along the ridges. Down in the hollows where there is more moisture, often swamp, it doesn't go at the same racehorse pace. Thanks to the great glacier of twenty thousand years ago the ridges are roughly parallel, and in this area several crews are simply trying to block the advance along several adjacent ridges. It doesn't seem to us that it can possibly add up to anything significant in terms of the overall scheme and we're probably correct. However, the idea seems to be, "You can't do much but dammit do what you can and pray for rain." In this frail world maybe that's not a bad strategy. Hold the fort until God arrives.

The heat is terrible but the nozzle force is just sufficient to keep us at a bearable distance from the flames. The fire moves in stages. It burns its way forward through underbrush, seems to loiter for a moment at the base of trees, then suddenly surges upward. The cedars crackle for a moment before being engulfed in an upward roll of flames, but the balsams almost explode. A stand of balsams is all proud and green one moment and then, with a sound like a cannon, the whole stand is instantly in flames. Once the flames are in the treetops they can rush forward at alarming speed — an airborne assault.

Sometimes we can soak the trees ahead of the advance and actually beat the flames down while they are still in the brush, but when we lose the battle on the ground we have to retreat. Occasionally, but only occasionally, a free-standing tree ignites and we are able to hit the upper branches and sweep downward, wiping the flames off as if we were stripping feathers from a freshly killed fowl.

It is a frightening, terrible place to be, and Alex and I both know we wouldn't exchange places with anyone at this most exhilarating moment of our lives. Others don't necessarily feel the same way.

We are in the process of battling a surge when the water stops and the hose goes limp. We drop it and run, following its inert length several hundred feet to where the little red Wajax is sitting alone, deserted and silent, its feeder hose running uselessly down to a creek. The poor derelicts who were our pump tenders have not only run, they've shut off the pump. We are enraged. We get the pump going and manage to retrieve our hose and retreat. The men rejoin us, sheepishly. They'd been watching other ridges and thought they were being cut off.

At the end of the day we compare notes with the other four guys and find that all six of us are worried. We tell the Ranger we'll go anywhere he says and we'll do what he orders but from now on we'll do it as a team. At least we know we won't run away on each other. The Ranger agrees.

At the end of the next day the Ranger doesn't return to camp. We want to look for him but nobody seems to remember where he was last seen. There is a rumour that he has been trapped. Just before sunset he walks into camp looking tired and dirty, but uninjured. The rumour was correct. He had found himself surrounded by flames, completely cut off.

He saw a slight gap and charged through, not to the outside but to the inside, into the burn. It was his only chance, and the odds against him were huge, but he took it and won. He had a long walk through appalling conditions before he could make his way out again, but here he is. Our admiration for this man is enormous.

It rains. The heavens collapse and our fire goes away in a night and a day. Or almost.

Most of the men are flown out, but our gang and a few of the more dependable types are kept on. We are sent to patrol a portion of the burn. As yet no one has assessed the whole damage, but we figure that at least one hundred square miles of forest has been turned to smouldering ashes in this little Dog Lake fire. It is the smouldering that is now of concern. What lies in the middle of the blackened desert bothers no one, but along the edges the sparks from a fallen log or a smouldering stump can be fanned back into flames and the whole thing can take off again. Other patrols are being sent out from other base camps.

The six of us have one perimeter sector several miles in length as our domain. No, not six of us. There are now seven in our group. A big, good-looking, soft-spoken lumberjack has been gradually assigning himself to us. His name is George. He is intelligent and certainly not afraid of work and we like him. George is older than any of us and we are amused by the way he seems to be adopting us. He tells us he is a good cook and he keeps cajoling Ray, our intrepid team leader, for permission to join us as our company cook. George has learned that our team is scheduled to remain in the bush for the rest of the summer.

The burn is a frightful place to patrol. Except for the green fringe of the forest beside us it is black as far as the eye can see and deep in rain-soaked ashes. There is no underbrush. Many trees still stand but they are charred, lifeless sticks. We are walking through a world that looks like the scenes of no man's land from the First World War.

Each of us carries an axe and a pack-pump. We carry these pack-pumps on our backs; the tank of water is connected by a short hose to a long nozzle with a sliding section that we pump back and forth to create pressure. We call the contraptions "piss-pumps," because that about sums up their effectiveness. When we see something smouldering too close to the forest's edge we chop it open and let the pump piss into it. When the packs run dry we go off into the surviving woods in search of a stream or a spring for replenishment. In this country one never has to go far.

In the woods the mosquitoes and black flies are ferocious. At least the mosquitoes are big enough to swat. Some are big enough to shoot. But the black flies are misery incarnate. Every evening when we return to camp we strip and fall into the lake, and we are always streaming with blood from fly bites. The only part of me that's not perforated and blood-smeared is from the calves down, where I am kept secure by my tight-laced, hobnailed, high-cut leather boots. Evening is blessed relief. There's nothing to be achieved except rest. We light a small campfire on the shelving shoreline rock, as though we've not had enough of flames and smoke, and the six of us gather around and sing, softly, not wanting to disturb or annoy exhausted sleepers. After "Home on the Range" and "The Red River Valley" we slide into "Along the Navajo Trail," then fall silent. A gravelly voice growls out from one of the darkened tents. We recognize it as belonging to one of the now-sober derelicts. "Don't stop, boys."

It's our third day on the burn, chopping, pissing, re-filling, packing, and plodding, when we make an amazing discovery. Two discoveries. We stop to rest beside a big limestone outcropping where the heat must have been enormous. Not only is the underbrush all gone, but so is the moss. The rocks have been burned clean and the one we are resting beside has had its whole surface chipped and flaked by the searing heat. At the base of this rock there is a crevice in the Precambrian stone; we peer into this crevice to find that a mere three feet below the surface there is solid ice.

The other discovery is even more amazing. We see a lump in the fork of a charred tree. The lump is about six feet from the ground and when we investigate we find it's a porcupine. Its quills are burned. Its claws are burned. Even its teeth seem to be burned. It is probably blind. But it is alive!

Out here in the aftermath of Nature's Armageddon we get into a bizarre debate. Should the porcupine be killed or not? I say kill it. Others say definitely not. It has survived the unsurvivable, therefore, they argue, it deserves to live. I listen in disbelief. This is higher education gone mad. We put it to an open vote. George and I vote for euthanasia. The others vote for life. Five against two. Democracy must rule and we go on our way.

A while later George and I move off together to attend to a smouldering root system that is perilously close to the bush. Smouldering roots are dangerous. Fire can run along underground and burst up again, much later, at a distance. We call to the others that these roots will take us a while and that we'll catch up.

We attend to the root, but when the others are out of sight we circle back to the porcupine. It's still clinging both to the tree and to life, but barely. A clean axe blow ends its suffering. On one level I am relieved, but on another I feel guilty. George and I have denied democracy.

A day or so later George is in difficulty. His left arm has been so badly mauled by black flies that he has developed blood poisoning and the arm is raw and swollen. Ignoring his protests, the Ranger ships him off to the Lakehead in the Norseman. George seems distraught at not being able to remain with us, but we soon find that it's not from sentiment. At the Lands and Forests air base the police are waiting for him, and pick him up as he steps off the float. Our friend George had escaped from a penitentiary, where he was serving time for armed robbery. The police knew where he was but had no intention of interfering with him while he was being useful on a fire.

I think of George and of the porcupine and remember that at least once in my life when compassion came into conflict with ethics and democracy I opted for compassion, and in doing so saw eye to eye with a convicted criminal.

We are airlifted out of the Dog Lake burn. We are still north of Superior in the bush of the Thunder Bay Region but now we are doing what we signed up to do. We are finding suitable sites for new forestry fire towers. To permanent staff down in the Lakehead we are simply "the tower crew." To ourselves, we are wilderness adventurers, map-makers, and high riggers.

Fire towers are a common sight in the more southerly areas of Ontario's forest wilderness. They stand on commanding hilltops, where they thrust themselves another hundred feet into the air. They are four-square timber towers, and on top of their sturdy frames they support a square wooden room, fully roofed, well windowed, and equipped with a two-way radio, a map table, a telescope, a compass, and the rudimentary comforts of home. Access is via a ladder within the framework of the big tower.

During the summer months these towers are manned by students like ourselves, two to a site, who live in a small cabin near the base but who spend their days aloft, spelling each other off, constantly scanning the surrounding hundreds of square miles of heavily forested Precambrian Shield for any signs of smoke that might indicate a blossoming fire. If smoke is spotted the observer radios the compass reading to the nearest ranger station. If luck is with them another tower will also radio its sighting, and together the two will give accurate map co-ordinates. A bush plane is then dispatched to check it out.

We are up here in the Thunder Bay Region finding suitable sites for the expansion of the tower service. The theory is simple. Find the highest hill in a given area, raise a temporary tower, and on existing topographical maps shade in the areas that can be viewed from on high. Move on to neighbouring areas and repeat the procedure. The resulting maps, when juxtaposed and analysed for line-of-sight observation, should show the best locations on which to raise permanent towers. That's the theory.

The execution is damned hard work. We are equipped with a portable tower. It's composed of ladders, in sections, each section a little over ten feet long. There are two half-sections. All these pieces interlock. When the tower is fully raised it is composed of two parallel ladders twenty-two inches apart, cross-braced every few feet and soaring one hundred feet into the air. It is guyed at intervals by strong ropes reaching out from each corner and firmly secured at ground level to stumps or trees. About three and a half feet below the top, the cross-braces support the boards of a floor. On top of the tower a map table with a hole in its centre the same dimensions as the tower surrounds all four sides. The map-maker stands on the floorboards, his body protruding up through the table, and has a breathtaking view of the surrounding wilderness of hills, trees, rocks, lakes, rivers, and swamps.

We fly by bush plane to each new site. The planes are float-equipped Norsemen, the workhorse of the north. Ray, our leader, having already checked the topographical map of the area, has an idea where he wants to locate, but at each location holds his final decision until the pilot has given him a bird's-eye view of possible hills. Then Ray and the pilot look for the nearest campsite. It has to be on a body of water large enough for the Norseman to land and take off. The plane has the six of us on board, along with tents, food, cooking gear, axes, ropes, and other miscellaneous inventory. Outside, lashed on top of the floats, are two eighteen-foot double-skin canoes. In spite of this cargo the pilot often does some fancy flying. At one site there is a small L-shaped lake whose full length is required for a laden take-off, so here the pilot raises the outer float just enough to permit him to do a sliding slalom at full speed on the corner. Another short lake has a high cliff at the downwind end. To get down to water level as quickly as possible our pilot does a slideslip over the cliff, straightening out just in time to touch down. These pilots are a special breed. A few years ago they were jockeying Spitfires and Hurricanes over Britain and Europe. I doubt we will ever see their kind again.

At each new location we make our way ashore and off-load the gear. While some of us make camp the others fly out with the pilot to pick up the tower. The Norseman returns with the ladder sections lashed to the floats and with the rest of our ton or so of gear on board. The Norseman leaves and we are on our own.

Once camp is secure we make our way to the top of the designated hill. Depending on the location of base camp, it may mean a trek of a mile or more. On the hilltop, Ray often climbs the highest tree to see if the prospect still makes sense. Then we take our axes and create a hill-top clearing. And the pathway up has to be cleared of brush, because we're going to cart ladders up here and then backpack the rest of the tower gear.

The daily journey to work varies with each location. At Leopard Lake we strike straight inland. On the Nanewaminikan River we stay in a log cabin at an abandoned gold mine and canoe half a mile up the river each morning before thrusting uphill into the bush. Here the commuter can round a bend and confront a full-racked bull moose standing knee-deep in the water lilies. We spend the July 1st national holiday of 1948 cutting a trail that will permit us to portage the canoes so that we can shortcut across a swamp so full of weeds it is like a putrid sponge. Now, on the hottest day of the summer, it reeks of decay. One can thrust a paddle deep into this morass without bottoming, but in a few hundred years this will probably be solid ground. We dub it "coonshit pond," and carry on through the black flies and the heat and think of friends at home enjoying barbecues, parades, and fireworks.

When the designated hilltop has been cleared of trees and the tower gear has been carried to the site, we assemble three interlocking ladders to make a thirty-foot section. This is hoisted upright and guyed four ways. It then acts as a gin pole to raise a thirty-five-foot section facing it. We climb these two ladders, cross-bracing them together as we go. The extra five-foot height of one side provides a high point to which we attach a hoist that is used by the ground crew hauling on a rope to hoist the next section of ladder, and so on to the hundred-foot level, alternating the hoist from one five-foot extension to the other and guying every fifteen feet. It's a one-man job up top, swinging each section into place, cross-bracing it, and securing the guys. Some of us have a better head for it than others. Eventually, Ray and I take turns doing most of the high rigging, though he usually does the final heart-stopping section. I tell myself I'd rather be up top, precariously perched on almost nothing, gradually climbing above the trees into a panoramic world of visual splendour than be sweating down below on the end of heavy ropes and surrounded by steaming air and black flies. To each his own.

Once the tower is in place everybody takes turns up top doing the "visible area mapping." Again it's a one-man job, standing in an eighteen-inch-square manhole, a hundred feet above the top of the highest hill in the area, fully exposed to the scorching sun of summer. It's a job that cannot be rushed and is dependent on the weather. If visibility is limited by mist or rain, there's no point going aloft. If it is too windy we don't dare. Even a moderate wind can be a hazard. Although the tower is thoroughly guyed, the whole contraption sways slightly in a breeze. One day it gets to me. Me and my damned stomach. I get seasick, throw up, and come down pale and shaking.

The tower is always being fine-tuned. At the end of each day we slacken the ropes just a little, in case of rain. Next morning, first thing, we snug them up. One evening we forget to loosen them. It rains and the ropes shrink. Next morning the bottom thirty feet, below the first guys, has a bow in it almost beyond belief. Another morning we find that a bear has been clawing the bottom ten feet the way a cat claws at a scratching pole.

Mapping days are good days. While one of us is aloft the rest of us can goof off and relax, write letters, go fishing, canoeing, or swimming, or just sleep. Each day ends with a swim. Out here in the wilderness we never wear swimsuits, until one day we wind up at a campsite that is within a half-mile of a ranger station. The ranger says his wife objects to us skinny-dipping within range of her binoculars. We don't like to ask whether she feels shocked or deprived.

Our regular free time is during the long peaceful twilight of the Ontario summer. This is the time to do laundry, play cards, read, or just relax.

It's during an idyllic evening calm on the shores of one of a million isolated Precambrian lakes that I slide a canoe into the water and wander off by myself, skirting the rock-bound shoreline.

I am not an expert, but I'm very comfortable in a canoe. Happy might be a better word. It's a state of mind I learned from Dad one memorable afternoon when I was about fourteen, and Stoney Lake was being creamed to foam by a good west wind. We took our canvas-covered cedar-strip canoe and, together, fought our way up the lake, mainly to see if we could stay afloat. (Dad was a stickler for kneeling and not sitting, for carrying a spare paddle, and, if one miscalculated, for remaining with an overturned canoe.) Having made it as far as the ragged Jack

pine on the west end of Salmon Island, we managed to come about in
seas that would swamp a motorboat, and then we were up and away,
heading for home.

Although we couldn't beat the waves we could almost stay with
them, and suddenly everything became quiet. I had not realized how
much noise there had been before, with the canoe slapping into the
oncoming waves, with the wind in my face, with the noise of my own
breathing. Now the canoe was almost sighing, the wind was on my back,
and the wave crests made softly foaming sibilant supportive sounds as
they broke and capped on either side of us. It had been a hard haul to
get there, but the result had been exhilarating happiness.

A canoe can be the most silent of all watercraft, and now, at the age
of twenty-one, in this northern wilderness with not a breath of evening
wind, I revel in tranquility. By using the correct stroke one can even
eliminate the sound of paddle drip. I like cruising these shores, which
constantly change from out-thrusting rock to overhanging forest to
mysterious swamp. One never knows what one will encounter. I see the
small V of the wake made by the head of a bank beaver swimming for
shore. He sees me and simply dives, giving only a half-hearted tail-slap
of alarm. An adult loon and two youngsters also slip under, but I suspect
they're more interested in fishing than upset by my quiet presence. A
blue heron lumbers overhead, its long neck curled back, its head resting
comfortably near its shoulders and its long legs trailing behind, the slow
rhythm of its three-foot wings carrying it casually home to roost. I round
a rocky point and ahead, at the water's edge, a doe is drinking. No doubt
a game trail leads down to this spot. We are constantly crossing game
trails in the course of our days' work. When they lead our way we make
use of them ourselves, although we have to cut away the deadfalls that
the deer can clear at a bound. These trails are mini-highways in the wild.
The doe watches me a moment but I don't move, so she takes another
drink, then turns without haste and vanishes up the path. I begin to
convince myself that I am not an intruder.

A hundred yards offshore there is a rocky outcropping. Gulls are
wheeling around it. I know they know I'm here so I don't worry about
paddle drip and simply head out to take a look at the shoal and the
birds. Suddenly I'm in trouble. There must be nests out here, and two big
birds don't want me around. The first warning is the sound of rushing air
and a heavy swoosh as a gull swoops in from behind, almost brushing my
head with its wings. I look up in time to see another one coming straight
down at me, wings spread, trailing edge feathers splayed in the wind,

talons out-thrusting, beak half open ready to seize or to impale. I raise my paddle to ward the bird off and it veers aside at the last moment. These are the biggest gulls I have ever seen, but then I've never seen any gulls flying this close before. There is a movie that is set in the Scottish Isles in which fishermen execute a man by tying him hand and foot, putting a float under each armpit, tying a fish to his head, and setting him adrift in the sea. The gulls, dive-bombing scavengers, do the execution. My gulls aren't scavenging. I've invaded their nesting area, so they're out to kill. It occurs to me I may not only be the first human to pass their way but possibly the last. I seize the spare paddle (thank you, Dad, for the spare paddle rule) and with my left arm hold it upright, tight to my chest, the blade above my head. Only their own sense of self-preservation prevents the swooping birds from crashing into it. With my free arm I back-paddle out of there. The gulls return to their lazy, graceful evening vigil over this idyllic land.

Most of the time we eat heartily on this job and most of the time we're lucky enough to have a camp cook. Not always the same cook. They come and go. It's too bad George got extradited to prison. We could use him. For a time our cook is Harry, an elderly Ukrainian whose career was spent in lumber camps. He has a little trouble scaling down to a six-man crew. The first day he's with us we return from the tower site to find he has been baking peach pies. After a full meal of steak, potatoes, and vegetables each of us finds himself confronted by an entire pie.

"Harry," I say, "I'm not sure I can eat a whole pie."

Harry grabs a butcher knife and jumps up and down in front of me, screaming, "You don't like my peaches pie!"

"Harry, it's the best pie I ever ate." We all agree and tuck in.

Harry is not strong. The poor old chap should be in a home, not out here in the bush. Eventually he falls sick and is flown out. We are without a cook for a week and then Jim is flown in to our rescue. He's a seventy-year-old Metis and tough as nails. After the Norseman has departed and we have welcomed him ashore, he asks about his duties.

"You're the cook," says Ray, somewhat surprised.

"No, I'm not," says Jim, equally surprised. He's a quiet, gentle man, but one with whom you don't argue.

It's agreed that Jim will join us as a backpacker, axe man, and rope puller, while the rest of us will take turns at cooking. Jim asks if he can put his sleeping bag just inside the door of the sleeping tent. This puts him on the boughs next to me. Taking me aside, he explains, diffidently, that he snores.

"Just belt me," he says, "and I'll shut up."

Jim seems to enjoy working with us young fellows. At first he is a little embarrassed when he finds we're all university men. But gradually he seems to realize that for the life we're leading here he knows more than all the rest of us put together. Even so, I have to do some prodding to extract marvellous bits of wood lore.

He likes to watch us swimming, but confesses that he never learned. He seems envious. We finally convince him that he should give it a try. He strips down, but only to his long johns. Jim is of a generation that wears long johns winter and summer. He doesn't actually sew himself into them, as I understand the early settlers did, but almost. I suspect his long johns could stand by themselves — until now, that is, when he takes them swimming. We are very careful to lead him into water where the bottom shelves gently and there are no sudden surprises. He wanders gingerly around, water up to his chest, a blissful smile of discovery on his face.

The day we are closing down our last tower site we are all in a good mood and compete to see how fast we can backpack the gear down from the hilltop. We are heading up for the last few loads when we meet Jim on his way down. "This is it, boys," he says. "There's no more."

He has the big backpack and it's bursting at the seams. He has laid iron stakes and an axe crosswise on top of it and coils of rope on top of that. Jim doesn't use shoulder straps but carries the whole weight on a tumpline across his forehead. He must have hundreds of pounds on board and he's seventy years old. We feel like children.

A few days later, after we're disbanded at the Lakehead, I try to find Jim to say goodbye. I'm told he's in a beer parlour and I eventually locate him. Jim is a beer-sodden, trembling mess. He shakes my hand with tears in his eyes and says, "I didn't want you to see me like this."

I can't help seeing him like that, but I also see a kind, gentle, friendly man, gifted with enormous physical strength, like the rock-ribbed land that bears us.

7

CHOICES

THE AUTUMN OF 1948 finds me at a new home, this time in Lindsay, Ontario. Dad and Mother have moved here because Dad has become minister of Queen Street United Church.

Now that I have graduated from Queen's, it is time for me to lay out a course for the future, but I haven't a clue where I'm going. I spread out the charts, try to figure out where I am, lay in a few close co-ordinates to somewhere, and prepare to set sail on the first reach of a journey that has, at best, a nebulous destination. It's mostly a matter of making choices, one after another, and whether I'll be guided by brains, God, or hormones is not for me to pre-judge.

While I've been studying for my B.A. I've told myself and everyone else that I'm headed for journalism. Officially it's my intention to go to the States for post-graduate studies. I've been talking about either Columbia or Northwestern Universities, if either will have me — and if they have any standards, that is by no means certain. But there are no post-grad courses in journalism in the Canada of 1948. However, one thing is certain. I'll have to work for the winter to make it possible.

But I am no sooner out of the bush and at home in Lindsay than I am notified by the Queen's University Drama Guild that I have won the one-act category of a national playwriting contest the Guild had sponsored. I had written my entry as a means of relaxing during my final exams. It was a nationalistic farce called *Sunstroke*, and it never gets produced — probably fortunately. But the win does help me alter my objectives. It occurs to me that drama is a lot more fun than journalism. Some of the happiest moments in my life have been on stage in amateur theatricals in both high school and university, and I enjoyed every minute of my involvement with the Queen's radio station. Moreover, CBC radio is doing breakthrough work in broadcast drama in Toronto. The CBC

Stage series, sparked by people like Lister Sinclair, John Drainie, Len Peterson, and Esse W. Ljungh, is establishing worldwide standards.

I hare down to Toronto and, with remarkable ease, am granted an interview with Lorne Greene, later of *Bonanza* fame, who has recently founded a broadcasting school, The Academy of Radio Arts. Lorne listens to my voice and tells me to avoid radio. I get the same advice in Kingston from my Queen's drama professor, Dr. "Doc" William Angus. Doc advises me to go to Cornell and study playwriting under his old professor, A.M. Drummond. I have enormous respect for Doc and I decide that if Cornell will have me, that's what I'll do.

I still need to work for a year, and winter jobs are scarce. I find temporary work in a Lindsay feed mill. It consists of heaving hundred-pound bags around for eight hours a day, but after four months in the bush I'm in the best condition of my life. In order to fill my spare time, I begin directing a one-act church basement play, *Mr. Bean from Lima*, a nonsense item from the Samuel French catalogue.

Then along comes a letter from the Regional Forester at Thunder Bay suggesting I return to the Lakehead for the winter to correlate the mapping information gleaned during the summer. I loved that summer in the bush. It occurs to me that if I go I might be permanently hooked. Forestry could be a worthwhile career. And I can do post-grad studies in Forestry without even leaving Canada!

There is a dilemma here. Drama or the bush? Am I veering off course? Do I even have a course? If my ship has a rudder it's not doing a very good job.

One day I drop into Woolworth's on Lindsay's Kent Street, wishing to talk to June, a clerk in the store and an actress in *Mr. Bean from Lima*. June introduces me to a new girl who has just been hired as a pre-Christmas temporary. She's a marvellously pretty girl with extraordinarily blue eyes, light brown hair, an English accent, that amazing complexion that seems to be a product of England's abominably humid climate, and an entrancing figure that does wonders for a sweater. Her name is Hilda Davison and she has just arrived from Manchester, England, on a one-way ticket. She is here to visit her sister, Anne, who is married to Bob Smith, a former Canadian merchant seaman from the Lindsay area who is now superintendent of Lindsay's Riverside Cemetery. It is Hilda's intention to work for a year in order to buy a ticket for home.

My eyes meet with those of this Lancashire lass and I'm snared. Our destinies are entwined and I know it. (Later, comparing notes, I find that she knows it, too.)

I feel an overpowering urge to by-pass the forestry offer and remain in Lindsay for the winter. I rationalize this by saying that Dad is not well and an extra hand during the winter will be useful. Anyway, heart and hormones rule. I stay put, romance flourishes, and I apply to Cornell and am accepted.

A career course has been charted by fate, and fate is a lassie from Lancashire.

Hilda Davison — her middle name is Mary — is two years younger than I am, but what a difference in life experiences! We were both youngsters when the Second World War broke out, but when the air raids began ten-year-old Hilda had been evacuated from Manchester and sent to strangers in the country. She had not liked the experience and had un-evacuated herself. When she arrived home her parents had let her stay. She and her mother decided they didn't care for the backyard bomb shelter, so when German planes came over they would shelter under the kitchen table. While I'd been studying airplane silhouettes Hilda had been evading the real McCoy. She had gone to work at the age of four-teen but had studied assiduously in the company school and had acquired highly coveted English secretarial diplomas, with her short-hand clocking in at eighty words per minute and the certificate pro-claiming "distinction." For her holidays she had joined the "Land Army" and picked vegetables.

Now, having migrated to Lindsay, Hilda goes in the space of a few months from the Woolworth's clerking job to a secretarial job at a seed company, then on to Lands and Forests, where she sells waterfront Crown Lands for ten cents per foot of frontage, and finally to a position as private secretary to the General Manager of Visking, the first Ameri-can branch plant to hit town. I soon realize that a charmingly pretty exterior and an outwardly shy personality house an individual who is both adaptable and determined. When I also discover her bubbling sense of humour I am totally captured.

My own jobs are useful but, for me, insignificant, other than as a means of earning much-needed money. I go from the feed mill to the egg-grading plant of Silverwood's Dairy. When the summer of 1949 rolls around I drive a milk truck on a rural route. But for that whole glorious winter and summer Hilda and I spend all our free time together. We stroll in the moonlight through old Riverside Cemetery. We join a dys-functional Little Theatre group, sing with an eighty-voice community choir and with the smaller church choir, attend boring meetings of the

Young Peoples Union (Hilda protestingly, me from a sense of duty), go canoeing on Stoney Lake — and at every opportunity make love clandestinely, sinfully, and oh so devotedly.

The future may be unclear, but I have the strongest feeling imaginable that this Lancashire lass is the nucleus around which my entire career will orbit.

8

GETTING
INTO MOVIES

DURING MY LAST SEMESTER at Cornell, in the summer of 1950, I almost panic. I want to work in Canada but my post-graduate studies have been in theatre, with a major in playwriting and a minor in dramatic literature. There are almost no professional theatres in Canada. The only one I know of is the Canadian Repertory Theatre, in Ottawa. I make contact in the spring and, not knowing the politics of the place, am quite buoyed up by the director, Sam Payne. Sam says "Yes," but apparently there is another director, Amelia Hall. I never meet Milly but she says "No." Milly wins.

One of the professors tells me of a teaching job at a college in the southwestern U.S. and urges me to apply. Says he'll recommend me and I'll probably get it. But no, the blood is strong, the heart is Canadian, and I, in dreams, behold the Precambrian Shield. It is Canada or bust. The only reason I am studying here in the States is that as yet no Canadian university offers post-graduate studies in drama, or in any related field.

And then a miracle happens. I attend a weekly campus film screening and see a marvellous Canadian short called *The Loon's Necklace*. The sparse credits say it was made by Crawley Films Limited, Canada. They don't identify a city, but I soon find that Crawley Films is based in Ottawa. I am excited. Film is a possibility. After all, it is related to theatre. I already know about the National Film Board of Canada and that it, too, is in Ottawa. I fire off a letter to Crawley Films and receive a courteous reply from the company Vice President, Graeme Fraser. He invites me to pay them a visit.

I complete my studies and, feeling well armed with an A.M. (Ars Magister) — which from now on, in the interests of clarity, I turn around, probably illegally, to the Canadian "M.A." (Master of Arts) — I make tracks for Ottawa. The Crawley company is located in an old church on Fairmont Avenue in the city's west end. I seem fated to be drawn to churches. Mr. Fraser greets me in a friendly fashion but says it's too bad but the man I really have to see is away on location. That man is Mr. Crawley himself. I promise to return.

The National Film Board is downtown in a long, ugly, ramshackle, barn-like building sandwiched between the beautiful Rideau Falls and the aristocratic French Embassy. I go to the NFB to submit a job application and am instantly granted an interview. It is all very strange. A long thin man carrying a questionnaire on a clipboard ushers me into an almost barren room. There are only two chairs, both straight-backed and cushionless. He places these two chairs dead centre in the room, facing each other, and we sit down. Our knees are almost touching. He peers at me earnestly, glances at his clipboard, then peers again and asks, "What is a good citizen?"

What is a good citizen? The question has never occurred to me. I have been raised to *be* a good citizen, not to analyse it. Perhaps I should just say "me" and get on with it. But he looks so earnest. He must want something deeply profound. I don't want profundity, I want a job. I have no idea what I reply or what else he asks me, but there is no job for me at the National Film Board of Canada. In retrospect I decide that the "good citizen" question had been induced by the Gouzenko revelations, which had recently — and temporarily — given rise to a witch hunt for communists in Canada and had created a lot of angst within the Film Board. Maybe I bungled the citizen question and sounded like a commie.

I have friends in Ottawa, Margaret and Jack Bray. Margaret went to high school in Almonte and her husband, Jack, was in the RCAF. While courting he drove a marvellous Ford coupe with a rumble seat. I have fond teenage memories of all three of them. Jack is now a civil servant. They take me under their wing in their small apartment. Jack lends me some old clothes and I get work as a labourer on a construction site while I wait for Mr. Crawley to return to base.

After ten days as a hod carrier I am happy to hear that Mr. Crawley has materialized. I go to the studio and climb an old oaken staircase that leads to what was once the church balcony, but which has now been converted into two offices, each with a window opening onto the sound stage down below. Mr. Crawley is a handsome, solidly built man with the ruddy complexion of an outdoorsman and I will soon learn that he would rather be in a lumber camp with a camera than here in an office. Presumably Graeme Fraser has given him a briefing, because he apparently knows that I was here before and have been lying in wait for him. I wonder if he is going to ask me to provide the recipe for a good citizen.

"What have you been doing?" he asks, and instinct tells me he is not interested in an account of my academic studies.

"Wheeling bricks and mortar on a construction site."

It's the magic question and the magic answer. He hires me. I'll earn $25.00 per week and will be assigned as an assistant to a director. What I will actually be is an apprentice. I don't know it but I am about to enter the best film school in Canada. No one has asked about my M.A., or for that matter my B.A. It is twenty-four years before the fact of having an M.A. is ever said to be relevant and that is when I go briefly to the University of Guelph as an Artist in Residence.

I go home to Lindsay to bear the good news and collect my things. Dad and Mother seem pleased and take the meagreness of my pay in stride. They take everything in stride. Even when I had announced I was going abroad to study, of all things, drama, they had never so much as flinched. Their forbearance has been monumental.

Hilda doesn't handle it as well. She now has the best secretarial job in Lindsay and when I tell her what I'll be earning in Ottawa she bursts into tears. I propose anyway, and after she has accepted she says she was only crying because she figured a guy earning such a lousy wage would never propose marriage. I guess I have no honour.

Hilda has already told me she'll never gamble more than three years on one man, and we've been going together now for two years. We agree on a one-year engagement. I'll be coming in just under the wire.

Meanwhile, I am on the absolute bottom rung of a career ladder.

My first day in the film business is probably a record-breaker, although I am too green to know it. I've been assigned to work with Producer/Director George Gorman but this first day I am seconded to Producer/Director/Editor Sally MacDonald as an extra pair of hands. Sally is "negative cutting" (whatever that means) a film that she has just edited and, I am told, is running out of time. It doesn't occur to me that if she is short of time the last thing she needs is the job of teaching me, and it is only later that I wonder whether this whole thing is some weird Crawley trial by fire.

I find myself wearing clean white cotton gloves and seated at a workbench that is covered with soft, immaculately white paper. I am learning the mysteries of rewinds and synchronizer. I find that there is a black and white "workprint" that has been edited to length and that there is the negative — which isn't negative but is the pristine original colour film — that must be cut to match the workprint. This is done by lining up tiny matching numbers found on the edge of the two films. Later I will realize that those tiny numbers aren't "found," they are put there. During the months ahead thousands of them will be put there by me, painstakingly, before editing takes place, with white ink and a sharp pen, a set of numbers every foot, one number on the workprint matched by the same number on the corresponding original, foot after foot after foot after foot, each foot containing forty frames, the synchronizer tabulating every foot to the frame.

But today I am matching numbers that already exist and am carefully winding through the original to find them. Next, under Sally's watchful eye, I verify that the numbers are lined up in the synchronizer and then roll gently forward to the next splice in the workprint and cut the original to match, allowing an extra half-frame, which will eventually disappear in a splice. To me it is a technical challenge that simply calls for concentration and care. It is only later I discover that the idea of a first-day novice not only handling original but actually putting scissors to it is unheard of. I also realize, later, it wasn't that anyone had confidence in me. They had unlimited confidence in Sally.

Sally graduated as a chemical engineer and entered the film world via the processing laboratory at the National Film Board before migrating here to Crawley's, where she makes a specialty of producing technical films for industrial sponsors. Sally is of the old school. She calls guys like me by their last name in a clipped, rather British fashion that brooks no disobedience. She is also a feminist pioneer and goes where few women have gone before — into the bowels of deep mines and hydro developments, usually a thousand miles from nowhere. She drives a car that is always full — food, files, clothing, a sleeping bag — and usually has a canoe on the roof. She likes to wear capes and long scarves and to camp out in winter and to take holiday canoe trips to back-of-beyond places like the Nahanni. Her father is Manley MacDonald, a prominent artist, and her mother is Beverley Lamb MacDonald, also an artist. Sally is both brilliant and eccentric, and comes by it honestly.

The film company was started by Budge Crawley (no one knows why he's called "Budge," but it's better than the Frank Radford that his parents saddled him with) and his wife, Judith. Since the war it has expanded rapidly and by the time I join in the fall of 1950 Crawley Films Limited is a going concern.

Among the folk here ahead of me are Producers Peter J.B. Cock, George M. Gorman, Quentin Brown, and Stanley Moore; Cameramen

Tom Glynn, Stan Brede, and Frank Stokes; Soundmen Rod Sparks and Tony Betts and an assistant, Paul Harris; Writers Judy Crawley and her sister, Cecily Chrzanowska. Neither of the sisters actually holds down office space. Cecily functions as a freelance. Judy is a power behind the throne but specializes in child development films and does her own thing. The two carpenters, Ignatz and Fred, are incomprehensibly Polish, and Wanda Nowakowska, the lady who eventually becomes the film librarian, is charmingly Polish. Two junior juniors, like myself, are Bill O'Farrell and Glen Robb. Both will far outlast me and are destined to keep the company on track long after its chief pilot begins to lose course. Another junior is Jean-Pierre Senècal, "J.-P." for short. J.-P. is from Montreal and along with George Gorman is destined to teach me how to make films. The oldest man on board, outranking everyone else in age by about 100 percent, is the janitor, Abe Clutterham. Abe's age gets added in with that of everyone else by Vice President Graeme Fraser when he writes company propaganda extolling a hundred man-years of film-making experience.

This gang is a diverse crew, some of whom have been shaped by the rough years of the recent World War. Peter Cock was the youngest Lieutenant Commander in the Canadian Navy and he still runs a tight ship. He is a descendant of Captain John Bligh of the *Bounty* and his middle initials, J.B., proclaim that heritage. He hides a compassionate heart under a firm exterior. Quentin Brown, too, was a naval officer and was on a Canadian minesweeper that was one of the fleet that led the way to the beaches of Normandy. Quentin, like me, carries an M.A. in drama from the States, but unlike me he has administrative ability, and is a party animal who can sing hilarious songs in a Scottish accent. Only once does he have to be carried home on a door. George Gorman is ex-RCAF. George is the type who, when the going gets tough, starts dancing. I see him, when lights collapse, the camera jams, and actors foul up, simply perform a soft shoe shuffle or tell a dramatic shaggy dog story until everyone's nerves unjangle. George is almost incoherent when he talks to actors but they always know what he means. Bill McCauley, head of the music department and destined to be music director for Toronto's O'Keefe Centre, is a talented composer and a rap artist ahead of his time — particularly when half cut and inspired by a party. Stan Moore is a handsome Irishman who has kissed the blarney stone more than once, but Stan's charm is not false — he *is* charming. Frank Stokes is from Germany and we call him "the Baron" more because of his accent than his bearing. Frank is very patient with apprentices like me. The Polish folk are what at this time are called Displaced Persons, or "D.P.s," and they are willing to work twenty-four hours a day to become undisplaced. The two carpenters are buying real estate and Wanda runs a rooming house while maintaining the aura of a society lady. Rod Sparks is Judy Crawley's brother. He is an extraordinarily quiet, introverted sound engineer who smokes a pipe, and occasionally on a Saturday uses the P.A. system to broadcast a clandestine and flatulent CBC record, *The Crepitation Contest*, on one occasion much to the consternation of a visiting Anglican bishop. Tony Betts is from Birmingham, England. He's a Cambridge grad, smokes a pipe, and has a devilish sense of humour and a notch in one ear where a boyhood arrow pinned him to a tree. Paul Harris, from Nova Scotia, the youngest of the whole crowd, likes to eat seaweed and liver and to drink dandelion wine. He came into the film business when he joined Budge on a Newfoundland whaling ship to lug sound equipment. In this establishment, apprentices get thrown straight into the deep end.

At the moment Paul and Tony are manufacturing more sound for a film called *Newfoundland Scene*. When I first meet them they are on the sound stage. Tony is manning a microphone while Paul, on a tall ladder, is lowering a large chain into a tub of water. Apparently a Newfie whaler is dropping anchor. Cecily has written a beautiful commentary that uses Newfoundland names to adorn the English language. I will come to regard this as one of the best documentaries ever made — before it gets pruned down to a state of political correctness. It will lose Stan Brede's scenes of the seal hunt and of the Toonerville Trolley train that used to circle Newfie on days when the wind wasn't high enough to blow it off the rails. At this time, Stan Brede is probably the best documentary cameraman the country has ever produced. His life is all too short.

For the first year I share a Spartan apartment with Tony and Paul, just two blocks from the studio.

As time goes by, other staff come and go. There is Ivan Herbert, who begins as a truck driver and ends up as head of the lighting department. Ivan was a submariner in the Royal Navy and is a good man in adverse conditions. There are two cameramen from Britain's J. Arthur Rank Company — Norman Allen, whom we nickname "Crikey" because that's his favourite expression, and Ian Matheson, who is sometimes, and unfairly, called "Mother Matheson" because he likes to have details under control. These two come from the feature film world of 35mm film, whereas the Canadian documentary/commercial field uses 16mm. The Brits have the unfortunate habit of referring to 16mm as "substandard" — "meaning no offence you understand." Years later I am privileged to be with Ian Matheson in the interior of China on a remarkable shoot for which he quite cheerfully and very professionally uses 8mm, about as substandard as one can get.* There is another Brit, a soundman, David Howells, nicknamed "Lofty" because of his height. There is a big, handsome Irishman named Patrick "Paddy" Reid, who breezes through the Crawley sales department before frustration with the general administrative chaos induces him to leave. He heads up the Federal Exhibition Commission during the 1967 Centennial and is the Commissioner General for Expo 86 at Osaka. There is an even bigger, handsome black from Chicago, Fred Casselberry, a lab technician. Fred hates police and loves progressive jazz. There is Kay Shannon, who goes on to the National Film Board and creates the trail-blazing Studio D, where films are made by women for women. Donald Carter, a highly experienced administrator from the British feature industry, becomes Production Manager. Donald arrives already talking about a book he has read that should be turned into a feature film. It tells the story of the "Black Donnellys" of southwestern Ontario. He is a couple of decades ahead of Canadian playwright James Reaney, who will popularize the savage Donnelly tale, but Budge, as usual, is not listening. Donald's son, Peter, comes on staff with him. Peter was in the British Army in Korea and when he eventually leaves Crawleys to freelance in the Canadian feature film industry his military toughness makes him a formidable Assistant Director in a ruthless business.

Two Producers come over from Holland. They are Ted de Wit and Gerard Raucamp, co-owners of a Dutch film company called Carillon Films. They are here to assess the Canadian industry and, possibly, either to set up a branch of Carillon or to join Budge. Gerard is the friendly, buttoned-down administrator type and Ted is a mutton-chopped, beaming-eyed extrovert. They and their wives only remain one year in Ottawa, but for Hilda and me it is the beginning of an enduring friendship.

Once I have finished my little stint as Sally's negative cutter, I am assigned to George Gorman as a Production Assistant. Jean-Pierre Senè-cal is already on board as George's Number One Assistant. The three of us are a Production Unit. George, as Producer, is assigned productions and the three of us work together, taking each project through from conception to finished print. J.-P. has a head start on me so he teaches me everything he has learned, including how to swear in two

---

*　See Chapter 29, "Global Glimpses Along the McClure Trail."

languages. George teaches both of us. There is not a person on staff who is not willing, even eager, to teach the apprentices.

The first film in which I am involved from the beginning is made for the Canadian Plumbing and Heating Association and the Canadian Pump Association and is called *Water on Tap*. It is shot on location, in the winter, on a farm near Ottawa, and shows in detail how running water is installed in a farming operation. We have to cope with the largest sponsors' film committee George has ever seen. There are forty-eight members. We all vow never again to be subject to such a committee. It becomes a standard goal, whether dealing with an advertising agency or directly with the sponsoring company, to keep the liaison committee to a mere handful — and preferably to no more than one.

The farm location is diverting. The male and female lead actors, both from New York, have some adjusting to do. John McLiam, whose TV image I spot off and on for many years, takes to his role with gusto. One day pigs make an unplanned escape and the entire crew, including John, indulge in a pig roundup. It is dirty, rough, and great fun. The crew also takes time out to supervise when Basil the bull puts the blocks to a cow.

We arrive on location one morning to find that another cow is about to give an unscripted birth. The farmer is away but his hired hand is here and needs some help. John mucks in and acts as midwife in the delivery of a bull calf. We are all standing around, suitably impressed by the marvel of birth, when the farmer arrives, sees that the calf is a useless bull, boots it on the head, and stomps angrily away.

We are filming in colour and the film speed is very slow compared to later standards. A great deal of lighting is required and we have a few nighttime setups for which we use the huge arc lights. The muscle for these set-ups is provided by juniors like me and J.-P.

During the course of that first winter there are other films. We shoot a basketball sequence in the gym of an Ottawa collegiate. Bill O'Farrell and I race each other in carrying lights to the top of a scaffolding.

I injure my back hoisting lights. At the time it seems like a simple strain, but soon it feels like a rupture. Eventually it turns out to be a ruptured disc. I am hospitalized in the Ottawa Civic Hospital for a couple of weeks, and then encased in a full body cast for most of the summer of 1951. No longer doing physical work, I am now on the job as an assistant director.

The summer is hot as Hades and we are shooting on the sound stage, where the lights make Hades seem like a cool retreat. The heat in my rubber-lined cast makes me throw up, and I lie down during breaks. Actress Barbara Hamilton is the first to autograph my cast, and other actors follow suit. The company frequently draws on the local Canadian Repertory Theatre for its actors, an eager crew with names like Ted Follows, William Shatner, Christopher Plummer, and William Hutt. I forget whose names I collect, but it doesn't matter, because I am too stupid to keep the cast as a souvenir.

I tell Budge I am going to be married in the fall and he tells me not to be an idiot and spoil my career. Hilda and I do postpone our wedding for one month, because it seems a good idea for the groom to shed his body cast before taking a bride. We are married in Queen Street Church, Lindsay, on September 29, 1951. It is a grand occasion. Hilda's sister Anne is Matron of Honour and my brother Doug is Best Man. Brother Don is in England studying for his surgical fellowship, but, pleasure of pleasures, Hilda's mother has come from Manchester. She is a lovely, diminutive lady whom everybody likes. Hilda and I are an unusual couple in that we both love our mothers-in-law. Dad officiates at the wedding.

During the reception that Hilda has engineered and paid for (I'm still on 25 bucks a week), Dad gives me a copy of the service. Doug and his wife, Jean, who are constantly supportive, having already subsidized me at Cornell, have lent us their Pontiac coupe. As we are driving out of town, Hilda says, "Wasn't it nice of your Dad to leave out the 'obey'?"

"Who are you kidding?" I say. "He wouldn't do that. 'Love, honour and obey,' that's what you promised."

"I did not!"

We pull over to the side of the road and stop, right there, by the ditch, while I unpack my copy of the service. Sure enough — she is correct! Dad has betrayed me. Did Mother have a hand in this? We continue on our way with me suitably docile. I never manage to get Hilda to obey. I learn to con her, when necessary, but never dare give her an order.

We have an apartment in the basement of a new apartment building across the river in Hull, Quebec, near the mouth of Brewery Creek, where the concrete piers of the MacDonald-Cartier Bridge will eventually embed themselves.

The ruptured disc has been a blessing. Not only did it postpone our wedding until the gorgeous weather of autumn, but it becomes a career boost as well. Budge has known all along I want to specialize in writing, so he moves me from the production unit and makes me, officially, a scriptwriter. The thought of a freelance career has not, as yet, occurred to me.

9

CRAWLEY FILMS
LIMITED

ONE YEAR AND A MONTH after we are married Hilda returns to England, not because she is leaving me, which would not be unusual in the film business, but because both her mother and brother Tom are sick. She goes by sea with a one-way ticket because that's all we can afford. She is away over Christmas and is hoping to return early in the New Year on the *Empress of Canada*. We are trusting that the year-end Crawley bonus will make her return possible. Recognizing this as wild optimism, the rest of the staff prepare to see me as a white-haired old man still waiting for a bonus to bring my wife home from England. As it turns out, the bonus is $5.00. So is my end-of-year monthly pay raise.

It also turns out that the *Empress of Canada* burns at her dock in Liverpool and Hilda's journey is radically delayed.

Hilda has adapted more rapidly to Canada than any other Brit I've ever met. She is already more Canadian than we Canadians are. The Mancunian fog, smog, grime, and raw weather are not to her liking. She writes that she cried when the *Empress* burned, but that if she can find a canoe she'll be right home. By early spring she is home, having pulled Mom and Tom through the winter. (I have no recollection how we financed the return. Did I rob a bank?)

Before going to England, Hilda had been employed at the headquarters of the Conservative party. Now she becomes a civil servant. She aces the obligatory civil service exam, scoring 98 percent in shorthand and a comfortable 64 words per minute in typing, a full 24 words more than is required for the highest grade. She is assigned a job as secretary in the Department of Supplies and Services, where her skills are totally wasted. The lethargy of that establishment drives her on to the Historical Section of the Army as secretary for, among others, the head historian, Colonel Stacey. As usual, she is out-earning me by quite a bit, thank the Lord. She enjoys the Historical Section and regales me with stories of the secretarial life, including the names and proclivities of certain mid-rank officers a girl must keep well away from when they're both in the stacks.

In the meantime I am busy becoming a film writer. The first script I write is for a film called *Immediate Action*. It is sponsored by the Toronto Stock Exchange and stars beautiful Toby Robins, along with William Needles and Robert Christie. George Gorman is the director. *Immediate Action* wins first prize in the sponsored category of the annual Canadian Film Awards.

I write films for sponsors such as Abitibi, Inco, Alcan, the Wheat Board, and Moyers School Supplies. The film for Moyers stars James Doohan, a young actor who later becomes famous as Star Trek's irascible engineer, "Scotty." Some productions are structured as dramas, many are straight documentaries, and a few are blatantly promotional. The industrials I like best are the ones we call "institutional." They are not about the sponsoring company but about the business the company is in. The subjects we deal with vary greatly — shipping wheat, making paper, generating electricity, weaving cotton. I visit factories and hydro installations, I travel to Montreal and Toronto, and numerous times to Winnipeg, and on one glorious research trip Budge and I are driven around most of Saskatchewan planning a film for the province's golden jubilee.

Here I am, exploring Saskatchewan fifty years after Dad arrived as a homesteader, and I can hardly believe what I see and hear. Our guide is historian Jack Herbert, who shakes me loose with his description of General Middleton. As an easterner I think of Middleton as the heroic leader who suppressed the Riel Rebellion. Now I hear him described as "a discourteous bastard and a pompous, thieving asshole." My perceptions are being altered. Guided by Jack's trained eyes, we can still see the delicate shadings in the wheat that delineate the now ghostly tracks of the Red River carts that brought settlers to these vast prairies. We meet an elderly couple who describe being evacuated from Fort Carlton by the North West Mounted Police during the Riel Rebellion. They tell of seeing the fort in flames. We meet an elderly lady in North Battleford who describes war-painted Indians riding along the shore of the river. I meet a giant of man who, in his nineties, dwarfs me. He worked on the Hudson's Bay Company York boats, and I can imagine his massive hands tossing barrels and bales like featherweights. To me, all of this — Indians on the warpath, the Riel Rebellion, burning forts, York boats — has until now been ancient history. I have the perspective of the easterner. Suddenly it's all real, and it happened only yesterday.

In Ontario when you ask people about their roots they usually name some place in Britain or Europe. Here in Saskatchewan, unless they are Ukrainian, most people say "Ontario." In this context I was born in the Old Country.

I go on location with George to the Abitibi paper mill at Sturgeon Falls in north-central Ontario. I am fascinated by paper mills. The paper-making machines are the largest machines I have ever seen. They have personality all their own. When the paper breaks and a machine begins to vomit paper by the ton the sirens sound and men come running to their action stations to take part in a titanic struggle. There is no question of shutting the monster down. It must be tamed and re-fed while its great gears and belts and webs and rollers continue to roar on their way. Lumps of pulp become trapped in the towering calendar, where many tons of high-speed steel rollers are stacked one on top of the other. If not soon cleaned, the rollers begin to bounce and pound in thundering unison. On the other side of town old-timers sitting on the golf club verandah feel the boards begin to tremble beneath their feet; these veterans test the vibrations on their chair arms before pronouncing, "Paper break on Number Two," or "Damn! Old Number One just let go."

The whole paper-making process is awe-inspiring. From the great tumbling de-barking machines the wood goes through massive grinders, the pulp then into giant blenders, along rushing conveyors, through the thundering calendar stacks; at last the finished product hurls its way onto gigantic rolls that are craned off and away. Almost stupefied by the sights and sounds of this heavy, high-speed industrial operation, I become aware of the mill manager standing by my shoulder. He is a big, grizzled man in his early sixties, almost deaf from years spent in this awesome world of thundering machinery. We both watch as a monster roll of newsprint is hoisted away. He bends over and shouts in my ear. "And now they take it away and print god-damned comics!" He turns on his heel and marches off.

I begin to gain enormous respect for workers in heavy industry — and nothing but disdain for distant executives who consider them expendable.

We are here in Sturgeon Falls because the workforce has not yet been made safety-conscious and the law of the land is still insensitive. Abitibi is trying to encourage mill workers and bush workers to wear safety helmets, gloves, boots, and glasses. In the mill, the company is laying down the law that no mechanic must ever enter a machine without shutting off the power and hanging a "Hold Card" on the switch. And these are machines that you can "enter." Some toothed gears are six feet high, and unwary millwrights have been ground to hamburger. In one mill a worker lay down on a wide, temporarily stationary drive belt for a lunchtime nap and didn't wake up in time. He went around a drive pulley.

Accident-prevention films are a genre to themselves. They invariably pit men against tools. George and I enjoy making them because they are not only inherently dramatic, but also, we hope, useful.

This Abitibi film, *It's in the Cards*, in black and white to suit the nature of the subject, is a synchronized-sound dialogue film with a professional cast. We have great hopes for it at the 1955 Canadian Film Awards. It does get both an Award of Merit and an Honourable Mention, but the top award goes to a film by a producer from Toronto we have never heard of. His name is Anson Moorhouse. He is an ordained minister, a clergyman! Not only that, he has won the top award with *The King's Man*, a film he shot in Angola virtually by himself! Apparently he is creating some sort of a film unit for the United Church of Canada in an old church (where else!) on Berkeley Street in Toronto. I don't know it at the time, but it's his opinion that *It's in the Cards* should have won, and he puts my name on file.

Crawley Films expands by sticking an entire new building onto the front of its old church. Most staff members are vying to establish their personal claim to space in the new quarters, but I fancy Budge and Graeme Fraser's old suite, with its view of the sound stage. By now I am being introduced to clients as the senior writer, which is a gracious fiction, because Judy Crawley is still going strong, although she does have four children and doesn't work in the building. I am also said to be head of the script department, a notion that bears more credibility. The balcony suite is indeed assigned to me, and we hire two other writers, Donald Jack, a transplanted Englishman, and Joan Hind-Smith. Don Jack and his wife Nancy and Hilda and I become life-long friends.

Other staff members like to drop in to the script department eyrie because it is always full of laughter and bizarre ideas. Joan eventually leaves, and enjoys a lengthy career at the University of Toronto Press. One bleak day Budge calls me into his big office on the main floor of the new building. He tells me he has decided Don will never make a writer and that we have to let him go. Don has no sooner left than he writes the first CBC-TV drama not only to be simultaneously aired by the CBC and an American network but also to be published at the same time, as a short story, in *Maclean's* magazine. He writes *The Canvas Barricade*, the only fully original Canadian play ever to be performed on the main stage of the Stratford Festival Theatre.* He creates the character of Bartholomew Bandy for a series of novels, *The Bandy Papers*, which make him a three-time winner of the Leacock Medal for Humour. He also writes extensively for the National Film Board. Don is living proof that the only thing more advantageous to one's career than joining Crawley Films is leaving it.

I am privileged to write the script for a promotional film for my old alma mater, Queen's University. The film will eventually be directed by a young director, Ed Reid, another P.K., but the research and writing is up to me. I am accustomed to meeting with sponsors — usually high-level executives, often including the company president — and have learned that showing a genuine interest in their business is the best ice-breaker there is. There's no use bluffing them. They expect ignorance and are keen to erase it. At the research stage the writer has to be an empty vessel eager to be filled without being brainwashed. At the writing stage the roles get reversed, because the writer is now teaching the sponsor about film. It can be a delicate transition.

I arrive at Queen's unusually perturbed. It is less than a decade since I graduated from here. I have seen the names of my advisory committee, and they are the names of gods! Principal McIntosh himself will be here, along with the Dean of Arts and others. A few short years ago, when I met these men in the halls of academe I would feel like genuflecting. My God, I wonder if they have checked my less than distinguished academic record. I always used to put more effort into the Drama Guild, the swimming club, and the campus radio station than I did into formal subjects like English, History, and Political Science, which were supposed to be my subjects of specialization, although I switched from Political Science to Spanish, thinking of South America and a career in journalism — and misjudging the pace of history. My instincts told me that South America would soon burst onto the world scene. My instincts were wrong.

I enter the boardroom, where I am to meet with the gods, and I find the committee members totally distraught and distracted. For a while I

---

*   There have been some fine Canadian adaptations from other media.

wonder if they know I am here. Even when we begin to talk about the film there are messages being sent hither and yon. Eventually I catch on. This very morning, when the young ladies inhabiting Ban Righ Hall, the women's residence, arose and peered from their windows, they saw a naked male corpse hanging from a tree in the garden. A swift investigation has shown that it is not a fresh corpse, thank Heaven, but has been purloined from the medical school morgue. (Gasp! Horrors!) There is the potential here for a monumental scandal, and everything is being done to keep a lid on it, even though the instincts of these administrators are to carry fire and sword through the ranks of the medical students.

I am delighted. There is life in the old school yet. As a student, I myself never did anything less law-abiding than shinnying up a rain pipe one Saturday afternoon to a second-storey window and climbing in, only to be confronted by the elderly head of the Spanish department. He almost had apoplexy at the prospect of apprehending a break-and-enter artist, until I explained that I was trying to retrieve a coat that had been left by a young lady before the building was locked. He looked out and saw the said young lady shivering down below, and, overwhelmed by what he mistakenly took to be a romance, the gallant old soul swept me effusively on my way. I had watched this professor, with some concern, weep profusely as he read poetry, but now I realized romance was embedded in his genes.

Dad has stories of an earlier Queen's — indeed I remember a snapshot of him wearing a turtleneck sweater and holding some guy down with one knee and an armlock, in the middle of a lawn that's littered with signs of combat. According to him it was always the engineers or the medical students who got out of hand, and I never have the heart to ask him what the theolog was doing applying that hammerlock. He claims that the engineers once dropped a piano down a stairwell and had to be cleared out with a firehose. Doug's father-in-law doctor says that when he was studying medicine here the medical students engaged in an occasional bit of grave robbery, but of course he never participated.

It's not long before today's little flare-up is under control, and it seems to me that a university whose Gaelic war cry has been heard in Upper Canada since 1842 should be allowed an occasional aberration without society going into convulsions.

An abrupt deviation from the writing trade occurs one winter morning when I wheel our eccentric fire-engine red four-seater MG convertible into the Crawley parking lot. By this time Hilda and I are living in the country near Stittsville in a little two-bedroom bungalow. We didn't have the money for it but Budge guaranteed the bank loan for the entire $2,000 down payment, and our two mortgages together total exactly what we were paying for rent in Hull — $60 a month. Commuting is only possible because of the MG.

This morning I'm running late. I've already dropped Hilda at the Army Historical Section, and now, as I wheel into the parking lot, here is Tom Glynn, Head Cameraman and at the moment Production Manager, waving at me to hurry up.

"Phip's broken his leg," he announces. Philip Wiegand is a relatively new young director who just yesterday began shooting a series of mini-films on *How to Play Hockey*.

"Gee, that's too bad. Is he okay?"

"He'll live. But the crew's on the rink at Ottawa U. They're waiting for you. You're directing."

Oh-oh! I have written the scripts for this series, with technical advice from Bill l'Heureux of the University of Western Ontario. Bill is a good educator. He helped create the popular Five-BX exercise series for the RCAF. It's one thing for the scriptwriter to absorb the information, sift it, sort it, analyse it, select from it, and then organize it — but direct it? No thanks.

Tommy is adamant. "Nobody else knows the material like you do. Bill's still here for technical help. The players are booked. The high-speed camera is here from New York. We're into it."

So I direct a series of instructional hockey films. Me, whose ankles were so weak as a kid that I never played anything but shinny. Me, who fell on a frozen pond in Stirling and threw up twice before I got home, thanks to a touch of concussion. And we're having a fiercely cold winter, and we are shooting most of the footage on an outdoor rink. It is fun, though. And the players are great. They are all professionals — not from the NHL, but fellows who come and go on the European circuit. Sort of mercenaries of the hockey wars. We are working with just a few of them at a time, because the series is structured to illustrate basics like skating, shooting, goaltending, and stickhandling.

We use the high-speed camera to study in slow motion everything from the angle of a skate blade in a fast start to what happens when a player tees off with a slapshot. As far as we know this is the first time a slapshot has ever been studied in slow motion, and when we screen the rushes Bill l'Heureux can hardly believe his eyes. The stick is bent like a fully drawn longbow. The power of the shot is enormous. Our players can destroy a one-inch plank with a few shots. We put bulletproof glass in front of the camera.

Because we are using a high-speed camera we are shooting the whole series in 35mm, but the bigger 35mm equipment doesn't function well in cold weather that "substandard" gear takes in its stride. Crikey is the cameraman but Tommy backs him up by keeping a little 35mm wind-up combat camera from the Second World War tucked under his parka for warmth. It takes a combination of high-tech and low-tech to get us through.

The series ends with two night-long sessions inside an arena in Hull with two full teams functioning to illustrate both Offence and Defence. For the next fifty years I will watch NHL games in fascination to see whether the players are doing the power play properly. Too often they are not.

Hilda is waiting with the MG as we finish our last night's shoot. I am too tired to drive, so Hilda gets us home. It's been a grand adventure, but thank goodness Phip, in a leg cast, is able to take over as director for the editing and completion. Phip and I together deliver payment to the University of Ottawa for the use of their rink. It has to be "delivered" because it's in the form of a large TV set, a typical Budge deal that's not quite under-the-counter but almost. The priest who takes delivery looks on Phip and me with compassion.

"Here," he says," what are your names? Why don't I give each of you boys a 'charitable donation' receipt for this?" Phip and I demur.

Phip Wiegand does a fine job of completing the series. I write the commentary. The Secretary of the American Hockey Coaches Association writes to his membership saying, "They are without doubt the greatest instructional films I have ever seen in any sport." The series gets a Gold Medal at the Sports Film Festival in Cortina, Italy, and I take a great deal of perverse pleasure in sticking that on my resume. The players who really put the series to good use are the Russians. They buy prints of the entire series. Their power play is a dream.

By 1957 the Crawley gang, particularly George Gorman and I, are in a state of high excitement. Budge has a deal with the CBC, the BBC, and U.S. backers to produce a series of half-hour dramas for TV based on the exploits of the Royal Canadian Mounted Police. It is to be an anthology series, drawing upon a rich variety of stories — lonely manhunts in the High Arctic, a confrontation with Sitting Bull after he destroyed Custer, inner-city narcotic deals, the maritime unit's high-speed rum-running adventures, its achievement of the first circumnavigation of North America, the aerial service's far-flung exploits, perhaps even a cavalry unit's service on the steppes of Russia in 1919. The RCMP patrols more territory and is involved in a wider range of activities than any other police service on earth.

To satisfy his financial backers Budge takes an American producer on board as head honcho. His name is Barney Girard. Barney brings the holy tablets down from the mountaintop of American TV and lays down the law that if a police series is to be successful it must have a compact central location and the continuity of continuing characters. The series is to be tailored to meet American preconceptions, and the essence of the RCMP goes out the window. Right off the top we are turning our backs on the Mounties' motto, "Without Fear, Favour, or Affection." Never mind. We all forge onward.

I frequent the library at RCMP headquarters, read case histories, and interview officers. The dapper RCMP Commissioner, Colonel Nicholson (he has carried his wartime rank and impeccable military bearing into the Force), gives several of his men permission to meet informally with us at Budge's home in the Gatineau Hills. Their orders are to let their hair down and tell it like it is. There's a supply of booze on hand to help with the telling and we hear tales of wonderful derring-do, the kind that veterans call "war stories." The tales that remain in the mind are full of self-deprecating humour.

A sergeant who looks tough enough to crack rocks with his teeth tells us about his first use of ju jitsu-like police holds.

"It was one of those hilly northern mining towns. Police detachment at the bottom of a hill and the main mine gate at the top. I get a call to go up, because the mine guards are being annoyed by a drunk. Get up there and find this big bastard of a brute's been annoying the guards all right. He's taken their guns off them! Anyway, I arrest the guy and put an armlock on him. Don't forget, this guy is fried, boiled right to the eyeballs, but big! Muscles hanging off his ears. Anyway, I start him off down the hill and find the armlock isn't working. I try another hold and it doesn't work either but we're going faster and faster downhill. I go through the whole damn manual. Arm bends, finger locks, hammerlocks, crotch holds, you name it. Nothing fazes this guy except gravity. I start to panic. When we get to the flats and stop running he's going to damn well kill me. We get to the bottom of the hill, the guy trips, falls, knocks himself out. We're right in front of the detachment. I drag him in and lock him up."

An Inspector reminisces about his first stake-out.

"One of the local merchants had his safe robbed several times. It wasn't cracked, just robbed. We figured it had to be an inside job. I was detailed off to stake the place out for a few nights. The safe was in a back storage room full of boxes, bales, and general hardware. I hunkered down in a dark corner and tried to stay awake. I don't recall how many nights I was there but one night a guy lets himself into the room. It's almost pitch dark. Bit of light from a street light near a window but that's all. The guy has a small flashlight but all that does for me is put him into silhouette. He looks big, dark, faceless. For all I know he has a gun. I suddenly realize this isn't exciting, it's damn scary. I crouch there, sort of shaking, letting him open the safe, waiting 'til he gets what he wants — and getting me a little more time to live. Finally he stands up and turns around and I stand up in the dark and say in a real squeaky voice, 'You're under arrest!'"

The Inspector pauses to let the drama sink in. George and Budge and Barney and I are all waiting for the climax.

"What happened?"

"I fainted."

Laughter. "So you didn't get him?"

"Oh, sure I did. He fainted too, right on top of me, but I came round before he did."

A grizzled Superintendent who is participating in our bull session disappears partway through the evening. Soon one of Budge's youngsters comes up from the recreation room looking wide-eyed and impressed.

"Who's that man? He came into the rec room and sat down. Didn't say anything, but the dog's there!"

Budge looks nonplussed. George and I both know that the boys' aggressively territorial English bulldog considers the rec room to be out of bounds to strangers.

"Is he okay?"

"Well, sort of shook up. The dog I mean."

It seems that when the Superintendent arrived and settled comfortably into an armchair, gently cradling a glass of Scotch in his right hand, the dog had uttered a roar and leapt at him. Switching the Scotch to his left hand without spilling a drop, the policeman belted the dog into a corner, where it remained, lost in thought. The Super's only comment to the boys was, "Vicious but inaccurate."

The initial series story editor is Lister Sinclair, CBC's Renaissance man. Film is not Lister's medium, but he is a Canadian dramatist and full to his erudite eyebrows with national lore, both mundane and esoteric. He is a skilled conversationalist in an era when TV and commercial radio are gradually killing that most refined of arts.

Hilda and I invite Lister to join us for Thanksgiving dinner. Dad and Mother are visiting and we wonder how the clergyman and the CBC intellectual will get along. But Dad is no slouch himself. I suspect he has never met anyone he can't talk to on even ground. The conversation at that Thanksgiving table ranges far beyond my comprehension, and I am spellbound.

For some reason that escapes me, Lister's term as story editor is short-lived, and with the series still in the planning stage a new story editor is imported from England. Probably it's to keep the BBC happy. But by this time I have gone freelance.

10

GOING FREELANCE

THE MOST IMPORTANT DECISION in my life is to marry Hilda. The second most important is to abandon a steady job and a salary in order to go freelance. Both decisions are made without a great deal of either debate or angst. The freelance decision may appear to be the less rational one, but, since just about everything that follows in this narrative is a result of it, perhaps it is useful to loop back into the Crawley years and delve into a deeper layer of memory.

It's a good life being staff writer for Crawley Films Limited of Ottawa, Canada's leading private film company. A great bunch of people work here, and for quite a few years most of us are full of enthusiasm. Budge's exuberance is contagious and it generates a great deal of company bonhomie. The Crawleys live in a modern ranch bungalow on a hobby farm in the Gatineau Hills, across the river from Ottawa. They throw parties there and sometimes recreate quaint folklorish events that Budge and Judy have experienced on faraway, even foreign, locations. And the whole studio gang certainly knows how to throw a wingding of a New Year's Eve bash, for which the company cheerfully surrenders the shooting stage and uncounted hours of staff time. But there is, alas, a downside, involving poverty, boredom, and exploitation.

Poverty is, of course, the companion to abominably low wages, and it can be tolerated in the interests of acquiring an education in film. There is, however, an old maxim that one's wages should keep some semblance of pace with one's productivity, a maxim Budge does not understand. He pretends to understand it, but claims that his hands are tied by his father, Arthur A. Crawley, the head of an esteemed accounting firm that appears to have control over the film company's purse strings. I never find out whether this is true, and have the distinct feeling that old A.A. is simply a handy decoy to attract flak. Budge himself trained as an accountant and is quite expert at double entry bafflegab. During one set of wage negotiations I call him a bloody pirate, and then immediately apologize, saying he isn't a pirate at all, but a privateer — a buccaneer with a licence. I also tell j13 him he's a son of a bitch, meaning no genealogical offence, to which accusation he agrees most humbly, then escorts me to the office door with his arm across my shoulder, assuring me that "We'll all be driving Cadillacs, kid." I don't think many of us really aspire to drive a Caddy. His own choice for an executive car is a Checker Cab, and he carries baled hay in the back seat. One can't help but like the guy, but there's a living to be made.

I survive in this cheerfully bohemian salt mine largely because Hilda is working, bless her. Her income suffers a temporary hiatus in 1954 with the birth of our first child, a boy, who is, alas, stillborn. Undaunted, she returns to work at the Historical Section until 1956, when another son, David, is born, at which point she leaves the Civil Service and puts her skills to use as a homemaker, and as my accountant, secretary, and general keeper. When the freelance decision is made it is not based on the security of two incomes, it is partly propelled by the paucity of one. There are, however, other motivations.

Given that I am privileged to enjoy the spectacle of paper mills and prairie fields, it may be difficult to understand how boredom can become a reason for going freelance, but boredom is certainly part of the job, and it comes in large doses. Far too often I find that the sales department has dropped on my desk a bunch of brochures it has received from a prospective client. Out of this material I am expected to concoct a short "treatment" to help that client imagine his factory or institution at the centre of a spellbinding film. Sometimes there's sufficient preliminary budget to permit me to go into the field to do some real research, but too often it's a matter of reading other people's blarney and then trying to synthesise my own. This is "service writing," useful to commerce but of little value to the soul. Even if a client signs on and a full budget materializes, there's no guarantee I'll get to go on location in search of inspiration. The final straw comes when I develop an idea for an institutional documentary to be filmed in a remote and mountainous corner of France and virtually all the senior staff goes on location except me. This is not what I have in mind as a writing career.

Exploitation is a heavy word, and not totally fair, in that, as I have said, the company is a great film school. But one does hope to graduate.

And as a family man I don't take kindly to being asked to devote Saturdays to staff meetings in the Gatineau Hills, an eighty-mile round trip from Stittsville, for which I am privileged not only to donate my time but to pay for my own gas. I get this rectified, but suspect that in doing so I have strained my relationship with Budge. He doesn't consider me a good "company man." And of course I am not. I don't take easily to being owned.

I am never sure exactly where I stand with Budge. Apart from the Saskatchewan jubilee film, we seldom work together, other than to attend sales meetings with sponsors in the very early stages of a project. But I do enjoy being with him. He's entertaining, mischievous, and afraid of nothing. Not only is he an accomplished documentary cameraman, but he can ignite enthusiasm in a sponsor the way a match ignites tinder, with a flourish and a flair. I once see him leap onto a sponsor's boardroom table and walk its length pretending to be making a trucking shot along a factory production line. The executives are spellbound. Even so, Budge makes me uneasy.

We come at film from different angles. I think it's a good idea to know where you're going, to research, to pre-plan, and, yes, to script in advance. Budge's approach is that of the cameraman. See it, like it, shoot it, and worry about structure afterwards. I call this the garden hose method of production. He tells me once, "All we want are ideas." Apart from the rather denigrating word, "all," it seems to me there should also be a place for planning and structure. A beginning, middle, and end are quite nice. It's not surprising that I write more for George, the actor/director, than for Budge, the cameraman.

But George tells me I'm the one who makes Budge uneasy! In explanation he points out that Budge comes from a rather pious, teetotal family, old A.A. being a pillar of the church with two maiden sisters who are both missionaries in India. According to George, Budge, who is beginning to slide away in several directions from the old family values, finds me, the P.K., an uneasy reminder of those values. I consider this to be totally unfair, although the only sliding I am doing is some tentative exploration of booze, a commodity that Hilda and I are finding to be definitely an acquired taste. Our first sampling, at a friend's cottage, involves dry martinis, which are so repellent that we dispose of them down a gap by a loose board.

I suspect the truth is that Budge and I understand each other better than either of us knows. We may even complement each other. We're both restless and impatient. We both revel in Canadiana, and a project like the RCMP series turns both our cranks. This is something that certainly has to be pre-planned, and early in the game Budge assigns me to a quest for story ideas. Very soon, though, I realize that he intends to import foreign story editors. I suspect my chances of even writing for the series are thin. Too many frustrations have accumulated and too many tantalizing mountains have appeared on the horizon, so I tell Budge I am going freelance.

I have misjudged him.

Budge not only agrees to the freelance idea, even telling me that he'd expected me to make the break sooner, but suggests that I write some of the RCMP episodes. I go freelance with contracts to write six episodes of the RCMP series. God is in his heaven and Budge is a great guy.

Hilda is in full agreement with the change of status. We know film wives who mutiny when their husbands threaten to opt for the instabilities of the freelance life, but my Lancashire lass is made of more independent stuff.

I am instantly introduced to the vagaries of the business world. I have been dealing at a service station whose owners are, like us, into sports cars. They have been urging me to get a credit card, a plastic device that is just beginning to catch on. Now that I am freelance I apply for one, but the oil company turns me down. As a freelance my income has just quadrupled, but I am no longer in thrall to an employer. It seems that credit cards are for the salaried poor.

With the RCMP contracts completed I take off on a three-month documentary assignment in Africa (which is a story for another chapter), and when I return I find that Budge and George have been looking for me. A second story editor from England has been and gone and I am conscripted as the new story editor for the RCMP series. I am story editor for twelve episodes, the last third of the series, but am uncredited, craft credits being treated with cavalier parsimony in these pre-guild days. R.C.M.P. is a good series, and a trail-breaker, but never the sprawling anthology it could have been. Here, as usual, expression of the Canadian experience is hampered by the accountants' demand that we conform to the perceived requirements of the American market.

The story of Crawley Films could fill a book, and has.* But the world in which the film folk of the era were living was larger than any book. Years later, I try to sum it up in one speech in a stage play.* The principal character, Frank, a retired pioneer filmmaker who outrageously resembles

---

*   Barbara Wade Rose, *Budge: What Happened to Canada's King of Film* (Toronto: ECW Press, 1998).

Budge, is being interviewed by a mysterious young woman, Terrie, who is posing as an oral historian:

> FRANK: It was a simple world then, and it's gone. But we filmed it.
> TERRIE: A simple world? The Cuban Crisis? The Berlin wall? Selma, Alabama — integration riots — beginning of the Vietnam War — Jack Kennedy assassinated — Martin Luther King. A simple world? Come off it.
> FRANK: That was somebody else's world. My gang and I were filming Kitimat. Power dams rising in Rocky Mountain canyons, tunnels carving through the mountains. We were hanging by the ass from camera planes, watching the radar domes of the dew line, branding cattle in the foothills, laying pipelines across the prairies, flooding the seaway, flight testing the Avro Arrow — my God, girl, the world was our oyster and we were being paid to be there! That was the real world. We weren't high on hash or LSD. We were hooked on the religion of progress and our patron saints were INCO, Hydro, Noranda, Alcan, and Atomic Energy. Banks were beautiful, the Stock Exchange was the entrance to Ali Baba's cave, and St. Laurent and C.D. Howe and even Diefenbaker were leading us to the gates of the Promised Land. Different gates, mind you, but it was a big land.

And to that I still say, Amen.

But what else do I say, for the record, about the real Budge Crawley, the remarkable man who creates the most dynamic private film company of his era and eventually destroys it? Well, I say nothing, until he dies and it's too late. Then I say it, in 1987, for a newspaper column. I call it "A Letter Too Late." **

> Dear Budge,
>   They held your funeral recently in Ottawa and this is the letter I should have written to you before you died. Leaving letters until too late is one of my several serious flaws. But you had a few flaws of your own so will understand....
>   Since this appears in a family paper I'll have to be careful. Many people will be happy to know you came from a good Christian

---

*   *Corpus Delectable*, Theatre Aquarius, 1995. Directed by Robert Rooney, starring Mary Long and Aron Tager. Available from Playwright's Guild of Canada.

** *Lindsay This Week*, 26 May 1987.

background and others will be relieved to hear you led a model private life — if viewed by a Mormon or a Moslem.

The *Star* says you left an "immeasurable" legacy. Since I was privileged to work for you during most of the '50s, I'll try a little personal measuring.

... I get mighty annoyed when I hear the Film Board being touted as the father and mother of all things creative in Canadian cinema. Nonsense. Compared to you the Board was lolling around a government oasis while you were hacking your way through the commercial, uncharted, forest primeval....

Time and again I watched you con sponsors into increasing their budgets but it was never to increase the profit margin. It was always to improve the film. You inflicted all of us with your enthusiasm for bigger and better sequences. The result was that many sponsors got much better films than they really deserved....

Thanks to you, there's a whole underground of Crawley alumni who have Canada in our bones. You and I wandered the boondocks of Saskatchewan prior to her jubilee and I was never again simply an Upper Canadian.... You never flinched as we all crowded the screening rooms to see each other's rushes and final prints. We kibitzed while on your payroll and vicariously drenched ourselves in Canada....

Following in your tracks we learned to hobnob with the weak and the mighty, and became totally confused as to which was which. We graduated into all corners of Canada's communication business and must be having some impact out there, somewhere. Are we your legacy?...

When we first met, you were planning to shoot a feature film in the Labrador. When I saw you last you were planning another wilderness feature. Neither dream ever materialized, nor did a host of dreams dreamt in between. It's too bad, and it's Canada's loss.

We didn't deserve you, Budge. We with our endless hypocritical lip service to cultural sovereignty while refusing even to seize control of something as elemental as cinema screens!

Now that you're dead I suppose the academics will analyse you and your films. Good luck to them! As for me, I'll skip the cerebral exercises and simply say that if we can preserve your enormous spirit of enthusiasm then that's a legacy worth having. Thank you.

11

AFRICA

MY FIRST FREELANCE DOCUMENTARY assignment is thrust into the midst of the RCMP adventure, and it is a direct result of Rev. Anson Moorhouse's having noticed the film *It's in the Cards*. Mr. Moorhouse is the executive producer of the United Church of Canada's Berkeley Studio film unit. When I meet him, I find a tall, friendly man who gives the impression of being slightly high-strung, but well contained. My brothers and I had learned to classify Dad's clergyman friends. A good handshake was a good sign. The ones who offered a dead fish were best avoided. Mr. Moorhouse passes with flying colours. Anson, as I soon come to call him, has a test of his own. He takes me on a brief scouting trip to remote corners of northern Manitoba, and then, since I have apparently passed his boondock trial, offers me a three-month research/writing trip to Africa.

This is what I've been hoping for, and I'm terrified. I lie awake nights wondering whether I'm up to the challenge. In the years ahead, I will come to realize that the more I am intimidated by a project the more satisfying it will be, but that's future knowledge. And right now it doesn't help that the medical shots intended to protect me from African hazards such as tetanus, typhoid, and yellow fever send me straight to bed with a high temperature.

There is a slight family problem. Hilda has been completely behind the freelance move, but was not counting on my sudden exit for three months to the heart of the "dark continent." The problem is solved. Hilda and eighteen-month-old David accompany me as far as England for a well-earned visit with her parents in Manchester. While there she also manages a visit to the south of England to touch base with a good friend and neighbour from Stittsville, Ivy Szobonya. Ivy, who has just completed a one-year stint as Budge Crawley's secretary, is visiting her parents in Surrey along with her two small girls, prior to emigrating on to California with her husband, Karl. It's a small world and everybody is on the move.

My path takes me from England to Lisbon, Portugal, where I link up with Anson, and we soon find ourselves being admonished in an elegant government office. A tall window opens onto Lisbon's famous arcaded square, the Praco do Commercio. If I were to walk to the window I'd see the imposing statue of a black horse in the centre of the square and, beyond, the triumphal arch that opens to a view of the Tagus River, but right now I don't feel relaxed enough to stroll to any window or look at any view. A senior Portuguese bureaucrat, seated behind an unbeliev-ably handsome desk, has my full attention as well as that of Anson.

"Gentlemen," he says, in an accent that reveals just a touch of Oxford, "we can only give you visas to enter Angola if we feel you fully understand the conditions there."

"Our film unit, which will follow us eventually," responds Anson, "is from the United Church of Canada. Our church has had missionaries in Angola for many years, as I'm sure you know. We've been fully briefed."

"As far as the work of your people goes, I'm sure you have. Unfor-tunately, it has been our experience that journalists ..." — he smiles — "I believe that documentary film people come under that classifica-tion?" We nod, obligingly. "Journalists tend to have misconceptions that lead them into error. For instance, they think Angola is a colony. Quite false."

"We understand that," says Anson. He seems to know where this is going, probably because he's been to Angola before, but I am mystified.

Senhor Noguera* turns to me, as if assuming that the writer is more ignorant than the producer. "Angola is a province. Its people are citizens of Portugal with all the rights and freedoms of any other citizen."

I know this is true, but I also know that to be a Portuguese citizen, with the dictator Salazar still in full control, is not necessarily to enjoy a bountiful supply of either freedoms or rights. Taking my cue from Anson I merely nod agreeably.

Noguera, too, is affable. "We understand that your films will deal solely with the work of missionaries and with the daily life of the Africans. Politics — so confusing, so difficult to understand — politics will not be your concern." Is it a question, or an order? He looks at a file on the desk. "I see that some of your people — Dr. Gilchrist for one — he and others will soon come to the end of their current terms and be going on — what do you call it? — leave? It would be most unfortunate if valued people like that were unable to re-enter the province."

---

*   This is probably not quite the correct name.

There it is. So smooth, so polite, so genteel, with no tone of hostility, just a simple warning that we had better mind our Ps and Qs or sundry missionaries who have devoted their lives to the Ovimbundu people of Angola will simply be barred from the "province." We get the message.

Anson adds a footnote. He can be quite suave himself. It's the clergyman in him. "We are pleased to have your co-operation, Senhor. As you know, our film assignment is backed by the United Church of Canada, the Canadian Baptist Church, and the American Board of Commissioners for Foreign Missions." Does Noguera know that this last one is part of a blanket group headquartered in New York City and representing a sizable proportion of American Protestants? I am sure he does. Anson has just let him know that many interested and discreetly powerful people are watching this project. Genteel blackmail is a two-way street.

With our visas approved and the path paved for the rest of the Berkeley Studio unit to follow from Canada within a month, we take the TAP Super Constellation flight to Angola's capital, Luanda.

Luanda is on the Atlantic coast about ten degrees south of the equator. It is horrendously hot and humid. Almost instantly I develop a great deal of respect for the early explorers. David Livingstone crossed the continent east to west and arrived at Luanda from the interior. He then turned around and retraced his footsteps! I consider myself to be suffering simply because the shower in my Luanda hotel room is a bucket on the end of a rope. I am going to have to alter my perspective.

Later in the year I write a book about this film expedition and call it *African Manhunt*, because our main purpose is to attempt to capture some sense of what makes an Ochimbundu* tick. Memory does not even begin to contain the detail entrenched in the book. What memory does contain are scenes hanging in space, as though etched by the light of a cooking fire.

Luanda is modest, but some of its public areas are quite lovely. Here as in Portugal concrete is used with far more flair than it is by us stolid Canadians. Public buildings have graceful curves that please the eye, and pastel colours that soften street scenes. Many sidewalks are formed of lovely mosaic. This is true even in interior frontier towns.

There are scars on the pastel scenes. Here in Luanda we see road crews at work. Piles of stone have been dumped on the road, and old men, women, and children are crouched down, tap-tap-tapping away

---

*   The language is Umbundu; a person is Ochimbundu; the people are Ovimbundu.

with hammers, turning the stones into gravel. The same scene is repeated in the interior. The Portuguese tell us that these are employment
projects. The missionaries tell us they are slave labour projects — or,
euphemistically, "forced" labour. We will not film these. We have had
our orders.

We fly into the interior in an old reliable DC-3. After traversing
about 100 miles of coastal plain at several thousand feet I am suddenly
nonplussed to see solid rock looming just beyond one wing tip. The
plane labours upward to clear the rock escarpment that borders the
planalto, Angola's prairie-like heartland that lies at an elevation of 6,000
feet. The oppressive humidity of the coastal area gives way to the dry
heat of the grasslands and I am much relieved.

At a small airstrip deep in the heartland of the high veldt we are met
by Rev. Murray McInnes, a round-faced, cheerful, muscular son of
Musquodoboit Harbour, Nova Scotia. He is our guide, mentor, interpreter, driver, and general all-round companion for three months. Murray speaks both Portuguese and Umbundu. His vehicle is a half-ton pick-
up truck with benches in the back under a wooden roof that doubles as
a camera platform and makes the whole contraption look like a mobile
table. Very soon we adopt the Portuguese word *carinha* when referring
to our vehicle.

Our base is a mission station called Donde. It is a self-contained community of comfortable adobe brick homes, a school, student dormito-
ries, a church, and a sprawling one-storey hospital. The missionaries
here run the gamut from single women to married men with families.
Some are relative newcomers, while others are veterans with many
decades of Angolan experience. They come from both Canada and the
States and from a variety of Protestant denominations. This mission is
not tagged with one of our denominational titles. These folk are here to
co-operate with the Angolan church, not to run it. They are here by invitation. None of them has come here without first attending language
school. It is essential for them to be able to function in both Portuguese
and Umbundu.

Anson and I are billeted with a charming young American couple.
They have a strong evangelical bent and like to pray. They also like to
count the heads of the "saved." Finding this constant holiness and tally-
keeping more than we can take, we flee to other billets.

To begin with, Murray, Anson, and I travel as a trio into various corners of the "field." We visit mission stations and we visit villages. We

squat under the thatched roofs of palaver huts and speak, through Murray, with headmen and hunters. We stand by the "pounding rocks" listening and watching as the village women pound corn into flour with the rhythmical strokes of wooden mallets. They sing as they work. I notice that one voice often takes a theme and the others chime in at intervals as a supporting chorus. It is charming to hear but the westerner in me is struck by the seemingly hard, relentless toil of it all.

"Surely," I say to Murray, "a simple mechanical grinder of some kind could make this task a lot easier?"

"Sure," he says. "We used to think so. Technology is great. But we've learned to be careful. You think they're just singing to make the work easier but that's not necessarily so. Hear that woman who's taking the lead? She's describing a family problem that's got her real upset. The others aren't just providing musical backup, they're reacting, sympathizing. There's a whole communal, psychological thing going on. We bring in a machine and all that goes up the spout. It's easy to see ways to help but important to learn when not to."

I have an agreement with Anson — a condition of my employment, laid down by me and agreed to before we left home. I had the misconception that missionaries spend their time under palm trees, praying. Even though, or maybe because, I was raised in a clergyman's family, overt piousness does not appeal to me. And to be asked to lead in prayer or, for that matter, even to speak publicly on matters religious, well, it didn't bear thinking about. So Anson and I made a deal. If, at any time, anywhere, some misguided person, missionary or African, should say, "And now Mr. Scott will lead us in prayer," that would be Anson's cue to rise instantly and, yes, lead in prayer, or say a few words. Whatever is required.

It's a good arrangement and it works. Inevitably Mr. Scott is called upon and right on cue Rev. Moorhouse rises and does the necessary. We follow this routine for the next decade. Here in Africa, in Canada, in the Caribbean, and in Asia we leave behind a string of innocent folk who wonder why they have difficulty remembering who's who.

Much of the terrain here is reminiscent of our own rolling prairies, except that it is covered with waving elephant grass, dotted with isolated and deformed trees, and bedecked with clusters of mud huts. This time of year vast areas of grass are being cleared by fire, a risky enterprise when most roofs are thatched with grass. We see very little wildlife, but we hear blood-curdling stories of leopards, and I buy a cheetah skin from a hunter who has killed the beast with a trap baited with meat tied with string to the trigger of an ancient muzzleloader. The face has lost half its hair, thanks to the blast. One day we enter a village where the headman has just killed a python. The snake is still lying in all its fifteen-foot splendour on the earth in front of the hunter's doorway, and he proudly displays his weapon: a bow and arrow.

Another day we leave the prairie and go on foot into a rugged, rather heavily wooded area. This is neither jungle nor the impenetrable rock and evergreen of our Canadian Shield, but rather an open hardwood forest with a heavy ground layer of grasses and ferns. We are forced to stick to the path, but are suddenly stopped by a strange, black, low-lying, moving barrier. It looks at first like a black conveyor belt sliding through the undergrowth, and where it is moving the undergrowth has vanished as though cut with a mower. The moving belt is about a yard wide and, as far as the eye can see in either direction, it is endless. It is composed of army ants. There is no walking through this. We have to run and jump across, as one would with a stream. But to fall into this stream would be fatal. Several hours later we return by this same pathway and the column is still marching.

With the *carinha* as our steed we travel hundreds of kilometres, visit a myriad mission stations, venture into leprosy camps, wander into a variety of outlying villages, and talk, question, observe, and take notes. We sit in on midwife classes, visit village mother-and-child clinics, attend enthusiastic church services where at least the singing is heavenly, tour remote hospital wards, and watch emergency operations in mud huts. We meet a variety of missionaries — evangelists, well drillers, agriculturalists, teachers, doctors. One of them, Dr. Bridgman, is a distant cousin, but I don't know that until I return home and Mother brings me up to speed on the family tree.

Doctors such as Walter Strangway and Sydney "Sid" Gilchrist are household names among United Church folk in Canada. They are totally different personalities. Strangway is a quiet, calm, almost gentle man. Gilchrist is talkative, energetic, always on the move.

Gilchrist has a knack for PR. When writing to folks at home to describe current challenges and current medical needs, he uses scraps of paper — backs of envelopes, pieces of brown paper bags. The salvaged paper is a witness to the fundamental truth that much is being attempted with very limited resources and that time is finite.

All the doctors share a common frustration — they would rather prevent disease than have to cure it. They know that in Canada the "fee for service" structure of the medical profession doesn't permit a doctor to make a living *and* devote much time to preventive medicine. Because the doctors here on the mission field are salaried, they can theoretically program their time as they wish. But so urgent are the immediate needs of the people that the doctors spend most of their time and energy healing rather than preventing, fully aware that many long-term solutions depend on improvements in nourishment, personal hygiene, and public sanitation. These matters are the primary responsibility of the agriculturalists, teachers, and other team members, but the doctors have a powerful role as motivators.

I am with Sid Gilchrist in a mud-walled, thatch-roofed hut as he performs a skin graft on a hunter. Logistics don't permit transporting the patient to Sid's base hospital at Bailundo. The unfortunate hunter has fallen into a cooking fire, and one knee and part of his lower leg are in terrible shape. His wife is standing to one side, watching. At one point Sid's capable nursing assistant has to slip out for supplies and Sid conscripts me to hold two small blocks of wood that, pressed firmly on the thigh skin and moved apart, stretch the skin tightly so that the doctor can shave off delicate layers, which he then transplants to the wound. I find myself assaulted by the conflicting emotions of fascination with the procedure and empathy for the patient. I glance at the wife. All she appears to be feeling is intense interest.

"Sid," I say, "this guy's wife seems pretty cool about his suffering."

"She is. She's being very analytical. She's thinking, 'Will he get better? Or will he be a useless cripple? If he won't get better, I may as well leave him now.'"

I am aghast.

"Think about it," says Sid. "He's her hunter. Her provider, her security. She's his cook, his gardener, the bearer of his children. When either one can't fulfill their function it's madness to stay together."

It is then I realize that in a society without social security nets — no welfare, no funded health care, no disability pensions, no long-term hospice care — human relationships can be reduced to the ruthlessly practical considerations of sheer survival.

While journeying around the Angolan *planalto* — if Saskatchewan were at 6,000 feet we too would call it the "high prairie" — I write the shooting scripts for several short documentary films on various aspects of

Angolan life. Anson, as producer/director, wants to be ready for action when the rest of the film crew arrives from Canada, and I want to be able to keep a script ahead of them.

The crew does arrive, headed by cameraman Ed deFay, a stocky, handsome, soft-spoken Hungarian immigrant who will always carry an accent as charming as his manners. The assistant director, who will also be the editor, is dark-haired, fair-skinned Shirley Tyte. Anson and I are both about six feet tall, but Shirley looks down on us. She is one of those rare good-looking tall women who are not embarrassed by their height. The other member of the team is diminutive Jitsuko Sada, a second-generation Japanese-Canadian. We call her Dickie, but where that name came from none of us knows. Dickie is an accomplished still photographer and filmstrip producer. Much of the time she will be doing her own thing.

One team member is missing. The sound engineer. Last-minute health problems aborted his trip, but his equipment has arrived. These are the days when highly portable professional-quality reel-to-reel recording equipment is in a state of flux. The ubiquitous Nagra is just around the corner, but in the meantime film sound engineers are using their own ingenuity. Len Green, the Berkeley Studio engineer, has designed and built a portable unit that is superb. But now Len is not here. We try to use his one-of-a-kind prototype to record an Ovimbundu choir and something shorts out. A missionary provides a domestic machine and we do the best we can. The entire Angolan shoot is plagued by sound problems, but Anson, who is an old hand at solving location catastrophes, comes through with flying colours. Eventually our major half-hour production, *I'll Sing, Not Cry*, is awarded a Blue Ribbon "First" at the 1960 American Film Festival in New York with special commendation for the sound track. We believe it is because you can't go wrong with a track that has lots of Ovimbundu music.

There is music everywhere. These people sing while making adobe bricks, mud-plastering a wattle wall, or grinding corn on the pounding rocks. Trucks loaded with male forced labourers rattle by on their way to the coastal cities, and out of the clouds of dust comes the sound of voices, singing. Men building a palisade of sharpened stakes to keep leopards out of a goat pen not only whistle while they work but whistle in four-part harmony. We are told that other tribes consider the Ovimbundu to be *the* singers. They are the Welsh of Africa. We are also told that in this society, rife with adversity, music is a survival tool; it not only reflects a buoyant mind set, it creates the attitude. This is voiced in an

Umbundu expression, "N'jimba si lili," which translates as "I'll sing, not cry." It is this upbeat philosophy that motivates our major film.

Their musical instruments are supplemental voices. There is the *umbumbumba*, a long slender bow with half a hollowed gourd fastened to one end. The player holds the gourd against tight stomach muscles and taps the bowstring with a slender stick while singing softly. The result is mesmerizing.

The drums. I hear the drums even in memory. There is the wedge-shaped drum, about two feet long, hollowed out through a slot that runs the length of one apex. Its sound is satisfyingly throaty. There is the common *onoma*, which can vary in length but is made from a hollowed log and tapers toward the open end, the other end being covered with cowhide. Since the lengths vary, a team of *onomas* provides its own blend of voices. It is the *onomanguita* that is the spellbinder. It looks somewhat disreputable, more like a battered wooden barrel than a drum. Cowhide is stretched over one end, but on the inside, fastened to the centre of the cowhide, is a long slender reed about a foot and a half long. The drummer tightens the moistened drumhead by holding it close to a fire, and then lays the drum on its side and kneels beside it, a gourd of water close by. He moistens the fingers of one hand in the water, reaches inside, and strokes the reed. The result is a deep, thrumming *zoom-zoom* that goes right through the chest. The other hand beats out intricate rhythms that play in and out among the majestic *zooms* like children romping through a stately grove of trees.

One evening we hear a *kudu* horn blowing an invitation to dance. Murray and the film crew board the *carinha* and follow the sound through the darkening twilight until we come to a village of mud huts where the hard-packed earth at the village core offers a fine, hard floor. A fire is already burning and people are drifting in from other villages. Our arrival is greeted with friendly enthusiasm and the *kudu* horn invitation becomes even more persistent. Soon the village is dancing, and before long we are dancing too. I am not a dancer. The two-step, the quick-step, and a careful waltz are all I can manage, and, preferably, only with Hilda. But here it is not a matter of *being* a dancer, one *must* dance. The feet dance, the soul dances. The drums demand it.

Eventually we are in the hill country at a mission station called Elende. It is paradoxical hill country, because it lies just over the western edge of the *planalto*, about a thousand feet lower than the plains above. But paradox is common in Angola, so I am not surprised to meet Paulino

Ngonga Liahuca, an African pastor. His father was a witch doctor. As the eldest son he had been expected to learn the craft, and had been apprenticed to his father for that purpose. As a boy Ngonga had come to work at the mission, simply to earn some coveted cloth, which at the time was used as currency, but he began to learn to read. Soon his cousins were plotting against him.

Pastor Ngonga and I sit on an Elende hillside under the shade of an ancient tree, the valley spread out below us, and he tells me all about it. Ngonga is one of a mere handful of Ovimbundu who speak English. He speaks it beautifully, with a rich, deep voice that matches the smooth and remarkable ebony of his skin. He appears to be ageless, but is somewhere in his sixties, more than twice my age.

"To our people reading was magic. To many it still is. How else can you explain the fact that a few marks on paper are able to speak to a person? Sheer witchcraft. No one person's eyes could possibly be strong enough to master this magic. The reader would need the strength from someone else's eyes. To get that strength the person wishing to read had to kill some member of the family, so the dead person's spirit would join his and add power to the living eyes."

"Did you believe this?"

"Not after I started to learn. But my father sent word that my cousins believed. They were planning to seize me when I came home. They intended to send me off to the coast before I had a chance to kill one of them."

"What happened?"

"I didn't go home." He raises his eyes from the valley below to stare off at the top ridge of a distant hill. That is where his father's village was, not far from what used to be the *ombala* of the king whose royal blood also flows in Ngonga's veins.

"And then," he says, "my sister died."

I wait patiently.

"My father saw me secretly. Very angry. 'Ngonga,' he said, 'you were very bad to kill your sister.' He scolded me but told me my cousins were now determined to kill me. I must stay away from the village for a long, long time. So I did."

I look at the man beside me. He is one of the calmest, most dignified yet reassuring men I have ever met. He is revered throughout the region, respected even by the Portuguese.

The Portuguese have a tendency to be paranoid; they suspect that African pastors are fomenting rebellion. This is not illogical, since Christianity properly understood is nothing if not revolutionary. We hear numerous stories of pastors who have been sent to prison to cool their subversive tendencies. Their colonial masters still use the ancient Portuguese technique of the water prison, where the prisoner is immersed for days in water up to his chin. Eventually one tends to recant, give information, betray one's associates, and generally alter one's political philosophy. If one is too stubborn and drowns, well, the body can be dumped by the Cuanza River, the unfortunate victim of a travel accident. The water prison leaves no signs of physical violence.

As I listen to Pastor Ngonga I become certain this remarkable man has reached such stature in the region that by now he is exempt from such treatment. The Portuguese are not idiots. Indeed, they are paradoxical themselves. They can be ruthless, but at the same time they have great admiration for education. They admire achievement and tend to be colour-blind.

Ngonga talks about colour as we sit there on this idyllic hillside, the mission nearby, its buildings embroidered with the brilliant red of poinsettia flowers blooming on bushes that are almost trees. The pastor is the blackest man I have ever seen. "Ebony" is the only word to describe his skin. And now he gives me a gentle lecture about colour prejudice. It is not what I expected.

"You are going to be accused of being colour-prejudiced just because you are white. There will be those who will try to make you feel that you have a monopoly on prejudice. Do not ever believe it."

I am intrigued, so I say nothing.

"They will blame you for the slave trade and all that went with it. I tell you, we too are prejudiced. We sort people out by the colour of their skin, only we do it in shades of brown to black, with black being the least desirable." So here is another obstacle this man has overcome. "As for slavery, our tribe was part of it. We Ovimbundu were great travellers, great traders. We bought slaves deep in the interior, often from Arabs, and we brought them out to the coast and sold them to your traders. Without middlemen like us your trade could not have flourished."

He looks thoughtful for a moment and I wonder where his mind is going. Then he smiles. There is a warmth about the man that is amazing. "Colour prejudice and slavery — never carry that guilt by yourself. We all share it."

One day when Murray and I are on the road we once again hear drums. Murray wheels the *carinha* off the main route, which is somewhat like a dusty riverbed, and follows a branch that is more like a dried-up stream bed. We come to a village. Skull-like gourds and other fetishes hanging from the palisade tell us this is a pagan village, but the drums are calling, so we leave the truck and enter on foot. In the centre of the village, near the *palaver* hut, a funeral service is underway. We move quietly to the edge of the crowd and watch. Our presence is noticed, but there is no suggestion that we are unwelcome.

We are both carrying still cameras, but we keep them in their cases, slung around our necks. Some pagan folk believe that in order to capture a likeness the camera must extract a portion of the subject's soul. In non-Christian villages it is wise to ask permission to take a picture.

The funeral service is being conducted by a witch doctor. As the drums thrum he chants his mantras and shakes a basketful of bones and trinkets. Various items come to the top, some of which appear to have special significance. Pastor Ngonga and several of the older missionaries have already told me not to be too judgmental of witchdoctors. They appear to be dealing in magic but are often dealing in psychology, and their knowledge of herbs can be impressive. Today it is the psychology that counts. In the presence of death everyone needs reassurance.

Eventually the ceremony is completed; the pallbearers lift the crude coffin high on their shoulders and lead a procession into the surrounding fields. I must have a picture. After assuring Murray that I intend to keep my distance, I run out of the village parallel to the funeral cortège, keeping a full field-width between myself and the mourners. My whole attention is on the procession, but suddenly I look ahead and skid to a stop in consternation. I have almost run directly into the open grave. An Ochimbundu's grave is the usual deep slit in the sandy earth, but it goes sideways at the bottom so that the body is lowered down and then slipped into a niche. When the grave is filled in, the earth does not land on the body. But I am not taking time at the moment to admire a gravedigger's handiwork. I look up to locate the cortège. It has already turned to advance toward the grave, the pallbearers in front, holding the body high on their shoulders.

I throw caution to the winds. I have probably already violated custom, so I might as well go for broke and get my picture. I slip the camera out of its case, cock it, and raise it to my eye.

The procession stops dead in its tracks. The pallbearers freeze. They are standing, staring at me, immobilized, the deceased suspended at head height.

I take a deep breath, click the camera, and lower it. Now for the retribution.

The pallbearers unfreeze and the procession continues. This may be a pagan village, but these courteous people have paused to let the silly *ochindele*, the crazy foreigner, get his picture.

When I leave Angola I have no idea that these kind, proud, intelligent, well-mannered, and musically gifted people will soon be going through years of turmoil, strife, and bloody civil war, the all-too-common aftermath of colonial rule in Africa. As the years roll by I never hear reports from Angola without feeling deeply depressed.

My assignment takes me deeper into the continent to carry out some additional research for the Church. I travel by train through the southern tip of the Belgian Congo.* It is a lonely trip. The passenger car I am in is almost empty, and I have been assigned a compartment to myself. There are some young Belgians farther down the corridor but they remain aloof. On the third day one of them speaks to me as I am returning from the dining car. His English is quite good. "Where are you going?"

"Northern Rhodesia," I answer.**

Then, tentatively, he asks, "Where are you from?"

"Canada."

He turns and calls down the corridor, and my French is just good enough to understand what he says. "He's not American, he's Canadian!" The Belgians sweep me into their compartment. They are recent forestry graduates on their way to the excitement and adventure of a colonial frontier. We visit until their journey ends at Elizabethville,*** but I am troubled. I have been ignored for three days because of a misreading of my citizenship, and then accepted because of my citizenship? I have American cousins of whom I am very fond. I am not sure Americans deserve this, and I can only hope that Canadians do.

I stay overnight in the city of Elizabethville. Late at night, restless and unable to sleep, I walk the streets and marvel at how peaceful, civilized, and safe it all feels, deep in the heart of Africa, in the fabled Congo. At the moment I am a tourist, simply in transit, afflicted with the tourist's innocence. Within a year independence will strike here, accompanied by political chaos among tribal groups, foreign interests, mutineers, and various secessionists, all of it leading to violence and heavy

---

* The Belgian Congo became independent in 1960 as the Republic of Congo. In 1964 it became the Democratic Republic of the Congo, and it was renamed Zaire in 1971.

** Northern Rhodesia became Zambia in 1964.

*** Renamed Lumbumbashi.

bloodshed. I will remember my peaceful nighttime stroll as a naive interlude in never-never land, and I will wonder whether the young, friendly, enthusiastic Belgian foresters survived the slaughter.*

In Northern Rhodesia I find an extreme version of a colonial problem that was subtly apparent in Angola. The Africans have difficulty telling missionaries from masters. In Angola very few of the Protestant missionaries were Portuguese. There, most of the missionaries spoke English as a first language. But they also spoke Portuguese, were of "European" extraction, and were often seen consorting with Portuguese officials. Most Africans did not realize that behind closed doors the "consorting" was often abrasive. The missionaries might denounce administrative excesses, but they didn't make a habit of doing so publicly. The Ovimbundu had never met Senhor Noguera.**

In Northern Rhodesia the paradox is even more extreme. Here, most of the missionaries speak the same mother tongue as the masters do, and indeed many of them are from Britain. Real colonial oppression is not as extreme, but here in 1958 there is complete segregation. Africans are barred from white restaurants, hotels, and theatres. Train stations have segregated public washrooms and drinking fountains. In African eyes this inevitably blends master and missionary. Even churches with mixed congregations that attempt to desegregate their seating run into societal turmoil.

I observe prejudice from several angles.

I tour a copper mine. It is immense. Never before have I been so far underground. The foreman who guides me moves at high speed, making little effort to conceal his dislike for a visiting journalist. I think he is attempting to exhaust me, but I am not in bad shape myself. In a rare moment of camaraderie he tells me what he thinks of African blacks as miners.

"They're stupid, so stupid. Had one bloke when he came in had never even seen a wheelbarrow. Doubt he even knew what a wheel is for. Loaded the wheelbarrow and carried it off on his damn head!"

My guide may think he is illustrating gross ignorance, but he leaves me gasping with admiration at the thought of a man so powerful he can carry a loaded wheelbarrow on top of his head.

---

*   This area was at the very heart of the major uprising.

**   In 1968 Sid Gilchrist kicked over the traces in a book called *Angola, Awake* (Ryerson Press). In his words, "The African church and the African people are in the tightening grip of a white government and gestapo-style police that make any protest, claim or expression of opinion by or from the people utterly impossible."

I spend some time with John, a well-educated member of the Bemba tribe,* an Anglican deacon about my own age. When we first meet he expresses pleasure at the brotherhood implicit in our both belonging to widely separated corners of the British Commonwealth.

We visit villages together and John teaches me some useful Chibemba phrases of greeting, along with an elaborate handshake. The greeting is a mixed blessing. When I use it, villagers bubble with enthusiasm, thinking they have found a non-missionary white who speaks their language. Then, of course, comes the disillusionment. At the end of our final day together, when John and I return to the city and are clear of the missions, I ask him if we can find a restaurant where he can be my guest for a sociable meal. He is both pleased and frustrated. There is no place where John and I can sit together in public as two friends, brothers in the Commonwealth, and enjoy a dinner.

Many missionaries rail against this social system. A few do it openly, but most do it quietly, in the background, attempting to change the system from within. Such efforts too often go unobserved. Many Africans merely see the veneer that makes it appear the "European" missionaries are in league with the European masters. Many fail to understand that the missionaries and the masters, although apparently members of the same tribe, often have diametrically opposed agendas.

This is a problem and a paradox that haunts me for years. I find myself wondering how we Canadians would cope if we were colonized by people from a vastly more technically advanced culture who are accompanied by others who are actually missionaries. Could we tell one from the other? I doubt it. Eventually drawing on my Angolan experience and combining it with a liking for science fiction, I write a novel, *Waltz for a Pagan Drum*.** Murray MacInnes and his wife tell me it is "the worst novel ever written," but my local pastor enthusiastically quotes from it in his Easter sermon. Mostly it is ignored.

A more useful book, *African Manhunt*, is written as soon as I arrive home from Africa. Commissioned by the United Church of Canada, it is my personal account of our Angolan assignment. It sells some 10,000 copies, which, by Canadian standards, makes it, or so I am told, a best-seller.

---

*   The Bemba people are Bantu. The language is Chibemba.

** Tri-M Publishing, 1988. Now out of print but available from the author.

12

HOLLAND, IRELAND, AND A LITERARY MAN

IT IS MID-FEBRUARY 1959, and I am away again. This time my destination is Holland. The Carillon Films partners, who decided some time ago not to throw in their lot with Budge Crawley, have invited me to do some writing for them. And this time Hilda, who is several months pregnant, has accepted an invitation for herself and David to spend the time with her sister in London, Ontario, where Anne and Bob Smith now live. Hilda and I compare notes and confirm that we both suffer from aching heartstrings when we separate, but both agree we've stepped knowingly onto this freelance trail and intend to follow it.

I fly from frozen Ottawa to blizzard-blown Montreal to Amsterdam's Schiphol Airport and find Holland in the midst of a heat wave. Ted and Ina DeWit meet me wearing summer attire. Flowers are blooming. Holland is green. I have come to another world.

Ted and Gerard have contracted me to write films for some of their industrial clients. The two principals are KLM (Royal Dutch Airlines) and Philips. It seems odd to me that a Dutch film company is hiring a unilingual English-speaking writer. I soon learn that in Holland language is not a major concern. Many Carillon productions are produced first in an English version, and later in several other languages.

Carillon Films is based in the city of Rijswyck, and the fellows have obtained room and board for me in a lovely home not far from the studio. My room overlooks a principal canal, and I am entranced by the passing traffic of Rhine barges. My landlady, Lottie Neimeijer, is a sophisticated divorcee who is offended when I innocently use the term "landlady," but she is a gracious hostess and becomes a good friend. She is well read, and speaks impeccable English. Lottie has three children, and they seem pleased to host a visitor from Canada. Even though the Second World War is almost a decade and a half behind us, many household items are still in short supply, and Hilda sends Lottie the occasional "care package" — being careful not to use the term.

I acquire a bicycle and use it to commute to the studio. On weekends I can ride into the Hague, or to Delft, or follow old towpaths beside the canals. I am fascinated by the architecture, the streets, the abrupt transitions from tidy city to tidy countryside. It's an amazing experience to ride casually from one city to another without traversing a hundred miles of either field or forest. There is a city in miniature at Madurodam, but miniaturization seems redundant. This whole country is miniaturized. Delightfully.

In the city square at the heart of Delft I come across a street organ. These large Dutch machines are beautiful instruments, ornately carved, gilded, painted. Their music is intricate, multi-voiced, and varied. I watch in fascination as the operator nonchalantly turns the large wheeled crank that powers the amazing contraption, sending its music dancing across the cobbles and echoing off the surrounding medieval buildings of this charming old city. I talk to the musician. (I cannot refer to him as an organ grinder; there is no grinding going on here.) He asks where I hail from and seems pleased when I say "Canada." He asks if I want to play the organ and lets me take the handle.

The music wails, howls, moans — and finally almost stabilizes. Pedestrians a block away turn to stare in disapproval. There is more to playing this thing than just turning a wheel. But I am thrilled. I am playing a Dutch street organ in the heart of Delft.

Lottie, Ted, and Gerard attempt to teach me some useful Dutch, but I seldom meet anyone who doesn't also speak English, or German, or French, or all three. I feel like a linguistic cripple.

My hosts describe living under German occupation during the recent war years. Ted tells of near starvation, and the sheer joy of catching the loaves of bread that were dropped from Allied planes. I begin to understand why he now takes such enormous pleasure in good food and fine wine. A Carillon employee, Karl Logher, who is Jewish but looks Aryan, takes me on a tour of the Hague. We walk through areas where the population was once predominantly Jewish. Karl gives me an on-the-spot eyewitness re-creation of the wholesale roundups and deportations. He himself fled on foot into Germany, hoping, correctly, the authorities would not expect him to flee to the centre and that with forged documents and his Aryan looks he could "pass."

I am almost embarrassed by the generosity extended to me because I am Canadian. I know the Canadian army made a major liberating drive through Holland, but I also know there were other Allies here as well. Lottie had the experience of being "occupied" by four different armies. I ask for her impressions.

"The most disciplined troops were the British and the Germans."

This is not what I expected, but it's interesting.

"The Americans were the noisiest and the Canadians were the happiest."

This is an assessment I have never heard, before or since. I ask for an explanation.

"I don't really know. I've thought about it. I think it's because the Canadians were the only soldiers who were all here voluntarily."

I think of the political foofaraw at home during the last year of the War when conscription was finally introduced, but only for home service. Those who volunteered for overseas service were designated as "General Service," and wore a little "GS" badge on their sleeves so the home citizenry could distinguish them from the slackers. There were many cynics who suggested that the GS troops were coerced, and I find Lottie's assessment reassuring. I press her a little further.

"The Americans tried to turn everything into a little slice of the States. The Canadians tried to become Dutch."

If that offers a clue to our national psyche, I have no idea where it leads. The sociologists may do with it what they wish.

KLM wants a public relations film to help introduce its new airplane, the DC-8. This will be KLM's first jet airliner, as it will be for many other airlines. They haven't yet taken delivery of a DC-8, but that's no deterrent to my doing research and writing a script. It occurs to me there are two angles here. KLM's routes girdle the globe, and many destinations are touted as exotic. I can think of the new planes as new exotic means to old exotic destinations. Not a bad promotional combination.

KLM is hosting a cocktail party for a mix of executives, diplomats, and friends. I am enjoying some good wine when inspiration strikes. I collar Ted and explain how difficult it is to do research in a vacuum. It would be very productive to travel KLM's famous "Golden Circle Route" around the world, with a research stopover in Asia. Ted absorbs this idea along with several shots of Genever Gin, and we go and find Pepe, the head of the airline's Public Relations department. We isolate Pepe for a little creative business chat. Before the cocktail party is over it is decided the three of us will fly the Golden Circle Route to Japan.

Within a few days we are ready to go — KLM is an organization that appears able to move with the speed of its own planes. It is early morning when we meet below sea level at Schiphol airport and prepare to board. At the last moment an attendant asks me to accompany him to the plane, where I am asked to identify my baggage. I do so. My case is removed. And I am removed from the passenger list. The Second World War has just caught up to me. When Holland was occupied by Germany, it was considered by Japan to be part of the Axis, and Dutch nationals still do not require a visa to enter Japan. A Canadian, because he comes from the Allied side, does require a visa. The Japanese bureaucracy is only a decade and a half behind the times. This minor technicality has escaped the expediters in the PR office of KLM.

We hold a swift tarmac conference and Ted and Pepe decide to carry on. I will follow as soon as my credentials can be improved. I watch despondently as the DC-7C, with my friends aboard, departs on its global journey.

KLM gets into gear. These folk must have good contacts. The Japanese embassy has a visa in my hands before the end of the day. The next morning I, too, am airborne. I have had an exhausting and nerve-wracking day and I had very little sleep last night, but I am now off on a trip around the world, following the fabled Golden Circle Route, on board a DC-7C that is cleverly labelled by KLM as one of their "Seven Seas" fleet. I am headed for places with names like Cairo, Karachi, Rangoon, Bangkok, and Tokyo. And I am travelling First Class. Ted, who flew this eastern route before the War, has told me that in those days the handful of passengers would rendezvous with their captain at the beginning of a journey so he could brief them about the first leg of the trip. At each stop they would get together again and the captain would tell them about the next leg. Very little of it would be pre-ordained by schedule. Times have changed.

We land at Cairo in the middle of the day for a two-hour stopover and leave the plane. Outside, the thermometer is more than 100°F, but I am feeling very very cold. I take a blanket with me and sit in the airport. Here I am, surrounded by desert, in the land of the Nile, the Pharoahs, and the pyramids, and I have to wrap myself up in a vain attempt to keep warm.

We land at Karachi for what is intended to be a genuine rest stop. We are bused away from the airport to a resort, where each first class passenger or couple is given a small, attractive, comfortable cottage in which to rest. I have finally got warm, but I am very tired. I try to sleep.

On to Rangoon and then Bangkok. Is this a special, holy occasion? I have a fleeting impression of airports full of young men wearing the saffron-coloured robes of Buddhist monks.

Finally I arrive at Tokyo. Ted and Pepe meet me at the airport. They are accompanied by a charming middle-aged Japanese filmmaker, Mr.

Kawaii. He speaks excellent English and is our guide and mentor. We are not here to see Tokyo. My baggage is taken directly to a plane belonging to a domestic airline. We fly straight on to fabled Kyoto. Our transport, a small plane about the size of a DC-3, gives us one of the roughest rides I have ever had. By a miracle I remain in one piece, but some passengers do not. One young man turns pale green, a colour that until now I have always associated with fiction. When we land at Kyoto he is removed on a stretcher.

Our hotel was once part of a palace. Its architecture is more western than Japanese, but the staff speak no English. I have a huge room with high ceilings and a large bed that seems to be adrift in space. Whatever affliction has been bothering me seems to recede. For the next few days we are constantly on the move within this most beautiful, ancient city of charming temples and understated palaces. We walk narrow, claustrophobic streets and are ushered through gateways in high wooden walls to find ourselves in lush gardens surrounded by luxuriant greenery and babbling brooks. We visit a monastery renowned for its gardens of stone, and here we participate in the ancient tea ceremony. It is cherry blossom time, and evening is pure enchantment, with the soft lights of street lamps shining upward onto delicate blossoms and glowing downward upon doll-like kimona-clad geishas gliding to assignments in neighbouring tea houses. Students approach us diffidently and ask if they may try their English. They also like to take our pictures. Ted thinks they are intrigued by our size — we both stand a head taller than most of the locals — but I think their photographic zeal has something to do with his mutton-chop sideburns, bull's horn moustache, and twinkling eyes.

We are walking through a market on the edge of a silk "garden," admiring lovely materials, clothing, and crafts. I am not feeling well. This time I am warm. No. Hot. Too hot. I begin throwing up, convulsively.

Ted and Pepe get me to the hotel and into bed. At the moment, Mr. Kawaii is elsewhere. A doctor comes. He speaks no English but seems efficient and compassionate. He talks in German to Ted, who translates into English. The Japanese doctor and the Canadian patient communicate via English and German through the Dutchman. And we Canadians think we're the world's brokers.

The diagnosis is simply that I am exhausted. Totally. The doctor puts me on intravenous glucose for the next few hours and orders me to rest for another day. Ted and Pepe are due back in Tokyo to catch a flight for

Holland. We decide they should carry on, but I will do as the doctor orders and stay put for another day to let the inner man rest.

All goes well. Two days later I am aboard a DC-7C heading northeast from Tokyo to Anchorage, Alaska. Now I am travelling Deluxe First Class. These seats recline almost to the horizontal. We are given an elegant menu that itemizes the meals for hours to come. It is illustrated with beautiful watercolour paintings and makes the reader salivate. The snack trolley, cocktail cart, and meal wagon arrive with attentive regularity. Eventually, each passenger is given a personalized "certificate," signed by the captain, stating that the holder has crossed the International Date Line.

As we approach Anchorage we drop down onto a scene of mountains, glaciers, and snow. I realize with a jolt that it is still midwinter. From Anchorage, we head off on an eighteen-hour flight over the North Pole. The polar route is even more spectacular than the name implies. As a child I made relief maps from flour and water, shaping hills, valleys, lakes, and rivers from the white material, which I would then paint. Now I am looking down from 20,000 feet onto a world that is a solid white relief map with no colour anywhere except in the changing heavens. The delta of the great Mackenzie River is an elaborate bas-relief maze. I marvel that anyone ever finds a way through it. We continue across Arctic waters that are invisible under snow-covered ice, and islands that are mere humps swelling out of endless vastness. It is difficult to conceive of this as a land inhabited, explored, and travelled by man. But it is more than that. It is part of my native land. The desolate, beautiful enormousness of it is almost frightening.

Passengers are presented with another personalized certificate, also signed by the captain, proclaiming that we have flown across the Arctic Circle on KLM flight 868. The seat is very comfortable and the trolleys keep coming. Never again, even in the jet age, will I travel more elegantly than at this very moment.

I write a shooting script for the KLM film and Gerard heads it into production.

Ted and I find ourselves on a totally different assignment, this one in southern Ireland, the land of my Scott ancestors. We are in Dublin to meet with the senior PR man of a large American oil company. He is that godlike creature we commercial film folk think of simply as "the Sponsor," and He is flying in today from the States. We are to meet with Him later in the day, after we have been thoroughly briefed by the oil company's

Dublin office. This is the beginning of one grand film assignment. Carillon Films has a contract to make a broad informational film, not about the oil company, but about Ireland herself. The plan is that once the formalities are out of the way Ted and I will be taken on a research tour of the whole country. A dream is about to come true.

But first we find ourselves in one of the oddest, most informal, most long-drawn-out business meetings I have ever attended. Do all the Irish do business this way? After meeting in the office for a little desultory chit-chat we head for a pub to talk business. Then back to the office to talk about nothing much in particular. Then off to another pub to talk business. By the middle of the afternoon we and the local staff, headed by the local PR man, whom we think of simply as Our Host and whose name is probably Patrick (although memory fails me), are feeling quite amiable.

A brief adjournment gives Ted and me the opportunity to walk down O'Connell Street to the River Liffey. This is a lovely old street with monuments commemorating both the parliamentarian Parnell and the liberator of the Roman Catholics, O'Connell. But I am equally impressed by a scene enacted by Ted in front of a fine old hotel.

As we approach along the sidewalk, a black limousine pulls up to the curb and a uniformed chauffeur gets out, opens the passenger door, and stands waiting, his eyes on the hotel entrance. An elderly lady emerges from the hotel. She must be well into her eighties but she is impeccably dressed and manicured, not ostentatiously but becomingly, and she carries herself with regal grace. We pause to permit her access to her limousine. It occurs to me this is one of the most beautiful elderly ladies I have ever seen, and apparently the same thought occurs to Ted. Being Ted, he does something about it.

"Madame," he announces, smiling through his large moustache and beaming past his mutton-chop sideburns, "Madame, you are beautiful!" He bows slightly — a genuflection that would look absurd on me, but from him is old world gallantry.

The lady nods ever so slightly in acknowledgement, but I swear she rises a full foot off the sidewalk and floats into her carriage. With four words and a gesture, Ted has made her day. How I envy him his charm.

We reconvene for more business and are driven to an exhibition grounds, where the annual fair is taking place and the oil company has a PR booth. The exhibition is like a modest version of Toronto's CNE, with more greensward and horses, and without the overwhelming presence of a monstrous midway. Here there is no adjournment to a pub, because there is a private pub in the back of the company booth.

Here is also a young lady, who is being feted for having just won some kind of company draw. The feting is well underway, and she, too, is feeling amiable. She seems to be attracted by my Canadian accent and my blue eyes, which seems odd, since blue eyes are common currency in this country. Hers, however, are very dark; perhaps she has Spanish blood in her veins, left over from would-be conquerors shipwrecked with the Armada. No, I'm wrong. Her ancestors are from the Balkans, as independent and unruly a crew as you'd ever want to meet.

Noticing the young lady's affinity for my accent and blue eyes, Ted, already affable, becomes magnanimous. He wants to hire her to come along on our tour, ostensibly as my research assistant and secretary. The suggestion seems to appeal to this gorgeous young woman, and I admit it's a very generous offer from my Producer, but I happen already to have a lovely secretary, to whom I am married.

Our hosts, apparently judging that business is getting out of hand, whisk the young lady away in a taxi. To her home, I hope.

It's now Happy Hour, although I don't know whether that is what the Irish call it. Here, every hour seems to be Happy Hour. Anyway, we are in another pub. We notice an attractive, well-rounded woman in her mid-forties talking earnestly to one or two men at a time. She approaches Patrick, who introduces us. She seems pleased by the alien presence we present.

"I'm having a party next Tuesday evening. Very quiet. Very discreet. Do come."

"We'll be out of town," says Patrick.

"Excellent. So slip back into town."

She aims a conspiratorial smile at us and moves on.

"What's that all about?" I ask.

"Don't be so naive," says Ted.

"To be sure," says our host, "she runs a grand high-class brothel. Her 'parties' are a treat."

Back in the office we finally meet the Sponsor Himself, just arrived from Head Office in the States. He is big and affable. He flew in this afternoon, so although the affability may be genuine, it may also have been induced by First Class airline hospitality, or by a swift indoctrination in Irish business practices. In any event, He and Patrick and Ted and I are all to have dinner together — eventually, sometime during the evening. In the meantime, now, during the lovely Irish twilight hours, Patrick takes us for a drive along a coastal road skirting the cliff tops that flank picturesque Dublin Bay. I suspect the Sponsor would prefer a catnap at his hotel.

When we return to the city, we settle in to enjoy what to me seems to be a very much needed and long-awaited injection of real fuel at an upscale restaurant. But first, we all take our bladders to the rest room. The Sponsor, Patrick, and I are the first to return to the table. The Sponsor orders wine.

While Ted is still absent, the wine steward presents the bottle to the Sponsor, who approves the label, smells the cork, and nods acceptance. The wine has now had the blessing of Himself. Our glasses are filled, with sacramental reverence.

Ted returns, beaming, refreshed, a new man ready for a huge meal. I marvel at his resilience. I know he has an enormous affection for women, wine, and food, and a very well cultivated palate for all three, but it beats me how he can continue to be so exuberant after the heavy day of deliberations we've just been through. But here he is. Wine and food are about to be presented in abundance, and his enthusiasm knows no bounds.

He seizes his wine glass. He beams at the three of us. He raises the glass to his nose for a little preparatory connoisseur's sniff.

The smile vanishes. His face freezes. My heart stops.

He takes one, tentative, careful sip, then puts the glass down and pushes it away with two fingers at the base as though wishing to avoid contamination.

"Who," he says, glaring around the table, "who ordered this! Waiter!"

The waiter comes and Ted presents him with the offending bottle. "Take this away and bring me the wine list."

God-the-Sponsor-Himself has just been offended and I wait for the earth to open, but nothing happens. God's affable good manners prevail and the meal proceeds, with copious amounts of food — accompanied by Ted's selection of wines.

Late in the evening the Sponsor and Patrick pour us out of a taxi in front of our hotel. Ted seems surprised.

"No, no," he protests. "The night's young. Where are the girls, where are the girls?"

I thank the Sponsor and propel Ted into the lobby, where he again laments the lack of female companionship.

"Ted, for Christ's sake, the day's over, the night's half gone. Bed time."

He looks at me balefully.

"You're a really talented, nice guy," he says, making it sound like a very sad pronouncement, "but my God, you're dull."

The next morning I have an abominable hangover and — thank you, Lord — so does Ted. I was beginning to think he had a special immunity to Irish hospitality.

Late in the morning we make our subdued way to the oil company office for a pre-arranged meeting with the Sponsor and Patrick. The Sponsor is not here, but PR Patrick is on hand, looking untouched by the previous day's labours. He, I decide, must be immune.

The meeting is very brief.

"It has been decided not to make the film. Himself thanks you for coming and says to send us your expenses. Thank you."

Ted is dumbfounded. "But why?" I have a damn good idea why, but keep my mouth shut.

"It's an executive decision." PR Patrick would make a good politician. "He hasn't confided in me."

And that's it.

Ted heads for the airport and Holland, but tells me to hang on for another day or two, to find out why the project has been cancelled. This strikes me as the kind of assignment that needs no research, but Ted's the boss.

During the afternoon I try to speak to Patrick. Apparently he is extraordinarily busy and I can't get an appointment. I camp in his waiting room. At the end of the afternoon I am invited into his office. He is friendly and courteous and apologizes for having had some difficulty in extracting an explanation from Himself.

"All I can say is that you are advised to tell Mr. DeWit that the cancellation has nothing whatsoever to do with you."

Apparently realizing I may find it difficult to absorb the idea of carrying such a message to my own boss, he suggests I go to the pub next door, where he'll join me for a drink when the office closes.

"By the way," I say on the way out, "that was a lovely drive you took us on yesterday evening. Great road that, skirting the top edges of those cliffs. Quite a thrill. You play a good mouth organ, too."

He looks puzzled. "When?"

"While driving. Quite interesting."

He turns pale. Aha, think I, so you're not immune. You were looped, me boyo, playing the mouth organ with one hand while driving with the other along those cliff-clinging goat trails. We're all bloody lucky to be here today and you don't even remember. "Right," say I. "See you next door."

This is a pleasant pub and, at the moment, rather quiet. The other customers look like regulars and probably are. I sit at the bar, stretching one beer out so long I begin to fear they will charge me stool rent. Patrick never turns up, and an elderly customer asks me if I am waiting for somebody. I say I was, but not any more. Privately, I'm not surprised. I rather expect the poor fellow is in his office awaiting the delivery of his own pink slip. Too bad, for he really does play a good mouth organ.

"What's the accent? American?"

"Canadian."

"A colonial! Colonials are the only bloody people worth talking to!"

The old gentleman joins me, and a very interesting guy he is, too. Affable, of course. I eventually decide it's time for a meal and invite him to join me. During the course of a hearty pub meal I get a crash course on a segment of modern Irish history. My companion was a young rebel, or a patriot, or a republican, or an anti-monarchist — as a Canadian I'm not good at classification — away back during "the troubles" that came to a temporary head in 1916 with the Easter Rising. He was a participant, or at least he tells me he was, in the Battle of the Post Office. I have no way to verify any of his tale, and he has probably dined out on it for years, every time he's run into a colonial, the only people worth talking to because they're the only ones who'll buy him a meal. But who cares? The old fellow is a grand storyteller and makes the scene live.

"It was the Thursday and there we were in the big old General Post Office, down there on Sackville Street, that's the one we now call O'Connell, and sure there were only a handful of us but we knew what we had to do and were going t' do it, and had been doin' it since the Monday. Sure and hadn't Patrick Pearse already told his mother he was goin' t' be kilt, and his own brother too. And Jimmy Connolly who was leadin' us at the Post Office had already told us we didn't have a hope in hell. But that wasn't the point, you see. We had t' try."

The names of Pearse and Connolly are familiar to me, but I have no knowledge of any details. For all I know, my friend's story is sheer Celtic fantasy.

"It was that very Thursday that the bastards started shelling us."

"Excuse me. The bastards?"

He looks at me in puzzlement. "The English. What other bastards are there?"

I decide it's a rhetorical question, so just nod, and ask my English ancestors to forgive me.

"Connolly got hurt but he didn't tell us, then they damn near blew his foot off and he had to allow as to how he was havin' some pain with that. There was women with us. I tell you, boyo, they could fight. You lads in Canada ever want to have a revolution get the women folk with you first."

I refrain from suggesting that revolution isn't very high on our Canadian agenda, and I also refrain from commenting that his Easter uprising didn't work, or at least not then.

"By Friday the whole damn building was ready to collapse. I swear the stones were red-hot. Connolly ordered the women out. We were still fightin'. Funny how y' remember details. A young English captain came around a corner across the street and one of our boyos shot him."

He pauses and looks off as though staring into the past. He is silent a moment before his gaze returns to me.

"Just a young fellow, that captain. Praise be to Jaysus we didn't kill him. He was a literary man."

Suddenly I believe him. This old-timer was indeed there. This is Ireland. They're all nuts, but they've got their priorities straight. Fight the colonizing bastards but don't kill a literary man. Perhaps I'm prejudiced, but it sounds like a good recipe for achieving enlightened democracy.

I arrive home a couple of months before the birth of our second son, Ian, and return to Holland and Carillon for an uneventful month near the end of the year. Before doing so, I manage to write an original one-hour drama for cbc-tv's anthology series, "General Motors Presents," but that's another story for another compartment. Documentary continues to call.

13

THE STRANGE WORLD
OF RANKIN INLET

I AM BECOMING TIRED OF AIRLINES. They all look the same. So do
the stewardesses, the stewards, the pilots, and the navigators. Their uniforms vary in colour, as do their skins and their eyes and their hair, but
they are all natty, neat, buttoned-down, sophisticated denizens of a
smooth and sophisticated world. I've only been flying on commercial
airlines since the early 1950s, but already they bore me. Bloody bus trips
in the sky.

Today, however, I walk out from the little shack that Ottawa thinks is
an airport terminal and realize that this time it's different. It's not
because the February wind is driving ground squalls of snow across the
airport. That goes with the territory. Nor is the difference in the fact that
I'll be flying in an old North Star. TCA (Trans-Canada Airlines, which has
not yet been rechristened Air Canada) has flown these planes for years,
with their big Rolls Royce Merlin engines that hammer passengers into
senselessness by the time they're an hour out of port. But this line I'm
boarding today isn't TCA, nor is it CPA, KLM, BOAC, TAP, JAL, or any other
member of the flying alphabet that I've travelled with. This one is Trans-
Air, a little upstart of a regional carrier that doesn't even use initials. As
soon as I reach the boarding steps my heart leaps, because *this* airline is
different. Its people are different. The stewardesses who usher passengers aboard are just as pretty as any others, but these girls are wearing
snow boots with fur tops. They are wearing windproof leggings and neatly tailored fur-lined parkas. In the plane they shed the parkas, but their
shapely contours are still neatly swathed in soft turtleneck sweaters. This
craft is not headed for Europe or the Caribbean or the Orient. It's flying
to the fringes of the Canadian sub-Arctic, and the crew, bless them, are
bent on survival. As for me, I'm off to research a film for the NFB about a
new breed of nickel miners, to be found only in the sub-Arctic.*

---

* *People of the Rock*, National Film Board of Canada, 1960.

The first leg of the journey is to Fort Churchill on Hudson Bay and is uneventful, but here the schedule dictates a two-day stopover that has nothing to do with my film assignment, so I indulge in a little serendipitous wandering. I meet a piano tuner from Winnipeg who has customers all along one of the world's loneliest railroads. It's the CNR line that wanders northwest from Winnipeg, crosses into Saskatchewan, and then turns northeast to head across the Precambrian wilderness, well above Lake Winnipeg, en route to here. It must be the longest piano-tuning practice in the world, and the practitioner is blind! I also meet a public health nurse, who asks me to join her on a visit to the local Indian community. I have been to Native communities before, at places as remote as God's Lake, Norway House, and Indian Lake, but this time is different. Perhaps it's because now it is midwinter, with sub-zero Fahrenheit temperatures. In this weather it is not uplifting to visit families living in wooden shacks where newspapers are used to block open cracks. There truly is a third world in Canada and the knowledge of it is deeply depressing.

The town of Churchill is just above the tree line, and beyond it the Churchill River is frozen solid, as is much of Hudson Bay. I give employment to a Native by hiring him to take me by dog team across the river to the ruins of Fort Prince of Wales, perched on the northern lip of the mouth of the Churchill River.

The first fort in this area was built by the British in 1689, but it burned. In 1732 they began to build the stone fort on whose ramparts I am now standing. It is star-shaped, which was state of the art for military engineering of the day, but was so weakly garrisoned that the French walked all over it in 1782. I am not interested in the fortunes of old wars, but I am interested in the weak garrison.

No wonder it was weak. The remarkable thing is that this fort was ever built, let alone inhabited. Even today, as I stand here on the frozen parapet, I see nothing through an arc of 358 degrees but absolute frozen wasteland. There are no hills, no trees. The only signs of current human habitation lie in the remaining 2 degrees of arc, which embrace the distant up-thrusting columns of the Churchill grain elevators visible across the ice to the south. I try to imagine what kind of men would put ashore here and not only build this cold stone fortification but settle down to inhabit it. It occurs to me life must have been tough back home.

The Trans-Air schedule gets itself back on track and I leave Churchill. This time the plane is a DC-3 and I am its only passenger. They say the DC-3 is the most reliable aircraft ever built, and I hope so, because this one is full of machinery and big crates. All but four seats have been removed. The four that remain are in line abreast across the front of the cabin. Every other available cubic inch of space is solidly packed with cargo.

The stewardess makes sure I'm okay for takeoff and then vanishes into the cockpit and closes the door. For the next three hundred miles I never see her, and I don't blame her. There is heat in the cockpit but there is damned little back here. I am wearing a parka and snow boots, and my body is warm but my feet are freezing. If there is any heat at all it has to be rising, so I slouch down in the seat and stick my feet high against the bulkhead. In this pose I follow my feet all the way to Rankin Inlet in the sub-Arctic.

We land on a single-strip snow-packed runway and are met by the large Bombardier snowmobile that acts as the airport limousine. (These are the days when the word "snowmobile" can still mean an enclosed snow machine the size of a large car, rather than the tiny Ski-Doo.) The horizon around is white, flat, and unbroken, except for an intrusion about half a mile away where a small community nestles into the snow and the headframe of a mine rises into the sky. The principal industry at Rankin Inlet is nickel mining and most of the miners are Eskimos (it will be some time before we are instructed to use the term "Inuit"). In spite of my cold feet I have warm thoughts for an airline that has such an unusual destination on its route.

The mine personnel are expecting me. I am assigned a room in a bunkhouse that shelters a cross-section of southerners who are here as foremen, middle management, and teacher-technicians. Some of my neighbours are fugitives, fleeing not from justice but from themselves. The man in the room on one side of me is an alcoholic when he's down south. Up here, in his spare time, he's an accomplished artist. The guy on the other side creates nothing but marital problems when he's at home in the south. He fights with his wife and is a compulsive woman-izer. Up here he writes poetry. These two guys warn me to keep one eye peeled for eccentrics.

If the mine manager gives a cocktail party, I am told, I must keep an eye on a certain executive. Apparently he is an extremely fine mining engineer but has a peculiarity that can be interpreted as hostility. He is a left-handed drinker, which is okay, but if one is talking to him and notices him shifting his drink to his right hand then one must duck, instantly. His problem is that, for no apparent reason and at highly inap-propriate moments, he likes to throw a haymaker with the left. They should post him to Ottawa and liven up the cocktail circuit.

I like the southerners I meet up here. (It should be "down" here but I can't get used to being "down north," even though the Arctic watershed dictates its correctness.) They may be eccentric but they are extremely interested in what they are attempting to do, which is to help Eskimos adapt to an industrial society without becoming slaves to it. A nice challenge. I get the impression that management is doing more adapting than the Eskimos are.

Management is attempting to make the shift system more flexible. Eskimos, I am told, are good workers and make good miners, but they are also good hunters and, not surprisingly, prefer hunting to mining. If a man working at the top of the crusher tower or high up in the mine headframe looks out over Hudson Bay and spots whales, he announces his discovery and the news speeds right down into the stopes. The miners all down tools and go on an instant whale hunt.

Instead of opposing such sudden dereliction of duties, management is trying to arrange stand-by shifts to take up the slack. It is not easily done, because of course the stand-by crews have gone hunting too.

I go down in the mine with an engineer, he of the supposedly uncontrollable left fist. Hard-hatted and heavy-booted, we are clumping along a tunnel that will lead us to an ore face. There is snow down here, or what looks like snow. It is actually frost. The mine is driven through permafrost. The tunnel we are in is not in hard rock, but because of the permanently frozen ground it requires no timbers to shore it up. Mines are fascinating places, but I can't say I like them. Even big ones with giant lifts and cavern-like stopes make me claustrophobic, and this is not a big one.

On the way to an open ore face to watch the drilling we pass two Native miners who are standing in a niche, talking and enjoying a smoke. My companion greets them as we go by and the two men reply in a friendly fashion. But we have not gone another twenty paces before an alarmed voice bellows from a side tunnel.

"Hey, you two — get the hell out of there! Fast! Move!"

My guide seizes my arm, spins me around, and we make an Olympic sprint. We round a corner just in time to escape having an explosion drive hard rock up our butts. We have come within an ace of walking directly into an ore blast. The two miners we have just passed were the lookouts. I tell my companion it was highly unfriendly of them not to have warned us.

"No," he says, "in their minds it would have been highly presumptuous of them. We're white men. Where technology is concerned we know everything." He sounds just a little frustrated. "They would consider it most impolite to tell us something that we obviously know."

"That we're about to get killed!" I am experiencing some culture shock.

"Since we know everything they'd assume that we wanted to get killed and they'd figure that's our business, not theirs. I should've asked them."

Back on the surface I'm still pondering the perils of being an all-knowing white man when a young Eskimo who speaks excellent English and is a deacon with the Anglican Mission draws me aside for a quiet conversation. He wants to talk to someone who understands films and who is not a member of the establishment. Establishment to him means the RCMP, the Anglican Mission, Mine Management, and the Department of Northern Affairs.

His problem is interesting to the point of being frightening. Apparently the company shows movies in the recreation hall and the whole Eskimo community likes to attend. They have just seen *The Fly*. I have seen that film and rather like it, even though it does get a bit out of hand. It's a black and white sci-fi horror flick in which a man is disintegrated and transported from *a* to *b* via radio waves and then re-integrated. The horror comes when a fly gets into the machinery, and the creature that is reassembled is part human and part insect.

The problem here at Rankin Inlet is that the Eskimo viewers *know* that the white man is capable of performing seemingly impossible feats of technology, and consequently *The Fly* has scared them out of their wits. They have been coming quietly to the deacon, who is the best educated of their number, to find out if what they have just seen on the screen is possible. And he's not sure. He wants me to point out the dividing line between fact and fantasy. He is waiting, nervously, to be reassured that fantasy *is* involved.

I think of all the outright fabrications, fantasies, and bizarre half-truths that are skilfully built into films and television and literature with every intention of making them appear real. I see a weird cultural avalanche coming down upon these unsuspecting people. I reassure my Native friend about *The Fly*, but I haven't the heart to tell him what is really on the way. When I think of my culture pouring into his world I feel cold inside. Empathy is a curse.

I tear myself away from gloomy thoughts, become a tourist, and, during a brief period of half-twilight, go on a shopping expedition with Ralph, a schoolteacher from the south, as guide and interpreter. Ralph and his wife, Louise, have already expanded my education by introducing me to delicious contraband caribou steak. Today we are on another cultural expedition. There is a ground storm blowing and the snow is travelling horizontally. If I look straight up I can just discern the blue sky. The "storm" doesn't extend more than fifteen feet into the air. Ralph and I pull our parka hoods well forward and lean into the wind as we cross through the community. When we come to a cluster of scattered bumps that look like snow-covered rocks I am guided around the perimeter. The bumps are a team of huskies calmly sleeping under the blanket of fresh snow. If we were to walk among them and accidentally step on one we could be killed on the spot.

We pass two Native gentlemen seated side by side on a snowdrift, their backs to the wind, talking and laughing. For them the "storm" does not exist. I have been raised on the philosophy that the only way to endure our bizarre Canadian climate is to dress for it and then ignore it, but compared to these two men I am an amateur.

Our shopping destination is the home of Daniel, a carver from Povungnatuk whose skill with soapstone has earned him a reputation in southern art circles. The Department of Northern Affairs has brought him to Rankin to help the local carvers improve their techniques and to stimulate their creativity. The Department doesn't approve of outsiders buying directly from the carver, but every Eskimo alive is a freelance at heart and so am I. I am not aware of any Act of Parliament that decrees the Department to be God, so I am dealing direct. Besides, Ralph assures me I'll pay Daniel more than he can get from the government-monitored sales agency. He also assures me that although Daniel doesn't speak English he is not some poor primitive who is going to let himself be gouged.

We plunge down a narrow, tunnel-like snow corridor into Daniel's house. This is not an igloo, it is a one-room frame house that just happens to be totally covered with snow. Daniel, a round-faced, smiling man with an open and direct manner, seems very pleased to show us carvings. I negotiate for one that stands about eight inches high and depicts a hunter striding along dragging an enormous sea otter over his shoulder. The piece embodies everything I like about Eskimo carvings — human and animal subjects with rounded, soft, flowing shapes captured in a moment of motion. While I am admiring Daniel's handiwork I have an image in mind of another carving I have seen up here. Long after I have forgotten what artist carved it or the southerner who owned it, even the recollection of it will make my heart muscles contract. The central figure was neither human nor animal; it was a large, square, hard-edged underground ore car. An insignificant human figure was behind it, pushing, and that figure was not rounded by the soft outline of parka and mukluks, nor was it momentarily frozen in flowing, rhythmical motion. It was petrified in an act of inhuman labour. That is the carving I should be carrying home, not as a trophy but as a warning, but it was not for sale. In the years ahead every time I look at Daniel's hunter I will see the ghost of that other, ominous carving.

After I have closed my bargain with Daniel he retreats into a corner and roots around in a deep dunnage bag. I have no idea what he is doing but while he's doing it I ask Ralph for some advice.

"Would it be all right for me to ask Daniel to step outside for a picture?"

Although I am carrying a 35mm Asahi Pentax camera I don't have flash gear with me. There is also another problem. "I don't want to intrude," I explain. "I don't know how he feels about pictures."

While I am engaged in making sure I don't commit any cultural indiscretions Daniel has been tossing things out of his seemingly bottomless dunnage bag. Apparently he finds what he wants, because he resurfaces, comes across the room, puts the soapstone hunter in my hand, and pushes me gently backwards into a corner. He then backs away about ten feet and, using a state-of-the art flash camera, takes my picture. I've got my trophy, for cash, and now Daniel has his, for free.

By the time I'm ready to leave Rankin I have also bought a pair of colourfully embroidered Eskimo mukluk liners and am wearing them over two pairs of heavy socks inside my snow boots. Even though I wear a heavy, nylon-covered insulated parka I can still feel the cold Rankin Inlet wind going right through me. It's a strange feeling. Like being transparent. At least my feet are warm. On this, my day of departure, the thermometer outside the RCMP post registers fifty degrees below zero Fahrenheit, which seems a little extreme even to a fellow from the Ottawa Valley.

The shore ice of the inlet is rough and chunky where large tectonic plates of sea ice have ground over each other in the shallows. I walk with some other folk out over the rough stuff to the level snow-covered ice prairie beyond, which stretches east across Hudson Bay as far as the eye can see. The big Bombardier is also going out, but via a longer, smoother route. A plane is waiting on the ice looking small but ruggedly square and solid on its big skis. Being ski-equipped and much smaller than the DC-3 it can ignore the airstrip and use the ice closer to town.

I am pleased to see that the plane is a Norseman. I haven't flown in a Norseman for years. It's good to see that they are still in use in spite of Beavers, Otters, Caribou, Buffalo — the whole menagerie of Canadian flying fauna. The Norseman, I tell myself, used to be old dependability itself, the half-ton truck of the north.

I read the licence letters on the fuselage and my insides twitch. CF-OBQ!* This is not just any Norseman, it is the first plane I ever flew in! It has changed owners, but these planes never change their registration. My heart sinks. That first flight was years ago — twelve years ago, in 1948! Where has the beast been since then? How many miles has it flown? How many *hours* has it logged? Has it been well maintained? Has the single engine been rebuilt, or are all the moving parts in that old radial mill the same moving parts that were already old when CF-OBQ was beating its way around Thunder Bay Region for Ontario Lands and Forests? I'm flying out of the sub-Arctic, in midwinter, in this thing? My God!

The passenger list includes an Ottawa man from the Department of Northern Affairs, me, and five and a half Eskimos. We are heading south for Fort Churchill. The Northern Affairs man is the first passenger aboard and he pre-empts the co-pilot's seat. The pilot, of course, has a reserved seat. The Natives get the bench seats along the cabin walls. I am the last man aboard and for me there is no seat. (This is educational. I have just learned the pecking order for film writers.) There is, however, a large bag full of Her Majesty's Royal Mail at the rear of the cabin and I am told I can sit on that. If Her Majesty doesn't mind, I don't mind. Besides, I've been sick on this plane before, so what else is new?

We begin the take-off run across the hard-packed, wind-rippled snow of the Bay ice and I suddenly realize that OBQ on skis is not like OBQ on floats. On floats, on choppy water, she was a rough steed, but none of the water-induced bouncings ever sent signals like those that are coming through from the tail skid as it bangs over the snowy waves of Henry Hudson's bay. And my own tail is on a hard-cornered parcel lodged at the top of the mailbag. I can't stand up because the cabin is too low. I can't move forward because of the other passengers. The unsprung tail skid is hammering away just abaft and below me, a genuine piledriver. I am about to holler for mercy when OBQ reaches tail lift-off speed, and its end and my end smooth out. A few moments later and we're airborne.

---

*   It could have been CF-OBL. We were served by both. Memory fades.

I have been hammered into a sombre mood. I wonder, blackly, whether the old machine has a one-way trip left in her. If that pounding happens every time she takes off and lands she should be ready to disintegrate like the wonderful one-hoss shay, not in bits and pieces but suddenly, totally, all at once. I wonder if all the pieces and all the passengers will land simultaneously, like the iron ball and the feather in the vacuum gravity test. But it's far more likely something will simply fall off the engine. I wonder whether these things can glide. A Norseman looks about as glideable as a block of cement.

While I ponder the implications of a forced landing in mid-February up here north of the tree line — north of anything, God help us — I take some consolation from the fact that five and a half of us are Eskimos, nature's best survivors. I can discount the half, because he, or she, is not yet born — although, judging from the size of the expectant mother and what the nurse told us before we left, he or she could be born at any minute. Certainly, the mother and her pending offspring can't be considered assets to our hypothetical overland expedition.

There is an elderly woman aboard who probably knows just about everything there is to know about survival. She and her people are survivors of the caribou famine of 1956 that Farley Mowat wrote about in *People of the Deer*. Unfortunately, the old woman is now stone blind. Even so, I suspect that in a crisis she'd be more useful than either me or the Department man from Ottawa. Finally, there is an elderly Eskimo man and a boy. The drawback with them is that they're both sick and on their way to hospital. There is one other Native passenger but she is lying full length along the bench seat on the port side of the aircraft. She is under heavy medical sedation. She is also in a straitjacket — full-length, neck to feet. The nurse told us the sedation should last until we reach Fort Churchill and if it doesn't, the jacket should hold.

I decide, all things considered, it will be nice if old OBQ can hang together for the entire run.

The old bucket is vibrating. Small waves ripple through her skin. Little shivers run through her frame. Her very molecules must be in motion. That's absurd, I tell myself. Molecules are always in motion. Or is that atoms? Anyway, what's it matter! I soothe my nerves by telling myself that the old girl always did vibrate. I'd vibrate, too, if I were carrying that 550-horsepower Pratt & Whitney radial mill in my nose. As a matter of fact, I am vibrating and that blasted parcel is up near my sphincter. I am also getting very cold and there's a wind in here.

Wind?

How come there's a wind in the cabin!

I look around in consternation. There is a door in the port side just a foot away from my left elbow. In this door is a window that slides up and down. Right now that window is gently vibrating downward, opening, and as it does so the breeze increases. I close it, hastily. It immediately begins to vibrate down again. It is fifty below zero on the ground, so what is the reading up here at 2,000 feet? And what's the windchill factor at 150 mph? I don't know, but I do know that my heavy parka is beginning to feel like tissue paper. I slide the window up again and try to jam it.

It won't jam.

So this is the way a Norseman begins to disintegrate. Not all at once. The windows first, probably the fabric next, then the struts, and so on. But it's supposed to be so reliable! I imagine that reliable old engine grinding along on its reliable way with nothing left except a pair of disembodied but reliable skis underneath and that damned tail skid hammering along behind.

For three hundred miles I sit here like a frozen hunter at a seal hole and every thirty seconds my left hand reaches out and closes the window and then for the next thirty seconds I watch it vibrate open again.

We are still half an hour away from home port when I am distracted by eerie sounds from up forward. The long, full-body straitjacket is beginning to writhe. The poor soul inside appears to be asleep, but she is making the most unnerving noises. Every now and then her legs, of necessity moving in unison, rise upward and flex at the knees. She is like a mummy testing her bonds at the first spasms of returning life. We all watch with compassion and helpless apprehension. We were assured by the nurse that the sedation should hold, but it isn't holding, dammit, any more than that window is holding.

Up front the pilot has his ears clamped under his headphones and his eyes locked off on his instruments, his map, and the ground below. He is a specialist doing a specialist's job. The Ottawa man beside him is enjoying the barren scenery. Neither man is aware of the passengers behind.

Suddenly I want to laugh. The Canadian symbolism is glorious. Here is this little microcosm of humanity, willy-nilly in the back of the bus and committed to the full ride, but knowing full well everything is on the brink of coming unstuck. Up front are the specialist and the bureaucrat, both supremely confident and oblivious of the reality.

This time we make it. OBQ lands about as gently as she took off.

Thank God there are medical people waiting; they take possession of the straitjacketed lady, the expectant mother, the blind woman, the sick old man, and the sick young boy. The bureaucrat and the specialist saunter off, happy in the knowledge that they themselves have the world under complete control. I limp off, thankful that I take with me nothing more serious than frayed nerves, symptoms of minor frostbite, and a case of impacted parcel.

As for Churchill, scattered on the frozen shore just above the tree-line, it looks positively metropolitan. It's great to be back in the south.

14

ON THE RIM
OF TOMORROW

IT IS LATER IN 1960 and I am wandering the rim of southeast Asia with Anson Moorhouse. Anson and his Berkeley Studio film unit have been asked to make a documentary film for the National Council of Churches, headquartered in New York. The energetic producer/director and I are once again gathering material that I can turn into a shooting script.

We pause briefly in Japan to visit a rural agricultural mission, but this Japanese interlude is less exotic, and less traumatic, than my Carillon visit of last year and little remains imprinted on memory. We soon move on to South Korea.

It is only seven years since the end of the Korean War and much of the country still looks like a war zone. The capital, Seoul, is crowded, busy, and very ragged. My principal memory is of Seoul markets at night, with most exterior lighting provided by torches and lanterns. In open spaces among the stalls entertainers are performing. There are jugglers, musicians, and a snake charmer.

Seoul is peaceful while we are here, but we are told that student riots are part of the fabric of life. Asian students are not docile and obedient. They are determined to help shape their own destinies. As in the western world after the Second World War, there is little chance of a return to a rigidly class-based social structure.

We travel southeast into the interior, heading for the city of Wonju. Our companion and driver is Dr. Florence Murray, a medical missionary from Nova Scotia.

Dr. Murray is a tall, gaunt, sinewy woman who looks as though she will last forever. She has already lasted since 1894. The only female in her medical class, she cut her medical teeth, while still a student, in the immediate aftermath of the 1917 Halifax explosion.* The following

---

* The explosion of a munitions ship in Halifax harbour on 5 December 1917 was the biggest, most devastating man-made explosion before the bombing of Hiroshima and Nagasaki.

year, before being licensed, she found herself in the midst of the great influenza epidemic of 1918-19* armed with little more than a thermometer and a stethoscope. She came here to Korea for the Canadian Presbyterians in the early 1920s and hung on until a year after the Japanese occupation during the Second World War. She returned in 1947 and was again forced out by war in 1950. She bounced right back in 1951. Dr. Murray is said to be a leading expert on leprosy and tuberculosis. From what I hear, she is expert in just about everything that plagues these folk, from parasites to malaria.

Dr. Murray drives an open jeep, tall in her seat, slightly hunched over the wheel. Roads are abominable and road signs virtually non-existent in terrain that is every bit as rugged as our own Canadian Shield, without the softening cover of heavy forest.

We come to an enormous gorge and my lungs seize up. The bridge ahead of us seems little more than a skeleton. It was all but destroyed during the recent war and has merely been repaired, not rebuilt. It looks more like an abandoned scaffolding than a bridge. The wheel tracks are single planks. There are no railings.

Dr. Murray drives onto the dilapidated structure as casually as I would wheel out of my own driveway. I peer over the edge of the jeep and find myself looking straight down upon a torrent rushing through a rocky chasm far, far below. The wheels are only a few inches from the edge of the plank. This is the closest I have been to eternity, and it's not a comfortable feeling. Anson and I are both white-knuckled.

Our driver seems unconcerned. She drives on, eyes focused straight ahead. Typical missionary doctor, I think. Head for your destination and to hell with the periphery.

Whenever we stop and have to leave the Jeep, Dr. Murray pays one or two local urchins to keep an eye on the machine. Apparently such children strip parked vehicles in a matter of minutes. It seems to me that we are putting the fox in charge of the henhouse, but Dr. Murray assures us that now the urchins have been given temporary employment their duties will be honoured both by themselves and by other potential thieves. The human social animal is amazing. Those outside "the law" make and observe their own laws.

Our destination at Wonju is a church-run medical establishment. It is staffed by both westerners and Koreans. Some of the nurses are

---

*   In 1918-19 an epidemic of Spanish influenza killed twice as many people worldwide
     as had recently died on all the First World War battlefields of Europe.

Canadians. The management is Korean. As in Angola, the missionaries now come by invitation and work as advisors and partners, not as overlords.

The arrival of North American visitors is an event, and in celebration we are invited to a feast in a large but primitive local restaurant. The roof is galvanized iron, the floor is hard-packed earth. There is nothing primitive about the meal. It is a delicious-looking spread of dishes. A Canadian nurse sits beside me.

"I'm to help you figure out what not to eat," she says.

"You mean there are prohibitions?"

She points at a red sauce. "That's *kimchi*. Made from red peppers. You've seen it drying by the roadside." She is quite correct. I have. Vast areas of it spread out on the rock-hard earth.

"Koreans love it," she says. "It's a staple. But eat that and your ears will light up."

I try a little *kimchi* and wonder what Koreans use for stomach lining. My education continues.

"Don't eat any of that," she says, pointing at a dish.

"What is it?"

"A kind of raw fish. Avoid it."

"Why?"

"It will make you sicker than anything else here."

Raw fish is a delicacy in many parts of Asia. Some of it is harmless, but some of it is downright poisonous. Some of it puts small parasites into your lungs that show up on X-rays and that doctors in the west diagnose, and treat ineffectively, as TB. I make a mental note that if in future years I develop TB symptoms I will get a second opinion from a retired missionary doctor. If I am lucky, I'll find Dr. Murray.

The meal presents challenges that are technical as well as gastronomical. Ever since my KLM visit to Japan I have taken every opportunity to practise with chopsticks, and by now am rather proud of my capabilities. But I haven't reckoned on Korean hospitality. On this special occasion we are using silver chopsticks that come to a point as fine as any knitting needle. I can't make them grasp, and I don't think I should stab.

Our Korean host, the hospital administrator, is watching me. He says nothing, but gestures unobtrusively to a waiter, who glides away and a moment later slips to my side and gently lays a knife and fork beside my plate. I am both relieved and humiliated.

Next day I quiz Dr. Murray about the fish and the parasites and begin to feel as though I am back in Africa. The medical challenge here is not just an Asian challenge, it is a Third World challenge, and the answer lies in the teaching of public health and preventive medicine, but, as always, the doctors, overwhelmed by the urgent need to cure, have little time to prevent.

My questions about parasites open up a metaphorical can of worms. Years later, in an Africa-inspired novel,* I blend conversations with Sid Gilchrist of Angola and Florence Murray of Korea into one fictitious mission surgeon's operating room lecture:

> I hate these emergency invasions. Never know what you're going to find. Most people have parasites. Goes with being born into the Third World. Usually one type. Sometimes two. I've seen as many as five different parasites in one patient. You saw that little *kwashiorkor** child today. Notice where she walked? Little dusty white patches on the floor left by her bare feet. That dust was parasite eggs being squished out of the soles of her feet. Imagine the health revolution if one could only put a decent pair of shoes onto every child.
>
> This time I think we're lucky. God knows what's in the intestine but there are no worms in here. Once pulled a twenty-foot tapeworm out of a bowel incision. I've gone in after acute intestinal obstructions thinking I might be after a tumour and found a hard ball of roundworms. Desperate thing is, you irritate them with the anaesthetic and they start to travel. Also build up a big backlog of toxic fluid. Try to drain it before operating and the drain tube gets plugged with worms. I've found them in the appendix giving all the symptoms of appendicitis. They get into the bronchial tubes. Was checking a patient once for a respiratory problem and suddenly a worm wriggled out of his mouth. Respiratory problem cleared up instantly. Had an Asian colleague ...

... here my fictitious surgeon switches from my memories of Sid Gilchrist to those of Florence Murray ...

> with a patient, a little girl, so full of worms she was worn out. In those days the medicine used to kill the worms could kill the patient, so the doctor went easy with the first dose. Girl expelled five hundred round worms. Repeated the dose a few days later and

---

*   Waltz for a Pagan Drum (Tri-M Publishing, 1988).

**   A condition brought on by malnutrition.

she came up with another three hundred. Child died anyway. An autopsy found another one hundred. In the stomach, the intestines, the bile ducts, the liver ducts, even in the liver itself. Imagine what a nightmare you can carve into in emergency surgery.

I cannot think of Africa without remembering Sid Gilchrist. I cannot think of Korea without remembering Florence Murray.

Anson and I travel onward to the island of Okinawa, a land of rolling, open countryside with hills in the interior. The untilled areas are clothed in tall coarse grasses and crisscrossed with footpaths. We are told it is a good idea to keep to the paths because of poisonous snakes.

The villages and homes are quite Japanese, and no wonder; for several hundred years prior to the Second World War, Okinawa, as one of the Ryuku Islands, was part of the Japanese empire. The native homes have the sliding partitions and the tatami-matted floors of the Japanese. Here and there throughout the rolling countryside the slopes are dotted with houses unlike any I have ever seen. They are small stone domes with one door and no windows. Some are fronted by a small round courtyard partially embraced by a low stone wall. I see no sign of human activity around them and eventually realize they are homes for the dead.

We are told that each dome serves one family through many generations. I am puzzled. These structures do not appear to be large enough to be private mausoleums honey-combed inside with body-sized niches, each dedicated to one body, forever. I am correct. These folk are more rational than we westerners are. At suitable intervals each family has a ceremony in which the bones of the last deceased are "polished" and carefully stacked with those of their predecessors. I suspect that it's a psychologically healthy ritual. Here there can be no denial of death and no illusions about the fate of human clay.

Our missionary contacts are Americans. One is an Episcopalian bishop. A handsome man, he stands well over six feet tall in his size-twelve shoes and is married to an attractive and charming Okinawan who by now speaks excellent English. When the bishop arrived here he was an ordinary GI and had just taken part in the storming of Okinawa. His wife tells of their meeting.

"You must understand that we had been told by the Japanese how cruel the Americans were. That they raped the women, killed the children, and ate babies. When the invasion came my mother and I hid in the hills until we ran out of food. Eventually we had to come out of hiding or starve to death, so we made our way down to a road. A column of American troops marched by and we stood, terrified, in the ditch, clinging to each other. We knew we were about to be raped but the urge to survive is very strong."

I am trying to imagine the sheer terror of the moment as the two helpless women watch heavily armed and alien troops go by, men who must have seemed, on the average, to be giants compared to the compact Ryuku islanders and the Japanese. Then the bishop's wife giggles.

"Mother and I got the shock of our lives. Those big barbarians — they ignored us!" Even now she sounds torn between indignation and laughter. "We thought, we're going to starve to death here in the ditch. But then a huge young soldier came along in a Jeep and took us to a shelter where we found many of our friends. He was very kind."

He is also now her husband and a bishop.

We meet another American, younger than the bishop and also a clergyman. Here as elsewhere the missionaries are not all clergymen. They can be doctors, nurses, well-drillers, agriculturalists, carpenters — and some of the clergy also have technical specialties. But all must have language training in both Japanese and Okinawan before they are thrown into their work. The evangelists have an additional problem in that they are trying to communicate on abstract levels. For them language training is a serious business, and their path is strewn with occupational hazards.

Our new friend tells us of his perilous journey into the Okinawan language. "When I conducted my first church service I offered up an earnest prayer to the Lord. But I translated 'O Lord' using what I understood to be the honorific equivalent of 'O.' Problem was, I was wrong. The combination I came up with actually translated into 'O Wolf.' I led in an earnest prayer to the Wolf. And once I managed to turn carrots into an ecclesiastical symbol."

I've heard this kind of story in Africa, in Korea, and among Canada's Native Peoples. The miracle is that the Christian message can survive the garbling.

"I gave a carefully crafted sermon about Christ's forty days in the wilderness," he says, "but managed to get it really mangled in translation. The congregation listened quite attentively as my Christ, instead of going into the wilderness for forty days, kept going behind a bush to relieve himself! Some evangelists hand out Biblical tracts, but I dish out the urinary tract!"

His wife nods cheerful corroboration of all this and there is much hilarity — tempered with appreciation for the courteous, compassionate, and patient nature of the people. "I sometimes wonder," he says, "how they can put up with us."

There are other stories here but many are not so cheerful. The bishop and his wife tell us about the after-effects of the wartime propaganda that painted the Americans as monsters. He introduces me to an islander who looks to be little more than a youth. He is in his late twenties and speaks excellent English. I find him personable, knowledgeable, and interested in our film project. We are left alone and before long the young man is telling me his own story.

"I was raised on one of the smaller Ryuku islands. I don't like to say it was a primitive society, but it was a simpler society. The Japanese didn't bother us much until the war came, and then they took away all the men and the older boys to fight the Americans. We were told about these terrible creatures who were beginning to sweep through the islands. My friends and I were in our early teens and all the older males had gone to fight. Except, of course, for the very old men, our grandfathers.

"We knew that if our island was invaded it was up to us to protect our sisters and our mothers. We made a pact together — I'm talking young boys here, barely teenagers, if that — we made a pact that the barbarians would never capture our families. We would kill our families and then kill barbarians and then ourselves. We all had knives.

"The invasion came. I personally killed my grandfather, my mother, and my sisters. Before I could kill soldiers or myself I was knocked unconscious. When I came to I was in a tent hospital and the barbarian soldiers were looking after me as gently as though I were a baby. They fed me and gave me chocolate."

He finishes his story and sits silently, gazing off.

I venture a question. "How can you cope with that memory?"

"It's not easy. But then, was I not a victim of propaganda? Were we not all victims of propaganda? We are always giving messages to each other. There are bad messages and there are good messages. We'd all been victims of the bad and I decided to try the good."

"I don't follow you."

"Oh, didn't the bishop tell you? Barbarians like him taught me and even sent me to university." He smiles warmly. "I'm an ordained Christian minister."

Anson and I travel on to Taiwan, where, in the north, near Taipei, the capital city, a Canadian Presbyterian minister had established a major mission in the 1800s. He was a maritimer named George Leslie MacKay and his nickname in Chinese had been "The Black-Bearded Barbarian."

I am intrigued, again, by the use of the word "barbarian" when referring to westerners. It tends to temper my cultural preconceptions.

Taiwan is beautiful, hot, and, superficially, very Chinese. The cities are bustling and, in the daytime, not attractive. Nighttime is different. Everybody seems to be out of doors enjoying the cooler night air. A pedicab ride along back streets is an adventure in itself. Buddhist temples glow in lantern light. Distant gongs can be heard. There is the mellow sound of monks chanting. Hawkers are calling their wares. Bursts of firecrackers sound like hail on a wooden roof. Dignified men take the night air for a street stroll wearing the light cotton clothing their exporters are selling abroad as pyjamas.

I suffer cultural shock when our Chinese-fluent Canadian hosts, Bruce and Marnie Copland, take us to sample genuine Chinese cuisine in a large Taipei restaurant. The main dining area is a vast open space with none of the ornate trappings Canadians associate with a Chinese restaurant. The tables are the round variety popular with the Chinese and are generously spaced so that there is ample room for patrons and waiters to circulate. The floor is solid, unornamented cement.

As we enter we pass large aquarium tanks containing several species of fish. Bruce asks me, as a guest, to indicate which particular fish we will have for dinner. I am not fond of fish. I never handle them and seldom eat them, but am willing to abandon my dietary foibles when abroad. With guidance from Bruce, I make my choice.

We are sitting at our table, engrossed in conversation, when I become aware of a waiter standing by my left shoulder. I turn to find a two-foot-long, wet, wriggling fish being held almost in my face.

"He wants you to verify that this is the same fish you picked out when we came in," says Bruce.

"How do I know? Is it?"

"They're very honest."

I smile at the waiter and nod enthusiastically. He accepts my endorsement and turns away. Then, much to my astonishment, he executes a sweeping overhand throw that sends the live fish arcing high over a nearby table to land with a heavy squishing thud on a clear area of the hard cement floor. An employee wearing the white garb of the kitchen staff scoops it up and vanishes into the kitchen.

I turn to Bruce, looking, I am sure, every bit as shocked as I feel.

"Don't worry," he says. "That's just to guarantee that your fish will be killed. They're not going to pop it back into the aquarium and serve us something inferior."

When the fish returns from the kitchen it is beautifully cooked and exquisitely served, but I tend to remember it high in the air, headed for a concrete floor, making the final journey of its life.

When we are ready to leave, the bill is ceremoniously brought to Bruce. He pays it at the table, but no sooner does so than the waiter turns and shouts something in Chinese. Another waiter, who is about to enter the kitchen, repeats the shout, and from deep in the kitchen itself we hear several voices united in a third echo. Again Bruce responds to my unasked question.

"It's very simple. When I paid the bill I added a tip. Our waiter simply called out the size of the tip. The other one repeated it so they could hear in the kitchen and the kitchen staff repeated it to acknowledge they'd heard. Now, as we leave, it gives us much face."

I am aghast. "And if the tip is not a good one, we lose face?"

"Of course," says Bruce with a little smile. "Interesting custom, eh?"

As we leave I am praying that the Chinese continue to export their cuisine without their customs.

We travel south by rail from the capital, Taipei, to Taichung, halfway down, and on to Tainan in the south. We have crossed the Tropic of Cancer en route and it is very hot. Attendants serve complimentary tea to keep us from dehydrating. It is served in tall glasses that are placed on the window ledge. The sunlight glints through the tea, which is quite extraordinary with its petals, leaves, submerged tendrils, and strange fragrance. To me it looks like the cross-section of a swamp.

The island itself is breathtakingly beautiful. The train follows the fertile western coastal plain and it is harvest time. Both rice and wheat are being harvested, and on the hard-packed earth of household yards workers swing threshing flails in steady rhythm while others winnow the grain by throwing it high in the air in front of hand-cranked fans that blow away the chaff. Taiwan is said to be on the cutting edge of modern technology in Asia, but human muscle is still a major power source.

The coastal plain is narrow. To the east, running the entire length of the island, lies a majestic range of mountains with a high point of more than 12,000 feet.

As in all research for a documentary film, we are trying to absorb as much as possible of the society we are in, but we rely for guidance upon our western contacts, who in turn pass us on to well-educated Taiwanese friends. This process of introduction is important, because we soon learn that educated Taiwanese are wary of inquisitive strangers. For good reason.

It is only twelve years since Chiang Kai-shek, the leader of the Nationalist forces on mainland China, sent advance parties here to prepare the way for his armies' retreat from the mainland under the onslaught of Mao Tse-tung's communist Red Army. We are told, at first cautiously then more and more graphically, of the way the ground was prepared for the establishment of the Nationalist regime in this ancient island "Chinese province."

The Nationalist advance guard did a swift survey of the island to ascertain who were the current and potential leaders. It appeared to be an intelligent inventory of the human resources available to assist in building the new China. Appearances were deceiving. A generation of Taiwanese leaders were rounded up and either imprisoned or assassinated. The purge paved the way for the Nationalists to establish the present government, the majority of whose members are appointed to represent mainland jurisdictions, while only a few represent the Taiwanese themselves. This is the "Free China" I have read about at home, our newspapers extolling it as the democratic model for Asia.

Even now, twelve years later, in 1960, Taiwanese families are still mourning the dead, while other men are still in hiding or in prison. Leading newspaper editors have been in prison for years. But such things are not discussed openly. We are learning about them in bits and pieces, sometimes from university professors who still expect to be swept up in late-night arrests.

As a Canadian, raised to be loyal to a "motherland," I search for an analogy. It is as though the Germans had overrun Britain, and Churchill with his government and army had fled to Canada after preparing the way by assassinating a generation of our own leaders. In this scenario, Churchill and his people would then have imposed martial law and claimed to be governing both Canada and the United Kingdom, the latter by proxy through a majority of parliamentary seats in Ottawa occupied by friends appointed to represent the various shires of occupied Britain. I have difficulty comprehending the enormity of the political crime committed on behalf of Chiang Kai-shek, the wartime leader of China who, all through the war years, was eulogized from Canadian pulpits (including Dad's) as "the great Christian general."

We travel to the coast near Tainan and visit a village where the dominant sound is not the laughter of children or the barking of dogs but the screams of pain from men incapacitated by "black foot disease."

This town's principal product is salt. It is not mined but is reclaimed from sea water let into large evaporation basins along the shore, where the waters of Formosa Strait mingle with the South China Sea. The evaporation basins look like paddy fields but without the greenery. As in paddy fields, the barefooted workers toil through endless hours of endless days up to their calves in water. Here, unlike in the paddy fields, the workers are mostly men and the water is saline. It is the salt that causes the disease.

We visit the local doctor. Dr. Kin Ho Wang is a well-educated, skilled physician who could be making an excellent living in Tainan city but who is following his own conscience by devoting his life to the people of the salt flats. He was born and raised in this area. Doctor Kin and his family are almost as impoverished as his patients. His "hospital" is in half of an old restaurant and here in his clinic he sees about 200 patients a day. Half of them have eye disease and far too many have black foot disease.

The doctor explains that often, after long exposure to salt water, the foot and lower leg begin to turn black and become extremely painful. If the condition is not treated, the outcome is a slow, agonizing death or, more often, a swift suicide. Once black foot disease is well established the only remedy he can offer is amputation.

We watch an amputation in his small surgery. It is done expertly but with simple tools, the principal one being a large bone saw that brings to mind the village butcher shop of my childhood. He has some anaesthetic, thank God, but not much, and he has to work quickly. His surgical assistant is a young man he has trained himself.

Afterwards, Dr. Kin shows us the wards. We reach them up a narrow stairway. The stairway is cramped, because halfway up a couple of small alcoves with narrow beds have been built into its side. These are Intensive Care Units. They are really shelves with wire mesh doors, hinged at the top, that keep the patients from rolling out. The small room at the top of the stairway is the Recuperation Unit.

Here in the Recuperation Unit several patients are in various stages of recovery. All have lost limbs. Some are busy with knife and saw fashioning their own wooden legs. The room smells of bodies, common antiseptics, and fresh wood shavings. There is chatter and laughter, and faces are wreathed with smiles for Dr. Kin. These men are survivors. Even so, they will live the rest of their lives as beggars. Of approximately one hundred black foot amputees, Dr. Kin knows of only one who is self-supporting.

We have been told churches are organizing to get help to Dr. Kin. I hope that in this isolated community we are seeing the beginning of that familiar pattern in which the compassionate heart comes to serve the few, a voluntary but limited organization expands the assistance, and then, finally, the government, shamed into action, moves in to serve the many. Eventually, if the pattern holds true, legislated labour regulations may even prevent the disease.

We meet a Taiwanese professor of theology. He spends a considerable amount of time counselling individuals and families who have decided to convert from their traditional faith to Christianity.

"This is not an easy decision," says Professor Liu. "Not only does your own personal belief undergo a radical change but the change can affect, even destroy, your entire relationship with the community. It is particularly difficult if only one member of a family converts."

He illustrates by describing the role of the Buddhist household god.

"There are a multitude of gods, but a family will have one that is special. It may be a god related to the family occupation. An effigy of the god occupies the god shelf in the family altar. They worship at this home altar. If only one member has converted, how does that person show respect while no longer acknowledging the family god?

"You westerners assume that non-Christians worship the effigy, but does a Catholic worship the effigy of Christ, or the god that is symbolized by the effigy? Only the worshipper knows. At any rate the figurine is a symbol, and here, when an entire family converts, they often surrender the symbol to me for disposal. It's a bit much to expect converts to destroy a family icon. Would you ask a Christian who turned Buddhist to burn the cross?"

Just before we leave Taiwan the professor presents me with a deposed household god. It is an eight-inch-high wooden figurine of a seated male clothed in golden robes with crimson lining. His right foot is on a coiled snake and his left foot on the back of a tortoise. His right hand, resting on one knee, probably once held a knife or a spear; his left hand is extended as though both teaching and blessing. Long black hair and a flowing black moustache make him look fierce, but his attitude is benign. I am told his name is Hsuan-T'ien-Shang-Ti.*

Hsuan-T'ien-Shang-Ti, so the legend goes, had been a butcher, until one day it occurred to him that he should not kill animals. He wondered how to dispose of his knives. If he buried them, one day they would be unearthed. If he put them in the sea, they would eventually be

---

* I have found several ways to spell this name and make no claim to be knowledgeable.

retrieved. So he removed his own insides, placed the knives in among them, put it all, knives and viscera, in the sea, and, not unnaturally, died. However, the God of Heaven, impressed by the sacrifice, made Hsuan-T'ien-Shang-Ti a god and put him in charge of the waters. Eventually two monsters, a tortoise and a snake, arose from the sea and began to terrorize sailors. Hsuan-T'ien-Shang-Ti was sent to intervene and discovered that the monsters had grown from himself — the turtle from his stomach and the snake from his intestines. He was able to subdue them and maintain control.

We journey onward to the British colony of Hong Kong and I am flabbergasted.

This is the most exciting, dynamic, exotic place I have ever seen. The island of Hong Kong is a great jagged jewel; the city of Victoria is already shooting its office towers upward. The mainland city of Kowloon is like a human hive, with streets alive at all hours of the day and night. I am told that in some areas there are 5,000 inhabitants per acre, per level. Beds are said to be occupied in shifts, each occupant crawling in as his or her predecessor leaves for work.

The hills that ring the city are alive with refugees from inland China. They are living in galvanized shacks, packing crates, and sections of concrete sewer pipes purloined from construction sites.

This entire place should be utterly depressing, but it is not. The government is busily moving refugees down from the hills and into "settlement houses," multi-storey apartment buildings containing the rudimentary infrastructure required for running water, heat, light, and sewage. These, too, are desperately overcrowded, but they are better than the hillside hovels. In the vicinity of settlement houses the air is laden with a heavy buzzing sound unlike anything I have ever heard. It is the sound of human voices en masse.

The harbour hypnotizes me. I am spellbound by it. I visit it at every opportunity. I rise early in the morning and make my way to the quayside. I visit it again before going to bed. Seventeen years later I will listen to Dr. Bob McClure recalling his youthful impressions of Shanghai harbour and will find that they correspond to my first impressions of Hong Kong. My description in *McClure: The China Years* of McClure's view from the deck of an *Empress* liner entering Shanghai harbour in 1912 will be based directly upon my impression of Hong Kong harbour from the deck of a Star Ferry as I cross from Kowloon to the island in 1960. It is a description that Dr. McClure will endorse.

He watched as tiny sampans scuttled out of their way, and peered down onto their flat decks where cooking fires burned just astern of the sleeping shelters. Old rusty hulks of coasters, grimy with the coal trade, smoked their laborious way out of harbour. Deep sea freighters off-loaded into lighters, their sides swarming with coolies. A gleaming liner aflutter with pennants, rails lined with waving passengers, a band playing on the hurricane deck, was moving out even as the *Empress* was moving in. Past liners, battleships, freighters, cutters, longboats, and sampans sailed stately Chinese junks, each rear deck towering high like the after-deck of an ancient galleon, each ribbed sail looking like a great single wing of a prehistoric insect.... Off in the distance the slanting rays of the sun backlit an entire fleet whose fan-shaped sails seemed to stretch to the horizon. They were incredibly incongruous and achingly beautiful. They were China.

We travel beyond the hills that ring Kowloon and enter the narrow stretch of the New Territory hinterland that separates the colony from mainland China. In comparison to the teeming cities this area is still, in 1960, almost unpopulated. There is, however, an old walled village on a plateau plain. It looks like something from a medieval storybook, isolated, grim, and forbidding behind high grey walls. The main gates are open and Anson and I walk into a street that is narrow and, except for doorways, almost featureless. We are eyed suspiciously by inhabitants clothed almost entirely in sombre black. The whole place is only a few miles from Kowloon, but seems centuries away. We get the distinct feeling that we are not welcome so we leave as unobtrusively as possible.

There is nothing forbidding about the back streets of Kowloon, and here I search for a rosewood carving depicting a Taoist scholar. I had admired one that belonged to a Canadian doctor in Korea and he had told me I'd find more like it in Hong Kong. I come forearmed with advice. He told me where to look and he told me how to bargain.

"Don't accept the first price asked. They don't expect it and if you take it you spoil their fun. In Asia, driving a bargain is more than a pleasure, it's a ceremony. There's a ritual to it. When the first price is named, you must feign outrage. A Big Nose — that's you — must act particularly outraged in order to establish that you're not just some gullible tourist."

"But how far do you haggle?"

"Ah, indeed. You want to make your deal while both parties feel they've got a bargain. That's the art of it, isn't it?"

I find the carving in a backstreet shop and put the advice to the test. The only intelligible English the vendor speaks is numerical, but we both understand feigned outrage, followed by indignation, and then interest, and finally pleasure. As I leave I thank him and he laughs and nods vigorously.

I still have my Taoist scholar. He is an elderly man with the high-domed bald head that signifies intellect. He is seated, half-reclining, legs out casually to one side, and he is clothed in a long flowing robe. His bright, piercing eyes are focused on an open book he holds in his left hand. But he is reclining against the side of a panther and his right arm rests along the creature's back, the hand spread gently on its shoulder. The panther is half-crouched, its tail lashing against the scholar's back, its mouth open in a snarl, with jagged ivory teeth gleaming dangerously. Only the scholar's calm intellect is holding the beast in check. The beast, of course, is the beast within.

The doctor had warned me that "rosewood" carvings are often inferior wood artfully camouflaged with shoe polish. That might apply to mine, but I couldn't care less. The value is not in the material but in the art and the idea. When I look from the scholar with the panther to the god seated with one foot on a turtle and one on a snake, I cannot help reflecting how universal is the human challenge to subdue the beast within, and how sophisticated are these attempts to illustrate in concrete terms the abstract reality.

Kowloon city has burst through the hills into an area where development is establishing Shah Tin, New Town, but at the moment it is more a promise than a reality. Already, however, there is a Christian college here, high on a hillside overlooking new construction in the valley. We meet two Canadian missionaries, Muriel and Walton Tong.

Muriel speaks Chinese like a native, and when I mention that I'd like to buy a small ivory carving she volunteers to take me shopping. I learn more about the gentle art of commerce. There is, apparently, a triple price structure. The foreigner who speaks no Chinese pays the highest price. The foreigner who speaks good Chinese pays a middle price. The customer who is Chinese pays the lowest price.

I wonder why Muriel is so willing to help me shop, but I soon find that she is interested in improving my education.

We go to a shop where she knows the proprietor and I find a carving that I admire. It is an ivory Goddess of Mercy and is quite unusual. The goddess is usually carved in a most elaborate fashion with a great deal of intricate traditional ornamentation that almost overwhelms the eye. But this one is tall and slender, and her flowing robes fall in decep-tively simple lines. One hand is delicately raised in blessing. The figure is like a Buddhist madonna.

Muriel conducts the purchase ritual and I am very pleased. But then she has an earnest conversation with the proprietor.

"You're in luck," she tells me. "He's agreed to let you meet the carv-er who made this figurine."

I am delighted but puzzled, because now the proprietor is lifting a large trapdoor in the shop floor. He gestures for us to follow and we descend a set of ladder-like stairs. We are in a basement — or, more accurately, a cellar. No, not even a cellar, it is a windowless pit with earth-en walls and an earthen floor. There are workbenches here and several men are busily carving ivory figurines. I meet the artist who carved my Buddhist madonna. He appears to be elderly but may only be middle-aged. He is working by the light of a naked bulb that dangles on a cord from an overhead floor joist.

My Goddess of Mercy is a small, elegant creation only about a foot high. It is made from ivory, a substance so coveted that its acquisition threatens to exterminate the earth's elephants,* and it was carved by an artist working in a pit beneath a trapdoor in the floor of a backstreet shop in Hong Kong. The lovely female figure is depicted rising out of a lotus flower, symbolizing the fact that beauty and humanity are rooted in mud. When I look at my Goddess of Mercy my heart weeps but my hopes soar.

I return home from the rim of southeast Asia with memories of various peoples who, although racked with the problems of wars, shifting colo-nialism, poverty, and disease, seem so vibrant, so vigorous, so deter-mined to move forward that when I write the shooting script for our film I call it *On the Rim of Tomorrow*.

I return to Hong Kong several times and go far afield in other parts of the world, but Hong Kong retains the prime place in my memory it established in 1960. But there is a blend of updates. In 1978 son Ian and I go on a tourist bus tour and one of the "sights" is a lone refugee shack on a hillside. We visit the same walled village that Anson and I found so intimidating. The walls are still intact and still just as forbidding, but now there is a bazaar outside the main gate. There is bustle, chatter, and

* This was not fully understood in those days and importing ivory to Canada was not illegal. I would not purchase ivory today.

laughter. Ian bargains for a rosewood carving that takes his fancy and eventually both seller and purchaser are happy. In Kowloon itself, many of the free-wheeling backstreet merchants are gone and tourists are now directed toward the Ocean Terminal building where all the merchandise is tagged and there is no haggling at all. By 1981 I find that the golden arches of a hamburger empire have impinged upon the Hong Kong exotic.

The years go by. Taiwan holds democratic elections that abandon the fiction that the parliamentarians represent mainland ridings, Korea's economic vibrancy earns it the nickname "the sleeping tiger," Japan is one of the world's leading commercial powers, and the People's Republic of China resumes control of Hong Kong. In the global marketplace, Tomorrow has arrived.

But what I trust will never change is faith in the calming wisdom of the Taoist scholar, the meaning of the sacrifice made by the Buddhist butcher god, and the hope implicit in the figure of the lovely Goddess of Mercy rising from a flower rooted in mud. For more than forty years the two gods and the scholar have had a place of honour in my home, where they remind me that their people have thought of my people as barbarians.

15

THE MILITARY MIND

I'VE BEEN STAGGERING AROUND an army camp in central Ontario for a week now and my head is so full of warlike information I feel like Attila the Hun on a refresher course. I must say, though, the Major has been very decent about it all. He was saddled with me on Monday morning just after breakfast when he probably had his heart set on a few routine duties. Instead, he was told to educate me, and fast. I've been sent by the National Film Board and my assignment is to write a scenario for a training film on Infantry Fire Power. The Major has been pounding information into me all week. He has given me blackboard talks, map sessions, sand table demonstrations, and straight lectures — all private — until I never want to see another classroom. Even graduate school was never like this.

In preparation for this assignment I've been subjected to RCMP security clearance, and I must have passed or I wouldn't be here. In the years ahead the NFB will tag me for numerous other military projects, such as a sobering look at the effect of alcoholic hangovers on fighter pilots and a training film for crash rescue firefighters. I enjoy researching films for the military partly because of the subjects, which can be odd to the point of bizarre and are interesting topics for a writer with a bent for drama, but mostly because of the people. I admire and like the men I meet.

This Infantry Fire Power project is no exception. The Major is so patient and so thorough that I feel honour bound not to let him down. He has loaded me with manuals on tactics, and in my barracks cubicle I've been burning the midnight light bulb reading about the ways and means of trapping the enemy on killing grounds.

I keep telling myself not to worry about the fact that the film we're to make is probably obsolete before it's shot. I've seen the classified manual for the atomic battlefield, which is a whole different cauldron of death, but that manual is not the one we're following. Of course, ours is not an atomic army. Or is it? Who knows? I can't blame the military mind for suffering a little schizophrenia.

Today, Friday, the Major announces to the camp commander that I am ready to command a company. The Colonel doesn't look particularly excited and I hope he's not worried. I have no intention of staging a coup. I've learned from experience that when I cram like this I remember details just barely long enough to get them onto paper.

I've enjoyed this place, although, as the saying goes, I wouldn't like to live here. But everything fascinates me, from the heavy tanks on the range to the conversations in the officers' mess. I can see why some men take to the military life. There is an orderliness to it that is reassuring, and, paradoxically, a sense of security. There is also the opportunity to set an objective for oneself and then become very good at achieving it. Dad would be horrified to know that I see anything good about it at all. During the First World War he left theological college to join the army, but being opposed to combat he chose to serve in the Army Medical Corps, remained a private, and came out the other end muttering forever after about "the military mind." In Dad's mouth that is a dark phrase that hints of hardened military arteries, ossified brains, calcified livers, and atrophied morals. He has the old-time preacher's knack of making a phrase sound obscene without uttering a single vulgar word. In his mouth "the military mind" is the embodiment of obscenity.

I feel guilty because not only do I like these guys, many of them being downright civilized, but I am using my talents to aid and abet the war machine. But around here the war machine doesn't seem hell-bent on aggression. I figure if the fellows ever have to use their Fire Power it will be to help save my hide, so I'd better do a good job with my end of it. (Mind you, forty years later my naive confidence will be shaken when Prime Minister Chrétien ignores democracy and sends our troops to war in Kosovo without asking for the approval of Parliament. When asked why the decision is not put to a parliamentary vote he will say, "What's a vote? They stand up, they sit down." I will find it appalling that the lives of our astonishingly fine service people can be put at risk by autocratic fiat.)

But now it is late Friday afternoon, and the Major has completed his task and handed me back to the Colonel. The Colonel drags me along on what amounts to a recreational tour of the firing range. Some Members of Parliament will be visiting the camp on the weekend, and the Colonel wants to make sure everything is in tip-top order.

We come to the rifle range where marksmen will be demonstrating the FN semi-automatic rifle. The Colonel is struck with a happy idea.

"Pretend that Mr. Scott and I are visiting M.P.s," he instructs the officer in charge. "Do your stuff."

We are given ringside seats at what, if it were for real, would be attempted homicide. The firing range is in a small forest of trees. Paths lead away from sandbagged firing butts and wind off among the trees and through the undergrowth. Two soldiers, each armed with a semi-automatic rifle, leave the butts, and each selects the base of a path. They stand ready.

"To begin with, gentlemen," says the officer to the two ersatz M.P.s, "we will demonstrate the FN on automatic."

He signals, and the two men walk away, following their separate paths. I wonder if they are after rabbits. Then I realize that the woods are full of automated targets. Behind us, raised several feet above ground level, is a control room from which an operator activates targets. In the woods, man-sized metal shapes rise ghost-like from the undergrowth, loiter a few brief moments, and then subside. The riflemen are hoping to flatten those figures before they go down on their own.

The figures rise and fall and the semi-automatics chatter in savage bursts as the two men walk, slowly and alertly, deeper and deeper into the range. I realize with some amazement that fully fifty percent of the time the marksmen are missing. There is a hail of bullets out there but it is achieving very little.

The marksmen return to home base.

"Now, gentlemen," says the officer, and I wonder how he can appear so imperturbable, "we will demonstrate the FN on single shot."

The exercise is repeated, and again the targets rise randomly and menacingly from the underbrush. This time there is simulated death and destruction. Each rifle is emitting only one single snapping crack at a time, but every target is nailed and flattened the moment it appears. I feel all cold inside and make a mental note: if a real marksman is ever shooting at me, I'd better pray that his weapon is on automatic.

"Excellent," says the Colonel. "What next?"

"Well, sir, we thought the visitors might like to try the FN for themselves. Single shots, firing from the butts."

"Good idea," beams the Colonel. "Mr. Scott and I are your guinea pigs. Show us what it's all about. Ten shots each."

The Colonel looks very pleased with himself, and why not? He has just found a legitimate way to expend a few rounds of Her Majesty's ammunition.

A sergeant is detailed to look after me, and he leads me to a sand-bagged butt. He presents me with a rifle and shows me the trigger, the barrel, the stock, the safety, the breech, and the sights, and he makes sure I know which end the bullet emerges from. He messes around with the rear sight, and finally the rifle is all mine. He gets me comfortable with my elbows on a sandbag and makes sure I know that the rear sight is to line up with the front sight. He seems very affable for a sergeant, and again I marvel at how good these guys are at PR.

"If you can see the targets," he whispers, "I'll suggest where you should aim."

I wonder why he's whispering, but it sounds like a fair deal to me. This is a heavier rifle than anything I ever used on groundhogs as a teenager, but not as cumbersome as the old .303s we used as cadets on the high school firing range, and I can't see that the principle is any different.

The Sergeant calls that we are ready and the Colonel sings out that he's ready and in a moment the targets begin to rise out there in the woods.

"Dead centre," whispers the Sergeant, and I fire. "A foot above ..." he continues; "... two feet over the head ... the knees ... dead centre...." He drones on quietly, giving me the precise range every time, his voice very low and confidential. I am relieved to find that we are both seeing the same targets at the same time. I do what he tells me and ask no questions. After all, he set the sights and he knows the distance. I may not be in the army but I know when to obey orders.

Off to my right I can hear the Colonel blasting away and can tell by the vibes that he's having a thoroughly good time.

We both squeeze off our tenth shot and silence falls over the range. The Colonel hands his rifle off and comes striding bouncily across to us.

"Well, Sergeant, how'd our visiting M.P. do?" He is beaming broadly and looks very pleased with himself.

"One, sir," says the Sergeant.

"Ha, ha, ha," laughs the Colonel, amiably condescending.

"Missed one, sir," says the Sergeant, inserting the knife.

The Colonel's face turns to stone. He stares past my left ear and for several seconds he doesn't focus. When he does, he ignores me and turns on his heel.

"Give me that goddamned gun!" he orders, and heads back to the butt.

I look nervously at the Sergeant. His face is expressionless. "Sir," he says quietly, and he is speaking only to me, "may I suggest a cold beer in the sergeants' mess?"

I follow him to a jeep and we drive off. From behind us comes the sound of the Colonel's rifle ripping away at helpless targets. The Sergeant is whistling softly to himself and he looks contented, as though he has just come to the end of a perfect day. Interesting thing, the military mind.

16

INQUÍRY

I AM INVITED TO CBOT, the CBC's Ottawa TV station, to meet a young public affairs producer who has just been imported from Toronto. He is three years younger than I am but has a lot of television production under his belt. So far, I've only dabbled casually in the public affairs realm, for some CBC regional productions. This chap, however, is charged with launching a network series that will take its impetus from Parliament Hill and associated federal doings — or misdoings. He is a slight, wiry, game man with a sparkling intelligence. The fact that he's game is self-evident, since although he has just recently lost a leg and is breaking in a prosthetic, he seemingly couldn't care less. He also has a guitar leaning against the side of his desk. I am immediately captivated by Patrick Watson and will remain so for years.

I sign on for one show only, but that contract leads to many more. I never do sign an exclusive contract. Freelance is freelance, a status I protect for the rest of my career, with only one partial relapse in 1984.

Pat's series is called *Inquiry*, pronounced "inKWY/ree" — none of this "IN/kw-ree" business for Pat. So that there can be no doubt, every time the main title appears on the screens of the nation the second syllable is marked with an accent: *Inquíry*. The slack of tongue and loose of brain don't mess with Patrick.

The series format is relatively simple. There is a live on-camera host — literally on-camera in the studio at air time. There are sequences on film that are plugged in from the telecine room during the live broadcast. There may be skits and interviews, also presented live in the studio. My functions are to research a subject, design the program, go on location as director with a camera crew to get film footage, supervise the editing, sound mixing, and so forth, write the narration, write the skits if there are any and the words for the on-camera host, and then sweat it out in the control room while Patrick knits it all together at air time. I am becoming a documentary writer/director. Others perform the same

function on their own segments. Warner Troyer (another P.K.) is imported from Winnipeg. He eventually follows Patrick to the series *This Hour
Has Seven Days*, then moves on to cbc's *Fifth Estate*, where he cements his
status as a nationally known incisive tv reporter and anchorman. Compassionate Ed Reid, a late-comer to the P.K. species, is imported from
Crawley Films (he is destined, alas, to lose his life while attempting to
serve humanity in South America) and shrewd Roy Faibish comes from
the back rooms of Parliament Hill. We have a young on-camera
announcer who is enjoying his first exposure on national network tv.
His name is Lloyd Robertson. While the series is underway he relocates
to Toronto and cbc-tv's *Weekend News*, en route to *The National* and, eventually, to ctv as the dean of its news anchors. Lloyd is followed into
Inquiry by an even younger and even more handsome on-camera
announcer, Alex Trebek, who will eventually migrate to a career as per-
petual host of *Jeopardy*. He, too, is getting his first national network tv
exposure.

In casting a host, Patrick performs a miracle. He entices Davidson
Dunton into the chair. "Davie" Dunton is a brilliant, erudite, massively
knowledgeable man who had just retired as President of the cbc when
Pat snared him. He attended several universities, but avoided graduating
from any of them; his string of university degrees are all honorary. We
writer/directors admire Davie enormously, not least of all because we
know that he, like Pat, will not put up with any bullshit.

When Davie eventually moves on he is replaced by French Canada's
gift to the nation, a history professor from McGill, Laurier LaPierre. Laurier, like Warner and Roy, eventually follows Patrick into *This Hour Has
Seven Days*. When I think of Laurier as host of *Inquiry* I think of an
evening when the telecine collapses with ten minutes of the show still
to go and Pat sends Laurier an SOS on the intercom.

"We've lost telecine. There's ten minutes to go. Fill it."

The show is mine, although the precise subject will not remain in
my memory. (It was undoubtedly political. Possibly electoral redistribu-
tion, or separatism, or even the moral state of the nation.) Laurier never
misses a beat. He looks straight into the camera and delivers a spellbinding mini-lecture on democracy and personal responsibility. He
weaves it seamlessly and passionately into whatever has been going on
before, so that only those of us in the control room know there has been
a glitch. It is the best ten minutes I never wrote.

It's fair to say most of us involved in this series are pleasantly left of
centre and tend to mistrust the establishment, which in this case is the

Progressive Conservative government of John George Diefenbaker. I maintain that a little pleasant prejudice is essential to good programming. Of course, a little judicious balance is essential to ethical programming.

My first network TV script is written for *Inquiry* and is called "Our Unreformed Senate." (Shades of the past, present, and future! The same show could be aired in the twenty-first century. Nothing has changed. The Senate is still an unreformed, unrepentant, undemocratic, and apparently irreplaceable institution. It has even managed to deteriorate to the point where it is totally under party control and no longer truly represents the regions. Even so, I would prefer to see it reformed rather than abolished. In my opinion, the appointment of Laurier LaPierre to the Senate in 2001 gives that anachronistic institution an injection of credibility.)

A program called "How to Get Government Action," in which earnest cabinet ministers recommend writing letters and staging demonstrations, seems, in retrospect, less than illuminating. We do have fun with it, though, staging a scene in which a Guy Fawkes character stashes explosives under the Peace Tower. There is a dandy explosion and an animated Peace Tower goes into orbit. (If we were to broadcast that today we'd probably be put in the slammer for advocating terrorism.)

Freelance cameraman Johnny Foster and I go to the Caribbean islands to look at Canadian foreign aid. Johnny is a genuine pioneer in cinéma-verité, the use of highly portable and therefore unobtrusive cameras to produce a heightened sense of reality and immediacy. He and I do a lot of work together, which is my good fortune.

In the Caribbean, as elsewhere, the most memorable (though not necessarily the most important) moments occur off-camera. In Barbados, an island that boasts the oldest parliament outside of Britain, we are granted a Sunday morning interview at the home of a judge. He is flanked, off-camera, by a couple of lawyer associates; they are possibly intended to function as witnesses, but as the morning wears on and the rum and coconut milk flows they become jovial companions. By the time we leave, a happy trio of legal beagles are waving a cheerful goodbye from the front porch. I am not a good investigative reporter. People are too friendly.

On a smaller island, St. Vincent, we arrive at an airport that has only one airstrip. That strip runs downhill into the ocean, and there is a small mountain at the upper end. This means the takeoff must always be downhill, and any overshoot will lead to a watery end. One can land either uphill or downhill, depending on the wind, but each alternative has potentially disastrous drawbacks. This runway typifies the infrastructure problems facing these small islands.

We are met at this airport by a taxi driver who has been courteously assigned to us by the government's Information Officer. Our driver is a fund of information, both touristic and political. He is not happy with the current administration. The islands of the Little Eight, of which this is one, are flotsam from the recent breakup of the short-lived West Indian Federation, and our driver says that the smaller the island the more autocratic and corrupt it becomes, because it's easier for families, cliques, or gangs to take control. We eventually discover that our taxi driver is the leader of the unofficial underground "loyal opposition." Apparently the government Information Officer, who assigned him to us, takes the information job seriously. He will certainly never qualify as a spin doctor.

On St. Kitts, an island almost devoid of sub-tropical growth and famous for its sugar cane, we choose a taxi driver at random and hire him for the next few days. Johnny Foster has connections in the travel business in New York and they have booked us a reservation at a local hotel. We give the address to our new driver, whose name, so he tells us, is "Coke." Coke eyes the address less than enthusiastically.

"You know where it is?" I ask. It's a ludicrous question. There can't be a square foot of this small island that Coke doesn't know.

"Yes, Man, I know." There is a long pause. "You say you got reservations?" He sounds incredulous.

"That's right, Coke."

"There's other places. A few."

Here's a guy, I think, trying to take business to his own friends. "No thanks. We've got reservations."

"Just want you boys to know there's choices."

"That's okay. We're fine. New York booked this for us."

Coke seems unimpressed by travel-savvy New York.

Our taxi pulls to a stop on a back street beside an almost windowless building with one small doorway piercing its blank wall.

"Coke, I think you've got the address wrong. This looks like a warehouse."

"No, this is it. This here's the back door. Why don't you men leave your bags here and walk through to the front. I'll wait right here. If everything's okay I'll take your bags in."

We don't trust this guy. Leave our bags? Our camera gear? Well, we are on an island and he operates a licensed taxi and this is a British colony, so what the hell.

We walk through the building. There are rooms on either side of a narrow hallway but each is little more than a cubicle with a bed. The dividing walls go only partway to the high, warehouse-like ceiling. These partitions are made of rough lumber and there's not a vestige of decoration. We emerge into an equally depressing lobby occupied at the moment by three female staff members. The desk clerk is incredibly buxom with cleavage a guy could get lost in. The other two are undulating enticingly in brief and clinging dresses that look as though they came out of a spray can. Apparently the clerk is expecting us.

"Hello, boys! We got your booking. You two boys goin' t' have a really good time!" It's not a question. It's a promise. Or a threat.

We retrace our steps to Coke's taxi. "This place is a whorehouse. Why didn't you tell us?"

"I don't interfere with other folk's business. You go where you want. I take you."

We consign ourselves into Coke's hands and he takes us to the harbourfront and a little hotel that is run like a family home. It is also primitive, with window air conditioners that don't work and cracked linoleum that hides warped floors, but we are treated with warm courtesy. In our spare moments we sit with our hosts on rocking chairs on the verandah and watch, as though through their eyes, as bizarrely dressed tourists come and go from a gleaming tour ship. In later years I will have no recollection of whom we interviewed or what we filmed but I will remember that little hotel, our hosts, the verandah, the spectacle of what might have been aliens landing from Mars, and the daily care taken by our taxi-driving shepherd.

With our Caribbean shoot finished, Johnny heads for home, but I go to Trinidad for a week or so to meet Anson Moorhouse and research a short film for Berkeley Studio. It turns into a sync-sound mini-drama called *Peter Mahadeo's Quest*. As usual, the principal memory has nothing to do with the film. One of our guides and gurus is a schoolteacher, Macdonald Tiklisingh, who invites us to a house party. In typical Trinidadian fashion the house is on stilts. Among the guests is an entire steel band, *The Sundowners*, who are warming up to be a top contender in the rapidly approaching Carnival competitions. I swear there is not a room in the house that doesn't have a steel pan or two in full action for the entire evening. The very house, high on its stilts, is inclined to dance. Before the evening is over I buy a pan from the band, but they can't let me have it until Carnival is done with. Macdonald will ship it to me later and it will become a family heirloom. The Trinidadian expedition provides a pleasant interlude before I return to the turgid waters of CBC-TV public affairs.

Inquiry takes me into the realm of fraudulent Canadian passports, and I am astonished to find myself in a depressed area of Montreal talking to a clergyman from the Caribbean who actually admits to acquiring forged passports for would-be immigrants. He comes to the Ottawa studio and cheerfully goes in front of the TV cameras to explain his unorthodox social assistance program. He appears voluntarily, but I worry that he will find himself in trouble. If he does, my conscience will bother me. If he does not, then there is something seriously wrong with my country's administration.

I do a series of programs on aspects of criminal justice. One involves the last hanging in Canada — two men, Arthur Lucas and Ronald Turpin, were both hanged at Toronto's Don Jail on December 11, 1962. Their cases have been appealed, but unsuccessfully. I interview the appeal lawyer, Walter Williston, a brilliant criminal litigator, and find him frustrated by the system. He has serious reservations about the adequacy of the defence, which was handled by a court-appointed defender who allegedly spent more time shacked up with a prisoner's girlfriend than he did preparing the case. Williston had important new defence evidence involving blood types, but was not permitted to enter it into the appeal. The executions took place while John Diefenbaker was prime minister, but in later years I will realize that Mr. Diefenbaker, who was a seasoned criminal defence lawyer, had no liking for the notion of death as a penalty.

While exploring the problems judges face when imposing sentences I am permitted to do on-camera interviews with outspoken and experienced magistrates. This material is edited into manageable form and I take it into the maximum-security penitentiary at Kingston, show the magisterial interviews to three convicts, and film their verbal reactions. The three are long-term residents, and include a safecracker and an armed robber. I am intrigued by their thoughtful approach to the subject. When their interviews are eventually intercut with those of the magistrates it's a toss-up as to which team has the most insight. When the cameras are not running and conversation is off the record, two of the convict interviewees speak forcefully in favour of indeterminate sentencing, in which the term can be left open-ended and the time served has more to do with rehabilitation than with legislated "one-size-fits-all" punishment. I want to put this opinion on film but they refuse, saying it would be dangerous for them to express that opinion publicly — meaning, of course, to the prison public. For some, they say, indeterminate sentencing can amount to throwing away the key.

In the course of researching and filming this Justice series I interview a friendly, exceptionally warm human being, Dr. Bruno Cormier of Montreal, who has been described as the father of forensic psychiatry in Canada. He is also a rebel, an iconoclast, and an art connoisseur. Dr. Cormier is studying habitual offenders. He takes great exception to the practice of throwing away the key after a person has been convicted of five indictable offences. He is convinced that middle age has a rehabilitating effect all by itself, and that we put "habituals" away just as they are about to be reformed by nature. A troubling paradox.

Also in the course of our making these Justice shows Patrick suggests that I phone another lawyer in Montreal and ask him for an on-camera interview. The lawyer is pleasant and courteous, but not interested in TV exposure. "Who needs it?" he says, and that's the absolute end of our conversation. His name is Pierre Trudeau.

One day Patrick calls me into his office, which is located in a former lumberyard, close, but not too close, to the CBC's Ottawa TV studios. It's a location that apparently gives a producer some flexibility in the choice of staff. Like me, most of the Inquiry gang are freelancers. I expect there is another assignment in the wind. Pat accepts program suggestions, but often throws in some of his own. Today he's following his own trail and gets straight to the point.

"Have you heard of an Ombudsman?"

"No."

"Well, you have now. It's a Scandinavian idea. A professor at Carleton is studying it. See what you think."

As it turns out, I think the idea of an independent agent — appointed by government but at arm's length from government — who protects us from government is a great idea, and why have we Canadians not thought of it all on our own? Patrick and I run an anonymous ad in the newspaper personals, giving a phone number and asking folk who are having trouble with government bureaucracy to call. We don't have long to wait. The first respondent doesn't even use the phone. He comes directly into the office and grills Patrick and me. He is an RCMP officer hot on the trail of subversion.

As far as I know, our *Inquiry* segment gives the first national TV exposure to the concept of the Ombudsman.

I get to dabble a little more actively in sedition by doing a program on the sillier aspects of security. This involves some off-the-record research, because people in the security business are not keen to talk on camera. There are some wild stories out there but they can't be used on air without corroboration. My favourite is the one about a politician who insisted that the Defence Research Board take a look at a friend's invention. The DRB passed it on to the Canadian Army Research Establishment (CARDE) for testing. Apparently the inventor's idea was to put a propeller on the nose of a shell, his theory being that since a shell rotates, the propeller would also rotate and the missile could go right around the world. CARDE was not pleased, but political pressure is political pressure. To save face, the "test" was classified as highly Secret. I am told the use of the "Secret" stamp is a well-used tool to avoid embarrassment.

Still following the security spoor I interview Major-General F.F. Worthington, CB, MC, MM, CD (ret.), who at this time is head of Canada's Emergency Measures Organization, the institution that is supposed to organize our response to floods, tornadoes, fires, and other disasters. This gentleman is known to his friends as "Worthy" and to vast numbers of Canadian veterans as "Fighting Frank." In the course of a jovial conversation he tells me how, as a First World War cavalryman, finding himself unhorsed and lying in a ditch watching German tanks rumble by, he decided that tanks would be the future cavalry. He is now known as the "Father of the Canadian Armoured Corps." This is a man to be respected, and he believes that a great deal of security is indeed silly, because it is so superficial — which is exactly our point.

Fighting Frank is happy to illustrate his opinion. He is an energetic, compact, wiry man with a roguish, almost elfin twinkle and he seems to enjoy his story, the gist of which will remain with me.

"I had a map on the wall right here that showed the location of certain sensitive installations. I had it because we were trying to figure out good evacuation routes in case of disasters, nuclear or otherwise. You don't want to evacuate an entire city into a cul-de-sac. Anyway, the security people came in and confiscated my map!" He is hugely amused by the clincher. "I took that map out of *Time* magazine!"

I am reminded of Hilda's experience in the army's Historical Section. On her first day as secretary she typed letters for the Director. When she came to work the next morning she found a security officer waiting for her, holding the ribbon from her typewriter along with transcripts of the previous day's letters. Apparently someone had been up all night painstakingly extracting information from the ribbon. She was given a little lecture on security. She wondered, but did not ask, how they managed to overlook her personal file in the desk drawer, where, following her private-secretarial habit, she had innocently filed back-up carbon copies of the same correspondence. She had also left her short-hand notebook in a drawer. But it was the ribbon that was the culprit.

Research trails lead into strange encounters, but don't always result in a program. One strange conversation, which takes place in a normal middle-class living room in Alta Vista, an Ottawa subdivision, is with a senior civil servant who believes, absolutely, in the existence of extra-terrestrial UFOs. His name is Wilbert Smith. In lazy Ottawa Valley speech the "t" gets dropped and the name comes out more like Wilbur. Wilbur was an engineer with the Federal Department of Transport* when he and a few associates began to suspect that there were real entities behind the UFO phenomena that were being reported around Ottawa and in various other parts of the world. The government was intrigued enough back in the early 1950s to give Wilbur and his colleagues a laboratory at Shirley's Bay on the city's western outskirts. Officially it was just a communications building, but every layman in the Valley knew of it as a UFO tracking station.

For some reason, the government's enthusiasm ran out and consequently so did the budget. But apparently Wilbur has not been deterred.

I don't record our conversation. Even a small tape recorder tends to be inhibiting. If I want to record, I'll come back with a camera crew. But the shape of our conversation remains with me.

"The people topside sent us information that changed our perspective."

"Topside" turns out to be Wilbur's term for extraterrestrials.

"How did you know it was from ... uh ... them?"

"Well, we picked up transmissions on Department equipment that puzzled us at first. They were just mishmash. Then we recorded them and slowed it all down and began to realize that they made sense."

"That doesn't prove they came from aliens."

"It was the speed of transmission that alerted us. We have no equipment that can duplicate that speed. Then we realized they were sending us radically new concepts related to physics."

---

* Like every government department, the name has gone through many chameleon-like changes; its most appropriate form has been "Communications."

Wilbur doesn't lumber my layman's brain with scientific detail, but says that he and some associates got working on an anti-gravity machine.

"Anti-gravity?"

"Yes. That's the way their craft function. By manipulating gravity. And it explains the way they travel. Almost instant travel in any direction."

He tells me that he and a friend have been working on an anti-gravity experiment in his garage. This doesn't surprise me. I sometimes suspect there is more original high-level research going on in the garages of Ottawa's boffins than there is in the labs of the National Research Council.

"We were getting ready to test it when the Department receivers got a message telling us we were making an error. We ran a test anyway, but triggered it remotely." He gets up and leaves the room, returning with a twisted piece of copper tubing about eighteen inches long that looks as though it might once have been circular. "This is all that's left of it. Almost wrecked my garage."

I think this man is nuts. And soon I'm sure of it, because he is telling me about the monitors.

"The monitors?"

I sit spellbound as this pleasant, seemingly intelligent senior civil servant with an engineering background tells me that he often spots spheroidal monitors about the size of a large football. They tend to hover and are frequently seen prowling around power installations. Wilbur believes they are observation units for the folk topside.

His wife comes into the living room with coffee and cookies. She sits and listens quietly as her husband describes UFO monitors from outer space.

"Mrs. Smith," I finally ask, "how do you feel about all this?"

"Oh, I used to think he was quite mad. Until I saw my first monitor. Once you've seen one, others are quite easy to spot."

I think of the three spots that flash on the cinema screen to signal a change of reels. They are virtually invisible until you see them once, then you never miss them again.

"It's the same for the children," she says.*

---

*   Mr. Smith died in 1962. I have confined myself to personal recollections of our conversation. There is a Wilbert Smith web site on the Internet: www.geocities .com/Area51/Nebula/5924

The series moves into its final stages. I have already done a segment on the new separatist movement in Quebec, but now toward the end of the third year of *Inquiry* I find myself structuring a segment that we call "To Be and Not to Be." It is based on the results of a poll conducted jointly by the CBC and *Maclean's* magazine. The current editor of *Maclean's* is Peter Gzowski, with whom we are co-operating. I have difficulty with the whole thing because the poll is asking Canadians whether we should join the United States. It is part of the perennial Canadian navel-watching, back-scourging, soul-searching, introspective abrasion of the national psyche. Self-analysis is a tool that helps rehabilitate the psychiatric patient, but we Canadians use it to make ourselves psychotic. Patrick has launched this aberration, but now he goes off to Toronto to prepare the ground for *This Hour Has Seven Days* and is replaced by a brilliant, underrated producer, Wilson Southam. Wilson views the subject with the same jaundiced eye as I do.

I feel that the only way to keep my sanity is not to take the whole thing too seriously. We are going to have some pundits discuss the poll results. The participants are to be in the studio on-camera at air time. I write a program structure that calls for an eccentric computer that not only presents the poll results but makes visual and audio editorial comment before the pundits have their egg-headed say. Some of the visuals for the computer screen are created by Noreen Young, a young Ottawa artist with a talent for creating puppets. At one point, puppets that look remarkably like prominent politicians Judy LaMarsh and George Hees sing a ditty to the tune of "The Maple Leaf Forever":

> In days of yore and since the war,
> Many brave investors came
> And planted firm the U.S. flag
> On Canada's fair domain.
> We must confess we like that rag.
> You ought to hear us holler,
> "God save the Queen and Heaven bless
> The friendly Yankee dollar."

During a brief studio rehearsal and warm-up, one of our pundits, a political science professor, gets annoyed by our frivolous and irreverent approach and walks out. He is retrieved in the nick of time by Wilson, who includes diplomacy among other useful talents.

Inquiry remains in memory as an exciting trial-by-fire introduction to the world of CBC-TV public affairs. I always feel fortunate having been able to apprentice, as it were, under Patrick. I hope I learned from the whole gang, and I certainly gained a great deal of respect for the extraordinarily efficient Cecily Burwash, who was Patrick's executive assistant throughout the entire process.

Neither Cecily nor I move on to *Seven Days*, having other stars to follow. We do work together again early in 1965, when Patrick, who has various irons in his numerous Executive Producer fires, asks us to take over a project for *Intertel*, an ambitious multi-national series of one-hour programs. This one is about the effect of TV on politics and politicians. Cecily functions as producer and I as writer/director. In this case a great deal of film material has already been collected. It's a genuine "bushel basket" project — one is presented with a mass of unedited, unorganized material and has to give it structure and content. There is a tight deadline on this and little time for fresh filming. The only new material I recall shooting is sparked by Winston Churchill's funeral. This is the first time satellites bring real-time coverage of an overseas event, so I take a cameraman into a CBC-TV Toronto control room and film the technicians and equipment as they receive the historic transmission and feed it into the network.

The freelance editor working with us is Don Haig, who is on his way to making a formidable reputation for himself. Pushed by a rapidly approaching air date, we go through the bushel baskets in extraordinarily short time and structure a program called "The Cathode Colours Them Human."

At one point I find Cecily looking a little depressed.

"What's bugging you?"

"I think we're being fed to the wolves."

"How so?"

She has no idea. Female intuition?

We go through the final editing and the final sound mix and feel very pleased with ourselves. Patrick vets the final product and drives me back to my hotel. He tells me what a great job it is and that he is very impressed and pleased.

The program goes to air. The reviews are not good. The wolves are there, clothed as critics. There seems to be some concern the program is too simplistic in suggesting that the electorate is more influenced by image than by policy.

Before *Inquiry* itself comes to an end Hilda and I have pulled up stakes. We move from Stittsville to the village of Manotick, where we build a home on a Rideau River waterfront lot purchased from the Right Honourable John Bracken, former leader of the federal Progressive Conservatives. We now have three sons, number three being Rob (christened Robert). The boys proceed to live the life of river rats, canoeing, swimming, and skating as the seasons permit.

Mr. Bracken, who likes to seize a companion by the elbow and propel him forward as he walks and talks, improves my education by explaining how the use of the parliamentary open vote kept him in power as premier of Manitoba for a remarkable twenty years. I begin to see why he introduced the word "progressive" into the name of the federal party. Also, after Hilda and I have been in residence for several months he observes that our supposed hundred-foot waterfront is only ninety feet wide, and gives us a ten percent refund. The adjective "Right Honourable" fits John Bracken like a glove. It's a concept the party will put into retirement in later years.

By late 1963, when *Inquiry* goes into oblivion, CBC-TV in Ottawa has already launched another national network public affairs series, called, not illogically, *The Sixties*. The mastermind of this series is Cameron Graham, not as iconoclastic as Patrick but a man whom I come to consider the very epitome of the thoughtful, level-headed, creative Executive Producer. He happens to be another P.K. There's one under every rock. My association with Cam goes on for years and leads down some odd pathways.

17

FROM JAMES BOND
TO BELL ISLAND

IT IS JANUARY 1964, and Hilda and I are having a dinner party in our Manotick home. Cameron and Jocelyn Graham are guests, along with a few other friends. We are chatting about TV in general and quizzing Cam about upcoming programs.

"Well," says Cam, "I'd really like to do an interview with Ian Fleming."

"Who's Ian Fleming?"

He looks at me in amazement.

"Ever hear of James Bond?"

"No. Who's he?"

"007? The secret agent with the licence to kill? Dr. No?" Cam obviously wonders where I've been. I've been off in the boondocks filming programs for Patrick and now for him, that's where.

He patiently explains that Ian Fleming is an Englishman, a genuine ex-secret agent and writer of travel books, who is the author of a series of novels featuring a fictitious agent named James Bond. Some of the books have already become hit movies. He says that he thinks Fleming is wintering in Jamaica.

For me the word "Jamaica" makes an interview with Fleming sound like an excellent program idea. "Well, why don't you ask him?" I suggest, naively.

"I called his agent and was told Mr. Fleming is not well and is off somewhere incommunicado."

"And you think that somewhere is in Jamaica?"

"Yes."

"What if I can reach him?" I have just taken the bait.

"If you can arrange it," says Cam, "we'll both go down. I'll direct, you be the interviewer."

Seems like a good deal to me.

"Of course," he says, "if we go to Jamaica it's only fair to the Mother Corp that afterwards we go to Newfoundland. They're shutting down the iron mine on Bell Island."

Newfoundland, out in the Atlantic? Bell Island, a rock east of The Rock? In mid-winter? I've just been suckered. But what the hell. "Sure. Why not."

In this business the name of the game is to stay adaptable enough that one can ricochet from one project to the next without becoming disoriented. This Ian Fleming gig sounds as though it will be a bit of a soak in literary froth, and it will be followed by a plunge into Newfie reality; according to the conditions just laid out by Cam, the whole crew, including himself, will be committed for the whole treatment. But is he really serious? As an executive producer he's more office-bound than I am, and maybe he's longing for a break. But does he really want to go from balmy Jamaica to frigid Bell Island in one bound?

"By the way," says Cam, "Fleming has already said no to the BBC and all three major American networks."

Okay, so he is having me on, and I've not really been suckered into a winter shoot on Bell Island. But let's see if we can make this joke, if it is a joke, stick.

"But if I can arrange it, we'll go?"

"Why not? I'll direct, you interview, you look after post-production."

Okay, a deal is a deal.

The next morning I'm calling Bell Telephone. I dial "O" and tell the operator I want to call Jamaica.

"Where in Jamaica, sir?"

"I have no idea but I want to speak with a Mr. Ian Fleming, who is a famous author."

"Just one moment, sir."

These are still the days when, if the operator leaves the connection open, you can hear her passing your request down the line. A beautifully accented voice answers from Kingston, Jamaica, and the Canadian voice asks for Ian Fleming.

"Oh, I don't think we have your Mister Fleming down here. I think the gentleman is on the north coast. Let me try Oroca Besa."

The next line is opened, the request goes through to Oroca Besa, and the operator there knows that a Mr. Ian Fleming is living in a house called "Goldeneye"; she will be only too pleased to connect us. By now, in this almost pre-satellite phone era, the connection is becoming a little fuzzy, but never mind.

A very English male voice answers the phone with that disconcerting British query, "Are you there?" Pronounced "theah." Of course I'm bloody well here.

"Is this Mr. Fleming, the author?" I inquire, raising my voice to penetrate the miles.

"In my office?" he shouts back.

"No, no. The author!" Is my Canadian accent that wild?

We overcome our communication problems and get right down to business. I explain that we — the CBC that is — would like to interview him for a public affairs TV program.

"When?"

Cam and I hadn't discussed this, the whole project being hypothetical, almost imaginary. "The sooner the better," I say.

"How many people and how long?" Cam and I had not really discussed this either.

"One cameraman, a director, myself as interviewer, and possibly one other. We'll be in and out in a day. We understand you're not very well."

"Who says so?"

Oh, oh. Time to confess. "Your agent."

"You've talked to my agent?"

"Mr. Graham, the producer has. Apparently you can't be reached."

There is a long pause. I've either blown it, or he's consulting his conscience.

"Very well, let's forget the agent."

A few minutes later I am phoning Cam to relay the results. We're committed to arrive at a house called "Goldeneye" on the north coast of Jamaica in four days time. But Mr. Fleming and I have not talked money. That's Cam's department. Mr. Fleming is expecting his call.

"Cam, whatever the fee is, he wants you to pay him direct." I guess the agent has been dealt out of this one.

By noon it's all nailed down and in the afternoon I drive in to Ottawa and go to the Public Library, look up a good profile on "Fleming, I., author," and then head for the best bookstore in the city. I find the "adventure" section and, much to my relief, a row of James Bond books in paperback. I insert one hand at each end of the row like a pair of bookends, extract the whole shebang, pay at the cash register, and go home.

I settle in to read. There are strange titles: *Casino Royale, Moonraker, Live and Let Die, Thunderball, From Russia with Love, Goldfinger, For Your Eyes Only, Dr. No*. As we fly from Ottawa to Kingston, Jamaica, I am still reading, while trying to ignore Cam, Paul Peguenat the cameraman, and Gilles Belanger, the unit business manager who is with us to watch over costs and as a well deserved reward for assiduous efforts in the back offices of the studio. In Kingston we hire a Volkswagen minibus with a driver to take us north to Oroca Besa, and, intoxicated by the climate and the scenery, we drive up through the Blue Mountains with the roof wide open, singing "I left a little girl in Kingston Town...." But whenever we stop I carry on reading.

Late in the afternoon we check into a moderately luxurious beach-side hotel in the tourist ghetto at Oroca Besa and phone Mr. Fleming, to announce our presence and assure him that we'll be on deck, as promised, first thing the next morning.

"No, no. Come around now. It will give us a chance to get acquainted."

We find Mr. Fleming and his wife in a relatively modest bungalow beautifully situated in a treed estate atop a high cliff overlooking the crystal-blue waters of the Caribbean.

He is pleasantly gracious. Not at all the stuffy upper crust Englishman I rather expected. His wife, however, is cool and withdrawn. Her manners are impeccable, but she is made of ice.

Our host uses Scotch as a social catalyst, but also provides a bottle of Canadian whisky. It wears a label neither Paul nor I have ever heard of and it tastes more like bourbon than rye, but we consider his offering it a hospitable gesture. Ian Fleming, Cam, and Gilles toast the project in Scotch and Paul and I wish us all well with pseudo-Canadian, while Mrs. Fleming watches balefully from the sidelines.

The living room, like the bungalow itself, is large, low, and comfortable. The master bedroom is immediately off the living room. With a view to selecting an interview location, we ask where the study is located. There isn't one. Apparently Ian Fleming writes in the bedroom, standing, as did Winston Churchill, at a lectern. We elect to film the interview in the living room, at an open window, with the sea beyond and below. Since we are filming in black and white there is no problem of colour balance.

Paul finds the main power box and takes some readings with his electrical test gear. He reports that he wouldn't want to run a heavy load, but that everything should be okay because he'll only be using a little fill light. We leave, promising to be on time in the morning, and, being a good film crew, we are.

Mr. Fleming is an easy man to talk to. He and I perch casually on the deep windowsill and the interview goes along quite nicely. Once, when

I ask about some obscure point, he says, "My, you have read my work, haven't you." If he only knew.

He is a chain smoker and I hope the damned cigarettes are not going to give us continuity problems. They are conspicuous, because he plugs each one into a long holder.

A small songbird lands between us on the windowsill and twitters away. Mr. Fleming gently acknowledges its presence, which is a nice touch from a man whose fictional hero is usually up to his eyebrows in blood, broads, and booze. He explains that he's very fond of birds and that he named his hero, the guy with the licence to kill, after the author of his favourite bird books. He has, however, never met James Bond the bird lover.

The morning flies by and, what with breaks to reload the camera, readjust the lighting, have coffee, and so on, it is noon before we know it. During the breaks we've discovered from Mrs. Fleming that her husband really isn't well. The agent was quite correct. We ask her how long she would like his after-lunch siesta to be and at noon we vanish for a slightly longer break than we had intended. It seems wise.

We return in the afternoon and continue to film. Mrs. Fleming seems much friendlier. During a break I ask her husband why he let us interview him when he had said no to other networks.

"Oh," he shrugs, "you people seemed so nice."

It seems so obvious that this is bullshit that I wonder if he actually needs the ready cash. But after a moment he explains. "They all wanted to move in on me for days, with a big crew. Said that was the only way to do it. You said there'd be four of you and you'd be in and out in a day. That's why."

Now I believe him.

Before long the inevitable happens. Paul's camera jams. It's not the cameraman's fault. These things happen to documentary crews — an occupational hazard. But it means an extra break while Paul unlaces the film, removes the magazine, cleans the gate, checks for problems, and withdraws into the cameraman's private trance, hands in the changing bag, to unload and reload magazines. At such times you leave a cameraman alone, do not talk to him, and never, ever, ask him to hurry.

This time no sooner has the camera stopped than we hear the doorbell, and in a moment the maid comes in.

"Mr. Fleming, sir, there's a man asking for you. He says his name is James Bond."

Yes. It is James Bond. The real James Bond. The ornithologist James Bond.

Our host excuses himself, saying he won't be long but that this is important — and of course it is. He introduces us, then takes Mr. Bond down to a conversation deck near the water. We watch in frustration from above while Paul works on the camera.

It is a brief visit and Mr. Bond leaves, promising to return in a few days time. By the time we are ready for action again, he is gone. We've missed recording a historic moment. *C'est la vie.*

Near the end of the day our host draws Paul and me to one side. "You boys are freelance?" he asks.

We admit that we are, and he draws a piece of paper out of his pocket and takes out his pen. "Well, look, the CBC has only bought the rights for one network showing of this interview. What say I give you two fellows subsequent rights?"

He isn't asking for money and he seems ready to start writing. But Paul and I are diffident, blast us. We can't accept. We are freelance, but on *this* project we are CBC. We thank him but say we'd better not cut in on any of the Corporation's business arrangements.

We leave on schedule, as promised. By now Mrs. Fleming seems quite friendly. We must have misread her initial hostility. Perhaps she was shy. The next morning Cam sends Paul back to Goldeneye by himself to get some exterior shots of the house. He asks him to be as discreet as possible. Paul returns to report that when he asked Mrs. Fleming for permission she said, "Where are the other boys? Why didn't they come with you?" She seemed sorry not to have had another mini-invasion.

We have enjoyed the gorgeous Caribbean climate and exotic landscape of Jamaica, but now it is time for the harsh rock-bound scenery of Newfoundland's Bell Island and the wild February weather along the North Atlantic coast. We've had our time in heaven; now this film crew must prove its adaptability by paying its dues, retroactively, in purgatory.

We touch base in Ottawa long enough to change our cotton shirts and Caribbean shorts for Arctic survival gear before flying to St. John's, Newfoundland, and commuting from there to Bell Island. The entire province is in the grip of the heaviest winter for many years, and Bell Island itself, although faithfully served by the trans-tickle ferry from Portugal Cove, is almost impassable.

Bell Island is a long slab of rock about six miles long by two miles wide that towers sheer out of the ocean on all sides. It is marooned in

Conception Bay, which carves into the northeast corner of the Avalon Peninsula. Now, in the winter, Bell Island looks about as forbidding a place as one can find anywhere south of the treeline. Cam hires an airplane and he and Paul capture an aerial view that drives home the chilling isolation. The island looks as solid as its principal — almost its only — product, which is iron ore.

Iron has been mined here since the 1890s and has been shipped as far away as Germany. That customer, of course, was not served during the Second World War, and in fact sent submarines into Conception Bay to attempt to sink ore ships. We are told that one memorable day the Royal Canadian Navy detected the sound of submarine engines, and some valiant corvettes took action, only to find they were dropping depth charges on the mine. The sound they had picked up was that of the giant air pumps in the mine tunnels that extend as far as three miles out under the ocean.

Apparently the mine has always been owned by people "from away," and now, with more profit to be made elsewhere, the mines are shutting down. When we visit, only one small portion of the mine is still operating. It is reached not by a shaft, but by a narrow railway track that plunges into a tunnel and heads out under the ocean. We ride down into the remnants of this strange undersea industrial rabbit warren of tunnels and I can't say I enjoy knowing the ocean is above us. We are assured that the thickness of the roof is never less than two hundred feet, and it can sometimes reach as much as 1,600 feet.

The problem is that this has been a one-commodity economy and there is nothing to replace it. The combination of ownership from away and a one-crop economy is becoming a far-flung modern curse. Most of the miners and their families have already gone. Now, and particularly in winter, the town of Wabana is almost a ghost town. But some miners, although laid off, have hung on, optimistically assuming that the stopes will soon reopen. They will not. These men and their families are trapped. Social assistance is limited, and for some has already run out. And those for whom assistance is not yet exhausted must travel to St. John's to collect it. There are two barriers to that — the cost of travel and the abominable weather.

We film an interview in the home of an unemployed miner and his wife who are almost destitute and feeling trapped, but are still dignified and still hoping. Their refrigerator, unplugged, has nothing in it but one small bottle of medicine for a sick child. As a documentary film crew we have no solutions. We can only report. We eventually call our program "Escape to the Mainland."

Before we leave the island we attend a Saturday night community soiree that appears to be held in total defiance of winter and of economic depression. There is exuberant fiddle music, moderate drinking, enthusiastic dancing, and an Irish tenor who sings "The Star of Logie Bay" and other ballads to great approval from the assembled islanders. Late in the evening, as I am reaching across the bar for a beer, the shutter comes crashing down, just missing my hand. As I stand somewhat shaken, the bar door opens and out comes the bartender. He looks at me cheerfully.

"Don't worry, b'y. The law says she has to close at midnight Saturday. The law don't say nothin' about openin' Sunday. She'll be open in a few minutes."

That's the same way these optimistic, kind, and deluded folk who have not yet escaped to the mainland feel about the mine. It will be two years later, in 1966, that the final shutdown comes

We return to Ottawa, a transition that doesn't require quite the same psychological adaptation as going from Jamaica to Newfie. In Ottawa we still wear survival gear. We put our Bell Island footage and tapes into the works for processing and transcribing and now turn our attention back to the Fleming footage.

Everything, as we say, has turned to rat shit.

When we view the rushes* we find that Fleming and I are both moving like characters in a Mack Sennett movie and our voices sound like Donald Duck. The unreliable Jamaican power source had slipped cycle on us enough to slow down the camera, so when the film is played back at normal speed the action and the sound are both speeded up.

We do some careful calculations and send the film to the lab to have every third frame double-printed in order to "stretch" the film and thereby slow down the action. The sound, being on tape, is also, thank God, "stretchable." The sound engineer at Crawley slows our voices down from their high-pitched babble. By the time the doctors are through with it the interview looks almost normal, and an edited version goes to air without any complaints. The only real giveaway is Mr. Fleming's smoking habit. When he puts the cigarette holder to his mouth and takes it away his hand seems to jerk slightly en route. Well, shucks, the man isn't well.

In fact, Mr. Fleming may have been more ill than we realized, because he dies not long after this. I think of him warmly not as the

---

*   Unedited film just returned from processing.

author of the James Bond novels but as a pleasant man without preten-
sion who seemed to genuinely enjoy talking to an ordinary film crew.

Later on I hear that the cbc has given the Fleming interview to the
Wolper organization in the States. I am told the operative word is
"given." Given or sold, I can't help but wonder who really has the rights.

As for the Bell Island footage, it comes from the lab looking pristine
and unblemished. It's only the content that is depressing.

18

THE SECOND
COMING OF
JACQUES CARTIER

WE ARE A FOUR-MAN film crew. I am the writer/director and the rest
of my team is made up of a very quiet soundman, Fred McCord, a technical assistant, Pete Warchow, and Jack Buss, a one-eyed cameraman. We
are just arriving on the outskirts of Alberton, Prince Edward Island, and
we are in search of a Roman Catholic priest named Gerald Steele and a
United Church minister named David MacDonald.

Something ecumenical is underway between the Protestants and
the Catholics and we're intending to shoot a segment on the subject for
Cameron Graham's TV series, *The Sixties*.

We stop to read a plaque on a cairn. It commemorates a missionary
from here who went to the South China Sea and got himself butchered
for his efforts. We hope the priest and the parson, the local missionaries,
will fare better.

On the outskirts of town we come to a new community centre. Out
front, a sturdy young man in dirty overalls is pounding a post into the
ground with a large sledgehammer. We stop.

"Hi. We're looking for Rev. David MacDonald. Any idea where we'll
find him?"

"Sure, boys. He's down at the beach by the river mouth. Can't miss
him. Teaching the Indians to build wigwams. Jacques's coming, you
know."

"Jack?"

"As in Cartier. He's helping us celebrate our Confederation Centennial."

This is 1964 and the rest of Canada isn't celebrating until 1967, but
P.E.I. is off to a flying start because the Fathers of Confederation came
here in 1864 for some preliminary talks. These P.E.I. folk are planning to

celebrate again in 1967 to commemorate the rest of us getting our act together. They'll have a real blowout in 1973, a hundred years after they actually did join the federation. They were cautious in joining but are swift to celebrate. There's nothing slow about these folk.

"We're also looking for Father Gerry Steele."

The man puts the sledgehammer down and sticks out his hand. "You're talking to him. Nice to meet you boys. David said you were coming."

We follow Father Steele's directions and find the mouth of the river where it opens into the salt waters of Cascumpeque Bay. This, it is said, is a spot where Jacques Cartier came ashore in 1534 in search of fresh water. Apparently he is expected to land again, and the local Micmac Indians (we have not yet been instructed to spell the nation's name as "Mi'kmaq") are busily erecting a welcoming village of wigwams.

We find the Reverend David MacDonald supervising the construction. He, like Father Steele, is a young man with an easy presence and apparently endless energy, but what impresses us at the moment are the wigwams he and his gang are building.

"Real birch bark! Thought making that kind of wigwam was a lost art."

"It is," says David. "Fastening the bark to the poles — that's been the major challenge."

"You've resurrected the ancient skills?"

"Something like that."

We watch as his enthusiastic companions bang bark into place with a heavy-duty staple gun.

"How does all this integrate with the second coming of Jacques Cartier?" I ask.

"We're not too sure. Just following orders. The mayor says the navy has it all in hand. Look, you fellows are just in time. Let's go meet the mayor and some of the council. Then we'll go meet the navy and find out."

A sleek grey frigate of the Royal Canadian Navy is dropping anchor in Alberton harbour even as we speak. It is touring these waters to help P.E.I. communities celebrate this preliminary Centennial. The captain's orders, so the mayor believes, carry instructions on restaging the arrival of Jacques Cartier.

Reverend MacDonald, Father Steele, the mayor, the council, and one film crew board a lobster boat and put out to sea. It is a bit of a journey, because the frigate is anchored well offshore. Apparently Alberton harbour contains more sand than water. Even out here the frigate's bow rests perilously close to a sandbar.

The captain is a calm man with a quiet air of authority who doesn't seem to mind the thought of a little sand and mud. He's probably from Saskatchewan. We meet his First Officer, known in Navy parlance as "No. 1." Before the day is done, No. 1 confides in me that they are navigating their pre-Centennial route using road maps provided by enthusiastic Chambers of Commerce. Apparently the Canadian government has been a little lax in charting Canadian waters.

Right now, however, we file into the officers' wardroom and are graciously invited to be seated. We prepare to hear details concerning the pending resurrection of Jacques Cartier. This miracle has been advertised for weeks, and both sailors and townsmen seem duly impressed by the fact there is a film crew here from Ottawa to record it. Granted, our objective is not their objective, but perhaps we can shoot a little Centennial joy to invigorate our ecumenical half-hour.

"Well, gentlemen," says the captain, "what can the Royal Canadian Navy do for Alberton?"

I study the faces of the assembled town fathers. They have turned pale with shock. They thought the captain had the script.

I study the face of the captain as the mayor explains that he understood the navy was to resurrect Jacques Cartier. Now I know how a frigate captain would look if he were ordered to ram the *Bismark*.

"All I know, gentlemen," says the captain, "is that I have a packing case on board that I'm to deliver to you."

It seems unlikely Jacques is coming in a crate, but a runner is sent to investigate. He reports that the crate contains sixteenth-century mariners' costumes. The captain realizes he is deeper into this thing than he thought. He looks as though he has just read confidential dispatches telling him to scuttle at sea, but it was not for nothing that he spent the Second World War aboard Canadian coracles in the North Atlantic. He rallies.

"Very well, gentlemen, I'll handle the arrival of Jacques Cartier. But once on shore," he adds — and it sounds prophetic — "once on shore he's your problem."

Everyone relaxes and the captain slips into PR mode. He invites the town fathers to bring the town mothers and grandfathers and grandmothers and other estimable folk out to the ship for a celebratory cocktail party at the tag end of this very day. He also invites us. I think he wants defence witnesses for a possible court martial.

Getting to the cocktail party becomes an expedition. Several lobster boats are pressed into service and the town fathers (and mothers, grandfathers, etc., etc.) are carefully handed aboard. It is a straight climb down onto the decks, and some of the elderly limbs are no longer supple.

The taxi-driving lobstermen, electing not to make the round trip, offload their passengers to the frigate but loiter nearby. It is a calm, quiet, sunny evening and everyone is relaxed. The lobstermen have jugs with them that help them relax even more.

While the cocktail party is going full blast on the decks of Her Majesty's Canadian frigate, the lobstermen start going full blast in their open boats, which are equipped with juiced-up V8 engines. Playing at being pilots of motor torpedo boats, they come in on kamikaze runs that are miraculously aborted at the last possible moment. Up on the deck with the genteel folk, we can hardly hear ourselves drink for the roar of V8s going full throttle the length of the ship, a foot out from the plates.

Another lobster boat appears. This one is loaded to the gunwales with the Miscouche Brass Band. The boat orbits around and around the frigate while the band plays watery marches.

As we are preparing to leave, a young sub-lieutenant draws me aside. "Thought you'd like to know," he says, "that the captain has solved his casting problem."

It is naval tradition that the chief engineer leads all landing parties. Jacques Cartier and his men are by way of being a landing party, so the chief has been assigned the detail.

"How's he feel about that?" I ask.

"Well, he's seen the costumes with the long leg stockings and the funny pantaloons ..."

"He's not pleased?"

"None of them are pleased." He looks around furtively before adding, "When the frigate's longboat lands, keep an eye on its flag."

By the time we go ashore there has been so much action at sea that the waters are rough with an artificial chop, and our lobster boat is dancing in time with our heads. An elderly fisherman who has filled his bunkers with the captain's grog spends the whole journey walking back and forth along a six-inch-wide gunwale.

"Man and boy," he keeps saying, "I been at sea nigh eighty year." We mainlanders watch him in consternation, but his friends, neighbours, and loved ones pay no attention.

While we've been away the tide has gone out, and it is now an even higher climb onto the pier. These amazing maritimers seem to float up, effortlessly, like dandelion fluff on an updraft. It occurs to me that a little Alberton sea air is a great tonic.

Day Two is clear, sunny, and warm. We take ourselves and our camera gear down to the mouth of the river to await Jacques Cartier. We can hardly believe our eyes. There are five thousand people here. They have come from miles around to see the pageant and are in high good humour.

Only the Natives are restless. The Micmacs are ready to give the whole show back to the French. They explain that although they and their wigwams are supposed to provide the shore side of the pageant, not one of them has any idea how their ancestors greeted Jacques and the boys. Whether he actually set foot here or not is, at the moment, irrelevant. The guy who is supposed to know these things has not arrived.

This guy is impresario Mavor Moore, Toronto's gift to the arts. Mavor is in Charlottetown this summer masterminding the provincial festivities, and he is due here at any moment. The town fathers expect Mavor to take full charge of the shore-side portion of the pageant. Cameraman Jack and I quietly lay odds with soundman Fred and assistant Pete as to whether Mavor even knows of the arrangements.

Jacques Cartier's longboat is spotted sailing into Cascumpeque Bay and there is still no sign of Mavor. The Micmac are planning on taking refuge in their wigwams and not venturing forth. The longboat is sailing parallel to shore, about a quarter of a mile out, and it looks very fine with its sail topped by a lovely fleur-de-lys flag. There is not enough wind to fill the sail but Jacques is no fool. He has a small outboard motor mounted on the stern.

The longboat turns and heads for shore. The crowd cheers. The Micmac head for cover, but just in time Mavor Moore materializes on top of a slight knoll. He is wearing his trademark beret, scarf, and cigar. The first coming of Mavor Moore is as much an event as the second coming of Jacques Cartier. The crowd is delighted. We are all delighted.

Mavor takes the cigar from his mouth. "Indians," he roars, "run to the beach!"

The Indians do so.

"You see Jacques Cartier! You are excited, you are excited!"

The players know that Indians are supposed to be stoical. What's with this excitement stuff?

"No, no!" roars the impresarial voice. "Action! Action! Be excited!"

The actors jump up and down in a frenzy of excitement and stage fright. All our misconceptions are shattered.

"All right, Indians. He's coming nearer. Now you're frightened!" They already are. "Run!"

Mavor's voice, groomed by a lifetime in the theatre and related aberrations, holds the crowd in thrall. The Micmac too are enthralled. They stir not.

"Run, Indians! Run! Hide, hide, hide!"

The tribal ranks break and the actors scurry, thankfully, for the privacy of their wigwams.

The captain has been standing on a slight rise with binoculars to his eyes. Of the five thousand he alone has been paying no attention to the impresario and his pupils. He is now bearing down upon me. He looks his usual calm self but his colour is purple. He heaves-to alongside.

"I hope your cameraman is using an ordinary lens?"

"Oh, yes, sir."

Jack has just adorned the Arriflex camera with an "ordinary" long lens that can spot a flea on a buzzard.

The captain sheers off and comes up abeam of Jack. "What do you see out there?" he mutters.

I hold my breath but Jack knows all about Horatio Nelson. He puts his blind eye to the finder. "Nothing unusual," he says.

The captain veers off for his knoll and I sidle up to Jack. "Now try the good eye."

"Interesting," says Jack. "The fleur-de-lys flag ... down in one corner ... a bloody great bullfrog on a lily pad."

I smile across at the captain and nod reassuringly.

"What the hell are they doing out there?" mutters Jack.

Cameramen often talk into their cameras — I never know whether or not their questions are rhetorical. It's a good question, though. What the hell are they doing? The longboat is bearing in toward us following a very erratic course.

"He's got no wind but he's trying to tack!"

A nearby fisherman answers. "Nope, not tacking. Got no water, no more'n a couple inches. Figure he's looking for a channel. Somebody should've told 'm."

I know another possibility but I am not about to voice it. I've already been informed that the chief engineer and his crew were ripe for mutiny by the time they struggled into their pantaloons. Drastic action had to be taken. Jacques Cartier and his men may indeed be zigzagging ashore searching desperately for a few inches of keel room, but it is highly probable they are tight as ticks.

The captain drifts by and growls to me, "Somebody is going to have his hide nailed to the mainmast." He doesn't sound happy. It is impossible to know whether it is the bullfrog flag that has him so itchy or the men who are flying with it. I find my naval confidant and suggest that at the first opportunity they furl flags and batten down for pending rough weather.

I must have a warped sense of the dignity of history, because I consider this to be the perfect pageant — not only historical, but itself historic.

The day scurries on its way.

Remembering why we're here, we actually film some ecumenical interviews with the parson and the priest, but soon it is afternoon and pageantry beckons once more.

The community has gathered by the quayside in Alberton harbour to watch the christening of two wooden boats that have been built for the Department of Northern Affairs for sub-Arctic use. The boats are sturdy craft, adaptations of fishing designs, and are being given the full champagne treatment.

Our two clergymen are participating in ecumenical fashion along with the town fathers and some imported dignitaries. It is difficult to hear the speeches and prayers, because the Miscouche Brass Band is still blowing its way around the harbour. I am becoming fond of that band.

The first boat is christened by the wife of a cabinet minister from New Brunswick. She is an attractive woman and stylishly dressed. We watch in amazement as she beats on the bow of the boat with a cloth-wrapped bottle of champagne. It is the only time I have seen a glass bottle give up slowly and simply go limp. The poor lady eventually stands there in full public view slapping away with a wet rag. The boat goes down the skids with a sigh.

The premier's wife tackles number two. She and her husband are both built with firm centres of gravity, like good maritime ballast. She intends to take no nonsense from a champagne bottle, domestic or French. There is an air of expectation as she winds up and lets fly. For one horrible moment I fear she'll knock the stem clean off the boat. The bottle shatters and at the end of her swing champagne is sprayed over the assembly.

"Well done!" cries the premier. The crowd cheers and the band plays on.

This most joyous day ends with a lobster bash at the Royal Canadian Legion. Everyone is here, including the captain and his entire

complement of officers. Well, not entire. I have a suspicion the chief
has drawn duty watch.

Boiled lobsters are provided literally by the tubful, and assorted
maritime mouthwash is available at the bar. Everyone has a cracking
good time.

The captain is making mellow conversation. He tells me of a young
Nova Scotian folksinger who is a member of his crew.

"Say, I'd really like to film him." This has nothing to do with ecu-
menism or Jacques Cartier, but could be useful in a Nova Scotia show
Cam has on my slate.

"No problem. I'll send the ship's cutter in for you fellows first thing
in the morning."

Contrary to opinion, most film crews like to stay in focus until the
end of a project, so the four of us slope off early. A soft mist is forming
as we drive to our motel.

We wake up to find the whole town wrapped in fog, a gift from the
Almighty to wrap aching heads and soothe tender eyes. We do not know
whether or not the ship's cutter will be able to come for us, but we
resolve to keep our end of the appointment.

The harbour is opaque. The mist-shrouded pier is a mysterious
world of fishing sheds, stacked lobster traps, and piled nets. As we walk
along it, recumbent bodies slowly levitate off beds of fishnets and we
gradually realize that these fogbound wraiths are the captain and his
complement of officers.

The ship's cutter, which was due at 2:00 A.M., has not arrived. The
captain would have commandeered a lobster boat, but their batteries
seem to be missing. The captain's jaw is now roughened by a stubble of
beard, but his manner is still impeccable.

A fisherman comes singing cheerily down the pier. His course is
none too steady but he is in high good spirits, and he has found a lobster boat that has its battery. The captain is a little dubious but he
makes an executive decision. Placing his trust in a fisherman's legendary sense of navigation, he decides to put out to sea with half the
complement of passengers. On behalf of my team I volunteer to wait
for the second sailing.

We cast them off, wave them into the fog, and settle down for a
long wait.

Ten minutes later we hear a heavy engine approaching at high revs.
The lobster boat roars out of the fog and narrowly misses sinking the
pier. The captain and his men come ashore.

"Hang in there, men," says the lobsterman as he rolls away down the pier. "I know a fella who'll be able to find that damned frigate."

He returns, accompanied by a fisherman I recognize from the Legion party. This man is quiet and dour; he is still wearing his Sunday suit. He seems sober as a judge, although right now I wouldn't lay any bets on P.E.I. judges.

Our hopes soar when the newcomer refuses to put out to sea until he and his mate can outfit themselves with a compass. They raid another boat for the precious equipment.

This time, feeling more confident, we all climb aboard and motor off into the fog. The captain is looking as dignified as if he were standing on his own quarterdeck. Everyone is straining for a first glimpse of the frigate.

We do not see the frigate, but we do see the frigate's cutter. It is angling toward us out of the mist. Our pilot shifts his engine into neutral and our big lobster boat sits burbling on the idle while the cutter approaches.

The naval cutter makes a brave sight with its uniformed crew standing nattily alert in the midship cockpit. I feel a great sense of relief, confident that they can rescue us from any unknown perils. From the cutter comes the sound of a bosun's whistle, and then the cutter, too, coasts to an idle, twenty feet abeam of us.

The ensign in command hails us. His voice seems to quaver slightly, but he is young, and command is a heavy responsibility. He may also be aware that the captain will want to know where the cutter has been since 2:00 A.M.

"Sir," comes the plaintive call, "can we have a tow?"

Where the cutter has been since 2:00 A.M. is on a sandbar, or, to be more precise, on every sandbar in Alberton harbour. It has been hunting them down, one by one. I hope the ensign has been keeping notes for the road map cartographers. The motor has drawn sand into its cooling system and the crew are afraid to run it for more than a few minutes at a time.

Our lobstermen pay out a line and we proceed with the cutter in tow.

What a grand sight it is to see the warship emerge from the mists in front of us, its clean-cut lines mirrored in a glassy sea, its rails lined with sailors who have heard the sound of our engine. They are all there, ratings, oilers, gunners, signalmen, everyone from the engine room to the galley, all at the rails to see their gallant officers return to ship.

The captain stands surrounded by his officers on the deck of that lobster boat with the salvaged cutter towing along at his heels and it truly is a brave sight. The men on the frigate think so, too. They cheer madly and lean over the rail to beat on the ship's side. Some of them are almost hysterical with pride.

I watch the captain, that colossus of imperturbability, to see if he is showing any signs of emotion. There is a slight quivering around the mouth. He may be fighting a losing battle to maintain the legendary stiff upper lip. I wonder if British naval tradition has been too diluted with colonial impurities for him to withstand the emotions of the moment. It has been. He loses the struggle and smiles, broadly.

I am all choked up. This is my kind of a navy. All we need now is the Miscouche Brass Band playing "O Canada" and we'd all be primed for war.

At home, I tell my brother Doug about the second coming of Jacques Cartier and its attendant marvels. Not only was Doug a naval officer in the Second World War but he was an engineer officer to boot! He has quaint memories of an old four-stacker destroyer that billowed immense clouds of smoke until it was ordered to lay smoke screens, at which point it became pure as an environmental virgin; of a minesweeper that dropped its ash cans on a sub and blew off its own stern; of another valiant warrior that, having accidentally shelled an island chicken house, adopted a shell-riding chicken as its emblem; and so on. Doug knows the truth when he hears it. He believes everything I tell him, right down to the road map. He laughs until the tears come. I am afraid he is going to re-enlist.

As usual, the completed film only scratches the surface of the whole occasion, because the Cartier celebrations are really used as decorative framework for the program about the ecumenical efforts of Father Gerry Steele and Rev. David MacDonald. The segment is called "The Priest and the Parson." Its network airing has an unusual aftermath. The two clergymen get such enthusiastic personal feedback they decide one of them should be in politics. I don't think they actually draw straws, but almost. David MacDonald runs for parliament and is elected as a member of John Diefenbaker's Progressive Conservative party at the time when it is Her Majesty's Loyal Opposition. He is a successful advocate for the establishment of the Canadian Film Development Corporation, stands in the House to oppose the imposition of the War Measures Act in 1970, becomes heavily involved in attempts to ameliorate the Biafran tragedy, in which a million people starve to death, is described by a journalist as "the best-loved member of Parliament," becomes a much-admired Secretary of State for Culture (while also Minister of Communications) in the short-lived PC government under Joe Clark, masterminds the official logistics for the Pope's first visit to Canada, heads up a commission on African famine, is made Ambassador to Ethiopia during the Brian Mulroney regime, and eventually becomes — as his instincts should have dictated in the first place — a dedicated member of the "socialist" New Democratic party. He blames his initial impetus toward politics on Jacques Cartier and the TV show, which I think is a bit much.

Father Steele leaves the priesthood and joins the federal civil service, where regional development can make good use of a man of strong intellect and vast compassion. He marries a former nun. Here, too, I am unwilling to claim any credit.

GREAT SLAVE LAKE
REFLECTIONS

THE MID-1960S IS A TIME for introspection. A remarkable night on
the turbulent waters of a sub-Arctic lake gives me a new perspective on
human beings in relation to the physical world, and a family calamity
gives me a new perspective on my own mortality. In recollection, this
time will be a blend of great pleasure and deep sadness. The pleasure
comes first.

It is August 1965 and I am north of the sixtieth parallel, more than
500 crow-flight miles north of Edmonton, out of sight of land, standing
at the rail of a powerful diesel tugboat that is ploughing northwest
across one end of Great Slave Lake. I am on this boat almost by accident.
An unavoidable delay in Hay River during a film assignment for CN
Telecommunications and Toronto's Chetwynd Films has turned into an
opportunity to make a free round-trip crossing of Great Slave Lake. A little friendly curiosity and politeness can take a fellow a long way in this
part of the world!

My attention is alternating from the watery expanse around me to
a telephone book I am holding in my hand. I don't know which
impresses me the most, the sight, the sound, the smell, the feel of this
vibrant tugboat pushing a great raft of barges loaded with railway freight
cars, trucks, canisters, crates, construction trailers, and bulldozers, or
the names in the new CN Telecommunications phone book.

CN has just completed a telephone pole line to the Arctic Ocean!
The line crews have hacked, slashed, clawed, climbed, and pushed along
the Mackenzie River valley, leaving behind a long distance phone system
with instruments hanging in houses, shacks, rustic hotels, offices, even
on posts outside Indian tents. I am looking at names that are among the
most exotic in the world — Fort Simpson, Norman Wells, Arctic Red
River, Tuktoyaktuk, Lady Franklin Point, Coppermine. They are names
that conjure up stories of Indian trappers, lost explorers, wartime oil

supplies, Mounted Police exploits, and indomitable Eskimo hunters. It seems incredible that we Canadians have finally expanded our frontier to the point that one can casually pick up a phone in Halifax and dial an Eskimo in Tuktoyaktuk on the Arctic Ocean.

I know it's true, not just because of the shiny new telephone book I have expropriated, but because back in Hay River, on the south shore of this same Great Slave Lake, I have just been talking to some of the men who made it possible. One of them was a truck driver. During construction he drove his truck the length of the pole line, rafting his truck back and forth across the Mackenzie as the line zigged and zagged. He finally dipped its front wheels into the Arctic Ocean. Overland to the Arctic, by truck, on a thousand miles of non-road. Such men impress me.

Everyone up here impresses me. I have met truck drivers who, when winter comes, will head due north into the sub-Arctic driving big tractor trailer transports following in the wake of bulldozers that are beating a path over the frozen lakes, rivers, and tundra. Caterpillar tractors will haul long trains of heavily loaded sleighs over the same routes. Sometimes a cat will go through the ice. If the driver becomes disoriented in the turbulence and the suction he will probably come up under the ice and be drowned. If he hangs on until the heavy brute hits bottom, then he may be able to swim straight up and find the hole to freedom. One just prays that the water is not too deep. These are men. An Easterner in this part of the world should walk quietly, sit small, and listen to his betters. I've been very comfortable doing all three.

Today, however, we are crossing open water, and we are finally approaching land. The tug with its raft of barges creaming ahead of it is beginning to slow down as it nears the channel leading into the head of the Mackenzie River. Our supply barges are completing the first stage of a multi-stage journey that will distribute them among communities along the Mackenzie River. The tugs began plying this route during the Second World War, carrying supplies to Port Radium on Great Bear Lake and bringing radium out. In a strange paradoxical way I think of the new telephone line as a communication link into a storied past, and I think of the older tugboat line as the highway of the atom.

The big tug rounds a sheltering island and nudges its barges to moorings in a marshy bay. Another swing of barges is waiting to be taken back across Great Slave Lake to Hay River, to civilization, where the best hotel in town is built of logs and the railroad goes down the centre of the main street. Soon a river tug will collect the barges we are leaving here at the entrance to the Mackenzie. And we do leave them here, where there's no sign of human habitation, no shacks, shelters, tents, or even guards. A million dollars worth of supplies is left moored to buoys at the head of the Mackenzie River. There's so much involved in that casual trusting action that I can't begin to comprehend the full meaning of it, but if I were a northerner I'd not even be wasting time thinking about it.

It is August, and already the days are short. By the time we turn south and leave land behind, it is dark. Once again we are pushing a huge raft of barges ahead of us, lashed side by side and end to end. The barges are riding high because most of the returning freight cars are empty.

It's blowing up a storm. Earlier, during the latter part of the afternoon, dark clouds were beginning to glower around the horizon, but they remained low and distant. Now that darkness has come they are still there, still distant. The sky directly overhead is clear. The stars are incredible. There's something eerie about all this. There are heavy clouds all around the horizon … I'm beginning to see lightning … there are stars overhead … a high wind is rising. Already the spray is beginning to show around the front of the lead barges. I am told that this west end of the lake is shallow and that it can get very rough very fast.

It's a northeast wind tonight and it's coming at us broadside across almost two hundred miles of lake, at least a hundred of which is wide-open water. I wonder if an east wind is as unpredictable and unfriendly up here as it is back home in southern Ontario. Something tells me it is. Certainly the waves are rising quickly. Very quickly. If this west end of the lake is as shallow as they say then the water must be literally piling up around us.

Lightning flickers low along the entire eastern horizon and suddenly our whole ship lights up. I wonder what has happened, then realize the tug's powerful work lights have been turned on. Spotlights probe the darkness. Deckhands go over our wide squat bows and drop, light as cats, onto the barges ahead, which are beginning to heave and groan and strain at their lashings. Spouts of water are jetting upward between the barges as though that huge articulated raft has spouted geyser-like leaks at the joints.

The tug slows almost to a stop and I realize we have problems. The captain does not dare push the unwieldy raft through heavy seas. Something is bound to come unstuck and then we'll be ramming into our own cargo!

I watch bewildered but fascinated as barge after barge is unlashed and turned loose. Soon all around us on the now tumultuous seas are lonely barges bearing shapeless, anonymous cargoes. They are rudderless, powerless, mere shadows against the darkness, true orphans of the storm. They are no longer clustered. They appear to be scattering, swiftly. Some are already mere dark ghostly impressions, almost lost, until silhouetted against the flash of distant lightning. But I know there are men out there. They are walking narrow ledges alongside creaking, swaying freight cars and calmly coiling ropes around bollards on slippery decks awash in black water. I am sure our captain and his crew have all gone mad.

The tug shudders and comes to life. The entire steel mass vibrates as the great diesels open up and the boat takes off in an arc to port, going so fast that she leans to starboard like those destroyers we see in old war movies. Our spotlight jabs into the darkness, pinning a barge to the water like a black beetle to a board. We roar alongside and then wallow to a crawl. Ropes are thrown and made fast, and we are away again with one barge in tow. Our pace is now steady. We are like a seasoned, wise, exceedingly powerful sheep dog rounding up its flock, in a wild, wet, moorland storm, but our flock is being brought into line astern, towline on barge on towline on barge, barge after barge after barge. It is the most fascinating performance I have ever seen.

And then I look upward, out of the wind and the spray and the searchlights. The heavy clouds still layer the horizon and they are still lit by the fitful flicker of sheet lightning and torn by the jagged knives of chain lightning. But above that the sky is radiant! It is alive with the northern lights, which grow even as I watch, swaying mauve and green and cold blue, spreading out and out until their base entirely circles the heavens and their undulating probing fingers reach almost to a single apex. Only dead centre in the peak above us is there a circle of sky devoid of light. We are sailing a storm on Great Slave Lake with only water around us, with lightning encircling the distant horizon, with the aurora's corona above us. I am almost crying with joy at the sheer privilege of being alive and here at this moment.

The years move on. At home, summer of 1966 gives way to the glorious spectacle of autumn. Our area around the Manotick millpond is vibrant with colour, but Hilda and I take the mandatory drives across the Ottawa River and into the Gatineau Hills in search of deeper ambers and richer reds. Our senses crave colour. Once addicted there is no such thing as surfeit. The trees are alive, but their leaves are dying and we bathe in the spectacle of their passing. We know that soon the carpet of colour will be replaced by the pristine comforter of snow. It's this relentless march of the seasons that makes Canadians cautious but optimistic. "O, Wind, if Winter comes, can Spring be far behind?"

And then, late one night, Doug phones to tell me that our brother Don has died, suddenly, with no warning.

After Doug's call I lie in the dark, weeping, overwhelmed by a sense of my own mortality. Don is just 44 and becoming well established as a surgeon with what everyone says should be a brilliant future. He has a loving wife, also a doctor, a gynecologist, and also, like Hilda, from England. They have four young daughters, roughly the same ages as our own three boys. The girls dote on their dad. And now Don is gone. Instantly. Dead. Vanished.

For the first time I realize how tenuous is my own grasp on life. Already I am 39. Where am I going? Nothing done yet. I, too, could vanish tomorrow. I am wasting my life.

It is a fevered, waking nightmare.

Doug and I have agreed to rendezvous early the next morning at Mother and Dad's home in Lindsay, not wanting them to get the word by phone from overly eager sympathizers. Much later in the day Hilda and the boys will drive to Elizabeth's side in Belleville, but now, in the still dark hours of early morning, I take the long drive along No. 7 Highway where the road winds its way through the rocks and past the forests and lakes and rivers of the old Precambrian Shield that I love so much. The rugged tranquility is soothing. The drive gives time for reflection and my thoughts inevitably slip back into childhood.

We three brothers have always been close, although Doug, being seven years older, has always seemed to me to be grown up, more of a protector than a pal. Doug is the big one, the strong one, the athlete. Don is no shrimp, eventually comfortably exceeding the coveted six foot mark, but even though five years older than me he always seems willing to come down, literally and metaphorically, to my little brother level. If it is a wet Saturday afternoon and we are trapped indoors, it is Don who lays the kitchen stool on its side, covers it with a car rug, and uses a metal pie plate for a steering wheel, creating the illusion of a racing car. If I am struggling to build a model of a simple cardboard fort, it is Don who joins in and helps create an exotic castle. Doug builds big things like a real kayak and a three-foot model of a boat, hewn from solid timber and powered by a real steam engine. Don takes an old alarm clock and turns it into a silly owl with rotating eyes.

It is Don who volunteers to help Mother gut the Thanksgiving turkey and then gives a lesson in turkey anatomy. He lays the guts out for examination and, inserting a drinking straw into the windpipe, inflates the lungs, or takes a pair of pliers and pulls the tendons of a severed leg to show how the feet contract. For a time, I think of my own insides as looking like those of a turkey, complete with gizzard.

As we grow up, we all read voraciously, devouring books by writers as varied as A.A. Milne and Sir Walter Scott. But Don is the artistic one, the talented one. We all three take piano lessons, but with Don they stick. Don takes violin lessons from a mad professor. Don can paint. Don likes dancing. Don understands things like fine china and good clothes. It is Don who is ambidextrous and can manipulate small things with either hand, a requisite for a surgeon.

I can't believe how stoically Mother and Dad take the terrible news. I am sure they weep and pray privately, but outwardly they are calm and accepting. I watch them and marvel. Is such control based on genuine faith in a Hereafter, or on recognition of an inevitable end? Does their faith really see the resurrection of Spring following the frozen sleep of Winter?

After the funeral and the trip to the cemetery, as we slowly leave the graveside, I walk with Mother and Dad down a gentle slope to the car. The others are dispersing to their own vehicles. Mother pauses by the car and looks back to where her son's coffin sits partially visible above its grave on a grassy knoll. Obviously the routine is to finish lowering it after folk have gone. There is no one with it. Even the cemetery attendants are waiting discreetly out of sight.

Mother gazes a moment and I know exactly what she is thinking.

"Oh dear," she says, "it looks so lonely."

Never again can I view with equanimity an unlowered casket or an unburied urn. Seeing earth go to earth, ashes to ashes, dust to dust, gives closure to the human heart. It is no accident that humankind refers to "Mother Earth."

20

DRAMA AT THE CBC

YOU MAY HAVE NOTICED that so far in this narrative, apart from some yarns about the RCMP series nothing has been said about television drama. With your indulgence, I'm inclined to make up for that now and package a whole decade, perhaps more, into one chapter. It may take a while in the telling and if you're not into TV drama you may wish to skip a chapter and go travelling again. There'll be no permanent escape, though. Stage drama is ahead too, but as yet it's still over the horizon.

From a writer's point of view there is nothing speculative about film documentaries or public affairs TV. It's in drama, whether for radio, television, or the stage, that speculation comes into play. Here one risks the time and the energy it takes to conjure up an idea, put some or all of it onto paper, and then convince a director or a producer to commission it. And yet the lure of drama is irresistible. In the late 1950s I write a one-hour drama on speculation and submit it to CBC-TV in Toronto. The CBC story editor is Nathan Cohen, better known as an acerbic critic. Nathan terrifies many people. I find him charming, even though he doesn't like my play and says so. He turns it down and says why. At the same time he gives me an enormous amount of encouragement. I am rejected but uplifted. Except for a brief exchange of correspondence in 1970 in which he and I both deplore theatre's shameful treatment of Donald Jack, that is my only contact with Nathan, but he occupies a warm niche in my memory.

One day in 1960 there is a knock at my front door. My visitor is a retired United Church clergyman and he has a story idea he thinks I should run with. It has to do with an incident that took place near Hamilton in Upper Canada in 1827. A couple of men were to be hanged for the theft of an ox. The Reverend John Ryerson (brother of Ontario's famous Egerton Ryerson) and Dr. John Rolph (who would later found the University of Toronto Medical School) took umbrage and circulated a petition for clemency. Rolph rode off to Toronto (Muddy York in those days) with the petition, but had not yet returned by hanging time. Ryerson demanded permission to pray on the scaffold, and did so. But he wouldn't stop. It was a filibuster prayer that went on for hours, until Rolph returned with a Governor's reprieve.

This story enchants me. It is Justice in conflict with Religion over Law and Order. It is true Canadiana. My clergyman friend has just enough documentation to give me some assurance that the story is true, which is all that the dramatist in me requires. With my documentary background, too many facts can be a hazard. My friend also assures me he has no intention of exploiting the idea, but thinks I should.

I take the idea to CBC in Toronto, to Ed Moser, the Executive Producer of the drama anthology series, *General Motors Presents*, and am commissioned to work the idea into a one-hour drama. The story editor is David Peddie. I already know David's father, Frank, a fine, grizzled character actor who has graced numerous Crawley films and enlivened the off-camera ambience. Right from the start I feel completely comfortable with David and never get the sense he is a novice story editor. It is only years later that I find I am his first writer.

We are in the early days of videotape and the stuff is almost impossible to edit. My play, *The Devil's Petition*, is done on tape, but it is shot at one go, as though it were going on air live. It is directed by Leo Orenstein. Ryerson is played by Ron Hartman. I am enthralled. I cannot keep away from the TV studio behind the CBC's Jarvis Street radio building, which the staff refer to as "the Kremlin." It doesn't matter whether actors are there or not. The big studio, the sets, the lights — this is my idea of heaven.

I am commissioned by the CBC to write another drama. The anthology series is now known as *Playdate*, but the executive personnel are the same. This play is based on the career of an Ottawa Valley rogue, the Laird of McNab. He had fled from debtors in Scotland in the early 1800s and had managed to become an immigration land agent in Upper Canada. As an agent he settled many Scottish highlanders along the Ottawa River in the Arnprior area, but posed as their Laird, neglecting to tell the simple highland immigrants that they, not he, owned the land. His attempt to establish the feudal clan system climaxed during the final spasms of the Upper Canada Rebellion of 1837, when, without authority, he declared martial law. However, he discovered that the highlanders were not as gullible as he had thought. They rebelled, vowing they would fight for the Queen under anyone other than the supposed Laird. The local Irish settlers were willing to fight under anyone, so the Scots and the Irish had a donnybrook as a sidebar to the other rebellions. Only in Canada, you say?

It so happens that I have been onto this idea for ten years. In 1950 I used it as my play thesis at Cornell, where I was exploring the charm of the "open" or "thrust" stage, whose time in Canada was soon to come. I called it *The Thirteenth Laird*. That first version was a bad play that used an overabundance of the word "it." My mentor, Prof. A.M. Drummond, wrote "the It play" in a large scrawl on the first draft. I am determined to do better for TV.

This new *Thirteenth Laird* is directed by George McCowan. George is married to Frances Hyland, whom I consider one of the finest actresses Canada has produced. George is a powerhouse and the only person I've met who has a genuine photographic memory. He can absorb a script at a glance. He can also absorb Drambuie and Scotch.

The romantic leads are played by Sharon Acker and Peter Donat. Peter is a nephew of British actor Robert Donat, whose performance in the film version of John Buchan's *The Thirty-Nine Steps* is etched in my memory. But Peter is capable of carving his own niche. The Laird is played by Norman Ettinger, a fine Australian actor who eventually returns home. I will never forget Norm, as the Laird of McNab, doing a dandy highland sword dance on top of a banquet table.

As with my previous play, *The Thirteenth Laird* is a taped production that, thanks to the early technology, also has to be done non-stop. It is all staged in the CBC's Studio 7 on Jarvis Street and everything — love scenes, crowd scenes, house burnings, donnybrooks — has to be choreographed in such a way that the cameras can flow smoothly from one scene to the next. It occurs to me the kind of drama I like to write tends to have large casts and is going to be tough to confine to studio live action. Fortunately, however, videotape editing will become less cumbersome, and also CBC-TV will discover film.

In the mid-1960s quiet George Salverson writes an hour-long comedy drama set in Upper Canada in the 1830s. It is called *Hero at Hatch's Mill* and orbits around a family who run an inn. George's play spins off into a CBC series under the name *Hatch's Mill*. It is the baby of film producer Ronald Weyman, and his full-time story editor is David Peddie. The principal director for the series is George McCowan. This is to be CBC's first venture into drama in colour.

I submit an idea to David, and Ron commissions me to write episode number one of the main series. I write a horse drawing contest into the climax of this episode, which is called, fittingly enough, "The Contest."

Ever since my teens in the Ottawa Valley I have been a devotee of horse drawing contests, in which teams of great Percherons, Clydes, and Belgians compete to haul enormous weights loaded on flat, ground-scraping stoneboats. Some people consider it a cruel sport, but I suspect the horses enjoy it as much as their masters do. You can see the great beasts starting to paw with anticipation as they wait for the first lunge into the harness that breaks friction and begins the haul. I've come to know some of the drivers well enough to believe that there is no way most of them would dream of intentionally injuring their teams. I say "most," knowing full well there is a small sub-culture that is not above administering a little stimulant, but they are despised by their peers.

The *Hatch's Mill* series is being filmed north of Toronto at Kleinburg Studios. Outside, on the partially forested, stream-fed, rolling farmland an entire pioneer village is created.

There is one major problem with "The Contest." It requires horses. Real horses. Big horses. Stoneboat-hauling horses. It also requires a technical advisor who can guide director and actors in the intricacies of handling several tons of mobile horsemeat.

I have the answer and have known all along that I have it. It rests with our former rural neighbours, the Hartin brothers of Stittsville. I recommend Beattie and Milton Hartin as technical advisors for "The Contest," knowing full well they will be fascinated by the foreign world of Toronto film production and that the film gang will be fascinated by them.

Beattie and Milton go to Kleinburg and I manage to drop in a few times during the shoot. I get the feeling they are like sociologists in a lab, thoroughly entranced by the specimens around them. A horse throws a shoe and the production manager panics, because Toronto is not well populated with blacksmiths. The Hatch's Mill blacksmith shop, however, contains a genuine forge, and the Hartin brothers cheerfully demonstrate the fine art of horseshoeing. I recognize something that I will reconfirm throughout the years. Technicians who are good at what they do, as is this film crew, respect others who are good at what they do, as are the Hartin brothers. The gulf between the Ottawa Valley farm and the Kleinburg back lot is not as wide as some think.

I am less pleased with some of the acting, and it's not necessarily the fault of the actors. If anything, it's the fault of low budgets and production pressures. George McCowan produces at a furious pace. Speed becomes and remains his stock in trade. He spares little precious time for rehearsal. He will sometimes shoot a rehearsal and tail-slate it, and by the time the actors find out the scene is already in the can, it's too late. Another problem is that too many Canadian actors have not yet realized you simply act comedy straight, but take great care with the timing. They tend to say, "This is funny, I'd better act funny." Too many of the Hatch gang are overacting.

Sometimes, though, the overacting is inadvertent. One day I watch in consternation as Robert Christie, who is playing the head of the Hatch family, mugs his way through a rehearsal; the camera is on the far side of the set. I slide over to take a peak at the camera and then mosey over to Bob and do something a writer is never supposed to do to an actor — give a directorial hint. "Bob," I whisper, "George is using a long lens."

Bob is nonplussed. He is in close-up and he thought he was in long shot. When the scene runs again he erases the mugging and plays it straight. I develop a great affection for Bob Christie. He is always courteous, kind, and very professional. I can't imagine Bob Christie being rude to the technical crew or throwing a tantrum on set. He endears himself to Canadians as a TV reincarnation of Sir John A. MacDonald and has a long and honourable career.

Hatch's Mill is a writer's dream. This is the big breakthrough. In my mind's eye it is now onward and upward to TV heaven. The series is to be run in 1967, Centennial Year, when Canadians are supposed to be discovering their roots, their stories, their mythology.

In the mid-1800s a sect known as the Millerites was wandering Upper Canada preaching the end of the world. Their gullible disciples did quaint things like fashioning wings and hurling themselves off high balconies. In "The Prophet" I bring a family of end-of-the-world believers into Hatch's Mill.

In the National Archives I find that a man from Upper Canada who worked in the far north as a Hudson's Bay factor had left instructions that when he died his body should be returned home for burial. In those days the simplest way to do this was to pickle the body in a barrel of rum. Because the superstitious voyageurs who handled the inland freight routes would probably have dumped such a grisly cargo en route, it was sent by sea. The barrel, discreetly and inaccurately labelled — because sailors, too, are superstitious — travelled by ship to England, then back to Canada and up the St. Lawrence River to home.

It's not the journey that intrigues me so much as what would happen at Hatch's Mill if a similar mysterious barrel, unlabelled but apparently full of rum, were to arrive in the village. The thought of burying good rum would surely be too much for the hard-drinking denizens of the Mill. In "The Cask" the seed of the real-life story blossoms into a comedy (so I hope) of greed, larceny, and mistaken identity. Johnny Foster's actress wife, Pam Hyatt, plays a grieving and highly confused widow.

Medicine in the 1800s was an imperfect art, and again I learn from the archives that many rural doctors were also lawyers, carrying medicine in one saddlebag and legal briefs in the other. Some were modernists who almost understood how the body works, and others were medievalists who interpreted every ailment in terms of the humours — phlegm, blood, choler, and black bile. One of the latter doctors was said to be so spry that in his eighties he could still shoot a crow off the ridge of a barn roof. He also believed in bloodletting as a primary remedy and surrounded his bed with spring traps for fear of witches. He lived in a cabin whose door was many feet above the ground; it was accessed by a ladder that he could pull up after him. It occurs to me that if Mother Hatch is seriously ill, and her two men strike out in different directions to find help, and each comes home with a doctor, one of whom is a modernist and the other not, the resulting clash could be interesting. It is also helpful to know that duels to the death were not unknown in Upper Canada. "The Consultants" becomes one of my four credits for the series. Six other episodes are written by Donald Jack, George Salverson, and Leslie MacFarlane, a multi-talented writer who was the principal author of the *Hardy Boys* books.

By this time, research is taking all the writers into the period in which William Lyon Mackenzie is fomenting rebellion in Upper Canada, and we are all beginning to make use of the bizarre politics of the era. The series has been uneven to date, but David Peddie tells me that in these political scripts everything is beginning to gel. This, so the Americans and Brits tell us, is normal for a TV series. They don't produce many of their early scripts, and they scrap some of the shows they do shoot. CBC can't afford such a luxury. We all know that some of the first ten shows could have been tighter and we are gung-ho to improve.

I am inspired by a book by the Ontario archivist/historian E.C. Guillet, *The Lives and Times of the Patriots*, which is full of verbal sketches of the Rebellion period. It soon becomes clear to me that the "patriots" were the rebels, which is a nice thought; most considered themselves loyal to the Queen while rebelling against the appointed governor and his cronies who ruled from Upper Canada's capital, Toronto. Among the patriots he describes are some who, after the Rebellion dust had subsided, became pirates in the Thousand Islands. They toured the islands in a forty-foot rowboat, raided settlements on both sides of the St. Lawrence, and burned a steamship, the *Sir Robert Peel*, in retaliation for the Canadian militia's having burned Mackenzie's supply ship, the *Caroline*, just above Niagara Falls. But they were loyal pirates, who bore no grudge against the Queen, and they declared their hideaway island to be the only independent piece of British territory in North America. Again, only in Canada. I write a two-segment script for *Hatch's Mill* based on these buccaneer patriots.

A few days later, however, I enter producer Ron Weyman's office and find him and David staring dejectedly at a pile of unproduced scripts, including my latest.

"What's the problem?" I ask. "Too much rebellion politics? Afraid we'll put ideas in people's heads?"

"No. Not really." They name a senior CBC executive whose name I have consigned to limbo, where it belongs. "He doesn't like period pieces. Says no one is watching. He's cancelled the series."

In a way, the bureaucrat is correct. Very few people in Toronto are watching and the city reviewers are not kind. Out of curiosity I ask to see the correspondence file. It tells another story. Rural Canadians, who almost by definition know about their roots, have definitely been watching and enjoying, and writing in to say so. We are moving into the era when rural Canadians don't count.

Almost simultaneously with the termination of *Hatch's Mill* a letter arrives saying that "The Contest" has won a prestigious award in Australia.

A desire to tell authentic tales of early Canadian life continues to drive me. I am still intrigued by that post-Rebellion period late in the winter of 1837-38. Groups of armed Americans conducted unauthorized raids across the border, striking at points as far apart as Windsor and Prescott. There was a battle on the ice at Pelee Island and another at Windsor. Entire American families followed their "soldiers" across the ice to be entertained by the spectacle of Canada being invaded. All were under the misapprehension that Canadians would welcome their liberators with open arms and that the British garrison troops were all away suppressing rebellion in Quebec. The National Archives contain descriptions of American families picnicking on the ice while the children chased spent cannonballs. The archives also reveal that not all the

British troops were absent; on at least one occasion, when the invaders charged, a small detachment of the "thin red line" of British regulars moved onto the ice. The flat surface of frozen water was the absolutely ideal terrain for the otherwise archaic formation of the British firing line. And here, as in other engagements, the Canadian citizenry, instead of opening their arms, picked up arms. Mounted on farm horses and wielding muskets, flails, and even pitchforks, the rustic cavalry swept past the regulars and closed in from the sides.

A militia officer in the Windsor area, Colonel Prince, promised the locals that any invading "officer" caught by him would be hanged out of hand. He kept his word and was applauded by the citizenry. It was ironic that in some instances captured invaders found that the hated Redcoats were their only protection from the inhabitants, who were supposed to be eagerly opening their arms.

Such episodes fascinate me, not least because behind some of the invasions were Canadian dissenters who, having failed in rebellion, went south of the border to mislead Americans about the Canadian state of mind. This deceit was compounded by the American propensity to believe that republicanism is the only form of government approved of by God Himself and that liberating Canada was, as one agitator claimed, "a mere matter of marching." For the dramatist it presents a chance to explore chicanery, naiveté, bravery, politics, martyrdom, betrayal, and national hubris.

Ron Weyman commissions a two-hour script that we hope might become a feature film. Although fictitious, my story is an amalgam of some of the real incidents of that remarkable post-Rebellion winter.

In the National Archives I come across a song of the time that was popular south of the border:

Come strike the bold anthem, the war dogs are howling,
Already they eagerly snuff up their prey,
The red clouds of war o'er our forests are scowling,
Soft peace spreads her wings and flies weeping away;
The infants, affrighted, cling close to their mothers,
The youths grasp their swords, for the combat prepare,
While beauty weeps fathers, and lovers, and brothers,
Who rush to display the American Star.

I give this to the invaders as a theme song and name the script *Bold Anthem*. I always consider it one of my best scripts, but it never gets produced. The official reason is undoubtedly partly true. CBC doesn't have the budget for a rather large mid-winter film epic. But I'm convinced there is another problem, and it has to do with the fact that too many of Canada's cultural czars are not Canadians. This is brought home to me one evening in 1967, Centennial Year.

Hilda's father, Joseph Davison, is visiting from the Old Country. The old gentleman is a dab hand with the banjo, even though he is quite deaf and plays with the stem against his cheek so he can pick up the vibrations. Dad likes to whip off little numbers like the overture to *William Tell*. The boys are fascinated by him. So am I.

Someone else who is fascinated when I describe Dad's prowess is Patrick Watson. Patrick is no mean hand with a guitar, and one evening he and some Privy Council guitarists have a guitar-and-banjo fest in our Manotick living room. A non-playing friend, Michael Spencer, has come along with them. Michael is head of the Canadian Film Development Corporation, the federal government agency that is charged with helping to finance Canada's infant feature film industry.

I have known Mike since my days at Crawley Films, when he acted as industry liaison for the National Film Board, which meant that whenever the Board in its magnanimity felt like letting some crumbs from the government table fall down to the private industry Mike would act as middleman. In one case the crumbs turned into a whole loaf, and he and I were associated in the production of *Canadian Wheat* (1956), which was for many years the definitive film on its subject.

Anyway, here is Mike, Mr. Feature Film Himself, a guest in my home while I'm all fired up by *Bold Anthem* and Canada's Centennial. While the banjo and guitars are hammering away in the living room Mike and I are sipping rye and chatting in the kitchen. I begin to rhapsodize about the romance and action and politics of the post-Rebellion era, but Mike cuts me off.

"Nobody's interested in people running around in red uniforms."

I am aghast. Is he that anti-British? He has an English accent. As far as I know he is originally English. Or is he just against costume drama? That can't be it.

"You approve of the CBC doing *Jalna*?" I ask. According to the hype, CBC is preparing to create a TV adaptation of Mazo de la Roche's *Jalna* books and it will be the greatest thing ever to hit Canadian airwaves.

"Of course I approve," says Mike. "But everyone has read *Jalna*. It's internationally popular."

"You're wrong. It's only internationally that it is popular. Canadians don't give a damn about the Whiteoaks of *Jalna*."

Mike is almost irate. "I was raised on *Jalna*."

"Oh? Where?"

"England."

"I rest my case."

I have a damn good case, too. One of the best educated women I know, my mother, who at the time is 82, has always been an avid reader of Canadiana. Not only that, she was raised in southern Ontario in what was supposedly Whiteoak territory. She tells me she had never heard of the *Jalna* books until the CBC started all its hype. She has gone to the library and rounded them up and has read every last one.

"I find no single point of recognition," she tells me. This from a woman who is old enough to remember stagecoaches. She is particularly amused by a description of Ontario farmers standing by the roadside on a Sunday morning and doffing their hats as the Whiteoak carriage rolls by.

"I can tell you this," says Mother, "your great-grandfather came from England in 1832 determined never again to stand by the roadside and tug his forelock to the squire."

A good case can be made that Canadiana is being selectively preserved according to the preconceptions and misconceptions of bureaucrats who have their roots elsewhere. As Canadian icons, the fictitious and highly irrelevant Whiteoaks are in, but the Redcoats and farmers from the National Archives are out.

Hatch's Mill is dead and buried and *Bold Anthem* is doomed to languish in limbo, but I go to David and Ron with an idea for a contemporary drama with a religious theme. I recently wrote another film for the United Church, a documentary about the problems encountered by old established congregations marooned in the hearts of today's big cities. The film was called *Inner City*. George Gorman directed it and a young Toronto composer, Herb Helbig, wrote masterly music for it. With Anson Moorhouse as producer, Ed deFay on camera, Shirley Tyte as editor, the film won a Blue Ribbon at the 1967 American Film Festival in New York. It was while researching this documentary that I had an idea for a drama.

I am intrigued by the dilemmas that plague those clergymen who are theologically liberal but preach from Biblical texts their flocks interpret literally. I myself have a father and a maternal grandfather who are theologically liberal. During these fascinating 1960s the United Church brings out its "New Curriculum" for Sunday School study and reaps a lot of flak for being almost heretical. Again, Mother settles down to read the new material to see what all the fuss is about. I wait for her analysis and when it comes it is remarkably brief. "I don't see anything there that would upset your grandfather."

So now, near the close of the 1960s, I present Ron and David with an idea for a TV play featuring a liberal inner-city clergyman who has a motley group of youths on his hands. As a result of a variety of misunderstandings and subsequent conflicts the youths put him on trial, charging him with intellectual dishonesty, and, to make their point, demand that he swear to his belief in the Apostle's Creed. He cannot.

Ron and David like the idea but feel it is not suited for film, so pass me on to the VTR (Video Tape Record) wing of the drama department and to Executive Producer Robert Allen. A script is commissioned under the banner of a drama series called Festival. This is a flagship weekly anthology series offering ninety minutes of drama unbroken by any interruptions, commercial or otherwise, and I am genuinely excited.

My story editor is Doris Gauntlett. I miss David Peddie's gentle guidance but find that Doris, too, is insightful and professional. My only concern, as time goes on, is the CBC's tendency to polish scripts to the point where they lose their spontaneity. If Shakespeare had been subjected to the CBC procedure, all true-to-life inconsistencies would have been ironed out and his plays would have been faultlessly logical and blindingly boring. Obviously, it's up to the writer to know when to stop polishing and dig in his heels. There's a catch. Such a writer can be labelled "difficult," and be unofficially blacklisted.

The script I am working on is called Reddick, after its fictional protagonist, Reverend James Reddick. When I am close to a final draft I show it to Berkeley Studio's resident communications expert, Dr. Robert Reid. Bob is an ordained United Church clergyman with a Ph.D. in communications from the University of Syracuse. We have become good friends and I want to see if I'm committing any technical gaffes with respect to the clergy. I don't expect him to be enamoured of the notion that my character might be guilty of "intellectual dishonesty," but he is.

Bob clutches Reddick to his breast and is off and running. While the play is being shot, mostly on location in Toronto's old Bathurst Street United Church, Bob is talking about it at the United Church head office, known in cheerful clerical circles as "Cloud 85" because of its 85 St. Clair Avenue address. He is also talking about Reddick to his Anglican and Catholic counterparts.

The play is being directed by a Jew, Mervyn Rozensweig, whom I consider one of the most creative, perceptive, and under-appreciated of TV drama directors. Because the editing of videotape is still a complicated nightmare, Merv is experimenting with transferring his rushes to 16mm film, editing the film, and then editing the tape to match. From a production point of view it's an excellent idea, but from a budgetary view it has drawbacks.

Merv casts Donald Harron in the title role, as Rev. James Reddick. I feel truly blessed. Don is brilliant. This is not the rustic Charlie Farquharson of his comedy routine. This is the fine dramatic actor who is, and will be, alas, very seldom revealed. As Don Jack says when he joins me to watch some rushes, "You can see the intelligence shining in his eyes."

By the time *Reddick* is ready to air, a strange phenomenon has occurred. Bob Reid has the United Church, the Anglicans, and the Catholics all promoting the show. They are arranging to put TV sets into church basements so people can watch in groups. Study guides have been produced to help with post-screening discussions. None of this has anything to do with sponsorship. They are acting absolutely at arm's length from the CBC. They have not attempted to interfere, alter, or in any way shape the script. Bob tells me all this activity is simply a result of the churches' recognition that the play has something of value to say to contemporary society.

I am in a daze. It seems to me this opens a door for the promotion of thoughtful TV drama without the CBC's relinquishing editorial control. I am, of course, enormously naive. The CBC brass seem unimpressed by the fact that a vast grassroots audience is being lined up for one of their dramas.

The Wednesday the play is to be aired I am at home in Manotick in bed with the flu. I am running an unpleasantly high fever but am reading the *Ottawa Citizen*. The TV reviewer is Frank Penn. I always read Frank's column because I think he is a good reviewer. Today he almost gives me apoplexy. He announces he has learned that this evening's offering on *Festival*, a play called *Reddick*, will be interrupted at intervals to bring us bulletins as President Nixon announces appointments to his cabinet. Frank thinks this is a lousy idea and so do I.

There are no commercial breaks in *Festival*. *Reddick* has been tailored with a great deal of care and can be utterly destroyed by arbitrary excisions and interruptions. I am distraught, but it is already early evening.

I phone Merv Rozensweig. He, too, is distraught and has tried to call the top brass of the CBC drama department in Toronto. Those with authority are not available. They and their counterparts from the news department have gone to a hockey game at Maple Leaf Gardens. The orders are written in stone and the duty station manager at Toronto's CBLT, the originating network station, says he can't change them on his own initiative.

My fever is making me unusually intemperate. I phone our sister-in-law, Margaret Davison, who lives in Ottawa. Margaret claims that her friends are my fan club. I suggest to Margaret that she get the club to phone the Ottawa station manager and complain mightily about the announced interruptions. I phone Don Jack in Toronto and ask him to do the same. Don, diffident chap that he is, doesn't bother his friends, but goes one better. He makes frequent calls to the CBLT duty manager and, being a frustrated thespian, on each call alters his accent and verbiage. "Hey, mister, what's this about Nixon's damn cabinet, eh?" "Hoot mon, y' canna do this t' your loyal listeners." "Mama mia, I'ma not believing this!" "I say, old chap, mixing Nixon into *Festival* has got to be a new intellectual low, even for the CBC."

And, of course, I phone Bob Reid. Bob also goes into action and I am sure he is the one who actually turns the tide. Contacting the CBLT station manager, he draws vivid verbal pictures of all those people who even now are gathering in church basements to watch *Reddick*, and describes how nonplussed these drama viewers are going to be to find themselves assaulted with news bulletins about a non-elected cabinet being appointed by a foreign president. He also points out, diplomatically of course, that the CBC is about to alienate the communications bureaucrats of the three most influential church establishments in the country.

The station manager makes an executive decision. He takes his career in his hands and cancels the orders to insert news bulletins. *Reddick* runs without interruptions. I am told later that the manager had also received a call from the Ottawa station saying there seemed to be some angst among that city's population.

The play is, apparently, a success. The reviewer in the Montreal *Gazette* writes of "power and sensitivity," the *Ottawa Citizen* finds it "a joy to watch," and the *Toronto Star* congratulates me personally (a rare experience for a dramatist) for "an honest, well-constructed, and dramatically exciting script." *Reddick* is picked up for rebroadcast by PBS in the States and by the BBC in England. CBC commissions a ninety-minute sequel.

In *Reddick II*, which is also shot mostly on location at the Bathurst Street Church, the youths, by now attempting to protect Reddick from his own elders, stage an "occupation." During shooting, Merv Rozensweig has the budget hounds snapping at his heels and loses much of his rehearsal time. (My memory says he is also deprived of one camera.)

Lack of rehearsal time is not too apparent to the uninitiated but is obvious to me. One virile young actor, stymied by lack of time, substitutes the expletive "bastard" whenever he runs into a memory blank, but he manages to knit it into a seamless structure, and Merv has little time for retakes. I begin to think of *Reddick* II as the "bastard" play. Senior CBC brass get into the act and try a little censorship. In a scene with upright and uptight church elders, one of the youths uses the phrase, "You give me a pain in the balls." It is used, intentionally, in a sexual context. The phrase is vetoed but I fight and we negotiate. A reluctant Doris Gauntlett tells me that the brass say if I delete the one set of "balls" I can use "ass" at least three times. This strikes me as an interesting Canadian compromise, particularly as it seems to add a touch of perversion, which is not my intention.

Anyway, in 1970, a year after the first broadcast, the two parts of *Reddick* are aired one week apart. By now the series has commercial breaks built into it. However, there are not enough sustaining commercials, so CBC interlards the play with breaks promoting upcoming dramas. This prompts a senior Ottawa civil servant to complain to the editor of the *Globe and Mail* that such interruptions are the equivalent of a symphony orchestra pausing between movements to play a selection from next week's concert.

Part 2 appears to be well received by the viewers and reviewers. The Hamilton *Spectator* finds it "a reaffirmation that the CBC still can live up to its old reputation as a fount of first-rate drama." But not everyone agrees. A fellow writer, reviewing it in Winnipeg, judges it the worst TV drama to come out of any network in living memory. It is possible that CBC Vice President Eugene Hallman agrees with him. Eugene tells me that the play has far too much bad language in it. It's my impression that there is no attempt to sell Part 2 abroad.

In the meantime Bob Reid continues to be active. He sends the *Reddick* scripts to Professor Richard Barnhill at Syracuse University. Until recently Dick Barnhill has been Vice President in charge of programming for CBS television. Dick makes an enthusiastic pitch to CBS that the Rev. James Reddick would make a dandy character around whom to build a TV series. Interestingly enough, Dick prefers Part 2, the "bastard" play. He eventually tells me that our submission has made it to the final cull.

I receive a letter directly from Bob Wood, President of CBS. Dick really has connections. Mr. Wood is friendly but reports that *Reddick* does not conform to the more fundamentalist religious profile of the average American viewer. He suggests there could be some interest from CBS if I were to reshape my theologically liberal principal character to be more of a Billy Graham type. I am sure he doesn't realize the irony inherent in the suggestion. If I were to agree, I myself would be guilty of intellectual dishonesty.

This divide between theological liberalism and fundamentalism always fascinates me. It seems for many years to be a major defining difference between Canadians and Americans, but in all our self-absorbed soul-searching I never see this recognized. In the twenty-first century, as Canadian hearts and minds begin to ossify, the difference may disappear.

But where am I? Oh yes, 1971. Perhaps *Reddick* as a series is not dead. I have had to turn my back on CBS, but I pitch the series idea to Executive Producer Robert Allen at the CBC. Eventually Robert phones to inform me that "no one is interested in religion any more." I wish he had put it in writing, because the very day of that phone call I walk across the dam to the Manotick post office, open my mailbox, and remove a copy of *Time* magazine for June 19, 1971. The front cover heralds "The Jesus Revolution."

For the next decade TV drama is, for me, unfertile ground. I write a couple of half-hour episodes for a series called *The Winners*, which is aimed at young people and is intended to showcase, dramatically, the achievements of famous Canadians. One is about my favourite Canadian poetess, Pauline Johnson, the Mohawk "princess." This segment goes on to have a long life. I write another on Armand Bombardier, the inventor of the Ski-Doo, but run into conflict with the Executive Producer. Perhaps I am handicapped by my documentary background, but in mini-dramas that are presented as profiles of real people there is a point beyond which I refuse to go in distorting history. I become "difficult." I like and respect the producer but we may have a cultural problem. Her roots are in the States, and Americans have turned the distortion of history into an art form. The Bombardier script is passed on to a more malleable writer. I never see the resulting production.

If you have come with me this far you will realize that we have covered somewhat more than a decade in the arcane world of TV drama. Fortunately for me, there was always a parallel universe of documentary film and TV public affairs, so let's step back into the memorable year of 1967.

21

CENTENNIAL YEAR

1967. CENTENNIAL YEAR. It has arrived at last! This fantastic country of ours is finally celebrating its hundredth birthday. Everybody has been looking forward to this for years. And not only is it Canada's one-hundredth, it's also the year for Expo, and Expo is being held in Montreal.

It seems that most of the world has its eyes focused on Expo 67. Already our own friends and relatives are saying they're going to visit us this summer — and, of course, they'll mosey on to Expo, another two-hours drive away. I understand their enthusiasm. I stumbled across Expo 58 at Brussels, en route from Africa to Holland. This show should be even better.

But it appears that I will be going to Indonesia. Anson Moorhouse and Berkeley Studio have another assignment from the National Council of Churches in New York, and again I'm the writer. It occurs to me there's an opportunity here, and late one evening I broach an idea to Hilda.

"You and I are going to Japan."

She puts aside a book she's reading. Something to do with the Duchess of Marlborough. Hilda relaxes with stuff that paralyses me.

"Where? Why? When? How?"

She should have been a journalist. Only the "where" was unnecessary.

"Why? Because we've not had a real holiday together, just us, for years. When? When I head for Indonesia. I'm meeting Anson in Hong Kong and my air ticket permits a stopover. Japan is on the way."

"We can't afford it!"

"If necessary we take out a bank loan for your ticket and our expenses."

"Who'll look after the boys?"

"Those are details. How about the idea?"

This is Hilda's first flight across Canada. For me there's usually a cloud cover for at least half the trip. For Hilda the entire country is laid out, bright, green, blue, clean, and clear, like a highly detailed model. The serpentine Saskatchewan River, with its branching coulees and draws, looks like a great dragon uncoiling across the prairies. The incredible spires of the Rocky Mountains thrust up at us with startling clarity. I feel that Nature is preening herself for Hilda's inspection.

After flying almost non-stop across both North America and the Pacific we arrive in Tokyo with our biological clocks in total disarray, and go directly to bed. We are staying in the old Imperial Hotel, which was designed by Frank Lloyd Wright and is, alas, very close to its final days.

We awaken at what must be a ridiculously early hour, because even Tokyo seems to be asleep. An envelope has been slipped under our door. It is a welcome, addressed to us personally, from the Japan Tourist Board. It assures us the arrangements I have made are all in hand and not to worry. This is PR for sure.

We go for a long walk while the city is rousing itself. Before long we find Tokyo so wide awake we are almost afraid to cross the street. You need an armoured escort to avoid being run over by taxicabs. I hire a pedicab to take us to view the Imperial Palace. I assume that a pedicab operator, being as vulnerable as ourselves, will have a highly developed sense of self-preservation and will be able to navigate these streets. I also think our transportation is exotic, but Hilda thinks it's undemocratic, exploitative, and patronizing.

I protest. "It's not a rickshaw. The guy's on a bicycle. He's not sweating between shafts."

We get out and walk.

As we pass along a quieter side street we come upon a modest Protestant church and realize it is Sunday morning. The service is about to begin. On an impulse, we enter, thinking it could be interesting to experience an entire service in Japanese. A smiling usher shows us to a pew. A moment later a young Japanese woman slides in beside us. In a whisper, she introduces herself in English and asks our names and origin. Later, when the offering is being collected, she slips a little note onto the plate and no sooner has the offering been dedicated than we hear the minister speaking our names. He is introducing us.

As the sermon gets underway our young companion begins to write swiftly on a small notepad. She passes the notes to us, a slip at a time. She is translating the sermon, swiftly and with great compression. I wonder if there is any church in Canada where such a courtesy is extended to foreign visitors.

We take a three-day bus tour that follows a historic route through the beautiful Hakone Mountains, en route to the fabled ancient capital of Kyoto. We pass near Mount Fuji, a national symbol that nearly always has her face shrouded in mist. Fuji does not hide from Hilda. For her, Mount Fuji is graciously unveiled. Such a sight is said to be a good omen.

The tour passengers come from various corners of the globe, but we are the only Canadians. The tour guide is a young Japanese man who speaks flawless English. At a lunch stop on the second day, he joins us at a small table. I compliment him on his English.

"What amazes me," I say, with the genuine envy that comes easily to a unilingual Canadian, "is that you have absolutely no accent at all!"

"Oh yes I do."

"Well, I can't hear it."

"That's because it's the same as yours."

He smiles, looks furtively from side to side, then slides his own passport across the small table. It is Canadian.

"That's right," he says, "British Columbia. Born and raised. Thank goodness my folks saw to it I also learned Japanese. I'm having a great time. Hope you folks are, too."

It's an amazing world.

The trip includes "educational" stops, including tours through the Yamaha piano factory and a Kobe beef cattle barn. We are told that the famous marbling of Kobe beef is created by the grooming each animal receives. We watch in wonder as a fat steer is massaged by a groom, who takes copious mouthfuls of beer, squirts it onto the beast's gleaming flanks, and vigorously massages it in.

In Kyoto we visit the ancient and exotic temples, gardens, and palaces that I was in no condition to appreciate fully almost a decade earlier. But it is our Kyoto accommodation that will remain enshrined in memory. We are at a western-style hotel but our room is in the annex. The annex is a genuine Japanese garden and the guest quarters are individual one-room cottages discreetly nestled among the shrubs, trees, flowers, and babbling brooks. It has been an unusually warm spring and all nature is lush. The floor of our room is covered with a wall-to-wall tatami mat. The bed is a futon unrolled on the tatami. Everything is charming, cozy, comfortable, and incredibly romantic.

This is, for once, a holiday trip. I am not conducting interviews or taking notes about the world's underprivileged, sick, or oppressed, nor am I constantly watching for events or locations that might be fodder for documentary cameras. It's most refreshing.

Reality does have a cloud. We are heading for Hong Kong, and Hong Kong is immersed in riots and demonstrations. In neighbouring mainland China, Chairman Mao's Cultural Revolution is underway and its leadership-induced chaos is spilling over into British territory. I check with the British Embassy in Tokyo and am told that the activity in Hong Kong is in a temporary lull. It should be okay to take my wife there for a day or two.

Hong Kong doesn't appeal to Hilda the way it has always appealed to me. We arrive late in the day, and as we emerge from the airplane Hilda exclaims, "Feel the heat from those engines!"

When we are well away from the plane and walking into the terminal I ask, "Can you still feel the heat of those engines?" And indeed, heat is still with us. We are teetering on the brink of the hot and humid typhoon season.

I claim our baggage and we force our way through a sea of taxi drivers, all of whom seem to think they are there exclusively to save us from the others. I insist on choosing our own cab.

Night has come. Kowloon city is aglow in neon signs gleaming on strange banners, and since most of the lettering is in Chinese each has its own mysterious look. At every street corner groups of men are huddled around oil drums of burning trash. These are not street people. These are demonstrators affiliated with Mao's Red Guard, simply biding their time and catching their breath, hoping to resume their activities within a few days. The huddled groups, the fires, the smoke, the strange neon signs, all combine to create an atmosphere that Hilda finds disturbing.

We reach our modest back-street hotel and the desk clerk is surprised that we have come in an independent taxi. He had sent the hotel driver to meet us. Apparently one of the crowd of drivers at the airport really was trying to save us from the others. I feel like an idiot.

A friend at home has asked us to take a gift to a child she is "fostering" through an international agency. We find ourselves on the dockside at Aberdeen, where the junks and sampans are packed in so tightly one almost forgets there is water beneath them. The agency representative is on hand supposedly to facilitate our meeting with the "foster" child, but there is something overly-monitored and staged about the whole encounter. We step onto the sampan. The boy, groomed, washed, and terrified, is duly pushed forward by his mother. We present the gift, words pass back and forth in mysterious translation, and we depart, feeling we have made about as much contact as space aliens landing for thirty seconds in Toronto at rush hour.

Our taxi stops at an intersection and suddenly Hilda is confronted by a wizened, deformed arm thrust through the open window, the hand cupped upward, as the owner, a gaunt, ragged crone, whines for money. The taxi pulls away and the driver laconically tells Hilda to close her window at stoplights.

This time I am seeing Hong Kong, the most exciting community on earth, through Hilda's eyes. It's a chastening experience. Either she is more compassionate than I am or she is less hardened by frequent exposure to poverty en masse. But wait, this is an economy that's touted as soaringly vibrant and is reputed to be creating millionaires by the hundreds. I appreciate Hilda's presence. Otherwise, like so many westerners I could easily become seduced by the glitz and glamour.

Fortunately there are no more riots. Even the street corner bonfires are extinguished. It happens almost effortlessly with the onset of torrential rains.

Hilda heads for home and I head for Indonesia. My passage is unremarkable, but her plane loses the use of an engine partway across the Pacific; it returns to Tokyo and then heads off again. All in all, it has been an interesting holiday. We both arrive at our destinations utterly ignorant of the fact that the Six Days War has been going on in the Middle East.

Hilda resumes her domestic duties and, as an escape from the mid-East, the Far East, and the contemporary West, settles down to read Henri Troyat's *Tolstoy*.

In Indonesia the typhoon season has ended and Anson and I move into hot, dry weather.

Did I say "in" Indonesia? How does one know? They tell me there are roughly 13,000 islands in the Indonesian archipelago. Anson and I are only visiting Java and Bali. Granted, Java has more people than the rest of the islands put together, but one must be cautious not to generalize, even in memory.

The capital, Jakarta, is a city of contrasts. There are sweeping boulevards, a few modern hotels and others arising, monuments honouring the founding revolution, elegant residential areas nestling in sub-tropical foliage, and, in contrast, the seemingly inevitable abject poverty.

Women are doing the family laundry in the muddy waters of the river as the bloated carcasses of animals float by just a few feet away. I say "the" river but have no idea which one is lodged in memory. A score of them flush through this city of several million people. Are all defiled? Probably.

Memory also contains stories of recent almost incomprehensibly savage violence, but they are temporarily pushed aside by recollections of a countryside that is lush and beautiful. We are less than ten degrees south of the equator, and we drive with relative ease to tropical jungle, to fields, to rice paddies, to hills, to mountains. An active volcano adorns a distant view that looks more like a painting than reality. Near Bandung, a former rural palace is surrounded by a treed park in which herds of deer graze with apparent unconcern. We visit the ancient Buddhist temple of Barabudur, more than a thousand years old, rising terrace upon terrace to the crowning pinnacle of a soaring stupa, the whole looking like an intricately carved stone hill. And indeed it is a hill. This temple has no interior. The ancient masons clad a hill in stone, upon which the sculptors enshrined an entire constellation of images depicting legends and beliefs.

I am fascinated by the shadow plays of wayang puppets, jarred by the clanging music of gamelin orchestras, and soothed by the liquid notes of Angklung bamboo instruments. The Angklung sound reminds me of Caribbean steel drums, except that these instruments are made from bamboo and each musician plays only one note. Sixteen players make an orchestra. I find myself imagining the Trinidadian "pans" of the *Sundowners* blending with Angklung bamboo, with an under pinning of the deep, mellow notes of the *onomanguita* drum from Angola.

We drive the length of Java via the city of Jogjakarta, where we are privileged to see an outdoor stage presentation of the great Hindu epic, the *Ramayana*. The stage is one of a kind. This is a nighttime performance, beautifully lit, exotically costumed, elegantly danced, and mounted upon a terrace of the magnificent thousand-year-old Prambanan Temple — in reality a cluster of 224 temples. The senses reel with an overload of beauty.

Later, in the centre of a Javanese village, on the hard-packed earthen square that has a modest mosque on one side and an equally modest church on the other, we watch a group of Christian dancers using traditional Javanese costumes and traditional music to portray the Old Testament story of David and Goliath.

We continue east and take the small, sea-tossed car ferry to the island of Bali. This island is even more exotic than its name. It is twilight as we drive toward Denpasar. The day's work is completed and the field workers are walking home. The women are moving with the incredible grace of carriage that comes from the carrying of head-loads and the enjoyment of dance. Their clothing radiates colours that outdo the sunset. There are small shrines in the fields and large shrines at the crossroads. The majority of these people are Hindu — no, not just Hindu, but Balinese Hindu. Here, the gods are everywhere. Worship and work are inseparable; the same word is used to describe both. Here, the arts are not simply a part of life, they are life. It is taken for granted that a field worker may also be a sculptor, and a painter, and a dancer, and a musician. The arts give joy to the gods. They are presented not as worship, but as a personal gift.

Bali is not yet wide open for tourism. Only the Indonesian Garuda Airline is permitted to land here. That will soon change. The Bali Beach Hotel has just opened. It has a diesel power plant that is larger than the one that powers the entire city of Denpasar. This hotel is the forerunner of more to follow, but at the moment its several hundred rooms are almost empty. Anson and I are among a mere handful of guests. The manager is a Canadian.

I meet the hotel's PR officer. She is a beautiful young woman just recently graduated from university. She speaks flawless English. She invites us to attend a coming-of-age ceremony at her own home. The principals are to be herself and her brother, who is also a university graduate.

The young woman's family live within a modest walled compound in the country. The day of the ceremony, guests are greeted at the main gate by the music of a cheerfully decorated gamelin orchestra. Guests arrive bearing gifts, which they deposit at the family shrine inside the compound. Here, too, there is a separate shrine honouring the high god trinity of Brahma, Vishnu, and Shiva. Everything is decorated, and I am entranced by the elegant beauty of the people who are gathering, all the more so because I understand these are not "society folk," but simply friends and neighbours. Beautiful Balinese.

As the ceremony begins, the brother and sister are carried from the house into the quadrangle. They are seated on canopied litters carried at shoulder height. Their costumes are vibrant with golds and reds and they wear helmet-like crowns. To the uninitiated, like myself, it has all the appearance of a royal wedding. The couple step from the litters to a raised platform, where a priest presides.

The priest's function is to release potentially evil spirits from the supplicants' bodies. He does this by using a chisel and a hammer to knock the corners off their front teeth. This is a "tooth-filing" ceremony!

Suddenly I am back to another reality.

It is little more than a year and a half since Bali and much of the rest of Indonesia was running with blood. There was fear at the time of a Communist coup. Communism, by definition, is atheist. Modern Indonesia is founded on five principles, of which the first and foremost is "Belief in God." A mere eighteen months ago, when the army was taking over during the anti-communist struggle, religion and politics became dangerous bedfellows. It was a sentence of death not to have a religion. More than half a million people were slaughtered. We are told the rivers of neighbouring Java quite literally ran with blood as the Moslems declared holy war. Here, in beautiful Bali, the elegant Hindus "cleansed" their island of impurities, the major impurity being communists. We are told that more than a thousand of the cleansed were teachers. Not surprisingly, many people with no religion, or with a poorly defined religion, have found it healthy to become religious. The Christian churches are gaining many new adherents. In earlier days, and elsewhere in Asia, such converts were called "rice Christians," a disparaging tag that suggested non-spiritual motivation. Nevertheless, here we find that many westerners, mostly evangelical protestants, are enthusiastically counting heads and jubilantly announcing an upsurge in Christianity. I am not convinced.

Java is overwhelmingly Moslem. Bali is overwhelmingly Balinese Hindu. But whatever their religion, Indonesians share a common history that leads them to defy westerners. Today's Indonesia is founded on a revolution, but nothing simple like the one in which the Americans merely overthrew the British. For almost three hundred years these islands were under Dutch rule. It was not until the Japanese invasion during the Second World War that the Dutch were forced out. At that time Indonesians noticed with a great deal of interest that their colonial European masters could be defeated by Asians. Those who were conscripted into the Japanese army took pains to learn military skills. When the war ended, the Japanese, following established protocol, were required to maintain the status quo until the Allies took over. The Allies in turn permitted the Dutch to return. The Indonesians revolted simultaneously against the Japanese, the Allies, and the Dutch — and won. These are tough-minded folk.

Right now I feel as though I'm on the edge of a volcano, and the seething lava that is waiting to erupt is religion. "Belief in God" as the primary pillar of a multi-religion nation poses some problems. The Moslems believe that "God" means Allah and that Mohammed is His prophet. The Christians, so say some Moslems, believe in more than one God. They believe in a Trinity of Gods. The Christians and the Moslems eye the Balinese Hindus with a similar suspicion, accusing them of having many gods and of ancestor worship. The Balinese Hindus say there is one Supreme God — Creator, Preserver, Destroyer — a trinity. But their religion is so deeply entwined with co-operative community welfare that they eye individualistic Christians as subverters of the community. The Christians and Moslems find the deeply personal, individualistic, contemplative worship of the Buddhists even more baffling. Each group eyes with suspicion verging on alarm any sign that another group is gaining power.

Before we leave I sit in on a meeting of representatives of several Christian denominations. Some American missionaries are enthusiastically planning a huge fundamentalist "crusade" in Java, to be centred around a prominent American evangelist. They are almost salivating at the thought of the new converts they will gather into the Christian fold. I think they are playing with fire. They should encourage the indigenous Christians to lead quiet lives of personal example and keep their inflammatory evangelist at home, but I say nothing. I am a mere observer.

It is time to leave. Anson and I check in at the airport, our tickets are validated, our baggage is checked, our boarding passes are issued, and our visas are cancelled. We walk across the tarmac to the airplane. There is a mechanical problem. The plane cannot leave today. We retrace our steps toward the terminal. Suddenly we are confronted by dangerous-looking uniformed, heavily armed men. Their officer demands to see our passports. He says that because we have no visas we can't enter the terminal. We cannot, as it were, disembark, even though we have not been able to embark. We expostulate. Of course we have no visas, our visas were just cancelled a few minutes ago. For a few long, agonizing minutes it has all the makings of a bizarre skit by some demented Kafka. Then an influential Indonesian associate who came to wave farewell comes to our rescue and we are grudgingly permitted one more night in Indonesia.

Anson and I fly to Thailand. From there he heads home, flying east, while I head home flying west. From Toronto, Thailand is halfway around the world and one can return either way at no extra charge. I happen to know that Carillon Films was recently in Indonesia making an industrial film, and we want to purchase stock shots. So, once again, I travel via Holland.

At home, in Canada, I write the first draft of a shooting script for our Indonesian film, which will eventually be named *Faith in Revolution*. I suggest that a final sequence make use of the Javanese villagers performing their David and Goliath dance, over which the commentator might say,

> Indonesia's Goliath is an ogre of poor communications, a struggling economy, over-population, racial and religious tensions, unstable government facing pressures from Communist and Western worlds.
> And David is very young.
> But his heart is strong.
> Indonesians know that if their David is to win his modern contest he must reach to the depths of his being and draw strength from the austere tough-mindedness of the Moslem, the sacramental awareness of the Balinese Hindu, the contemplative introspection of the Buddhist, and the strongly motivated, active social-consciousness of the Christian.

The script goes through a multi-denominational committee in New York. The more liberal members approve. The more conservative members come down on me very heavily. How dare I suggest that people should draw upon all the major religions! This is preaching syncretism! This is heresy!

I think of my father's frequent admonition that "truth" is usually found somewhere in the middle. But it's not my battle. Fighting with committees is what producers are for. I'm out of here. (I am pleased to note that the liberals won.)

Canada is still in the midst of Centennial Year and it would be pleasant to join in the festivities, but first I have to go to northern Newfoundland. I am accompanying a Toronto film producer, Richard Ballantyne. Dick owns the film rights for a novel called *Tomorrow Will Be Sunday*. It is set in Newfoundland and the author is Newfoundland's own Harold Horwood. Last year I wrote the script for a feature film adaptation and Dick and I are here now scouting for possible locations. Dick doesn't have all his financing in place yet but is confident that either the Americans or the Brits will come through. Canada's Film Development Corporation has made it possible for us to get this far. I like Harold Horwood's novel and, frankly, I like my script. So does Dick.

I lead Dick up to the Baie Verte Peninsula. I was here just last winter for a Berkeley Studio documentary called *Frontier Hospital*, and already have some locations in mind. We check them out and then Dick charters a single-engine float plane and we fly up the east coast of the Ste. Barbe Peninsula. For some time now the Newfoundland government has been closing down the outports and moving the residents to more accessible and more "civilized" communities. We land at incredible rock-bound outports, taxi in to deserted piers, wend our way on foot past the shore-side expanses of abandoned fish flakes, and walk through ghost villages with homes so intact and yet so empty that they defy description. I know it's natural for human communities to shift, change, grow, and even decay, but for them to vanish overnight by bureaucratic decree I find totally unnerving. At the same time, these remnants of a former society, perched here in wild isolation on their cliffs and inlets, are achingly and dilapidatedly beautiful. We take pictures.

The scenic wonders are only beginning. As we fly back to Baie Verte we pass over entire flotillas of icebergs. At home folks are sweating in the heat of July and here the ocean is seeded with ice. The pilot drops down and virtually motorboats through a stately field of bergs. We take more pictures.

Dick takes my film, together with his own, intending to have it processed in Toronto. All the film and his camera are stolen from his car. He doesn't get his financial backing for the feature film. His ambition to film a feature set in Newfoundland is too many years ahead of its time.[*]

Dick is an entrepreneur who has hammered his head against several cultural barricades and is finally becoming discouraged. He urges me to migrate to the States, which he says he intends to do.

"Go to the States," he says, "either Hollywood or New York. Even if you barely survive there, when you come home Canadians will think you're God."

He's correct. There is certainly a Canadian cultural mythology that any artist who doesn't prove himself in the States is, by definition, second-rate. I don't buy it, or perhaps I just don't care. I am too Canadian, too nationalistic, too little interested in achieving fame.

A little recognition would be nice, though. Fame and recognition are two different animals. The first can come quite accidentally or as the result of promotional hype, and can be quite unmerited. Recognition is more modest and far more meaningful. I know of no writer who does

---

[*]   Budge Crawley didn't produce Gordon Pinsent's *The Rowdyman* until 1971.

not hope for recognition from both public and peers. But to have the achievement of either fame or recognition as a career goal is surely a formula for misery. On the other hand, for the playwright or author, fame at least brings with it enhanced royalty cheques, but that's a whole different kettle of porridge.

By the way, Hilda and the boys and I do get to spend one excellent day at Expo 67, accompanied by a charming, mutton-chopped, gleaming-eyed, walrus-moustached, wine-loving, enthusiastic visitor from Holland.

22

THE TENTH DECADE

THE YEAR 1967 MARKS the end of Canada's first hundred years as a country, and, naturally, the end of Canada's tenth decade. And what a decade it is, with enough political turbulence to keep the ship of state constantly storm-tossed. As it begins, in 1957, John George Diefenbaker becomes prime minister. His Progressive Conservatives at first hold a tenuous grip on power, and then almost immediately afterwards win the largest majority to that date in Canadian history. From then on, he and the Liberals under Lester "Mike" Pearson are locked in mortal combat. The magnificent fighter aircraft, the Arrow, is scrapped, putting Canada's aviation industry into a nosedive. There is a Conservative caucus revolt. Pearson becomes prime minister but never achieves a majority government. The Red Ensign flag is scrapped in favour of the red Maple Leaf, and our armed services are unified into "the Forces," thereby theoretically doing away with the traditional "Canadian Army," "Royal Canadian Navy," and "Royal Canadian Air Force." The word "Royal" is being made obsolete while the monarchy remains strong. The social safety net is strengthened and the nation moves toward official bilingualism and biculturalism, while the Province of Quebec becomes more and more unilingual and French. The decade ends with Pierre Elliot Trudeau exploding into the political firmament, an event Cam Graham documents in a remarkable film called *The Style Is the Man Himself*.

And before the decade has even ended, Cam is busily convincing the CBC to underwrite a documentary TV series looking back at the political history of this whole remarkable decade. With the persuasive writing assistance of veteran journalists Peter C. Newman and Christopher Young, Cam has pried a considerable budget out of the CBC and has not only begun gathering archival material but has been filming fresh interviews with principal politicians, including John Diefenbaker and, more extensively, Mike Pearson. Cam is hoping, eventually, to spin off a series comprising Mr. Pearson's memoirs.

By 1970 the series *The Tenth Decade*, sub-titled *The Diefenbaker-Pearson Years*, is well onto the drawing boards and Cam has the script for an opening one-hour episode already on hand. However, he is unhappy with it. He invites me on board as a writer/director.

This comes at a crucial time for me.

There had been a period not long after Centennial Year when the bottom had apparently dropped out of the film business. Too many film and television budgets had been totally shot in Centennial extravaganzas. For a period of several months I had been certain I would never land another assignment. While pounding the streets of Toronto I had walked past hotels and had, metaphorically, pressed my nose against the plate glass windows of upscale stores certain I would never again enter their doorways. Was it possible the enormous surge in audio-visual creativity for Centennial Year had actually exhausted the nation's energies? Was it possible my own career was finished? I was accustomed to the momentary pause, the temporary hiatus, but this seemed otherwise. In the midst of these doldrums with no sign of an updraft I was experiencing the panic of the truly unemployed family man.

But then Berkeley Studio had suddenly come alive with a multi-screen project, *That All May be One*, and I had clambered out of the pit, that "slough of despond." And now here is Cam luring me into political history. Political history has not been my thing but I accept, feeling nervously inadequate. I protect my ego and my freelance status by initially agreeing to do only one show.

We decide to bend the format slightly by stepping backward in time and presenting thumbnail sketches of the earlier years of the two principals, Pearson and Diefenbaker. We also feel justified in re-creating the notorious Pipeline debate of 1956, because it paved the way for the fall of the St. Laurent Liberals at the beginning of the decade we are about to deal with.

Recreating the Pipeline debate is an interesting challenge. There are no visual archives from which to draw, cameras having been forbidden during any proceedings in the House of Commons. However, I am able to resurrect the actual words of the debate, which have been entombed in the pages of Hansard. We hire actors and recreate the sounds of the debate, complete with heckling, desk-thumping, singing, and general brouhaha. For visuals, we invade the empty House with a lighting crew and a highly experienced cinéma verité cameraman. While the sounds of the debate are played, lights illuminate the combatants' desks, and the cameraman tries to cover the event as though shooting a newsreel from the very floor of the Commons.

The sequence is filmed at night, when the House is empty. Indeed, most of the building is empty, except for the foyer of the House of Commons itself. This area is enclosed by heavy canvas drapes, and strange clanking noises are coming from within. During a break, I investigate. Behind the canvas barricade there is scaffolding, and on it two carvers, clad in coveralls and wearing breathing masks, are busily carving Canadian history into the limestone parapet of the balcony that surrounds the second floor of the foyer. One of the carvers is a woman, Canada's Parliamentary Sculptor, Eleanor Milne. I don't know her at the time, but she and her work will absorb much of my interest during the final decade of the century.

I love the ambience of this elegant Gothic building at night. It casts a spell over me that will last for the rest of my days.

When I began work on *The Tenth Decade* I agreed to do only the first show, but even so I am now commuting every day from Manotick into Ottawa. Not only that, but I am commuting to Crawley Films.

The CBC is renting editing suites from Budge not only for *Decade*, but, as time goes on, for other projects of Cam's. Working here gives me a case of déjà vu. I know all the senior staff, having apprenticed under some of them and alongside others. Whether I want to do some tricky shooting with old stills on the animation stand, or wish to expedite a final mix in the sound suite, or need the lab to rush an answer print, I am on familiar, friendly territory. Cam injects other staff into the mix. There are freelance film researchers Anne Acland, Bobby Turcotte, and Florence Smyth. They seem to have unlimited access to an endless stream of cards giving thumbnail descriptions of scenes in film archives in various corners of the world. When I read a thumbnail that interests me, they make the footage materialize on the editing bench. Political advisor/researcher Larry Zolf, a one-man CBC archive in himself, provides acerbic insight and wit. My indispensable associate is film editor Jim Williams. Jim is drawn from Crawley ranks and is a triple-threat player, being an experienced cameraman, picture editor, and sound editor. The series is to have original music by Larry Crosley, originally from Crawley staff but now freelance. Larry does an excellent job with the whole series and eventually migrates to the National Film Board of Canada to head up the music department.

With the first show of *The Tenth Decade* wrapped up, Cam is leaning on me to do more segments of the series, but I'm hesitant to commit to a long-term project that might appear to take me out of the freelance pool. While I'm hesitating, along comes the Opportunity of a Lifetime. I am offered the chance to write, nay, cajoled into writing, another Feature Film.

For most audio-visual freelance writers, the Holy Grail, the Brass Ring if you will, is writing for Feature Films, those entertainment flicks that adorn the cinema screens of the world. For the film writer a feature is the logical way to release the pent-up dramatic urge. Television is okay, particularly in the longer modes, but it tends to be fleeting. Feature films have a longer life. There's also good money in writing them. For years I've harboured the hope that sometime, some day, maybe, I'll break into features, and now, suddenly, just as I've taken the first hesitant step into a major political history series, along comes the opportunity. In the writing business, Opportunity is sometimes the gateway to Self-destruction.

It's the beginning of October 1970 when Graham Parker snares me. Graham (not to be confused with Cameron Graham) is a freelance film director who used to be with the National Film Board. We've known each other for some time. He directed the warlike training film I wrote for the army. Graham has lots of experience with scenes of violence, but right now he seems close to panic.

"Munroe, I need a shooting script for a feature. I need it fast. Cameras are almost ready to roll."

This is strange. Feature scripts are usually in the mill for ages, sometimes years.

"What do you mean, almost?"

"I mean, like in a few days time."

Apparently an independent film company owned by producer Bill Poulis is already renting the big Crawley shooting stage in the Gatineau Hills. A highly qualified art director has been on board and sets are ready for interior scenes. The wardrobe department is in full motion. The camera department is geared up. Lead actors have been contracted and extras are being assembled. The story is to be based on the real-life adventures of a Canadian army officer who risked his life in France during the Second World War. As an undercover liaison with the French underground, the Maquis, he helped downed airmen escape. But what's this about a script? Isn't someone a little late off the mark?

"I've got a script, but it's unshootable. I've got several. They're all crap."

Graham is a latecomer to the project and, although put off by the pile of scripts, is highly impressed by the team that Bill Poulis has assembled. So am I. Not only are the technical people highly qualified, but the two lead actors are impressive. One is Carole Laure, a young, very lovely Québécois actress. The leading man is John Juliani, a darkly handsome classically trained actor with feet already firmly planted in film, television, and theatre.

"These guys are good," says Graham. "We've got to give them something good to work with. Bill is willing."

I meet with Producer Bill Poulis, a big, pleasant man with Second World War experiences of his own. Yes, he has had other writers involved, but he has full copyright control, and, no, I am not being asked to do a patch-up of previous work, but a major rewrite. And whatever I can do, please do it fast.

This is madness. I am still waffling as whether to pick up the tools for more segments of *The Tenth Decade*. But this is an instant feature, so what the heck, this is the film business, where everything is nuts anyway, so let's go for it.

"By the way," says Graham Parker, "you won't want to waste time commuting the twenty miles in from Manotick for script conferences. Vice versa for me. I'm staying at the Château Laurier. We'll book a room for you. Bring your pyjamas and your typewriter."

So here I am away from home again, but only twenty miles away, chained to a desk in a room in the stately old Château Laurier in the heart of Ottawa.

By the time the draft of the script is half done the cameras are rolling and Graham Parker is shooting. At least I don't have to cope with story editors, a committee, and endless rewrites followed by a "polish." Polish? What's that?

At the end of each day Graham comes down from Quebec's Gatineau Hills and straight into my room. I figure things are getting a bit tight when he literally pulls the current page out of my typewriter and reads it. "Fine," he says, "I'm shooting it tomorrow morning."

I almost miss the fact that there is a "perceived insurrection" underway in Quebec. The Front de Libération du Québec radicals get out of hand and kidnap a British diplomat and a Quebec cabinet minister. They kill the latter. Prime Minister Pierre Trudeau invokes the War Measures Act, a draconian bit of legislation that sends the military to aid the police in Montreal and Quebec City and even puts armed soldiers onto Ottawa's Parliament Hill. And right now Bill Poulis and Graham Parker have a gaggle of actors running around the Gatineau woods re-enacting sabotage, subversion, and similar clandestine ventures. Suddenly the authorities take an intense interest.

The official interest escalates when several extras, taking a break, borrow a mobile prop, a genuine Second World War jeep, and slide into the city of Hull, still wearing Maquis costumes and carrying Second World War deactivated firearms. It's not the brightest of escapades. Production is slowed down radically while everyone and everything is carefully scrutinized by the RCMP.

There are other, stranger impediments. The budget comptroller for Batten Broadcasting, the distributor and principal financier, seems bent on hindering rather than aiding production. Wardrobe cannot rent sewing machines, and special effects are curtailed. A pivotal scene requires the blowing up of an old truck. To do it effectively, Graham needs either several trucks or several cameras. He gets one of each.

In spite of everything the film is completed. It's called *Inside Out*, and has a short, highly undistinguished career. As a film, it's a bad "B" but possibly a good "C," if there is such a thing. In retrospect, some of us suspect the major backer never wanted it to succeed. These are the days when Canadian feature film production is encouraged by more than 100-percent tax write-offs. A failure can be profitable. As for me, the project does nothing to enhance my resumé, and so is seldom listed. The only positive aspect of this whole fiasco, apart from the experience, is to have met John Juliani.

I return to the bosom of *The Tenth Decade*.

Production of *The Tenth Decade* is in full swing, and I, having exorcised the feature film demon, am fully involved. The series is composed of eight one-hour segments. Film editor Jim Williams and I, having completed the first episode, follow up with episodes two and three. Episodes four, five, and six are being masterminded by seasoned journalist Brian Nolan, working with film editors Bob Murphy and Peggy Chandler. Jim Williams and I move on and do shows seven and eight. The credits for some of the shows and, years later, the credits on Internet resumés list both Peter Newman and Christopher Young as writers. There is no doubt they were instrumental in selling the series to the CBC brass, but I don't believe that either of them wrote a single visual structure or narrative sentence that can be found in any of Brian's programs or mine. This is said merely for the record and not to denigrate any participant. Film and TV production is so complex that it's often all but impossible to recognize contributions. The behind-the-scenes interviewer for much of *The Tenth Decade*, particularly those sequences involving Mr. Pearson, was Bernard Ostry, but his voice is never heard, his face never appears.

The Tenth Decade is extraordinarily well received by viewers and most critics. Virtually the only reviewer who does not agree is Heather Robertson, writing in *Maclean's* magazine in December 1971. Ironically, it is her assessment that researchers prowling the Internet in the twenty-first century will find quoted at length: "[The series] contains extraordinary revelations about what kind of country Canada really has been — [a] gauche, provincial, pretentious, absurd, and incredibly colonial banana republic.... This banality is reflected, intentionally or unintentionally, in the style of *The Tenth Decade* — the pretentious, cliched titles for each program, the Gotterdammerung shots of Parliament Hill backed by Victory At Sea music...." The academic author of the encompassing article refers to this as "an all too typical example of self-contempt." I find it ironic that, in an article decrying Canadian self-contempt, the academic quotes only the self-contempt, ignoring enthusiastic reviews. "Canadian TV Comes of Age," says the Montreal *Gazette*; the series is "as breathtaking as this land." "A superview of fascinating men," declares the *Windsor Star*. "New series sees CBC-TV at its best," proclaims the *London Free Press*. (The same academic who ignores the eulogies lists the writers for the series but does not list me, who wrote five of the eight parts. The Internet is a marvellous tool but precariously unreliable.)

A year after the series has been aired, the production team is on hand as guests at a reception at Rideau Hall, the Governor General's residence. We are all delighted to witness our executive producer, Cameron Graham, receiving the Governor General's Award for Journalism. It is well earned.

By the time *The Tenth Decade* is completed Cam has another project underway. It's a series he is calling *The Days Before Yesterday*, and it is subtitled *The Struggle For Nationhood*. This series begins in the days of Sir Wilfrid Laurier at the close of the nineteenth century, and works its way forward to the beginning of the tenth decade of the twentieth. Brian Nolan is the principal writer/director for this series, although Cam throws the net over me to write and direct two one-hour segments dealing with Prime Minister Mackenzie King, one of which, "For King and Country," covers the period of the Second World War, while the other, "King of Canada," covers the post-war period up to the time of King's death in 1950.

Unlike *The Tenth Decade*, this *Days Before Yesterday* series is presented by an on-camera personality, a device that will become more and more prevalent as the years roll by. In this case, the personality is Canada's highly respected journalist and author, Bruce Hutchison. The viewer is given the impression that the "host" masterminds, shapes, and probably writes the entire program. This is seldom so. Brian and I each write the on-camera material for Mr. Hutchison for our own shows, which he vets, adjusts, and then delivers with professional aplomb. We shoot this material in the Centre Block of the Parliament Buildings. I can hardly believe that I'm being privileged to work with *the* Bruce Hutchison in this, my favourite building.

Brian and Cam have chosen actor Barry Morse as the off-camera narrative "voice" of the series. Mr. Morse has already had a distinguished career in theatre, film, and television, both in Canada and abroad. He has been so active that in a letter to a newspaper a viewer describes a nightmare in which Barry Morse plays all the positions simultaneously in a Stanley Cup hockey final. But until now I've never met him.

Mr. Morse arrives at the Crawley studios punctually. He reads my narration script, asks a few pertinent questions, marks his copy for phrasing and emphasis with his own pencilled hieroglyphics, enters the sound booth, and performs a read-through. He accepts direction from me, whom he doesn't know, with respectful attention. These are painless, pleasant sessions. I'm always impressed by our top Canadian performers. I have the distinct impression that the more famous they are the more courteous, co-operative, and professional they are. My perception seems to run counter to popular show-business mythology.

Before this, even while I am working on *The Tenth Decade*, I know that Cam has his eyes set on producing a series of half-hour programs comprising the memoirs of former Prime Minister Pearson. He has already filmed more than one hundred hours of interviews with "Mike." While structuring my shows for *The Tenth Decade* I have read the transcripts of all these interviews, have screened most of them, and have used some of them. Before *Decade* is completed I am certain that I want to be the writer/director of this memoirs series. I am captivated not only by Mr. Pearson's candour and personality but by the ease with which he responds to interviewer Bernard Ostry's questions. I also notice his answers are invariably complete. One doesn't have to hear the question to understand the answer. I become convinced we can fashion a memoirs series featuring just Mr. Pearson himself, aided by archival footage, stills, and music, with no supplementary intrusion by either a host or a narrator.

Cam agrees, and after I have disposed of Mackenzie King he launches me into what becomes a series of thirteen half-hour programs called *First Person Singular*, and sub-titled *The Pearson Memoirs*. I am again fortunate to have Jim Williams at my side as editor.

These memoirs call for a change of focus. Until now, I've been called upon to view subjects at documentary arm's-length and to make an effort to present both pros and cons — to present the conflict and the chaos; the good, the bad, and the warts. But in these memoirs the TV medium is being handed over to Mr. Pearson. It's his version, his story, his life. My function as writer/director is to fit his story to the medium by reducing more than one hundred hours of conversation to about six hours, structuring it so it has pace, interest, and progression, and at the same time attempting to remain ruthlessly faithful to the context. For me as a writer this is the ultimate "bushel basket" production. The core material, the Pearson interviews, already exists as endless hours of filmed conversation, but it is unstructured, unedited. I meet Mr. Pearson, but only a few times. We have personal conversations, but I, personally, never take a camera near him. Eventually, however, I feel as though I have been living in his brain.

There is no "voice of God" narrator, so all transitions in thought, context, time, and place must be handled by archival material such as newspaper headlines, old newsreels, and stock shots. Even when Mike's thoughts flow coherently, if the visual interview does not edit smoothly it will be necessary to bridge the roughness with suitable archival material. It's a nice challenge. I am "writing" something that is pure structure. This is where audio-visual writing parts company with all other forms. This is the writer as architect. No word of mine will be heard or appear. I am concerned solely with structure. But, since I am also wearing the "director" hat, I have to make it happen. Again, this is not the directorial function of popular perception, where the commander sits in a chair with a megaphone, issuing orders to the legions. This is the quiet, patient, behind-the-scenes design and assembly of an edifice.

The research crew is searching for visual material that will be specific enough to lead the viewer's mind and eye where I want it to go. At the editing bench, Jim is knitting it together. But more help is required. It must come from the music. Original music can close thoughts, open new ones, and set the mood. Cam agrees to hire Toronto freelance composer

Herbert Helbig, with whom I have collaborated before.* Herb is also a classical pianist and, as a freelance artist, has other strings to his bow. Not only is he the pianistic mainstay for the beloved children's TVO program *Polka Dot Door*, but for several years during this period he plays piano in Club 22 at Toronto's elegant old-world Windsor Arms hotel.

The challenge facing Herb is daunting. He comes on board when the visual for each program is virtually locked off with respect to length. He composes a number of themes that will be useful throughout the series to identify subjects subliminally and to reinforce memory. But he also has to take over from Mike's narration to change the mood, alter the pace, or set up a total change of location.

"Look," I may say to him as we peer at the view screen on the editing bench, "over the long shot of those troops marching off into the hills of Macedonia we've got to wind up that segment and switch to academia. When we come back to Mike on camera he's left Macedonia and is talking about military training at Oxford. We've got to be ready for it. You've got 46 seconds of screen time."

And Herb does it, musically.

Herb's task is completed in a sound studio in Toronto, where he brings together a hand-picked group of musicians who coalesce almost instantly under his direction into an orchestra. Again, the professionalism of these people is remarkable. Herb has a stopwatch on his music stand. I am in the control room, also armed with a stopwatch. We both know the selections that are the most sensitive. If music must enter the moment a heavy newsreel sound effect finishes and must stop, naturally, the moment before Mr. Pearson begins to speak, then it must be crafted to the half-second. When either Herb or I spot poor timing, he and his orchestra stretch the piece or condense it with laid-back aplomb. These artists are working inside a ruthless straitjacket that viewers should never realize is there.

Even as our series gets into production, Cam, Jim, Herb, and I know we have a non-broadcast deadline, but it's one that must not be allowed to jeopardize the overall project. Mike Pearson is dying. He has cancer. Before the interviews were all filmed he had an operation to remove one eye. It speaks volumes for the man that even under the severe scrutiny of the camera his deteriorating health is barely noticeable. We desperately want Mike to see at least the opening show of his series, but we don't quite make it. Mr. Pearson dies on December 27, 1972. The first

---

*   Berkeley Studio's Inner City (see Chapter 20).

print of the first show is in our hands a few days later, but the series air date is five months away.

During the build-up to *The Tenth Decade* the CBC promotional department published glossy brochures and issued press releases ballyhooing the show, without, however, mentioning either Brian Nolan or me. ACTRA (Association of Canadian Television and Radio Artists) protested rather vigorously. Now, the CBC, graciously accepting chastisement, sends Cam and me on a promotional tour for the Pearson series, first to the Maritimes and then to Alberta. CBC Halifax employees receive us courteously, but in Calgary we escape with our lives only by constantly reminding folk we are not from Toronto. Interesting country, Canada.

The series begins on the CBC network on Sunday, May 27, 1973, at 10:00 P.M.

Reviews are overwhelmingly positive, with the *Ottawa Citizen*'s Frank Penn greeting the first episode with startled enthusiasm. Apparently he expected an anti-climax to *The Tenth Decade*, and has instead found something "as close to a work of genius as we're likely to see on the screen for a long time." By the end of episode thirteen he has calmed down a little and settles for the adjective "brilliant."* For some time I have thought that Frank Penn is a good reviewer, and of course I see no reason to change my opinion, even though he has never mentioned my name.

---

* The Ottawa Citizen, 28 May and 20 August 1973.

23

THE RESURRECTION
OF GOVERNOR WU

DURING THE YEARS I've been involved with Cameron Graham's ventures in very Canadian political history an oriental story has been haunting me. It is the dramatic tale of a real-life Confucian governor and it has to do with cultural terrorism, headhunting, and leadership by example. As a project it comes to full fruition in 1974, but it has in fact has been hovering in the back of my brain for years, inhabiting, as it were, a parallel universe.

Let us leave the realm of public affairs television and step aside into that parallel world. Come with me again, back in time to 1960 and across the globe to Taiwan, on my research trip with Anson Moorhouse.

This Taiwan is a colonial society. At the moment, 1960, the colonial power is the Nationalist government in exile, which is ruling Taiwan while masquerading as the government of mainland China. But from the end of the nineteenth century until 1945 the island was under Japanese rule. Indeed, most educated Taiwanese can speak excellent Japanese. There was at one time a period of Portuguese colonial rule. But for centuries the principal ruling power has been Chinese. To the rulers in Peking ("Beijing" was not forced into the English language until the late 1970s) Taiwan has been, and still is, a "province." The majority of Taiwanese have their racial and cultural roots in China, just as my roots are in Great Britain. But they are Taiwanese the way I am Canadian. The "mainlanders" are recent immigrant Chinese who have come in, as we Anglo-Canadians would say, "from the Old Country."

But look to those rugged mountains that run down the spine of the island. They are the traditional home of the original inhabitants, the tribal folk of Taiwan. The tribal folk are not Chinese. They are themselves.

Traditionally the tribal people had been headhunters. For a while prior to 1769 the Chinese Emperor had managed to prohibit the custom, but that year there was a resurgence of the old urge and the Emperor's representative, Governor Wu-feng, had to suppress it. Being a Confucian pacifist he had adopted a most unusual diplomatic subterfuge.

I learn about Governor Wu from the Canadian couple with whom we are billeted in Taipei, Bruce and Marnie Copland (whom we met in chapter 14). They are in Taiwan with the Canadian Presbyterian mission, on loan from the United Church of Canada. Bruce is a clergyman with a flair for organization. He is gentle, calm, and cerebral. One would never guess that he has been through perilous adventures in mainland China during the recent Sino-Japanese War.*

Marnie is the one with China in her bones. Having spent her childhood in China, she learned Mandarin as a child and now is quite comfortable speaking Cantonese. She is at home in the culture. She paints Chinese style. She likes stories and she loves drama. She also likes old houses — there is an old stone house in the Ottawa Valley that is part of her family lore. I know that old house. Hilda and I almost bought it. Marnie and I have drama and one old Ontario house in common.

We visit temples. I am fascinated by Buddhist temples. Some are very poor, others almost opulent. All, to a westerner in 1960, are mysterious. Marnie explains the meanings of the fierce-visaged guardian gods and of the curved roofs with their dog-like figures that keep evil at bay. The symbolism of a multi-layered universe inhabited by a myriad of gods and spirits is almost too rich for a visitor to absorb.

The Confucian temples are quite different. They are serene to the point of severity. The roofs still curve gracefully and the pillars and carved woodwork are painted red, but here there are no effigies of spirits or gods, good or evil. There are name boards honouring ancestors, but it is not gods that rule here, but intellect and character.

We visit a Confucian temple dedicated to the memory of one man. His name was Wu-feng.

Marnie is bubbling with the story of Wu-feng. His father was what we would call an "Indian agent"; he worked with the tribal mountain people in the mid-1700s while the son was growing up. As a child Wu-feng, although Chinese, was immersed in tribal culture. As a youth in Peking he was formally educated in the Confucian tradition of leadership by example. As a man he was sent by the Emperor to be Governor of the tribal people he had learned to love as a child.

---

*   We like to think of this as merely part of the Second World War, but for the Chinese that "world war" was merely the final convulsion that brought their longer war to an end.

Among the tribal folk, headhunting had been part of an elaborate cultural tradition. For many years the Emperor had discouraged the practice, but during Wu-feng's regime a series of droughts, famines, and other problems brought a resurgence of the headhunting urge. The gods must be placated. So adamant were the tribes on this matter that Governor Wu realized there was no way he could prevent the taking of a head. He knew, however, that reckless decapitation of neighbours would not only spark inter-tribal warfare but would also bring down the wrath of the Emperor's army.

The Governor made a deal. Rather than allow a victim to be killed at random some dark night beside a lonely trail, he would select a candidate and designate a time and a place. The tribe could have its ritual. It seemed like a hard-headed but excellent political solution to a delicate problem, for it appeared likely the victim would be a condemned felon.

The designated victim was taken and beheaded. It turned out to be the beloved Governor Wu himself.

So appalled were the tribesmen at what they had done that an inter-tribal council was called and a great oath was sworn to abandon headhunting. The year was 1769. The oath has held to this day.

Marnie is enthralled by this story. So am I. It has incredible universal overtones. It has Christian overtones. It is Christ on the cross. It is the martyrdom of the saints. "Greater love hath no man than this...."

Marnie has been into the mountains to visit the descendants of the Ali tribe, whose forbears beheaded their governor. She has pictures of them in tribal costume. They look to me like our west coast Haida. She has a file folder full of information. She says she has already tried to write a play about Governor Wu but it doesn't work. She gives me her file and says she is throwing the torch to me, no strings.

The ghost of Governor Wu haunts me for years. I, too, try to write a play about him. It's a great story idea and I always take courage from the knowledge that there is a historical root to a dramatic situation. But I am neither Taiwanese nor Chinese. I am out of my culture. I can't make it gel. Something is wrong.

It is 1969 and the National Arts Centre in Ottawa is opening for the first time. Hilda and I go to an Open House and tour the building.

There is an Opera house, an experimental Studio space, and the Theatre. In the Theatre my heart almost stops. It is beautiful. Spacious but intimate. It has a proscenium stage, but — *Joy, oh joy!* — it can be converted to the open thrust mode, and right now, at the time of this my first visit, that is how it is displayed!

The last eighteen years dissolve away. I am at Cornell University taking my Master's degree in drama, and my chosen area of study is the open stage, the thrust stage, Shakespeare's stage gone modern. I love the concept. At that time there is almost no professional theatre in Canada, and there are certainly no thrust stages, so after graduation I get into film writing. Shakespeare would have been a film writer, too.

Now, eighteen years later, Canada is awash with thrust stages, the premier one being at Ontario's Stratford. And here, in Ottawa, nineteen miles from my own front door, is this pristine, gorgeous creation, the National Arts Centre Theatre.

But I see more than the theatre and the stage.

Hilda waits patiently as the tour moves on its way and I loiter behind, stretching a moment of wonder, even awe. I am seeing a phantom. The figure of Governor Wu is standing centre stage, clothed in the full ceremonial regalia of a Mandarin official, and he is beckoning to me.

This is it. This is the catalyst I have needed. This theatre, and this stage, have been created for the resurrection of Governor Wu.

For the next few days I am in a trance. I can't sleep. I slip out three nights in a row while it is still dark, creep through the backyard to our dock on the Manotick millpond, and slide the canoe onto the waters of the lazy Rideau River. I paddle quietly upstream, then drift back down with the gentle current, visions of the Governor in my head. I am obsessed.

The third night I am moving so quietly I almost run down a foraging beaver. He dives, not a foot away from the canoe, and his warning tail-slap sounds like a cannon. I almost have a heart attack. But it jolts me into action.

I write a letter to Hamilton Southam, the moving power behind the National Arts Centre and now its Director General. I am not rational enough to know it, but this letter is not my smartest move, although I begin rationally enough.

Dear Mr. Southam,

You have created a superb Arts Centre.

Your biggest challenge is to create at least one, please God, major Canadian playwright for English-language theatre, and how much raw material you are going to have to consume in that endeavour, God alone knows.

I go on, however, to present myself as eligible raw material, outlining my academic qualifications and my film and television experience, of which I've been accumulating a certain amount, and unfortunately I do the enumeration at length. It goes on and on for two pages, more than six hundred words. I am enthusiastic but I am quite out of my tree. Even so, I do end in a reasonably sane fashion:

> I saw the interior of the Arts Centre for the first time on the day of the Open House. I walked into "The Theatre" and went out of my skull! The last twenty years suddenly formed a pattern and made sense, and I have a play to write for you that has been wandering my mind for several years looking for a place to call home.
> Can you and the theatre use me?
> Respectfully yours,

But I'm not through yet. I have to throw in a postscript:

> P.S. Sorry to be so importunate, but ever since walking into "The Theatre" last week I have had the most pressing awareness imaginable of what Skakespeare meant about the tide in the affairs of men!

Within three days I receive a brief reply from Mr. Southam:

> … where English theatre is concerned we are … arranging for the Stratford National Theatre to carry the heat and burden of the day. I am therefore passing your letter on to Jean Gascon, Stratford's Artistic Director.

If Stratford receives the letter, no one reacts.

Hilda and I attend a gala opening performance at the Centre, which is followed by a reception for the general public. During the reception, an enthusiastic friend and old Crawley associate, Wanda Nowakowska, propels me up to Hamilton Southam, who is holding casual court. Wanda is one of those members of Ottawa's Polish-Canadian community who seem to move with great ease through the mysterious labyrinths of Ottawa society. She knows the influential Mr. Southam on a first-name basis. Wanda introduces me, effusively, as "one of Canada's best writers." There's no fan like a good friend.

Well, what the hell. In for a penny, in for a pound.

"We've almost met," I say, shaking the Southam hand and wondering whether I should kiss his ring. "I wrote to you recently."

"Yes, I know," says the tall and imposing Mr. Southam, looking down at me through the most impressive and homeliest face I have ever seen. "Because someone says he's good doesn't mean you commission him to write a play."

I back off, curl up inside, and turn to stone.

I hear fashionable Mrs. Southam saying to another society lady that with all the creative people around she'd simply love to establish a kind of cultural salon, a Camelot North.

I am still determined to write Governor Wu's play and so discuss Wu-feng with my two favourite CBC Drama story editors, David Peddie and Doris Gauntlett. Perhaps there is a home for the Governor on TV. I feel comfortable talking to both David and Doris because we meet on the ground of mutual respect.

"It's a marvellous story," says Doris.

"A great idea," says David.

I am elated. Then —

"It's not for TV." They both seem to agree. "You're right the first time. It's for the stage."

I am back to square one, but my two advisors are determined to be helpful. "How about writing for a specific actor? That can help clarify problems. It can also give you a theatrical toehold when you're done."

That, I agree, is an interesting suggestion.

"Any ideas?"

"Well," says David, "I can see John Colicos as Wu-feng."

As a matter of fact, so can I. So can Doris.

"David," she says, "you know John."

Indeed he does. Colicos was best man at David's wedding. And presto! Here I am in the Pilot Tavern on Yonge Street just north of Bloor, hoisting a late afternoon beer or two with one of Canada's leading actors.

Mr. Colicos is a little withdrawn, but has accepted the rendezvous most obligingly. Few actors actually shun free booze, but I'm flattered that such an established thespian is willing to take time out for an informal chat. He listens patiently as I rhapsodize about Governor Wu and his remarkable self-sacrifice. Mr. Colicos asks a few pertinent questions, makes a few minor suggestions, and is non-committal about my enthusiasm for the open stage. He seems to think it's an acceptable idea to write the play with him in mind, but makes no commitment other than to read the manuscript whenever it is completed.

I resolve to get to work, but still know deep in my heart that an ingredient is missing.

And then it happens.

October 1970. The Front de Libération du Québec, the FLQ, kidnap British diplomat James Cross and Quebec cabinet minister Pierre Laporte. They issue a manifesto. They murder Laporte. Prime Minister Trudeau, at the request of Quebec's Premier Bourassa, invokes the War Measures Act. The proverbial is well and truly into the fan.

As a Canadian I am appalled by the FLQ. As a democrat I am appalled by the War Measures Act. As a dramatist my creative juices are ignited. Suddenly I know what my play is all about. It's not about Governor Wu, or Taiwanese history, it's about the upsurge of one culture within the bosom of another. It's about tribalism within a federal state. It's about political blackmail with the threat of violence. It's about terrorism. It's about us. The Taiwanese background is merely a device that allows the dramatist to hold his subject at arm's length.

I write the first draft almost non-stop. I create characters out of whole cloth. The High-Chief's son, Margama, who leads the rebels, is a figment of my imagination. History be damned. Governor Wu is not a Confucian gentleman, he is *my idea* of a Confucian gentleman, austere in his habits, unfailingly polite, a little absent-minded, and childishly optimistic; he has a wry sense of humour and an ethical backbone made of carbon steel.

I see him as a man who can turn to a potential assassin and say,

> I am armed only with words. You may choose knives if you must, but it will be a poor discussion.

He is a man who has the power to summon armed might but who will not do so, as Margama well knows:

> To negotiate with troops would be to admit that your life's work has been a failure.

The Governor believes that personal example is a more potent weapon:

> When the Master wanted to live among the tribes a courtier said, "But they're so crude!" "Ah" said the Master, "if only True Man were living amongst them, how could they be crude? His very presence would alter all that."

Margama sees this as weakness:

> He will not oppose us with force. His religion forbids it, his vanity
> prevents it. The mere threat of the Act of Purification makes us mas-
> ters in our own mountains.

The "Act of Purification" involves the taking of a head. As tensions esca-
late, Margama and the Governor engage in debate:

> MARGAMA: We are done with being forced to be what we are not.
> WU-FENG: What is this thing you are not which you seem to fear so
> greatly you will become?
> MARGAMA: You ask that! Clothed in your foreign robes, speaking
> the foreign tongue!
> WU-FENG: You mistake the clothing for the man. The language for
> the thought!
> MARGAMA: Forgive me. "Become" is too strong. You would merely
> have us lose ourselves within them.
> WU-FENG: Only as a man loses himself in a woman, to merge the
> strength of one with the beauty of the other to see what new child
> the gods will send.

The rebellion escalates, Margama loses control, and the Governor is
faced with his ultimate decision:

> Am I a coward, afraid to use armed authority? But one in authority
> must lead through example. Will they see only the example of a fool-
> ish man going to a foolish end? Yet Father Confucius described the
> path to excellence and if I will not follow through a little darkness
> then I have no faith in the Wisest of the Wise. "Excellence will attract
> excellence." Since that is what I believe, what I must do I will do.

I complete the draft, make revisions, and go away on other business,
while Hilda, typing a clean manuscript, is the first to meet my Wu-feng.
I phone her. She has just finished the final scene. "I love it," she says. "I
want to cry." Crying is not high on the list of priorities for my Lancashire
lass. Her current reading is Barbara Tuchman's *The Guns of August*.

My first step is to send the manuscript to John Colicos, along with a self-
addressed stamped envelope. I give him some time, and then, having

received no reply, phone to ask if I may drop around to his place for a reaction and, if necessary, to reclaim my manuscript.

Colicos lives in one of those quiet Toronto residential areas that are comfortably gracious without being ostentatious. I go to the front door in great trepidation. This can be one of life's defining moments. I ring the doorbell.

John opens the door. He is wearing a silken dressing gown with a velvet collar and has a pleasingly theatrical air. I am prepared to enter the inner sanctum to discuss the magic of the open stage, symbolism in drama, and *Wu-feng* as a metaphor for our troubled Canadian multicultural state. Mr. Colicos has my manuscript in his hand. He passes it to me and makes only one comment.

"I am grooming myself for leading man roles. I see your Governor Wu as very fat."

He smiles courteously, nods good-bye, and closes the door.

It is now 1971. I send the manuscript to Toronto's St. Lawrence Centre. Eventually I am given an appointment with the Centre's dramaturge. He's friendly and complimentary but our meeting is held in the lobby, where he returns the manuscript.

"This has some very funny lines," he says, and heads for the door.

I decide to tackle the National Arts Centre once again, and here, at the NAC, I actually have a face-to-face chat with Jean Gascon, Stratford's Artistic Director,* who, apparently, really has been designated by Hamilton Southam "to carry the heat and burden of the day." I am overawed to meet him. Many years ago, in 1956, Hilda and I saw Stratford's *Henry V* when the main stage was still under canvas. The English court was played by Anglo-Canadian actors, headed by Christopher Plummer, and the French court was played by French-Canadian actors, headed by Jean Gascon. When the play ended I sat spellbound and almost in tears. I felt we had just glimpsed the enormous potential for creativity in the two mainstream cultures if only we could continue to bring them into catalytic convergence.

I find it somewhat ironic that Hamilton Southam has said that the fate of the Arts Centre's English language theatre will be in the hands of Stratford, and now Stratford's fate is in the hands of a French-Canadian. But I cannot be cynical in the presence of Jean Gascon. He is courteous,

Gallic, and thoroughly charming. He asks me to send a copy of *Wu-feng* to Michael Bawtree, his assistant at Stratford.

Don Jack comes to visit. We are both infatuated by the stage, but there is a difference — Don has already had stage plays produced, *Exit Muttering* in Toronto and (ultimate achievement!) *The Canvas Barricade* on the main stage at the Stratford Festival. As a sanity check I ask Don to read *Wu-feng*. He settles down in our Manotick living room and I discreetly vanish.

I manage to re-materialize just as he finishes reading. I walk in, sit down, and say nothing. He says nothing. He is looking very thoughtful. This is a tough moment. Friends assessing the work of friends can be a delicate exercise.

"It's okay," I say. "Be honest."

He nods. "I wish I'd written it."

I wish I'd written it. That's the best review I've ever had.

But Don continues. "Let me show it to Rolf Kalman."

"Who's Rolf?"

"He's a new Canadian. One of the mad Hungarians." There's nothing derogatory in this comment. Back in my Crawley days the staff, sparked by compassionate Ed Reid, opened an Ottawa refuge house for Hungarians who had been forced to flee after the spectacular uprising of 1956. They proved to be an assortment of volatile, eccentric, and highly creative people.

"He's in theatre?"

"No. He's a stevedore at Toronto harbour, but he's publishing a collection of Canadian plays." Of course.

"He's including my *Exit Muttering*," says Don, "but I want him to see this."

"But it's never been produced."

Don shrugs. "Like I said, Rolf's Hungarian."

Rolf Kalman is a character out of novel. He is a solidly built man, not tall, with the round head and broad shoulders of his people. He is ruggedly handsome, with heavy eyebrows and wavy hair. His English is excellent and is propelled by an eclectic mind. Rolf was raised in the cultured salons of Budapest and studied law. Here in Canada he actually apprenticed as a director with CBC-TV, but couldn't abide the cultural bureaucracy and has opted to work on the docks as a longshoreman, a proud owner of a union card, while simultaneously creating his own cultural niche. He and his Canadian wife, Betsy, a nurse, have an apartment in the Toronto Beaches area overlooking the boardwalk and the lake. They have two cats, a Siamese and a Blue Russian. Rolf loves cats.

Rolf has ambitious plans. He intends to publish several volumes of plays under the simple title, *A Collection of Canadian Plays*. The collections will be published in hardback, but each individual play will also be published in paperback to make it accessible for production.

"I want to include *Wu-feng* in Volume One," he says. "It will be the only one that has not yet been produced."

"But that means no production photos. You say the others will be illustrated."

"Yours will be illustrated. I know a fine artist. She's Chinese."

My diffident Canadian brain has difficulty with the fact that my play has not yet been on a stage. Very patiently Rolf explains the facts of life. While talking, he holds a cigarette in one hand and cradles a tumbler of brandy in the other.

"Everywhere else in the world," he says, "in the States, in England, in Europe, producers want to see a manuscript with the ink still wet. They hug it to themselves, hoping to get it on the boards before anyone else. In Canada that's not the case. Here they want to know that someone else has approved of it. If I publish *Wu-feng*, you can count on it, someone will produce it."

It seems possible that Rolf will preside over the resurrection of Governor Wu.

In the meantime I show the manuscript to George Luscombe, the founder and head of Toronto Workshop Productions (TWP). I met George back in *Inquiry* days, having cast him as a pyromaniac in a Justice segment. George has a penchant for ensemble productions in which the cast becomes a committee of writers. This is not, to my mind, the way to get powerful, cohesive drama, but I like George, admire him, and value his opinion. I don't expect him to produce this play.

George astonishes me. He reads *Wu-feng* and becomes quite excited. "I'll do it."

"You can't. It's too big." What's going on here? I'm the one who's supposed to be selling the idea.

"It's not big at all. It's a little fable. We'll treat it as such."

George is alive with ideas. His large expressive eyes fairly gleam. He will use life-sized puppets. Two extras can carry a whole tribe of puppets on a long pole. He will use black light. He will borrow from Chinese theatre. We will combine some characters and tighten up dialogue, but stylization can make the whole thing work.

"I'll ask the gang for a reading, just for you and me. Besides, I won't produce it without their approval."

"The gang" is George's current company of young actors, and sure enough, one afternoon when I happen to be in Toronto he assembles them all on the stage and assigns parts; he and I are an audience of two, and we hear a reading.

George seems pleased, and I am ecstatic. There are some dialogue clunkers, but in general the play works!

We all assemble in the Green Room, which at the moment is also the front office. There's nothing posh about TWP. The mood seems a little strained, and there's some whispered conversation. George asks me to take a half-hour walk.

I return to find George much subdued. Most of the company has gone. Those who are still here leave in a friendly but quiet fashion.

"I want to do it," says George, "but they don't. I won't force it on them."

"What's their objection?"

"You betray the beautiful young people who are trying to reassert their cultural roots. They turn out to be monsters." He shrugs apologetically and looks sad. I suspect that poor old George has himself created a monster by abandoning creative control to a gaggle of actors. But being a writer, I'm prejudiced.

Eventually Stratford reacts to the manuscript after a time lapse of a mere seven months, which is not unusual in Canadian theatre, where, I will find, a not uncommon reaction time is never. Michael Bawtree, Gascon's assistant, has just dug himself out from under a pile of material and seems genuinely apologetic. His letter, although a rejection, is far from standard. He writes,

> *Wu-feng* is, as you know, well-written and splendidly unusual in subject matter.... The idea of the play is spacious and heroic.

He makes a few critical comments that are well founded and helpful. It's the kind of letter that encourages a writer. There is, however, a paragraph that depresses a *Canadian* writer.

> As far as Stratford is concerned, the problem is one of size.... [T]he Third Stage, where from now on we will be doing the majority of our new work, simply will not have the budget for a play of such scope. You will reply, "What about the Festival Stage?" But our policy for the last few years ... is to keep the "classics" on the Festival Stage and let their inordinate success subsidize, in effect, the work

at the Avon and Third Stage. Eventually I hope this policy will be modified....*

There is no mention of the National Arts Centre, probably because the NAC now has a new Director of Theatre. Her name is Jean Roberts.

In the meantime, Laurier Lapierre talks with me about launching an assault on the NAC. He is, as usual, bursting with creative ideas and suggests we co-operate in creating a play based on John A. MacDonald and the Pacific Scandal. I write a nebulous outline for such a play. Laurier submits it to Jean Roberts and also passes the *Wu-feng* manuscript along, like a salesman submitting a sample.

Months go by and it is now 1972. I write to Miss Roberts in January and phone her twice in February. By this time I am merely hoping to retrieve my manuscript.

In March, Hilda and I go to Spain for a two-week holiday to preserve my brain from *Tenth Decade* overload. We return via London, where I have already contacted the agents Frazer & Dunlop Scripts Limited. I meet with a young man, Richard Wakeley, who promises to contact me as soon as he has read *Wu-feng*. A letter from Wakeley reaches home almost before I do:

> I would like to say straight away that it is, in my opinion, a very well written and constructed piece of drama.... [But] it is certainly not what managements over here are looking for. I fully agree that this is far more suitable for the open stage than for the Proscenium Arch and as I explained, theatres with the former are few and far between over here.

There is also a letter awaiting me from Miss Roberts. It is a courteous, apologetic, depressed letter that says no to both John A. and Governor Wu and, in a way, to the future:

> There was a time when there was a glimmer of light ... but that glimmer has now faded.

I am saddened, not by the rejection but by the tone of the letter. I suspect that the Ottawa bureaucracy is about to make a meal of the dedicated Miss Roberts.

---

*   Three decades later the policy remains unchanged.

Volume One of *A Collection of Canadian Plays* is published as promised. It is a "Bastet Book," named after the Egyptian cat goddess; Bastet is an imprint of Rolf Kalman's new publishing company, Simon & Pierre, which is named after his two exotic cats. Simon & Pierre is surely the only publishing company in the world to be founded by two cats and a stevedore. The moment when Rolf hands me my copy of Volume One* is enshrined in memory as one of the emotional peaks of my career.

The book is a production of high quality in every way, and, as promised, *Wu-feng* is adorned with magnificent full-page illustrations by Toronto artist Madame Shiu-Yu. The pictures are Chinese rather than Taiwanese, and certainly not evocative of the Ali tribe, but I am not about to quibble. The mood is perfect. Marnie Copland thinks so, too. She writes,

> It's a beautiful book…. And I'm terribly impressed with what you have done with *Wu-feng*. I realize that you have shaped history to your own ends, but the spirit of *Wu-feng* is served better because of what you have done.

Literary reviewers pay attention to Rolf's efforts and a few single out *Wu-feng*. I am not one of those writers who never reads reviews. I *always* read reviews. In this country, whose citizens like to be told what to think about cultural matters, reviewers can make or break a publication or a production. Unfortunately, many reviewers have no credentials to justify their opinions, but I have developed an easy way to assess a review's merits. If I agree with what is said, then it is a good review. If I don't, it's not.

I approve of Doug Bale's assessment in *The London Free Press*:

> *Wu-feng* … is an epic that would have done credit to a Chinese Bertolt Brecht…. It is also sweeping, subtle, profoundly philosophical, immaculately constructed and — incredibly — still unproduced two years after it was written.

Obviously, Bales is an astute man. Dave Woolner of the *Edmonton Journal* is another astute fellow:

> One result of the book — I hope — may be the staging of Ontario dramatist Munroe Scott's intriguing open-stage work, *Wu-feng*…. Almost Socratic in its theme, without being ponderous, it should be a pleasure for actor and audience alike.

---

* *A Collection of Canadian Plays* eventually consists of four volumes.

Now, armed with the paperback version of *Wu*, I get down to business and send copies to the artistic directors of ten theatres, including one to England and one to Michael Langham at the Guthrie Theatre in Minneapolis. Both Langham and his theatre are descendants of our own Stratford Festival. I hear nothing from abroad, but receive acknowledgement of receipt from four Canadian theatres and a follow-up from two of those, one of which is a rejection.

The positive follow-up is from John Juliani, in Vancouver, who has created a theatrical group called Savage God. John wants to present a public reading of *Wu-feng*.

John's first love is theatre, and Hilda and I have seen a production of *Peer Gynt* that he directed at Ottawa University. He draped the entire interior of Academic Hall with parachute silk. It was like entering a womb, and the entire area was both stage and auditorium. Audience members sat wherever they wished, mostly on cushions. Some were seated inside the risers, their heads protruding through holes and up through the silk surround. Hilda and I were ensconced cozily out of harm's way in the corner of a ramp, which was fine until we heard an actor declaiming just above us and looked up to see a totally naked *Peer Gynt* striding down the ramp. It presented an unusual perspective on the anatomy of the play. I know that whatever John decides to do will have flair.

Public readings can be useful. Ideally, they are followed by a discussion with the audience, and ideally the playwright is present to participate. In Canada, though, our geography is against us. It would be easier for me to get to London, England, for a one-night reading than to Vancouver.

It is now October 1972, and I have received a lengthy letter from John. He has finally managed the reading and encloses the one and only newspaper clipping. The headline banners *Humour Redeems Windy Play*. Christopher Dafoe, the critic, is less corrosive than the headline:

> The play is an ambitious work that cries out for spectacular presentation after the manner of Peter Shaffer's celebrated Royal Hunt of the Sun.... It is a fairly windy piece of work that is redeemed by a generous portion of humour, a touch or two of serene poetry and a measure of cool wisdom.... One hopes to hear more of *Wu-feng*.

John writes that he managed to lure Paxton Whitehead, Artistic Director of both the Vancouver Playhouse and Ontario's Shaw Festival, into the audience. The letter doesn't tell me what Paxton thought, but I can read between John Juliani's lines:

The cast quite loved the play and the majority of the "untutored" audience members did too — but the "experts" (oh god, spare us!) the experts quibbled like crazy. Or at least those in a position to get the thing on did.... In the meantime I am trying still to get *Wu-feng* on the Simon Frazer U curriculum — what an ordeal that is!!

Anyway, I take heart. The resurrection of Governor Wu may be slow, but at least people are working at it. Bob Reid gives it a try. He writes to Bob Wood of CBS telling him that the play has potential as a TV drama special.

CBS requests a copy of *Wu* and encloses a release form that seems to say that if anything appears to be pirated from my script I can take CBS to the New York Supreme Court. How reassuring. I send both script and form off by return mail and only two weeks later am reading a polite rejection letter. Americans don't mess around.

It is now 1973. The year gets off to a good start with a note from Maurice Podbrey, founder and head of Montreal's English-language Centaur Theatre, one of the four directors who received last year's mailing:

I seem not to have replied to you and I apologize sincerely for the oversight. We have just read your play and it has made a great impression on us all. Please allow me to hold onto the script a little longer so that I can consider possibilities....

So far so good. Things may be looking up.

It is March. Hilda and Rob and I see *The Tempest* in the National Arts Centre Studio. It is presented "in the round," with most of the audience sitting on the surrounding balcony peering down into the play, and it is a marvellous, innovative production starring internationally known John Neville as Prospero. I watch eleven-year-old Rob, whom most people think of as a jock, and he is enthralled.

I see by the program that John Neville has just been named Artistic Director of Edmonton's Citadel Theatre. Hey, the *Edmonton Journal* gave a good review of the published *Wu*. Neville should see that.

The next day I am on the phone to the Arts Centre but am told that Neville is in his dressing room and has no phone. I leave my name and phone number, but to no avail.

I try again the following day and am now told there is no matinee performance and Mr. Neville is not expected in until the evening. The switchboard has no Ottawa address for him. I call the Stage Door. They have no Ottawa address for their principal actor. I call the Theatre Department and they don't think they have an address but are willing to look. While they do so, the phone gets cut off. I phone Miss Robert's secretary. She gives me Mr. Neville's apartment address but has no phone number. I phone the apartment superintendent. He has no number for Mr. Neville. I try the fount of all communication knowledge, Bell Information. Bell has no Neville listing.

Does this man really exist or is he in town only as Prospero?

Well, there's no matinee today, so at noon I drive into Ottawa and go to the Algonquin Hotel Annex, 196 Metcalfe Street, and am pleased to find the name Neville on the building directory. It is spelled Niville, but never mind.

I push the button for # 607 and a man's voice comes from the inter-com.

"My name is Scott," I say, "and I am a writer. May I come up and talk to you for ten minutes?"

The voice says, "I am having a shower and I have an appointment at one o'clock." The intercom goes dead.

My watch says it is now twenty-five minutes to one, but there is a buzzing sound and the "Enter" sign lights up.

I enter and make my way up to 607, very nervous at the prospect of meeting one of Canada's, and Britain's, major actors. Selling one's product and one's self is not my favourite pastime.

I knock on the door and a voice projects through the wood. Actors have disconcerting vocal capabilities. "Who's there?" The tone does not sound hospitable.

"Munroe Scott, I just called from the lobby." Is my voice shaking?

The door opens and a wet, semi-naked Neville, partially wrapped in a bath towel, peers frostily out.

I am totally unnerved and begin to stammer. "You ... you did push the e-e-e-enter button did ... did you not?"

"I did not!" he says, and slams the door. Two inches closer and I would have a broken nose.

I make my way home, still clutching my copies of *Wu-feng* and the Edmonton review.

Out of curiosity I try Bell Info for Niville. No luck. For me, the man does not exist. Never mind. I make detailed notes of the experience and push on.

It is around the middle of the year and I am in Toronto on other business when I read a newspaper interview with Leon Major, the Artistic Director of Toronto Arts Productions. Leon is quoted as saying, "No one is writing for the open stage."

I lose my restraint, my diffidence, and my cool, and make tracks for the St. Lawrence Centre administration offices. Through an open door I can see Leon at his desk and there is no one with him. I ignore his secretary, march in on him, and present him with the published version of the play, my resumé, and photocopies of the literary reviews. I tell him that someone damn well is writing for the open stage, and, remembering Rolf Kalman's advice, refrain from telling him that his theatre has previously rejected the play in manuscript form.

Leon, who is one of theatre's true gentlemen, takes my outburst with startled politeness and says he will get back to me.

Within a few weeks Leon phones to say he is going to mount *Wu-feng* on the main stage of the St. Lawrence Centre in the fall of 1974. He himself intends to direct. Eureka, Hallelujah, and handsprings!

In the meantime, back in the other world, I have wrapped up 1973 by burying Mackenzie King in *The Days Before Yesterday*, and now the winter of 1974 finds me on a three-month stint at the University of Guelph, in southern Ontario, where I am an "artist in residence." I have an apartment on campus and a small office in the arts building. Fifty percent of my time is at the beck and call of the university and the other fifty percent is for my own pursuits, in this case the polishing of *Wu-feng*.

Every weekend I drive home to Manotick, where Hilda has taken time out from a myriad chores and her current relaxation of reading Frances Donaldson's *Edward VIII* to do some calculations. She figures I've been away from home for half our married life. I counter by saying that most husbands are away for around ten hours every working day and at least when I'm home it's for the full count. She's amazingly good about all this. Oh, we have our strains, our differences, and our spats, what healthy couple doesn't? Once, just after returning from some absence, I countermanded a discipline order and she left me. Packed a bag, took her little car, and vanished. But only for a day, which she spent with her farm friend, Iolene Hartin, at Stittsville; the two of them visited, drank tea, and giggled at the thought of me in shock, which I was. But we have an agreement never to go to bed mad, and she knows full well I could never survive the vagaries of the freelance life without her. I'm not sure the boys even notice my absences. (In later years David, the eldest, will say that rather than remembering my being away he remembers my being home — really home.)

I never figure out what I'm doing at the University of Guelph. I give a few open talks about TV drama and public affairs, using material cheerfully loaned by the CBC. These presentations are reasonably well attended and seem to be appreciated. Some professors are personally hospitable, a few ask for advice concerning the making of their own audio-visual projects, and students occasionally drop into my office for a chat, but to me this whole thing feels like a useless exercise. I don't think I'm sufficiently gregarious.

My personal time, however, is vastly useful. Next door, in Toronto, Leon Major is busily mounting a production of Bertolt Brecht's *The Good Woman of Setzuan*. I drive in to kibitz at auditions, first readings, and rehearsals.

And while I'm at Guelph, the annual ACTRA Awards ceremony is held in Toronto. I've been nominated for a writing award in documentary and also for one in radio drama. I don't win the documentary writing award, but the whole Pearson series is given a "Special Jury Award" and Cam Graham generously hands the parchment over to me, right there at the event. And I do win ACTRA's coveted Nellie for "Best writer in the dramatic mode in radio." This is for an adaptation of *The Devil's Petition*, and I am very pleased. The University expresses pleasure, too, but no professor ever invites me into his or her classroom.

I don't brood about my apparent inadequacies as an artist in residence, because in that other, parallel universe my first professional stage play is still headed for the boards in one of Canada's leading theatres, and life becomes even more complicated.

It is late spring and I am back in Manotick where I belong, with Hilda and the boys, when my damned back goes out on me. I take to my bed for the mandatory week or two of immobility, while thanking my lucky stars that once again the problem has struck at home and not on location. By the time school is out I am okay for gentle travel, so we take the travel trailer to Stoney Lake to spend some time with Mother and Dad. I am attempting to remain basically immobile, and am visited by Peter Wilde, the new dramaturge at the St. Lawrence Centre.

Peter arrives in the Kawartha land of Precambrian rock, pine, and blue water wearing tight trousers, a kind of medieval doublet cinched in at the waist, a white shirt with full voluminous sleeves, a trim spade beard, and immaculately groomed shoulder-length hair. The boys think I have a visitor from outer space, but I tell them he's from an alien world known as "theatre" and is friendly and very bright.

Peter and I discuss the dialogue revisions I have been making to *Wu-feng* and look very carefully at structure. I feel comfortable with Peter's advice and am becoming excited at the prospect of October rehearsals. Opening night is slated for October 22. There is, however, a sad break in the rhythm of this remarkable year of 1974.

Mother takes sick in the summer. I am reasonably mobile again and Hilda and Dad and I visit her in Toronto's Sunnybrook Hospital. She is 89 and has a blood disorder originating in her bone marrow. She is still a remarkable woman with an active mind. She passes the time in hospital reading, and working with a little weaving device made from thread spools rimmed with small nails. We leave the room, but I go back in and embrace her. She and I both know it is our final hug. One cannot explain such moments of certainty and the memory never fades.

Back home in Manotick my spine collapses again and I become total-ly immobilized in bed. Never before has my back been this truculent.

Mother's condition worsens. Doug and Jean have Dad with them in Toronto and are beating a steady path back and forth to Sunnybrook Hospital. Hilda and David drive to Toronto to see Mother and give Doug and Jean a weekend off.

David's teenage girlfriend, Janet Chapman, comes in to keep an eye on Ian, Rob, and me. The family doctor, O.B. Wilson, known affection-ately to us and his other friends as "O.B.," has given me muscle relaxant pills. I'm not sick, just in pain, but only when I move or laugh.

No sooner has Hilda gone than I slip into a massive drug reaction and my head swells up like a balloon. My eyes all but disappear. Within a day or two I put on several pounds of fluid weight, mostly above the shoulders. My skin turns blotchy like a snake's. O.B. wants to put me into hospital but I refuse, not wanting Hilda to know there is anything unusual afoot. O.B. consults with specialists, but he and Janet look after me where I lie.

This drug-induced illness climaxes late one night in what I can only describe as a near-death experience, something I have always enjoyed reading about but have never believed in. A logical mind can always find a logical explanation. This occasion, I am sure, is no exception.

Late at night, feeling feverish, in pain, and swollen, I attempt to concentrate my way into relaxation. I begin at the tips of my extremities and draw myself inward toward my centre of being. But suddenly I become aware of a black void in the cavity of my chest and I see my essence, liquid and dark, pouring into that void and being sucked downward and away. I fight away from the brink of that awful vortex, not directionally like a swimmer, but by expanding back into myself. I lie there, wide awake, perspiring as though in the aftermath of a nightmare, and then, amazingly, I feel an overwhelming sense of peace. I slide into a deep sleep and wake up feeling much better. In the morning, the phone rings. It is Hilda, telling me that Mother died during the night.

I should confess that I have long held a certain sympathy for the theory of extra-sensory perception, particularly as it relates to interaction between persons. Hilda and I each have a tendency to answer a question before the other has verbalized it. On at least two occasions we have spontaneously phoned each other from separate time zones, placing our calls so precisely simultaneously that each of us thought we had originated the call. Even the phone companies had not known which end to bill. Did I know Mother was passing on? Did I almost join her? Human ties are very strong.

There are no words to express the void in the hearts of her family created by the death of my extraordinary mother. It will be another quarter of a century before I even begin to comprehend what her passing means to Dad.

October rolls around and *Wu-feng* is in production. I am ensconced in the King Edward Hotel within an easy stroll of the theatre. For several years the "King Eddy" has been my home away from home. It's becoming rundown, in an elegant sort of way, and is not very expensive. A few years ago I was here so often that when I arrived from Ottawa the desk clerk would toss my room keys across the desk and keep on registering someone else.

Leon has assembled an amazing cast. There are seventeen principals and, eventually, about the same number of extras. The Governor is played by Alan Scarfe, and his antagonist, Margama, the young rebel leader, by Neil Munro. The entire cast list is a Who's Who of Canadian theatre — Sara Botsford, Gerard Parkes, Jennifer Phipps, Maja Ardal, Sean McCann, and on and on.

There is an initial period of three-way unease between director, cast, and writer, while each of us probes the others' insecurities and sensitivities. Every writer will automatically defend the territory of ideas, dialogue, and structure. I tell myself to be calm, to listen, and to remember that these are all experienced professionals and this is my first venture into professional theatre.

Very soon we all drop into the comfortable routine of communicating via Leon. Most dialogue suggestions are filtered through him. Nothing is more unsettling to an actor than having director and writer giving contrary instructions. My main concern is to defend the integrity of the play, while I listen carefully for dialogue that doesn't fit the players' tongues or that seems to irritate their sensibilities.

Leon sends an actress to me with a problem. She is acutely uncomfortable hearing a fellow actor having to mouth the phrase, "marriage mart."

"What's the problem?" I say. "It means 'market'."

"I know what it means. But surely it's too modern?"

Suddenly I realize that at forty-seven I'm an old man around here. This child is an offspring of K-Mart and the plaza age. I'm tempted to point out that "mart" is an ancient and poetic word and has only recently been resurrected for crass commercial purposes. I bite my tongue, thank her, and suggest that Lubomir Mykytiuk, who is playing a tribal chief of police, change the phrase to "marriage market." The trick is to give in gracefully often enough in harmless areas so when the battlements really need defending the actors know I mean it. The other trick is to know what is harmless and what is not. There's the rub.

My back begins to bother me again. Standing for any length of time is a problem. The props department presents me with an elegant "shooting stick," the cane-like contraption that English grouse-hunting gentry perch on while waiting for the beaters to flush game. It's a godsend, now and for several years after.

Two weeks or so into rehearsal I am in bad shape. My left foot has dropped, and the toe tends to drag when I walk. I am only comfortable sitting. I need help to walk the one block to the hotel, and I have to pause frequently to wait for the pain to subside.

I phone O.B. He is brusque and blunt.

"Your foot's dropped? You're only comfortable sitting? Okay, next plane home, you're on it."

"But we're in the middle of rehearsal!"

"To hell with it. Home! Now!"

I arrive at Ottawa airport to find Hilda waiting for me.

"We're to go straight to the hospital," she says.

At Riverside Hospital, O.B. passes me on to Dr. Agarwalla, an Indian orthopaedic specialist, who passes me on to a Haitian neurosurgeon with the words, "I have great faith in Dr. Dennery, he has done the same for me."

Years ago my surgeon brother, Don, speaking of disc removal operations, said, "Nobody is ever going to do that operation on me!" Fortunately, techniques improve.

Dr. Agarwalla could make a tidy sum doing this operation himself, but he recommends Dr. Dennery because he himself has been under the Dennery knife. Okay. Ask the man who's had one. Besides, the pain is agonizing. I tell the doctors I have only one pre-condition. Opening night of my play is October 22. I must be in Toronto by dress rehearsal time.

"No problem," says Dennery, "that's a week away."

They schedule me for o.r. the next day, and that evening O.B. comes in and draws pictures of what is to be done. Then Dr. Agarwalla comes in and explains what is to be done. Then Dr. Dennery comes in and he, too, draws pictures. Dennery is a small dapper brown man who speaks flawless English and, presumably, flawless French. Later on I will see a notice in his office advertising a lecture on voodoo; when questioned, he smiles affably and says, "Whatever works." Later on, too, I will find that his needlework is admired by the radiologists, who claim they can always spot a Dennery incision because it is so precise and neat. He is a specialist with an office in a relatively poor end of Ottawa and he doesn't charge more than OHIP pays.* He's in the habit of devoting holiday time to working gratis in a rural clinic in the hills of Haiti. I like Dennery. He is quiet, pleasant, sympathetic, confident, skilled, and admired by his peers.

I am discharged on Friday minus one lower disc and with a "window" that enlarges a portion of my spinal column cavity. Dr. Dennery has given me a couple of hefty prescriptions. Hilda and I fly to Toronto on Saturday. The St. Lawrence Centre has some publicity interviews lined up for me and dress rehearsal is Monday. David, Ian, Rob, and other family members will arrive for opening night, Tuesday.

Hilda seems very quiet, almost taciturn. I get the feeling she thinks I shouldn't be here.

I attend rehearsal and then dress rehearsal. The play seems to have changed somewhat. There is a great deal of toing and froing. Designer Murray Laufer has built an enormous bamboo structure on the thrust stage. It suggests a mountain and provides multiple levels for action. On the other hand, it is no longer a simple open stage.

* These were the days when doctors could charge additional fees.

There is a TV interview with broadcasting icon Elwood Glover in the basement lounge of the old Four Seasons Hotel on Jarvis Street. Erudite Arnold Edinborough is interviewed just before me. Arnold is an old pro and gets along splendidly by simply doing all the talking. My interview is rather strange. I want to talk about the play and the characters, but Elwood has some publicity pictures and keeps asking me about the costumes. No matter what I say, he comes back to costumes. Later on I am told that by this point in his career Elwood is deaf and would have had no idea what my responses had been. I make a mental note to learn from Arnold.

Opening night is, I think, splendid. The family is all here, including Dad and Janet. I have been supping on Dr. Dennery's pills. I don't know it but I am zonked out of my mind. I am in prescribed euphoria. Everything is marvellous. For all I know the cast may be speaking in glorious Greek. They probably are. Janet faints during intermission and I figure the world is just dandy. Nurse Betsy Kalman is here and eyes me quizzically. She tells me later, "I knew you were out of it. I could tell by your little piggy eyes."

Alan Scarfe makes a splendid Governor Wu. Neil Munro is dynamic as rebel Margama. Everybody is lovely, beautiful, fabulous. I go backstage afterwards to congratulate Alan and Neil and they look at me most strangely. Is something wrong? With me? With them? With the play? I did notice that there was something missing at the end of the play, but what the hell.

The next day it occurs to me that Margama's final speech has been deleted. He has just realized that the person he has beheaded was the beloved governor and is sitting centre stage cradling the head while his friends urge him to flee and to hide. He is supposed to cry out in anguish,

I have assassinated Excellence. I have murdered True Man. Where is the cave dark enough to hide Margama from Margama?

And the tragedy is complete.
But it is not complete. This speech has been deleted.
I talk to dramaturge Peter Wilde. He says that Leon doesn't like that speech because it can be interpreted as referring to Christ and as an attack on Jews. He also says he doesn't think Leon has fully understood the play.

Bob Reid tells me he was waiting for a post-performance bus when he overheard two ladies saying they didn't understand the ending. He told them the end line, and one said, "Oh, now I understand."

I plead with Leon to re-establish the line. He agrees to reinstate it the next day, only for the matinee, just for me. I attend that performance and hear my play, once, with its proper ending.

In the meantime, the critics are not kind. McKenzie Porter, writing in the *Toronto Sun*, takes me to task for not getting under the oriental skin, something I was never trying to do. He does say that *Wu-feng* voices "an eloquent and highly affecting philosophy that is pertinent to many of the political issues of today." He is not kind to Leon. "Director Leon Major in an excess of zeal for the visual has blurred the intellectual edge of Munroe Scott's dialogue.... But both author and director have over-reached themselves." Thank you very much. And thanks, too, to the headline writer who blazoned "*Wu-feng — why?*" across the page. On the other hand, Porter does make some valid points that are worth pondering. So, too, does Herb Whittaker in the *Globe and Mail*, who sees both strengths and weaknesses in the production.

Wu-feng is not exactly a box office success. It averages about fifty percent of capacity in a theatre capable of seating 831 people. The ticket prices range from $2.00 to $7.00.

My hometown paper, the *Ottawa Citizen*, runs a review of the entire Toronto theatre scene. The writer trashes the productions presented by Toronto Workshop Productions, Factory Theatre Lab, and Tarragon Theatre, and then pours generous doses of vitriol upon the St. Lawrence Centre's *Wu-feng*, with phrases such as "sophomoric ideals," "cheap and trite philosophizing," and "a sorry affair."

Most writers recognize weaknesses in their work, and I, for one, have great admiration for the perceptive critic who manages to put his or her finger firmly upon a soft spot without denigrating the whole, but a critic who sees nothing of value in the current offerings of four theatres and five writers is worthy only of scorn.

I am told that this guy is a part-time reviewer unchained from the mining camps of northern Ontario, so I phone Chris Young, editor of the *Ottawa Citizen*, and suggest that he should either send his own reviewer or at least use one with some credentials. This phone call, like my letter to Hamilton Southam, is probably not good PR, but who cares? The review in the *Citizen* is the only thing that my neighbours, friends, and associates in Ottawa will ever read about *Wu-feng*, and this knowledge makes for an unpleasant, tight, aching sensation around the heart. In our culturally insecure society, such a review will go a long way toward assuring that *Wu-feng* is never produced again.

Fortunately, I receive numerous letters from individual playgoers, both friends and strangers, extolling the virtues of the play and using words like "solid pleasure," "excellence," "superb," and "a rare treat." I am reminded of John Juliani's plaintive cry, "but the 'experts' (oh god, spare us!) the experts quibbled like crazy."

I do a post-production revision of the script, giving some thought to McKenzie Porter and Herb Whittaker and to my own instincts, and generally try to calm the structure down so that it's not quite so busy. As is the playwright's contractual prerogative, I retain production changes that I like and delete the ones I do not like. In 1982 *Wu-feng* is made available by Playwrights Canada and is incorporated into their catalogue. The Governor's story is now in two published versions, one pre-production and one post-production, which may some day be of casual interest to someone doing an irrelevant Ph.D. on an esoteric topic — something like "Can Canadian Drama Survive Canadian Criticism?"

Fast-forward to November 1995. I have not given up on *Wu-feng*. I'll never give up on *Wu-feng*. I believe in the play as both drama and contemporary comment. I write to Richard Monette, the current artistic director of Stratford, suggesting he might like to take a look at *Wu-feng* because of its contemporary relevance. Four months later I receive a reply from David Prosser, Stratford's Director of Literary Services, saying that in choosing Canadian works they tend to rely on the "cachet of a major literary name." *Plus ça change, plus c'est la même chose.*

But enough. Back to late 1974. Let us leave the world of theatre, critics, and actors, and return to the world of documentary, politics, and, yes, another actor — that consummate thespian, the Right Honourable John George Diefenbaker.

24

MAKING UP
DIEFENBAKER

THIS IS A SOMEWHAT UNUSUAL CBC film unit and, considering the purpose of our project, we are operating in a most unusual location. We are in Barbados and we intend to spend up to six hours every morning for the next few weeks making it possible for the Right Honourable John George Diefenbaker, Prime Minister of Canada from 1957 to 1963 and still a Member of Parliament at the age of 79, to commit his memoirs to film. We have him here in Barbados for two reasons, one being that he and Mrs. Diefenbaker like the island and find it relaxing, and the other that here we can monopolize his time without interference.

There's nothing unusual about the technical team. It's a normal, buttoned-down, compact CBC unit. There is cameraman Wilf Doucette, the shortest cameraman I've ever worked with — which I mention only because, in my experience, cameramen tend to be rather long beefy characters. (He and I meet diminutive entertainer Tom Jones while we are here and Wilf is delighted. "It's so great to talk to someone without having to stare at his navel!") Our lighting man is gregarious, wiry Peter Warchow. Sound is being handled by big, affable Laurent "Larry" Richard. I've worked with all three at various times and know they will quietly and capably deal with any technical problems that might arise. At the moment, I'm the director, with no commitment as yet to be the writer. In fact, I'm here in spite of myself.

This is another of Cam Graham's projects, and I've known for some time that it's been in his plans. I've been telling him I don't want to have anything to do with it. It's not because I have anything against Mr. Diefenbaker. Quite the contrary. But the man is larger than life. While working on *The Tenth Decade* I've already seen hours of "Dief" on film. I have maintained that Mr. Diefenbaker is too big, too bold, too overwhelming for a one-man series.

"Nobody," I've told Cam, "can watch Dief for thirteen half-hours."

My reluctance has had nothing to do with politics and a great deal to do with compassion and aesthetics. But I suspect the CBC is committed to giving Diefenbaker equal time with Pearson.

But Cam was persuasive. "Just go down to Barbados and take care of filming the interviews," he had said. " I'll sort it out from there."

"Hell, I'm just out of hospital. I still can't stand for any length of time. My back hurts." And indeed it does. I don't know it, but I'll be under the knife again within three months.

"It's a single location. John's doing the interviewing. Tommy is there as resource. You'll be wrapped up no later than one o'clock every day. That's my agreement with Dief. What's to sweat? Barbados will be good for you. No commitment beyond that."

The "no commitment" had sounded good. Hilda and I are thinking of moving away from the Ottawa Valley, probably in the coming year. But as for a one-location shoot in November near the balmy beaches of beautiful, laid-back Barbados — well, why not?

The technical crew may be standard but the remainder of the team is not. The interviewer is writer/historian John Munro, who is laying the groundwork for Mr. Diefenbaker's written memoirs, a function he has already filled as ghost writer, along with Alex Inglis, of *Mike*, former Prime Minister Pearson's published memoirs. Reinforcing John is Tom Van Dusen. Tom began his career as a journalist in the National Press Gallery, but moved into the political realm and was executive assistant to Mr. Diefenbaker when the latter was prime minister. (He will continue as a high-level backroom political advisor right through the Mulroney years.) Tom is here as moral support for Mr. Diefenbaker, whom he habitually calls "Chief," a habit the rest of us readily adopt. Tom and John are two very high-powered resource people. Between them, they will figure out the line John's questions should take. My interest, at the moment, is not audio, but visual content.

There are two others who are vital members of the group but who are not, strictly speaking, part of the CBC team. They are the Chief's wife, Olive (we call him "Chief" but she is always "Mrs. Diefenbaker"), and Tom's lovely blue-eyed artist wife, Shirley. Olive and Shirley do their own thing. Shirley never comes near the filming sessions but keeps us sane with compassion and humour during the down periods. Olive sometimes observes the sessions and sometimes does not, depending, I believe, on whether or not she thinks the Chief needs her moral support.

Although I've already seen more film footage of the Chief than is good for a fellow, I don't meet him until the night he and Olive arrive at the Barbados Bridgetown Airport. Cam, ever the diplomat, is here to hand the old warrior over to the tender mercies of the film unit. Cam assures me the Chief knows of my involvement with *The Tenth Decade* and, more importantly, the Pearson series. This latter has me worried. I know the conflict between the two men was more than political rivalry. It verged on outright antipathy. But Cam says the Chief has voiced no objection. I get the distinct impression he has voiced nothing. Of course he already knows John and Tommy. Wilf has filmed him before and the Chief seems to remember technicians Pete and Larry. I suspect he remembers everything, but he shows nothing more than affable courtesy when introduced to me. All may be well.

The crew's initial concern is to find a suitable location in which to film the endless interviews. After scouring Barbados, we decide that the living room of the house the Diefenbakers are renting for their holiday is as good a location as any. It's an oceanside villa owned by the mother of a Hollywood actress. We place bookcases in a corner of the living room and stock them with law books borrowed from a Bajan senator. Pete arranges his lights and covers certain windows so the shadows from transient sunshine won't create continuity problems. The Diefenbakers graciously accept these temporary but substantial modifications to their living room. The focal point of the scene is the firm armchair where the great man will sit to tell us about his life.

The camera position is established. John Munro will sit to the immediate left of it, off-camera but very close, so the Chief will be reacting almost into camera. I intend to sit on a low stool to the immediate right of camera and just beside cameraman Wilf's right knee.

Our budget doesn't run to either makeup or wardrobe. John Munro and I have an informal and, from a union point of view, illegal agreement that I will keep an eye on wardrobe continuity, and he will attend to makeup.

In this production, makeup is a special challenge. It's common practice to add a little cosmetic makeup to an interviewee, not to distort reality but to preserve it. The harsh lights tend to make an untouched interviewee appear unhealthily pallid. The Chief, however will be his own man every day from noon onward, and he likes walking in the Bajan sunshine. Over the coming days he will acquire more and more of a tan. John will have to "tan" him now, and then, each morning, apply a little less makeup than the day before. Later on the film editor may need to combine a statement made today with a follow-up made three weeks from now. We can't have the Chief going instantly from pallid to bronze and back again.

Wardrobe is a similar concern when interviews that are to be inter-cut stretch over numerous sittings. One can't have the subject's ties, shirts, and jackets changing colour, pattern, and style at the snip of an editor's scissors. That is known as bad continuity.

It's obvious, however, that once the camera starts rolling, the inter-viewer/makeup artist can't be expected to do anything about the inter-viewee's perspiration. That has to be my call.

This first morning of filming I'm very tense. So is the Chief. Wilf's camera has just begun to roll when I realize the Chief is perspiring. I call "cut," and move forward with a kleenex.

As I reach out to dab his brow, he skewers me with his blue gimlet eyes. Those eyes are famous in Canada from coast to coast. They have enthralled fans, impaled jurors, terrified recalcitrant backbenchers, and intimidated cabinet ministers. Now those eyes have me full in their scopes.

"You did that Pearson thing," he says.

I freeze, hand outstretched, kleenex almost touching his forehead.

"You did that Pearson thing."

It's not a question. Could it be an accusation? Those eyes have me pinned like a butterfly to cork. Perhaps the Chief did not approve of my editorial decisions. "Thing" is not a nice word.

No, there's more. "You did that Pearson thing," he has just said, and there can be no doubt he is referring to Mike's TV memoirs, *First Person Singular*, but now he continues. "Who was he talking to? Down a well?"

I am standing here, frozen, with a kleenex in my extended hand, and he is sticking a knife into my heart. He is demolishing my proudest achievement, an entire memoirs series crafted without the intrusion of either a host or a "voice of God" narrator.

Apparently Mr. Diefenbaker had been not impressed. "Who was he talking to? Down a well?"

I have no answer to either "the Pearson thing" or to this.

I unfreeze, decide to ignore the question, and simply ask, "May I touch you?" The Chief laughs. I dab the sweat from his brow and film-ing gets underway. But he is a mischievous devil and I know it. His tim-ing is impeccable. He has waited for just the right moment to let me know that he knows all about me and that I had damned well better use a different technique when I structure his memoirs. What he doesn't know is that I am here only for the shoot. I have no intention of being the one who completes the project. Tough.

John Munro asks questions and the Chief answers them. At length. Sometimes the old gentleman goes off at a tangent. John seems to know when to let him go and when to bring him back on course. At this stage, content is not my concern. What is my concern, and Wilf's, is the composition of the footage. We will be shooting thousands of feet of film with only one camera and from one camera position. But someone, sometime, will have to select, shorten, and intercut this material. If we had a more generous budget we would cover with two cameras, even three. Cam and I have already agreed not to use the technique of doing cutaways to shots of an all-knowing, nodding interviewer, re-asking questions re-staged for the camera. Both budget and technique put us into a straitjacket. I've always liked straitjackets. They can force creativity.

The only way we can swiftly change the visual composition is by using the zoom lens to go from wide shot, to medium, to medium close, or even to extreme close. Wilf and I work out a little code. When I tap him on the knee he will snap to another shot. We try at first to develop a code to indicate which lens position I prefer, but give up on that. I watch carefully for the Chief to pause while collecting his thoughts and I listen carefully for the moments when I expect he is about to go off at a tangent. I tap Wilf, and he uses his own judgment as to which frame to snap to. If I run my finger along Wilf's leg toward the knee he does a slow zoom in, and, of course, vice versa. A zoom is dangerous. Once it is underway it is difficult to cut out of. But it can be very useful if the Chief is beginning to show passion. Down here by the camera only Wilf and I are aware of what's going on visually. Is this "directing"? Who knows? It's certainly low-key. Tommy Van Dusen doesn't think I am directing. Later, in his own memoirs,* he refers to John Munro as the director. And, as I say, I don't really want to be here.

But Cam was correct. Barbados is good for me. I wake up early every morning, eat breakfast, and take one prescription Valium before heading off to work. Most of the time I am sitting, or crouching, beside Wilf. I also have the shooting stick from the St. Lawrence Centre props department, so I can sit virtually anywhere. If necessary, during the morning I take one of Dr. Dennery's little pain pills. After that, no more medication. The most healing relaxant down here is afternoon

---

* *Inside the Tent: Forty-five Years on Parliament Hill* (General Store Publishing House, 1998).

sunshine on the beach and one tot of Bajan rum, a potion that even a Jamaican diplomat once told me is the best rum in the world. I am temporarily wearing a fibreglass foot support that extends up the calf, and when I go swimming it is left standing in its shoe on the beach — a lonely symbol that reminds me how fortunate I am that the support is indeed temporary.

Shirley Van Dusen makes use of my afternoon indolence to paint my portrait in oils. The finished painting is very disturbing, not because it looks somewhat drawn, which I expect I am, but because it doesn't look like me. It looks like my brother Don, whom Shirley never met — nor does she know he even existed.

The shoot goes well. Wilf and Larry and Pete have no serious technical problems. Tommy and John have the content well in hand. The Chief himself is in good form. He leads us through his amazing career with great gusto, glowering, chuckling, telling anecdotes, excoriating his foes, and justifying his aberrations. He is a consummate storyteller and a consummate actor.

He is also an unabashed plagiarizer. There is a powder room close by the living room and in it a small wall plaque carries the statement, "No good deed goes unpunished." Pete Warchow asks the Chief if he has seen the plaque and at the next break Dief vanishes into the washroom. He emerges a few minutes later, chuckling. The camera has hardly begun rolling again before he announces, unblushingly and with a characteristic shake of his jowls, "What I always say is, no good deed ever goes unpunished."

It's easy to be spellbound by the old man, here, in the flesh. He's a raconteur of the first order, a role he enjoys hugely. And, as with any raconteur, details become a little exaggerated. In describing the cabinet revolt that ultimately lost him the leadership of the PC party, he says that in one cabinet meeting a minister, George Hees, was crying. "My trouser legs were all wet," says the Chief, his jowls shaking angrily but his eyes twinkling. I analyse this line. It conjures up the image of George Hees on his knees, his arms around the Chief's legs, weeping copiously, which of course is ridiculous and is not what the Chief actually said. But it is what he intended us to imagine.

He uses colourful metaphors with great dexterity. Reminiscing about earlier days on the prairies, he says, "Those were the days when the only protection a Conservative enjoyed in the province of Saskatchewan was under the provision of the game laws." We're not expected to believe him, but we get the point, just as did the audience he first used it on. He is self-deprecating enough to tell of a rural meeting where, after he had made an impassioned speech, he heard a farmer comment, "A half-hour rain would've done more good."

There is a side to this man that the public, particularly we easterners, have tended to overlook. Before making it into political office he was a highly experienced criminal lawyer. Not only that, he was a defence lawyer. One of the best. As a defence lawyer he had a highly developed antipathy to the establishment, which he mistrusted, often for good cause. As I listen to him describing his chaotic years as prime minister I think of the accusations that have been levelled at him — incompetent, paranoid, unwilling to delegate authority, and so on. Some facts might appear to justify these accusations, but I have my doubts about the usual explanations for his troubles. The man was, whether he knew it or not, in a classic bind. He distrusted, even hated, the establishment, but as prime minister he *was* the establishment!

Now, on camera, he attempts to explain and defend his government's cancellation of the magnificent fighter aircraft, the Avro Arrow, and I detect a high level of frustration. He says the Pearson government was preparing to cancel it anyway, he cites costs, and he claims the Americans wouldn't have bought it because of its limited range. (As I write this, in the twenty-first century, I am convinced that our aeronautical engineers over-achieved. They might have built the best fighting aircraft in the world, as we were told at the time, but what made us think the Americans would buy such a craft from a foreign country? There are areas where we Canadians are not permitted to excel. No wonder the Chief was frustrated. What I have never understood is how he, nationalist that he was, could have permitted the total destruction of the prototypes.)

I decide I really like the old gentleman. To him, we are all individuals. If one of us has a toothache, or an upset stomach, or is worried about someone at home, the Chief not only remembers but checks up in a few days time to see if all is well again. At the end of each day's session he and Olive unfailingly insist on serving us coffee and cakes. One day Olive is away shopping and the Chief produces beer instead of coffee. We are quaffing our brew when Olive returns. She stands a moment looking down upon all of us, but her only comment is, "When the cat's away...."

The Chief appears to be basically abstemious, but a member of our team claims to have been sitting one day at a thatch-covered beach bar when a towering, elderly, beach-clad former prime minister of Canada emerged from the shrubbery, climbed onto a stool, shook his jowls at the bartender, and ordered "One of those things you gave me last year." The bartender, not having a clue what he was referring to, decided that a planter's punch was a safe bet. The drink was absorbed with evident pleasure and the apparition sloped off down the beach. Perhaps the cat was again away.

The Chief arranges for the senator friend who had loaned us a portion of his library to take us all for an afternoon sail on the senator's sixty-foot schooner. I am perched on my shooting stick when the ship heels over under a sudden gust of wind and I fall heavily onto the deck. The Chief is worried about my back. He seems impressed by the fact I am here so soon after surgery. I think it's because Olive has back trouble, too.

I get along fine with Mrs. Diefenbaker. (A few weeks after we have finished our filming and are back in Ottawa, Olive writes me a note and addresses it to "My darling Munroe Scott." The addition of the surname is a deft diplomatic touch, but even so Hilda says she's going to sue for alienation of affection.) One day I suggest to Olive that we should be filming an interview with her. She refuses, making it iron-clad clear that she considers her role to be that of support for her husband. Mike Pearson's wife, Maryon, is reported to have said that behind every successful man there is a surprised woman. That does not apply to Olive Diefenbaker.*

In the meantime, I am having trouble with the Chief's tie and with his zipper. He is a bit of a squirmer, although not as bad on camera as Mr. Pearson, who used to twirl his hair, scratch his ear, and even explore his nose, thereby creating a lot of "outs" for the cutting room floor. (One day, in a fit of boredom, Jim Williams assembled a montage of these Mike trims, one of the most hilarious few minutes of prime ministerial fidgeting ever caught on film. It has, alas, disappeared.) The Chief's problem has more to do with haberdashery. His tie has a tendency to slip into disarray, which can cause problems with visual continuity, so every now and then I ask Wilf to cut camera while I straighten the Chief's tie and mop up a little excess perspiration. More alarming is the fact that the zipper on his trousers doesn't latch, and it tends, gradually, to slide open. This is no problem in a close-up on his face, but in a longer shot the sight of a gaping prime ministerial fly has the potential to be distracting. Every so often I find myself reaching forward and closing the zipper. A month or so later, back in Ottawa, I wander into the Chief's

---

*   Olive Diefenbaker died on December 21, 1976.

Parliament Hill office to say hello. The Chief leaps up as is his custom, and comes around the end of his desk, hand outstretched. He stops in mid-flight, looks down, and checks his zipper.

We return from Barbados with thousands of feet of film for processing, which will be a slow process indeed, because Kodak is struggling out of a protracted strike. We also have thousands of feet of interview audio to be transcribed to the typed page. There can be no editing room action here for some time, but that's of little concern to me. I consider my part in the project to be over.

I have another iron in the fire.

25

VISIONS

BACK IN EARLY NOVEMBER, as I was preparing to head for Barbados, two CBC producers from Toronto who specialized in documentary dramas paid me a visit in Manotick. They asked whether I had been giving any thought to writing docudramas. Well, it so happened I had been. *Wu-feng*'s theme of political blackmail with the threat of violence was still bothering me. And in this year, 1974, the hijacking of passenger planes was proliferating; we were now being scanned and searched whenever we boarded an airplane. It wasn't the search that bothered me but the apathy with which we were all accepting it. I told the producers that I saw the beginning of a police state and had an idea for a pseudo-documentary that I would like to set a quarter of a century from now, in the year 2000. I wished to "document" our slide into totalitarianism.

They seemed interested in my vision, and within a few days I had submitted an outline under the working title, "The Inversion of Intention." Then I had gone to Barbados.

Now, home again, I am keen to explore the future.

Strangely, my outline has been routed not to the two producers who approached me but to the senior CBC-TV drama producer, Robert Allen. However, a script is commissioned. I am now calling it "The Cattle Syndrome."

I am writing interviews to put in the mouth of a fictitious retired professor who is looking back from the year 2000. I name him "McIntosh." His interviews are intercut with those of other interviewees, equally fictitious — a TV journalist, a senator, a pastor — and with newsclips. I intend to begin with genuine archival newsclips.

Referring to my fictitious Prof. McIntosh, my equally fictitious TV journalist says,

> I think those airport searches unhinged him. After all, the States had the same problem.

McINTOSH: The most Canadian of all rationalizations for the irra-
tional. They were doing it in the States. That made it all the worse!
Here were two major nations sitting astride most of the air routes in
the world and unwilling to come to grips with the hijacking problem.

NEWSCLIP reporting a minor hijacking circa 1969.

NEWSCLIP, brief, of another minor hijacking.

NEWSCLIP, brief, of yet another (All three should be North American hijacks).

NEWSCLIP. The International Airlines Pilots Association demanding
that governments boycott all other governments that permit hijack-
ers to receive sanctuary.

McINTOSH: The pilots were right. The solution lay in the hands of
the international politicians. Instead, we pretended it lay in the
hands of our internal security people … Security! Bah!

NEWSCLIP re massacre at Rome airport.

NEWSCLIP re Tel Aviv bloodbath.

NEWSCLIP of hijacked airplane being blown up on the desert.

McINTOSH: And still we went through our little airport charades
like cattle through sheep dip. Looking back, I'd say it was good con-
ditioning.

So far, this calls for genuine newsclips, but I want to make this a
look back from the year 2000. Soon I am writing imaginary newsclips
that will have to be staged. I suppose in this kind of thing I have a tendency to go over the top. I can't help it. I've viewed a lot of politics and
religion and have seen a fair chunk of the world and I suspect there are
unpleasant things ahead.

I create a female pastor who expresses my concerns:

WHITING: Philosophically we were going two ways — hard right, if
you will, to an unthinking, illogical fundamentalism and away off in
the other direction to an almost equally mindless humanism.

Eventually I cast my mind well ahead. It's an Orwellian exercise and,
of course, I am influenced by Orwell. I can see so much of what he
feared coming to pass, but more violently:

A SPECIAL EFFECTS SHOT, staged newsfilm. It is an aerial from a
helicopter that is moving over a blanket of smoke. Here and there,

in isolated little spires, the jagged remains of skyscrapers thrust up through the smoke. The only SOUND is the rhythmical flutter of the helicopter blades.

SUPERIMPOSE: "1989"

McINTOSH: ... one crude nuclear device — one hijacked SST liner and a kamikaze dive into Manhattan. Now that really put the lid on.

HOST, on camera, colour background.

HOST: ... very early in the game Canada opted for Security and Stability ...

McINTOSH: "A Downward Spiral to Stability," that's what I called it.... We've come voluntarily to an unwanted state of totalitarianism.

Ah, well, I probably am going over the top. Some of this stuff is pretty far out. Too damned pessimistic. What's getting into me? My Reverend Whiting has already made a statement that's closer to the way I usually feel:

WHITING : ... I suppose I always felt we were a naive people with a great capacity for goodness.

Anyway, the CBC cuts off the contract at the first draft stage, which is its contractual right. Producer Robert Allen says, "I do not share your vision."

By this time the CBC-TV drama department has become strangely frustrating to deal with. Even though many of my ideas are appropriate for film rather than tape, I keep finding myself routed back to Robert Allen and his VTR kingdom — and I begin to realize that my vision does not coincide with his vision.

To me, this is a serious problem. I long for the days that I think of as the Weyman/Peddie era, when writers presented ideas and they were rejected or accepted on their merit. But with Ron and David gradually being forced into limbo another culture seems to be taking over. More and more producers listen to ideas and say, "That's great. But I've been thinking,..." and then, inevitably, "Now we could incorporate the germ of your idea into,..." and inexorably promote their own vision, not the writer's. I do not believe it is the function of writers of drama simply to serve other peoples' visions. More and more those other visions are geared toward what will sell.

One day a rueful CBC employee tells me, privately, that a confidential internal memo from on high has ordered TV drama producers not to commission any scripts that don't have the potential for sale in the United States. If this is true it is a travesty of the first order, a negation of the noble aim of telling Canadian stories to Canadians, and it is also an insult to American viewers. It is an insult that spreads throughout the Canadian entertainment film industry. The Brits carved their way into the global film world after the Second World War by being *very* British. The Australians won international acclaim by being themselves. We Canadians camouflage our cities, change our street names, subvert our stories, and generally sell our birthright in order to slide incognito into the American market. Eventually, of course, as accountants and investors take over the reins of internationally co-produced films, the rot becomes more widespread, but it is Canadians who are leading the way to cultural suicide.

26

HAIL AND
FAREWELL

RIGHT OFF THE TOP, 1975 unfolds in a most peculiar fashion. Hilda and I sign with a real estate agent to sell our Manotick home. It's a decision that's made with some angst. After all, our mill pond Utopia has been a great place to raise three boys, particularly while they were youngsters. But they are growing older, and the regional high school leaves a great deal to be desired in the areas of discipline, drugs, and academic standards. And the village is growing. Our semi-rural island haven is expanding into upscale suburbia. The taxes alone will probably force us out later if we don't go now. And I'm beginning to feel that too many of our friends are senior bureaucrats and that, through them, I could lose touch with reality. This is brought home at an Ottawa cocktail party soon after I return from some depressed boondocks location and voice concerns about the economy. "No, no," I am assured, "the economy is doing fine. We were discussing it just the other day when we were skiing at Whistler."

There is also a career concern. I am becoming heavily identified with public affairs at CBC Ottawa. Establishing a home base closer to Toronto but not in it might open up more opportunities. As it turns out, it's not that easy to make the break.

With the house on the market, I again go under the knife and come out shorter by one more spinal disc. Dr. Dennery says he was too conservative the first time. I have no problem with a conservative neurosurgeon. One chunk at a time is quite sufficient. While I'm still recuperating the house is sold, but the deal doesn't close for several months. We have until mid-July to relocate.

Hilda and I have drawn an arc, one hundred miles east of Toronto, that goes roughly from Cobourg up through Campbellford, Lakefield, the Kawartha Lakes, and on to Lake Simcoe. We want to be nearer Toronto, but not too near, and east of Simcoe, so Ottawa will remain easily accessible. Lindsay is not on our list because I've always said I'll

never move any place where I'm thought of as the preacher's kid —
even though I was only there the one season before graduate school,
and Dad is still in Lindsay, although for a long time now simply as a
minister emeritus. Nevertheless, the house that reaches out to us,
embraces us, and demands to be purchased is in Lindsay.

It is the middle of the summer, 1975, and Hilda, Ian, Rob, and I have
moved to Lindsay. Rob is ready for high school, Ian is already in high
school, and David is ready for Carleton University. We have always told
the boys that they leave home when they finish high school. With David
it's slightly different. Home is leaving him.

As for me, I move to Lindsay and begin commuting back to Ottawa!

The reason for this strange turn of events is that Cam has convinced
me I should shepherd the Diefenbaker project through to completion.
It's not been a difficult sell. I've become quite fascinated by the old man,
even fond of him. But now, for the entire winter of 1975-76, I drive from
Lindsay to Ottawa every Sunday evening and home again late Friday
evening.

Hilda seems happy to be back in Lindsay. She had thoroughly
enjoyed her three years here, and the first time she goes to the grocery
store she is recognized by a friendly former Visking employee. Her sister
Anne and brother-in-law Bob Smith are now in London, Ontario, but
Dad lives just a few blocks away — although she finds the old man a little intimidating. Within a year, Don and Nancy Jack will buy a house
across the street from us, which is marvellous, because Hilda and Nancy
are best pals. However, now, in 1975, Hilda is setting up a new home with
two teenage sons, and I'm commuting to Ottawa! It would not be surprising if she were less than happy, but the only deep concern that gets
voiced to me is her worry about my long twice-weekly winter nighttime
drive along old No. 7 highway. She needn't worry. I always travel with a
sleeping bag, matches, candles, a knife, and heavy winter gear.

For her birthday, David gives his mother Philip Magnus's *King
Edward VII*, and she's reading that while I'm away. Hilda is a socialist who
is fascinated by the history of the British monarchy. She's also reading
A.L. Rowse's *The Elizabethan Renaissance*.

Because I am now the writer/director for the whole Diefenbaker series,
I am, as I was with the Pearson project, responsible for selecting content,
structuring it, overseeing the gathering of archival material, giving
detailed instructions for stills on the animation stand, supervising editing, shepherding material through the lab, writing narration, conferring

in detail with Herb Helbig on the requirements for original music, directing the narrator, and overseeing the "final mix" recording sessions. This time my editor is Peggy Chandler, Jim Williams being totally immersed in a series on the history of flight in Canada, another one of Cam Graham's projects. I miss Jim, but he's a natural for the flight project, being not only an excellent editor but also a good cameraman and, believe it or not, a former Air Canada pilot. But Peggy, seconded from the Crawley staff, is no slouch. As usual, Herb Helbig comes through with flying colours. Throughout Cam's projects I am always working with very competent and congenial professionals.

I am weary by the time the series is completed and probably losing my touch. I am not completely happy with the technique I choose for narration, but I know only too well that the Chief didn't like Pearson talking "down a well." Not that the Pearson structure would work with Dief anyway. I decide to let the off-camera narrator's voice act as the interviewer. He asks questions, the correct questions, but in the course of doing so incorporates information that complements archival footage, creates transitions, and sets up context. It's a dangerous technique and just a little cumbersome. We hire Douglas Rain, that most consummate of actors, known globally as the voice of Hal the computer in Kubrick's *2001*. Inadequacies in the narration are all mine.

We call the series of thirteen half-hour programs *One Canadian*, a title that John Munro and the Chief will elect to use for Mr. Diefenbaker's published memoirs.

During the final recording session I contribute a sound problem to the series. Our standard visual opening includes an artist's depiction of a Diefenbaker log cabin. Over it I want to hear the Chief's voice, in an excerpt from a thundering archival speech, declaring, "I have one love — Canada; one purpose — Canada's greatness; one aim — Canadian unity from the Atlantic to the Pacific."

I must want it to be heard coast to coast unaided by modern technology, because during the final mix I insist that the level be set virtually as high as broadcast guidelines will allow. When he hears it at a private screening, even the Chief is terrified.

The project is completed. I am gone, off, away, and Cam does a little discreet re-recording. He has the sound engineer remix the series opening to bring the Chief's voice down into the human realm.

It is time for me to step away from film and television and write a book. As it turns out, two books. I am about to write a biography of Doctor Bob McClure.

From Pearson to Diefenbaker to McClure! Am I mad?

27

MCCLURE IN CHINA

WHILE I HAVE BEEN COMPLETING the Diefenbaker series, the United Church of Canada has been asking me to write a book, a biography of Dr. Robert "Bob" McClure. I've been stalling, saying I am not a "literary" writer. I've only written one book, African Manhunt, and that was years ago. My real reason for stalling is that I am tired — and, again, apprehensive. I don't know Bob McClure but I sure know of him. He's a larger-than-life missionary surgeon who, after spending the first half of the century knocking around China, and the next few years in other parts of the globe, became the first lay moderator, the head honcho as it were, of the United Church. I'm not sure I can handle two larger-than-life Canadians one after the other.

I relax. I take some time off. I meet with folk from the Church's head office at Cloud 85. The biography, they say, will be published by CANEC publishing house, a descendant of the distinguished Ryerson Press. Ryerson Press was established by the Methodists and eventually became the United Church Publishing House; now in co-operation with the Anglicans it has metamorphosed into "Canadian Ecumenical" — CANEC. The McClure biography will be CANEC's first "trade" book. The United Church will, for a maximum of one year, make a monthly payment as an advance against royalties, and augment it with a monthly research fee. They are making me an offer a freelance can't refuse. Dr. McClure has already given his approval and has promised to co-operate, "provided in the long run it doesn't cost the church a cent." CANEC is counting on recouping costs from retail sales. They also make it very clear that content and interpretation will be up to me. They will give me editorial guidance if I ask for it, but there will be no editorial censoring. My editorial liaison will be Norman Vale, from the Communication Division of the United Church. It is Norman who has been doing the initial arm-twisting.

These people have faith. They have more faith in me than I have. I talk it over with Hilda. This will radically affect her, too. More than ever before I will require her secretarial help. But she has as much faith as the Cloud 85 folk. Besides, she points out, we moved away from Ottawa and closer to Toronto partly to expand our horizons. Here, indeed, is a new horizon.

We go for it.

We begin the research at the beginning of July 1976, concentrating initially on China. The backbone of the research is, of course, endless hours of taped interviews with Bob McClure and his wife, Amy. I am aided here by the availability of audio tapes of interviews with McClure that a retired clergyman, Sandy Nicholson, has recently completed. The overview they provide allows me a speedy entry into the subject. Further help is given by the McClures' eldest daughter, Norah, who has been pondering such a project herself. As Marnie Copland did with *Wufeng*, Norah steps aside and passes her files on to me.

There is no question of going to China. That country is barely beginning to open its borders. I wouldn't be able to penetrate to the interior, where McClure functioned, and anyway, most of his Chinese associates were killed before 1949.

I enjoy interviewing Dr. McClure. He is relaxed, friendly, and amazingly candid. On most occasions we talk for an hour or two at a time in his apartment, located in an aging high-rise building on Thorncliffe Crescent in Toronto. The McClures' apartment intrigues me. Most missionaries of their generation retire amid souvenirs of adopted countries. I would expect the McClure apartment to be ornamented with Chinese screens and ivory carvings, rugs from India, ceremonial knives from Borneo, Peruvian artifacts, and other mementoes. It is not. It is comfortable — but unadorned to the point of being Spartan. It's the apartment of a couple who have travelled widely and experienced vastly, but who have never been lured into accumulating "things."

With me, the McClures are always informal. If the weather is at all decent, he is invariably in shorts. Shorts are almost a uniform. This is somewhat unusual for an "old China hand," because the Chinese, unlike people in many other regions, are not enamoured of shorts. There's a story that one time in Chungking McClure had an appointment with the British ambassador and borrowed trousers for the occasion. When he turned up at the residence he found the ambassador wearing shorts out of deference to him. But Dr. McClure practises Chinese courtesy. When I arrive at his floor after ringing from the lobby, I am always met at the elevator. When I leave, he always accompanies me to the elevator.

"In China," he explains, "you see your guest to the garden gate. I've decided that in a high-rise the elevator is my garden gate."

It's a charming courtesy and not unfamiliar. Mother and Dad insisted on seeing guests safely off the property. Hilda and I try to do the same.

Some people call him "Doctor" McClure, some call him "Reverend," which he's not, and I soon learn to call him "Bob," in harmony with the majority of people who know him, or feel they do.

Bob's ability to remember events fascinates me. When, in memory, he is reliving his childhood in the interior of China, or surviving an adventure with a warlord during the 1920s, or evading rioters during the Nationalist revolution, or acting as Field Director for the International Red Cross along the Yellow River, he throws out names and dates with casual confidence. Initially, I am sceptical of such detailed recall, but as the days go by and my research broadens I begin to find the details substantiated. Verification may come from a fellow Canadian associate, or from a nurse in New Zealand who worked beside him in operating rooms in the southern Chinese jungle, or from a Quaker pacifist who risked his life with him along the Burma Road. Amy turns over to me a vast supply of letters that Bob wrote to her during the tumultuous years of the Sino-Japanese War, after she had managed to return to Canada with the children and he had managed to have the Japanese put a price on his head. These letters not only chronicle dates, travels, and places, they also give insight into his moods, goals, achievements, and frustrations.

Bob is already into his seventy-sixth year as this project gets underway and I know full well that I am fortunate. He has mellowed. A younger, more demanding and hard-driving McClure would not be nearly as tolerant and patient with my fumbling questions and groping probes. I decide he is a very forgiving man. Even when he recounts horrific adventures and abominable atrocities he rarely sounds judgmental. When he describes his single, brief meeting with Dr. Norman Bethune in the Chinese hinterland, he remarks that they had so little in common that an opportunity to co-operate was squandered, but he expresses no rancour.

I am impressed by the man's open, frequently humorous accounts of his own foibles and his forgiving accounts of the foibles of others. Only once, and this is in general conversation, does he pass savage judgment, saying it's off the record. (Since it was, it is.) And only once, in hours of interviews, does he become truly agitated, even angry. He is recounting a wartime trip home to Canada during which he did a great deal of public speaking on behalf of war-torn, beleaguered China. It was his contention that Canada was allowing the shipment of Canadian nickel to the Japanese, who were using it against China, incorporated into bombs, shells, and bullets. Ironically enough, it was on December 7, 1940, one year to the day before the Japanese attacked Pearl Harbor, that McClure was summoned to the prime minister's office in the East Block on Parliament Hill and privately berated by Prime Minister Mackenzie King. According to Bob, King admitted that the nickel shipments occurred, but told him to shut up or be put in jail. But what fascinates me is Bob's account of a meeting with King's right-hand man, Norman Robertson, a highly respected senior civil servant. Bob claims that Robertson denied that strategic materials were being shipped, and now, years later, he is still enraged.

"I was disgusted to see a man of Norman Robertson's achievements prostitute himself, in doing a lackey's job for Mackenzie King. I was really disgusted, nauseated. I'm afraid it's one of the things I don't excuse, a gutless, gutless political lackey."

I use this account in the published biography and am taken to task by Professor Jack Granatstein, the highly respected Canadian historian. He doesn't believe the Robertson story; he believes that the meeting with King did not even take place. His authority, apparently, lies in the fact that King made no mention of the meeting in his diaries. I am intrigued that in a historian's mind the word of a living man of recognized integrity is not accepted because the event described was *not* chronicled by a devious prime minister.

As for Amy, after she has become accustomed to my frequent presence she permits herself to be interviewed. Amy is more reticent than Bob and not given to storytelling. She talks more easily about him than about herself, but I soon realize that beneath the calm, gentle, soft-spoken exterior there is a spine of steel. I also realize that she, like Olive Diefenbaker, is of the old-fashioned school that believes a wife's role is to raise her children and support her husband. This is something she has managed to do in spite of long periods of geographical separation forced upon them by international conflicts and Chinese civil wars.

I detect no separation of hearts.

The McClures were married in 1926, had four children, and for almost twenty years of the war-torn twentieth century were apart more than together, but Amy is the rock on which Bob's heart has rested, the centre of gravity that keeps him focused and sane. (We are a generation apart, but here, as with Mike Pearson's childhood, I find something that resonates with my own experience.) Even when Bob was trekking through the jungles of southwest China he would manage to write a letter every few days to Amy in Toronto. In those letters his love for her is clear. It is also clear that he counted on her to lobby for medical supplies and other aid. Here at home she has been his quiet, self-effacing, unofficial intermediary with the establishment.

Hilda and I send letters and blank audio cassettes to former McClure colleagues in Britain, Europe, the States, New Zealand, and Australia. Everyone who can responds. I also read, as extensively as time permits, books on contemporary Chinese history.

Early on, I luck out. Two of the McClures' closest friends and associates live in Montreal. They are, marvellous to say, none other than my own friends Bruce and Marnie Copland, but only now do I discover that Marnie and Bob were children together in the same mission station in China. Moreover, Bruce was a missionary in China and was associated with Bob even during the Sino-Japanese War. Marnie is the culturally sensitive one, with language skills and creative talents of her own, while Bruce is the academic intellectual. The two of them become my unofficial editors, steering me around pitfalls and offering enormous and constant moral support.

Throughout the remainder of 1976 and on into 1977 Hilda and I are immersed, vicariously, in the chaos that was China in the first half of the twentieth century. This is the era of the warlords, the Sun Yat-sen revolution, the Chiang Kai-shek Nationalist revolution, the war with Japan, which merged into the Second World War, and the culminating Communist revolution. We follow McClure's adventures from when he was a child in China, through his youth, to his time as a mission surgeon, as a Field Director for the International Red Cross on the Yellow River battlefront, as a Commandant of the Friends Ambulance Unit on the Burma Road, to his work in post-war hospital rehabilitation. Long before the China research is completed I am telling the folks at Cloud 85 that there's no way the rest of McClure's remarkable career, in Gaza, India, Canada, Peru, Sarawak, and Africa can possibly be inflicted upon the reader in one book. It will have to be a two-volume biography. They tell me to carry on and do China. We'll tackle one problem at a time.

Early on, I decide that my chronicle of McClure's life in China will be not so much an analytical biography as an adventure story. "Adventure" is the operative word. Right from the start Bob admits that his desire to become a missionary doctor was sparked by the hope for adventure. It was a well-founded hope, since the doctor he was sent to replace had just been murdered by bandits. And I soon find that adventure is of such interest to Bob that he has come up with a formula for it. Adventure, he assures me, involves Risk plus Purpose; $A = R + P$. It's obvious that Purpose is an essential factor.

My principal source of information is McClure himself, and many of his anecdotes seem a bit over the top. I check as much as possible with other sources and other people, and draw corroborating inferences, hoping to strike a happy balance between the truth and a good story. He has one great tale that really troubles me. According to Bob, while he and his multinational Quaker ambulance team were with a large Chinese army in the southern jungle near French Indo-China, the Chinese General threw a party for them and insisted that they sing their respective national anthems. The American medics were so intimidated by the high notes of "The Star Spangled Banner" that they substituted "I've Been Working on the Railroad." The hard-drinking general and his hard-drinking officers loved the tune so much that they called for the "American anthem" on all occasions. Which was all very well, until the Chinese army encountered an American unit, and a mutual flag-raising ceremony was arranged, which called for an American trumpeter to blow forth the real anthem. Bob had a confidential chat with the American commander and enlightened him concerning local politics, diplomacy, and the emotional nature of hard-drinking Chinese generals. Came the flag-raising ceremony and a heart-stopping moment of suspense. Much to the medics' consternation, the bugler burst forth with the opening bars of "The Star Spangled Banner" — then segued neatly into the railroad anthem.

What's a writer to do? Given another year's research I might corroborate this tale. At the moment, I can't. But do I want to corroborate it? What if I find it's all just a yarn? It's too good a story not to tell. So I tell it straight, but protect my back: "That is the story that came out of Yenshan. There has been no indication that it was documented in any military log, which is not surprising. There are those who have implied that the scene by the roadside and the flag-raising ceremony were a figment of a mc-curdled* imagination, while others maintain that even Bob McClure and his gang would not have fabricated a story that had a potential twenty thousand witnesses."

---

*   "McCurdle" was McClure's nickname among members of the Ambulance Unit. They painted it on the back of his bomber jacket.

The manuscript for *McClure: The China Years* is completed by July 1, 1977. It has taken one year to the day. Hilda and I are both exhausted. In addition to coping with correspondence, Hilda has typed several drafts of the entire manuscript, transcribed and indexed all my research interviews, and photocopied, summarized, and indexed Bob's wartime letters. She has barely had time for her own reading, although she has enjoyed Robert Massie's *Nicholas and Alexandra*.

CANEC, under publisher Alun Hughes, does a swift and professional job of designing and printing *McClure: The China Years* in a hardback version and it is launched in the fall. The book makes it onto the Best Seller list and is picked up as an Alternate Selection by the Book-of-the-Month Club.

I am sent on a book-signing tour with Bob. This is an adventure in itself. In Toronto, where we are booked for an appearance in a major department store, we find that the store has forgotten about us. Nothing daunted, Bob commandeers a card table and two chairs, orders the clerk to gather together whatever supply of books they have, and sets up shop. He then begins to tell the clerk an anecdote. The McClure voice telling a good yarn is full of both enthusiasm and volume. It is also highly recognizable, and begins to attract fans. Soon a good signing session is underway. The only other person I know who can tell an anecdote to a companion and cast a spell over everyone within earshot is John Diefenbaker.

Our signings follow a pattern. We sit side by side at a table. The customer wanting a book autographed hands it first to Bob. He signs it, then slides it to me, usually saying to the customer, "And now for the author." In Winnipeg, an eager fan gushes at him, "Oh, Dr. McClure, I've read your book and I do want another one. Oh, you're such a good writer." Bob signs, and beams at her kindly. "Ma'am, I couldn't write it if I tried. I only lived it. Munroe here wrote it." He slides the book to me.

In Edmonton an elegantly dressed, youngish, rather aloof-looking woman proffers a copy for signatures, all the time protesting, "I'm not interested in religion. I'm getting it for my aunt. Religion is not for me. I don't believe in it. This is for my aunt."

Bob looks at her sardonically. "Don't strain yourself, lady."

The frosting on the cake comes in Vancouver. A customer seems unusually alert as she watches Bob sign. When he slides the copy to me she pounces, snatching it to her bosom. "No, no!" she exclaims. "This one is special." She slopes off, having achieved her objective. She has acquired a book *not* autographed by the author.

Dad dies this fall, of a ruptured aortic aneurism, but not until after he has read *McClure: The China Years* and voiced enthusiastic approval. He seems to be proud of it and I take comfort from his having seen it. He is eighty-nine years old and has had a few adventures himself.

I have high hopes for the book in the American market. China is very popular these days. The publisher keeps assuring me that he has contacts in the States who will be interested. Eventually I decide that nothing is really happening and bring my agent into the act. After probing southward she reports, sadly, "The China crest has passed."

In the meantime I am annoyed, intrigued, and stimulated by Shakespeare. It's time for a change of pace.

28

SHYLOCK

IT'S THE SUMMER OF 1977 and, with the *McClure* manuscript safely out of our hands, Hilda and I go to Stratford to see *The Merchant of Venice*. We've seen an earlier production here, in which round-voiced, portly Frederick Valk played an impressive and stately Shylock, and we will see the play again with other prominent actors. This time Hume Cronyn is playing Shylock and Portia is played by Jackie Burroughs. Both of us are impressed by Miss Burroughs, but it is Hume Cronyn who is etched into memory. His interpretation of Shylock is the antithesis of Valk's dignified portrayal. This Shylock is agitated, nervous, frustrated, and utterly convincing. The director is Bill Glassco, the founder of Toronto's Tarragon Theatre. I listen to the play with new ears and am both appalled and fascinated.

I am appalled because, for the first time — a shameful admission — it dawns upon me that the "Christian" protagonists are a dreadful bunch of human beings.

I am fascinated, because the play is so beautifully constructed. It is cultural madness to boycott *The Merchant of Venice*.

Jewish folk condemn the play as being anti-Semitic; their condemnation is misdirected. Many of the characters are anti-Semitic, but the play itself is anti-Christian! Consider: Bassanio, the romantic lead, is a wastrel; Portia is raffled into his bed in accordance with her dying father's Christian wish; as a fake lawyer Portia entraps Shylock more in the name of sport than of justice; Shylock is forced by the court to desert his faith and accept Christianity; and so on ad nauseam.

But if this gang is Christian, I say to myself, may the Lord save me from the Church. What will these people have done to each other in another twenty years time!

On the long drive home to Lindsay I am already imagining a twenty-years-after scenario. When we arrive I go directly to the typewriter.

I have a lot of fun with this project. Language is a challenge. There is no way I want to attempt to fake Shakespearean English, but I do decide to use somewhat formal language; indeed, if one were to break down the dialogue, much of it would scan as iambic pentameter. When Shylock's daughter re-stages the trial, this time playing the false lawyer herself, I intentionally use less rhythmical and more vernacular dialogue. But, being weak-willed, I use verse to create a mad scene for Portia, who relives the lottery scene. She has become deranged, because she has finally realized that her husband, Bassanio, who won her in the lottery, is actually the lover of Antonio, the Merchant. This time around she knows what her dead father's dying wish has done to her:

> Old fool Father spouting divinity
> Ordains where I dispose of my virginity....
> Ah well, take sport, make sport, sport be as may,
> I am an actress in dead Father's Christian play.
> Let's play the play and play it on and on,
> I cannot win it but I can be won.

She relives the marital lottery but sees it with new eyes:

> Pray noble Lord, enter pray, please do.
> The Moroccan Prince you say? How do you do.
> A handsome man you are, I do declare,
> A trifle blacker than I had in mind, but there,
> 'Tis nothing. A handsome man of a handsome nation.
> You and I — my, what a handsome copulation.
> Choose. Gold, silver, lead. Make your call.
> My picture is in one. Winner take all.

This time, when Bassanio arrives to make his gamble she is under no romantic illusions:

> Ah, Bassanio, I hoped you'd never come.
> Who paid the passage? How large a sum?
> Antonio? Oh, yes, your paramour and friend.
> Of course I'm wealthy. Worth the risk no end!
> What? Don't like ladies? Are impotent in bed?
> Think nothing of it. Oh — you choose the lead?
> The lead's the one you like the most?
> You've won! Praise Father, daughter's Holy Ghost.
> My body's yours to sanctify the dead.

Toward the end of the script I find myself letting Shylock's old friend, Tubal, say how I really feel about the so-called Christian qualities of the characters I have extrapolated from Shakespeare:

> PORTIA: Is this an attack or a defence? Have my ears turned backward on my head? It sounds as though Tubal, the Jew, defends the teachings of Our Lord the Christ.
> TUBAL: Why, it is worth defending. You Christians do such a poor job of it, someone must. Antonio here did spit on beards, kick old men, and call them "dog", in the name of Christianity. I described a monastery devoted to exploitation and plunder. We brought forth this monstrous torture rack to stretch a man's bones. We waved a golden stick, an ornamented cup, a jewelled box, while chanting quotes, slogans, and gibberish with Latin endings, and some there be who accepted all in the name of Jesus Christ. Be not offended. Have charity. Forgive us when we say that the Jew of Nazareth must often tremble with dismay.

Within about three days I have a reasonably polished draft of a full-length, open-stage comedy, *Shylock's Treasure*. I use the classification "comedy" in the classical sense — a play with a happy ending. According to the sub-title it is "*A Reconciliation.*"

By this time the critics have savaged Bill Glassco's Stratford production and Bill, I understand, is mightily depressed. I don't blame him. I consider his staging of *The Merchant* to be one of Stratford's finer achievements, and I will continue to do so in the future.

But as for my creation — what to do with it?

I take it to Dennis Sweeting at the Kawartha Summer Theatre. I am in luck. Dennis, bless him, has just been studying Shakespeare at Trent University and is tuned to my wavelength. He slots *Shylock's Treasure* into his 1978 summer season. He is, and remains throughout his career, one of the few artistic directors in this country absolutely committed to presenting new Canadian plays.

Dennis elects to direct *Shylock* himself, and I am delighted. The summer stock schedule, with a maximum, at best, of two weeks rehearsal, is tough enough with an established play. For a new one, it's a cast killer. It's nice to know a real pro is in charge, and when it comes to theatre, who could be more experienced than Dennis Sweeting? He helped found both ACTRA (Association of Canadian Television and Radio Artists) and Actors' Equity as well as the popular Canadian Players touring company, which for many years took theatre to the far-flung cities and remote communities of Canada. He didn't found this Kawartha Summer Theatre, but he and his wife, Maggie, have certainly been its guiding lights almost since its inception. In this strange world of Canadian theatre the Sweetings are, quite simply, royal family.* My play is in good hands.

I, of course, agree to be on hand throughout rehearsals to write our way out of any quicksand we come upon. There are few problems, except for the very ending. We all struggle valiantly with the ending. I feel sorry for Jane Buss, who is playing my middle-aged Portia. She's doing a fine job, but some of the problems originate in her lines. I can't think of anything more frustrating for professionals working up a new play than to know that if they had just a few more days or even hours of rehearsal a problem that is plaguing them could be solved. Some problems, and this is one of them, are very subtle. The audience may never notice them, but they plague playwright, director, and cast. Even with input from veterans like Dan MacDonald, who plays Antonio, and Roger Dunn, who plays Bassanio, we never quite make it. By opening night the ending is acceptable but still not correct. I think I finally get it right when the penny drops during my post-production script revision.

This is my first immersion in summer theatre and I'm intrigued to find that most of the nine speaking members of the cast are rehearsing *Shylock's Treasure* by day while appearing on stage in another play at night. Their stamina, cheerfulness, and dedication amaze me.

There is one rehearsal glitch. A principal player, Jack Northmore, who plays a pivotal role as a domineering abbot, cannot join us for rehearsals until the second week. But Jack is an old pro with a string of credits that go beyond theatre right back to an earlier life as a member of the popular singing group, the Billy Van Four. No one is worried about Jack's not performing.

We receive a bonus on opening night when Norman Jewison shows up. Seems he is a friend of our female lead, Wendy Creed, who is playing Shylock's vengeful daughter. Wendy is a young raven-haired bombshell of an actress who brings an aura of sheer energy onto the stage. Not every actor radiates this energy. I doubt if it's learned. Probably one of God's little gifts. I like Wendy. She has no pretensions. She says she likes costume drama because her hips are too big.

———

*   Dennis died in 2000, at the age of 85, highly respected, much loved, and a worthy holder of the Order of Canada.

Opening night goes well as far as the audience is concerned, but Jack Northmore gives me writer's heartburn. Every now and then I hear him coming unstuck in his lines, and then, good old pro that he is, he manufactures new lines out of thin air. As a playwright, I find this hard on my blood pressure, and it's considerably disconcerting for his fellow actors, who like the support of cues delivered accurately, in place, and on time. But everyone copes admirably and there are no recriminations. Jack will nail it all into place during the run.

I am relatively happy. Dennis is quite happy. Most of the audience seem very happy.

"Isn't Jack wonderful?" people say to me as they depart. "I do so enjoy Jack!"

Well I enjoy Jack too, but I would have enjoyed my play more if Jack had had another week to rehearse and I'd had that damned ending right.

I get to meet Norman Jewison as he hurries backstage in a mad dash to say hello to Wendy before leaving. I introduce myself to him and get to shake his hand for three seconds before he vanishes. What he thinks of my play, good, bad, or indifferent, I never discover, although there may be a message in the speed of his departure.

After the opening night performance, as Hilda and I take the two-block walk home, breathing the balmy night air along Lindsay's quiet maple-lined streets, I say, "Honey, I think we're in luck. I think this one is really going to go places." As it turns out, "go places" is open to inter-pretation.

The local newspaper, the *Lindsay Daily Post*, prints a review that is lukewarm (pseudo-Shakespeare is not normal summer theatre fare) but not damaging. Both Dennis and I figure that *Shylock's Treasure* should have an afterlife. As soon as it's made available by Playwrights Canada I begin sending copies off to other theatres.

I accumulate some encouraging reactions.

Leon Major writes to me saying,

I think the writing is first class — it's literate and colourful, it has movement and texture....

But he also confides, later, over a drink, that as a Jew he has such a built-in pre-conditioning against anything to do with *The Merchant* that he can't touch it. I have some sympathy, but he's missed the point.

Professor Eric Salmon, at the time the head of the Drama Department at the University of Guelph, is very encouraging:

Shylock comes out of the matter very well.... What a marvel it would be, some time, to do a festival of all three plays — yours, St. John Ervine's [*The Lady of Belmont*] and Shakespeare's — side by side! As you will gather, I am enthusiastic about your piece.

Geraldine Balzer, writing in *Canadian Drama*, says,

Scott has emulated the quick wit and verbal play of Shakespeare.... [T]he language play makes this comedy a delight.... Shylock has created his second chance and used it to its maximum.*

As an added stimulant for my optimism, Dr. Rota Herzberg Lister, a Professor of English at Guelph, scatters some nine copies abroad onto the waters of Jewish academia. By the time I learn of this and inquire whether or not she has had any reaction, she has retired. I hear nothing further.

Most of the theatres to which I send copies never respond. One artistic director replies only to tell me I am turning the "beautiful people" of Shakespeare's play into middle-aged horrors. Another, Urjo Kareda, writes, with typical honest insight,

No matter what different perspectives you take on the characters, the fact and myth and knowledge of Shakespeare's play remain. They will challenge and obstruct you. Your play will not be received because too much is already in the way.

He may well be correct. Indeed, Portia voices a similar sentiment toward the end of my play:

Oh, we played a most vile play some twenty years ago and to this day Shylock is still thought mean, Antonio still thought noble, Portia still thought brilliant, Bassanio romantic, Gobbo gross — all such monstrous lies are still believed no matter what we say or do.

One thing is certain. *Shylock's Treasure* will have a few amateur productions, but no professional theatre will restage it. Stratford will restage *The Merchant* several times, and I will try to con lesser theatres into staging *Shylock's Treasure* simultaneously with the Stratford production and to

---

*   *Canadian Drama* 9, 2 (1983).

give discounts to holders of Merchant ticket stubs. No takers. I will ask myself the question that plagues many Canadian playwrights — have I failed, or has theatre failed?

Eventually, in desperation, I submit *Shylock's Treasure* to the CBC-TV Drama Department and, inevitably, to Robert Allen. He tells me, "There's nothing new here."

29

GLOBAL GLIMPSES ALONG THE MCCLURE TRAIL

WRITING *Shylock's Treasure* is, I suppose, recreational and therapeutic. It only temporarily deflects me from the saga of Bob McClure. *McClure: The China Years* is doing well, and CANEC is willing to publish a second volume. The United Church, however, is hesitant to advance royalties or underwrite expenses. I understand the problem. There are many many other missionaries who have made outstanding contributions, in China and elsewhere. The Church is well aware of diplomacy and is not immune to either internal jealousy or politics. There have already been calls for equal treatment for others. But not to worry. We all agree to look for ways and means.

I go to Ottawa with a copy of *McClure: The China Years* under my arm and attempt to penetrate the inner sanctums of the Canada Council. At this time, the Council's offices are scattered among several buildings; I approach a receptionist at one and explain that I wish to speak to someone regarding the possibility of a grant to complete a biography. I am asked if I am an academic — meaning do I have a Ph.D. I confess I do not, and am told that my quest might be fruitless, but to go to another office in another building. I do so. The receptionist here questions me in a similar vein, but is pleasantly helpful and sends me to yet another office. Receptionist No. 3 is also unsure where to channel me for a non-academic biography, but she, too, helpfully refers me onward. I find myself back in building No. 1, in front of receptionist No. 1. There appears to be no way to penetrate the front-line defences. I leave, despondent.

I spend the evening with John Munro, with whom I have kept in contact since the Diefenbaker expedition, and tell him about my abortive assault on Canada Council battlements. It's the kind of tale that narrates well in convivial surroundings and is particularly enjoyed by denizens of Ottawa.

John is superficially amused, but deeply irate. He stops laughing and goes to the phone. I don't know whom he is calling but he is relaying my saga. This is a fast grapevine even for Ottawa. John hangs up and tells me I have an appointment the next morning with Mr. Frank Milligan, a senior executive with the Canada Council. When I discover that the gentleman's title is "Associate Director for University Affairs," my heart sinks. The receptionists were correct. I'm venturing into the sacred realm of academia.

Mr. Milligan is friendly, diplomatic, and apologetic. He is diplomatic in that he listens politely to my impassioned plea to be given the opportunity to tell the remainder of the McClure story. After all, my protagonist is a surgeon who not only served for many years in the heart of China, but returned to serve in Canada, spent five years in the Gaza Strip and fifteen years in India, became, after his retirement, the first lay Moderator of the United Church of Canada, and after all that went on to volunteer as a surgeon in Zaire, Peru, the Caribbean, and northern British Columbia. This is no small saga.

Mr. Milligan apologizes for the problem I had with the receptionists, then also apologizes for the fact that they had been absolutely correct — there is no grant category under which I can apply. I leave him a copy of *The China Years*, which he accepts with some reluctance.

Our meeting is on Tuesday, November 22. He must be a fast reader, because on Thursday, November 24 he writes to me, describing *The China Years* as "one of those rare joys," but reaffirming that no program exists that would underwrite a sequel. "However," he writes, "the Council makes its own rules, and can, when circumstances warrant, waive them." He makes no promises but says he'll see what he can do to have my request "considered."

It will be at least five months before I know what's possible. During this time, Mr. Milligan becomes the Executive Director of the Humanities and Social Science Research Council when it hives off from the Canada Council. But by April 1978 I have a Canada Council Senior Grant that will permit me to spend the next year and a half researching and writing volume two of the McClure saga. Included is a budget for extensive travel.

Before taking to the road I do more interviewing, send off more letters, read more histories of more faraway places, and even write a draft of the manuscript. Lord, what a dull read it makes. This is not like the China saga, which was a roaring medical adventure set in the midst of social chaos. China was a large enough setting, but now the story wanders the globe, and, judging from my dismal first draft, it is desperately in need of authentic local colour. Fortunately, in most of the places where McClure has worked since 1949 the trail is still warm. I'll be able to see more or less what he saw, and meet his former colleagues. Now, eight months after stepping into this volume two project, it is definitely time to hit the McClure trail.

Ian has just graduated from high school and has been saying he doesn't want to go directly on to university. Hilda, Ian, Rob, and I are having lunch one day when I make a suggestion.

"Ian, your grandfather left you a few bucks. Enough to buy a fat air ticket. My expenses are covered. You buy your ticket, your mother and I will find the wherewithal to cover your other expenses. How would you like to come with me around the world?"

There is a long, silent pause. Rob, the sixteen-year-old, stares at his brother, his mouth hanging open.

"Hey," he says, "if you don't say yes, I will!"

But there's never any doubt. Ian is speechless only because he is stunned. I figure it's a good move for both of us. For him, it will be that happiest of combinations, education through adventure. For me it will mean companionship and physical assistance. At nineteen he is a strapping 6' 2". Before we are home again he is identifying himself as my "baggage wallah." He is more than that. He becomes my keeper. He has an unerring sense of direction and location. He always knows where we are in relation to where we have been, a useful talent in the back streets of Old Jerusalem and the crowded bazaars of India. I concentrate on gathering and retaining other information, confident that Ian always knows where our gear is and, better still, where we are.

My son and I follow the McClure trail. Our aim is to go where McClure went, to imagine or see what he saw, and to talk to people who knew him, all within the limits of budget, time, and practicality.

Ian and I are in Israel. For us this is the only route into the Gaza Strip, and there are people here who knew McClure. In addition, Bob, a missionary, visited Jerusalem, and my background, too, draws me relentlessly to the Holy City.

We are within the walls of Old Jerusalem, a strange, ancient, and mysteriously beautiful city with arched, stone-walled corridors, lanes, and streets. The past is alive. The past is real. The past is here.

We enter the Church of the Holy Sepulchre.

The church is massive and austere. It was built by crusaders more than a thousand years after the death of Christ, but is said to have been built around the hill called Golgotha, where Christ was executed. The hill, or some of the rock that composed it, is still here. Or at least there is some rock that can be seen through an opening in a wall beneath a staircase, and we are told that rock is part of Golgotha. There is a visible crack in the rock, and its presence is said to support the Bible's statement that at the time of Christ's death "the earth did quake, and the rocks rent." The stairway itself leads up to a chapel garishly ornamented with icons, gilt, paint, and candles. There is an elaborate altar and behind it stand three golden crosses; the central one, it is said, stands upon the very spot where Christ's cross stood. We are able to crawl beneath the altar to a brass-ringed hole in the floor. One can reach through the hole and touch the rock beneath. Of course, one is expected to make a cash offering.

On a lower level, away from the chapel but still within the ancient church, there is a huge solid rectangular block of what appears to be polished red marble. No, it is not solid. There is a doorway. And outside the doorway burn several tall, imposing candles. We are told this was Christ's tomb. We enter through a low doorway and find ourselves in a small outer chamber from which an even lower doorway leads us into the "tomb" itself, a rough-hewn cave of a room about six feet square. Along one side there is a narrow ledge wide enough to accommodate a body. Here, with an effort of will, I can imagine that I really am in the tomb. If it were not, that is, for the grey-bearded, grubby-looking priest standing beside the ledge soliciting money for the church.

Outside the tomb again, we sit for a moment on a stone bench. A tourist is sitting beside us. After a moment I realize she is weeping. I ask if she is unwell.

"Oh, it is all so awful," she says, and by her accent I know she is from England. "Everything is so ... so crass. So vulgar."

I know what she means. The "Golgotha" chapel is ornamented to the point of vulgarity, but it was probably the sight of the priest in the tomb that turned on the taps. But I also know one can't expect two thousand years of urban life to pass without the human animal destroying, rebuilding, ornamenting, mythologising, and generally altering any original reality. Besides, is there a reality? Is it not always subjective? Is it not always fleeting?

I tell her to exit from the old city via the Damascus Gate and follow the Nablus Road for a short distance to a certain narrow laneway that will lead her to a small wooden door in a blank stone wall. Inside she will

find a garden and within the garden she will find vestiges of a two-thou-
sand-year-old vineyard; she will also find a tomb carved into a cliffside. I
know, because Ian and I have been there. Archaeologists say this garden
tomb could conceivably be Christ's; it satisfies most of the criteria. There
is even a promontory at one end of the cliff that looks like a skull and,
after all, Golgotha means "place of the skull." Here, the imagination can
slip into unfettered action and one can ponder the imponderables.

The lady brightens up and departs, hoping to restore her faith, outside the church.

I am, fortunately, armed with introductions from Al Forrest, editor
of the *United Church Observer*, who has been here himself and has maintained his contacts. An Arab Christian drives us from Jerusalem to Gaza
City. There are Israeli military checkpoints to pass through and passports
to be scrutinized. Our companion, however, knows the drill, and in Gaza
City he takes us to a small private hotel that is like a family home.

Gaza City, with broken sidewalks and sandswept streets, looks as
though it had been ravaged by war, but we are told this is its normal
appearance. Near the city centre there is a walled compound containing
the hospital where Bob McClure worked for three years as surgeon and
administrator. At the time he was seconded to it, the hospital was
administered by Britain's Church Missionary Society. Now it is being run
by an American evangelical mission. We introduce ourselves at the
administrator's home, which is within the compound. We are received
courteously but coolly. Over tea and cakes the wife asks me, point blank,
"Are you a Christian?"

As far as I can recall, I have never been asked this before, other than
on a census form. Normally the answer would be a simple "yes," but
there is something about this lady that makes me think she wants to
know if I am *really* a Christian. Am I contrite, forgiven, re-born, re-bap-
tized, washed in the blood of the Lamb? I merely reply that I am a member of the United Church of Canada. She can interpret that any way she
wishes. I know that a few years ago, when McClure returned to Canada
and became Moderator of the United Church, he presided over the
adoption of a new, alternate creed that so nicely sidestepped the Trinity,
the virgin birth, the resurrection, and life everlasting that American
denominations like hers wanted the United Church of Canada
drummed out of the National Council of Churches.

There is a large refugee camp within the bounds of the city. Ian and
I walk through it. It's a hot, barren place, with streets of sand bordered
by rows of cement-block houses that are little more than rigidly regi-
mented boxes. We attract a group of teenagers. They walk with us, trying

out their English. They almost ignore me, but chatter in a friendly fashion to Ian. We've been told the camps are not a safe place for foreigners, but nowhere in Gaza do we ever feel threatened, except when we break for our daily swim at the pristine, amazingly empty beach. On these occasions we are always aware of the watching eyes of Israeli soldiers, who are manning a jeep with a machine gun mounted on its rear. They hover just above and beyond the beach, on the upper edge of a cliff-like sandy bank. It is possible they are lurking there to protect us, but I find myself wondering if they suspect we have contraband stashed aboard the rusty hulk of a shipwrecked freighter that protrudes a few hundred yards from where we swim.

We make a more formal visit to another camp, and here, with the aid of an interpreter, we meet other young people. Many are determined to go abroad for an education. They see education as the ticket out of here. I know that when McClure was here he put a great deal of effort into training X-ray technicians, believing, correctly, that it was a trade that would make his students employable abroad. Some of these young people are hoping to go to Germany to study medicine. I ask if they speak German. They look surprised. Of course they don't. How, I ask, will they be able to study? This is, apparently, an intensely stupid question. They will learn German. Of course.

Terrorism is not, at this time, on the upswing. No *Intifada* has as yet been launched. There is still hope here. McClure has a formula for terrorism. He has formulas for several things, such as "Adventure = Risk + Purpose" and "Satisfaction = Service ÷ Income." He likes to bait fellow members of the Canadian Medical Association with the latter formula, which suggests that Satisfaction will be diminished by too large an Income. His terrorism formula — or, more accurately, law — simply states that Terrorism grows in inverse proportion to Hope. As Hope dwindles Terrorism grows. If this law were understood and acted upon, the world would be a happier place.

In my files at home there is a letter from a New Zealand nurse who worked with McClure here in Gaza. She told me to ask Bob about "the sex change operation." I received the same suggestion in an interview with another former Gaza nurse, now living in Toronto. I did ask Bob, and he claimed to have no idea what they were talking about. Now, in Gaza City, Ian and I are in a local pharmacy talking to the Palestinian druggist and a couple of his medical associates, all of whom knew McClure, and obviously enjoyed knowing him. We are sitting, relaxed. The druggist has his feet up on his desk. I casually ask about "the" sex change operation. There is sudden, cheerful animation. Oh yes, indeed.

McClure turned a girl into a boy. Very, very culturally acceptable. The person was from the Jabalia refugee camp, they say. Not only that, McClure did it more than once. They are in no doubt whatsoever. Later research suggests to me that Bob may have been dealing with a form of "pseudohermaphroditism," which is, apparently, familial. But what is just as interesting is the jovial way these Muslim Palestinians reminisce about Christian missionary Bob McClure.

In another conversation, the Muslim doctor who is medical health officer for the city of Gaza tells me that Dr. McClure "had a very good relationship with God." Obviously McClure did not go around Gaza asking people if they were Christian, or he would not have had such a good relationship with the locals.

Our next destination is New Delhi, India, but the air route takes us via Iran, where we are delayed half a day at the Tehran airport. We decide not to venture into the city, because there is some sort of revolution underway and the Shah has put Tehran under martial law. There are times when it is wise to subdue the tourist instinct.

After we arrive at New Delhi in the middle of the night, the taxi taking us into the city runs out of gas and we reach our pre-booked hotel just in time to get up. Travel is such fun.

There are contacts to be made in this city, even though McClure didn't work here. But we also give ourselves a one-day break in order to take a bus ride the 200 kilometres to the legendary Taj Mahal. I can no more resist visiting the Taj than I could resist visiting Jerusalem. I have been pre-conditioned for both, but whereas the Jerusalem pre-conditioning emerged from the culture of my entire childhood and youth, the pre-conditioning for the Taj was achieved in one memorable day.

It was late spring in northern Manitoba, and the ice had gone out of the lakes and rivers only a few days before, permitting Anson Moorhouse and me to be flown in to Norway House, Cross Lake, and God's Lake on a research survey. We had landed on beautiful Island Lake, which was studded, not surprisingly, with a myriad islands. We had stepped off the bush plane's float onto a simple wooden dock and had walked up to the long low log building, the principal structure in a clearing surrounded by typical Precambrian rock and bush. We had entered the building through a doorway so low it made us stoop. It was like walking into the nineteenth, possibly even the eighteenth century. This was a trading post. A genuine trading post. This had none of the glitz and chrome, the transplanted-from-the-city-mall look, that one sees in northern Hudson's Bay stores. This was the real article. The aging owner-manager greeted us — no, he was not a "manager," he was a "trader," or, better still, a "factor," straight out of the history books.

It had been a slow day and the factor seemed genuinely pleased to have visitors. We sat in front of a log fire, drinking coffee and chatting. When he found that Anson had travelled abroad he began to ask questions about the world's great buildings. Had Anson seen Westminster Abbey? Apparently the factor had visited the Abbey, but only in books. Soon we found that this homespun man, who had never been farther than Winnipeg, had not been confined by physical isolation. I found myself listening to the clergyman and the factor discussing India's Taj Mahal — the poetry of its proportions, the white beauty of its marble walls, the aesthetics of its reflecting pool, the elegance of its four sentinel minarets, the way light filters into its interior through lace-like screens carved from solid stone, the facts and fictions of its burial crypts. Our host, sitting in this low log building whose walls were adorned with moose heads, snowshoes, beaver skins, and other artifacts of his trade, knew the Taj Mahal as intimately as if he had viewed it from every angle, walked every path, and admired every stone. My own ignorance was overwhelming.

But now, at last, twenty years later, I too have made it to the Taj Mahal.

This is the most astoundingly beautiful structure I have ever seen, or ever expect to see. The clergyman and the factor had been correct on every count. Our senses already overwhelmed, Ian and I continue next door to Agra Fort, more like a palace than a fort, itself an exotically amazing structure, but made all the more exotic by being built of brick-red sandstone, in sharp contrast to the gleaming white marble of the Taj. Finally, weary with a surfeit of crowded buses, appalling public sanitary facilities, questionable "fast" food, and magnificent architecture, we sit on a low stone fence to await departure time. We are surrounded, as usual and as everywhere, by vendors, all extolling, exhorting, pleading. We wave them off and they go. All but one. He is a somewhat nondescript-looking fellow in his twenties with a fist full of equally nondescript souvenirs. Ian and I have an agreement not to burden ourselves with junk souvenirs, anywhere — not even in front of Agra Fort or the Taj Mahal. I tell the vendor to desist.

He refuses to go. He keeps thrusting his wares at us. He exhorts us in nasal, whining pidgin English to buy his supposedly charm-laden bric-a-brac. He insists, he importunes, he pesters. Ian asks him to go. I order him to go. Later I find out from Bob McClure that there are Hindi swear words that let vendors know you mean what you say, but unfortunately our missionary contacts have not seen fit to educate us. Finally, in weary desperation, I shake my fist under the guy's nose and, lacking Hindi, use some Anglo-Saxon.

The fellow's face relaxes into a smile. He perches on the wall beside us.

"I say, where are you chaps from?" The pidgin English has miraculously been replaced by what strikes me as Brahmin-Oxford.

We tell him who we are and why we are in India, and he tells us that he is attending university, what he is studying, and what he hopes to do. I offer to buy a souvenir. "You don't want this junk," he says.

We visit for the remaining minutes before our bus arrives. We wish him good luck and he wishes us bon voyage. As we take our seats we hear a familiar, somewhat nasal, downtrodden, whining voice exhorting boarding passengers to buy charm-laden souvenirs. If I am learning anything in life it is that few things in this round world are exactly what they appear to be.

A few days later we are leaving New Delhi. Checking out of the YMCA, I ask for the room statement. The first night, pre-booked and guaranteed, is not on the account. I indicate the oversight, and the manager becomes quite irate.

"You were late. You did not arrive until the morning. How can we charge you for a night you did not have?" I wonder how many hotel guests in Canada have been asked that question.

We take a taxi to the New Delhi train station. We are hoping to catch the Frontier Mail, heading south.

"You have your tickets?" inquires the driver.

"No, we'll get them at the station."

"Oh no, no, we must go to the office. You cannot get tickets at the station."

I know this is theoretically correct. One cannot purchase sleeper accommodation at the station and we have a long day-and-a-half trip ahead of us. I also know there is, currently, a two-week waiting list at the booking office. I hope to sort something out at the station, even if it's simply permission to stand in a corridor.

The taxi driver is upset. All the way to the station he worries that he is betraying his passengers. They will be disappointed. He should be taking them to the office.

There is, in fact, a ticket office at the station and an agent who seems to have all the accoutrements for sales, but he informs us we are out of luck. I ask to see a supervisor. We are taken to the track and shown an office far down the platform. This is a big British Railroad-style station. It would look quite at home in Manchester or even London. We find the superintendent's office. He speaks excellent English and listens sympathetically to our appeal for swift transport. He looks doubtful, almost sad, as though it pains him not to help.

"And where may you be from?" he asks.

I tell him, and he brightens. "Ah, Canada. The very best of countries. Ah yes. I have relatives in Canada."

We are served tea. After a suitable delay I ask how long it might be before we can indeed catch a train. He looks almost surprised. "Oh," he says, "we will accommodate, we will accommodate."

When the Frontier Mail arrives he seizes a clipboard and leads us to the sleeping car section. We walk the train until he finds an empty compartment that seems to satisfy him.

"Ah, yes, yes, yes. You will be all right here until the morning. Then you will have to wait in the aisle, but it will only be a few hours more."

And we are all right until morning, even though, during the evening, a wandering passenger stands in the doorway quizzing us cheerfully, but unmercifully. He has all the earmarks of a con man. But before releasing us from his interminable chatter he says, "Lock your door tonight. There are bandits on these trains." (This seems unlikely, but a week later I will take a side trip on a rustic local that has recently been held up by bandits, who killed the engineer with an arrow.)

In the morning, when the pre-booked occupants board the train, they insist that we sit with them in their compartment until we reach our destination, the town of Ratlam. A handsome, charming young couple, they speak excellent English and seem genuinely intrigued that we are following the trail of a Canadian doctor. They are also immaculately clean and are wearing a great deal of freshly laundered white. I suspect they belong to a religious sect, but they bear no Hindu markings. I refrain from personal questions. The only thing that mars the remainder of the journey is the presence of a few mosquitoes. I manage to squash a couple of the more malevolent ones.

As we disembark, he of the previous evening accosts us.

"I see you had company this morning. Very fine people. Did they tell you they are Jains?"

Jains? The religious sect to whom all life is sacred? Who would kill nothing? Not even a mosquito?

I have just repaid kindness and courtesy with violence and desecration. I feel uncouth.

We disembark from the Frontier Mail at a major destination, Ratlam, in the heart of India, halfway between New Delhi and Bombay. This is a sprawling, dusty, teeming, lovely, ugly, attractive, repellent, mystical, crass, superstitious, enlightened town — in other words, a typical Indian community. The mission station here, with its two-storey mission houses and its low-slung hospital, was Bob and Amy McClure's home during their thirteen years in India. It is much like any other mission station. And the surrounding city, for all its inherently wild contrasts, contains that most western of institutions, a Rotary Club. Bob McClure was the first non-Indian to be president of the Ratlam Rotary Club. When Ian and I turn up, the Rotary Club greets us with enthusiasm.

The Rotarians let it be known that we are here doing research for a biography of the doctor. McClure's former patients seek us out, wanting to tell us about him. Too many have a disconcerting desire to show their scars. Some unveil themselves before they can be prevented, but what the heck, they wear those scars like badges of honour. They also leap to the conclusion that because I am writing a biography the subject must be dead. It is delightful to see their pleasure on learning that he is still gung-ho.

We are taken under the wing of a retired nurse, Sonu Canara, who had been McClure's Head Nurse in the O.R. She clears the pathway to former associates and opens the floodgates of memory.

In the hospital itself, some of Bob's former staff are still active. I am told they had nicknamed him "Dada," but now, eleven years after he left, they argue as to whether the name meant "brother," "father," "boss" — or "godfather," as in the mafia. Knowing McClure, I suspect it meant all four. The discussions, like those in Palestine, are always jovial. And on the gown shelf in the O.R. there is still a neat pile of gowns carrying the monogram "MC," for McClure, and a label on the shelf says "Dr. McClure's gowns." They are sacrosanct.

Ian and I journey on to Bombay. We are in transit to Borneo, but even in Bombay there are people who knew the doctor. Following the advice of Parsee friends of McClure, we go for a walk in a hillside park. Verdant and beautifully manicured, it is a topiary garden whose shrubs have been trained, moulded, and clipped to represent animals of many shapes and sizes. We have come here to enjoy the garden and the view. On the edge of this lovely, sophisticated park there is a Parsee Tower of Silence. A large round structure with an open top, not unlike a very large, squat silo, it has a function similar to that of our crematoriums — but with a difference. We can't see into the tower but we can see the vultures that circle lazily above it and then drop down inside to consume the dead. There is something about the whole scene that is peaceful, logical, and natural.

We fly to the Malaysian province of Sarawak on the fabled island of Borneo and are soon travelling upstream, on the Rajang River. Our destination is the town of Kapit, far into the interior, where McClure, accompanied by Amy, served as a volunteer administrator/surgeon for two and a half years after retiring as church Moderator.

Our water bus is a powerful twin-diesel launch with comfortable bench seats in a covered cabin. The river is wide, winding, placid, and muddy, with beautiful jungle-clad borders. There are occasional clearings in the jungle and every so often we pass a lumber mill or a small village. Houses are very long and thatched. They remind me superficially of Huron longhouses, except that these stand a storey above ground, on stilts. The jungle dwellers here are Iban. The Iban are Dayaks. The Dayaks have a long, celebrated history as head-hunters. The last head was taken as recently as 1949.

Our boat roars full throttle around a bend and suddenly the engines are cut. The craft wallows to a crawl and then stops. Our path is blocked by a dark, camouflaged gunboat. It rumbles alongside and heavily armed men wearing dark, ominous-looking uniforms come on board. Ian and I have no idea who they are or what they want and we are not about to ask. This is not India. Here, English is not a principal language. The men walk slowly down the aisle, staring for a long disconcerting moment at each passenger. Apparently satisfied, they leave. Our boat continues its journey.

It is quite stimulating to have a solid dose of apprehension injected into an otherwise idyllic journey.

It is a warm, humid day in the Borneo jungle. We are seated, Ian and I and an interpreter, on the verandah of an Iban longhouse. The river, the water path that led us here, can be glimpsed through the trees at the end of a short trail. The covered verandah runs the entire length of this longhouse and appears to occupy almost half of the available floor space. Doorways lead off it into the private quarters of several tribal families. Nearby are several other similar houses, all built from local materials — rough-sawn lumber, poles, vines for lashings, and leaves for thatching. We are seated, cross-legged, in a circle that is comprised, except for ourselves and our interpreter, of women. They are Iban wives and mothers.

The conversation seems remarkably relaxed and personal. It begins innocuously enough, with the women telling us how thankful they were for a midwifery program that McClure instituted when he was here from 1971 to 1974. A key component had to do with the technique for cutting umbilical cords. Traditionally, the cord had been cut with a piece of split bamboo, and the end of the cord was "purified" by rubbing it with ashes from the cooking fire. But these fire ashes were used by fastidious house cats as kitty litter, and even dogs made deposits. As a result, far too often the newborn infant would suffer an onslaught of tetanus, which would result in death in less than twenty-four hours. The women tell us that McClure supplied them with little sterile kits for cutting the umbilical cord and showed them a movie explaining their purpose and use.* They tell us how pleased they are that so many more of the newborns now actually live.

And then the conversation gets really personal. They tell us that traditionally a woman who has just given birth must sit with her back to the cooking fire for a month to dry out. During that period she eats only salt and rice. We need no explanation to appreciate that a woman can take only so much of this, when it's added to the natural trauma of childbirth. And a high rate of infant mortality encourages a high birthrate. Now I know why some of the mothers look so much older and more worn than their age should warrant.

In both China and India McClure had been a staunch advocate of family planning. Here in Sarawak he had again taken up the challenge. After a woman delivered her third child he would recommend a bi-lateral tubal ligation. Now, a mere four years after McClure had been here, my nineteen-year-old son and I are sitting on an elevated verandah in the Borneo jungle with a group of Iban housewives who are enthusiastically extolling the virtues of having their tubes tied. More than half of those present have been granted the favour. They are so pleased that I am afraid they, too, are going to display their scars.

We fly into Hong Kong early in the evening. There are two people here, a Chinese nurse and a Chinese doctor, whom I want to interview. Both worked with McClure in Sarawak and both now live in the New Territories. I know where the nurse is working but I have no address of any kind for the doctor. I hope the nurse will solve that problem. The other

---

* The film was made by a Canadian medical student, Lorne Direnfeld, working in Sarawak for the summer as a volunteer.

thing we don't have is a hotel reservation. Our schedule has become a little ragged. But never mind, this is Hong Kong.

Unfortunately, Hong Kong is full to the brim. The helpful folk at the airport travel desk have thrown up their hands in despair. Every licensed room in the colony is taken. There are lineups of other stymied travellers. Even the baggage lockers are full.

I con the airline into stashing our bags behind a desk in their office and phone the hospital where the nurse works and, fortunately, resides. My plea will be that if we can at least interview her for an hour or so this evening we'll return to the airport and continue on to Japan, or home, or wherever. Amy McClure has already warned us that the Chinese nurse, Miss Soeng, speaks a mixture of Mandarin, English, Iban, and various other languages that comes out as "Soengalese." But she is, apparently, a powerhouse of enthusiasm and energy.

Fortunately, my first contact on the phone is with an English-speaking supervisor, who simply tells me to take a bus to the hospital.

The bus takes us out of Kowloon into the hills and the darkness. We arrive at the hospital with only a hazy impression of our whereabouts, but find the supervisor, who in turn introduces us to Miss Soeng and a companion. They are both weathered-looking women of indeterminate age and are both dressed all in black, like the Hakka women one sees working as labourers on construction sites. The supervisor tells us that Miss Soeng and her companion will look after us.

These women don't walk, they flit, arms waving to beckon us onward. We fly in their wake, directly back to the bus stop where we recently alighted. The four of us catch a bus heading down, out of the hills and back into Kowloon. It's a winding road, and it's the dead of night, and the bus rockets downhill as though devoid of brakes. My damned stomach begins to act up. I begin the all-too-familiar sweat. I slouch down in the seat, put my head back, and close my eyes. Ian opens the window beside me as wide as it will go. He says I have turned white and am progressing to grey, or else the other way around. I begin to experience the familiar angst that accompanies acute seasickness. I know I'm in trouble when I begin to fear that I will live. This is almost as bad as the old S.S. *Manitoulin* of yesteryear.

By a Herculean effort of will I hold everything in place, eyes firmly shut, until the bus emerges from the hills onto level ground and rolls to a halt. There is no way, however, I can make it to the door. I thrust my head out of the window and throw up, voluminously. As my eyesight clears I realize that the bus has stopped in the midst of a crowded, floodlit

Asian bazaar. Hundreds of eyes are staring. Another uncouth foreigner has gone too far. Probably drunk. Barbarians.

Our two black-robed guides leave the bus and stand at the side of the street, arms waving, looking like two excited crows. Are they summoning the authorities? No, they are hailing a taxi. They stuff us aboard, and twenty minutes later we drive into the gated courtyard of a modest apartment building. We are ushered through another gate, up a flight of stairs, and into a small one-bedroom apartment. There's not quite enough headroom for either Ian or myself to stand fully upright, but there is a small living room, a tiny kitchen, and a bedroom shelf. Everything is immaculately clean and fresh. We are given to understand, in Soengalese, that these quarters are ours, free, for as long as we require them. We have arrived in Hong Kong with no hotel booking and no hope of any, but are suddenly in possession of an apartment. There are indeed miracles.

My main concern now is to find out how, when, and where I can interview Miss Soeng, and whether or not I can find McClure's other colleague, the doctor. Again, in a mixture of Soengalese, mime, and sheer telepathy, I am given to understand that there is no need to worry. The good doctor lives in the top-floor apartment. Nurse Soeng will return tomorrow evening, the doctor will interpret for us, and I can interview both of them. She and her companion flit into the night, arms still waving, black robes flying.

Ian is tired, but I am exhausted. We settle down for a good night's sleep. In the middle of the night my inner man erupts. I know these signs, too. This is not seasickness, this is the onset of *mal de tourisme*, Montezuma's revenge, the runs. This is a charming apartment, but it has one drawback. The toilet facilities are elsewhere. I exit down a flight of stairs, unlock a gate, and run across a small courtyard. I open another gate and run along a corridor to where a night watchman is sitting on a chair, half asleep. With frantic gestures I ask for guidance and am directed into a basement, where, indeed, there is a toilet room. The facility itself is the old Asiatic style, with a hole in the floor and two slightly raised footstands shaped like footprints. These are cleverly placed. If one stands in the prints and crouches sufficiently, one's aim will be more or less on target.

Every half-hour or so throughout the remainder of the night I plunge down the stairway, unlock the gate, run across the courtyard, open another gate, charge down the corridor, and dive into the bowels of the building. Each time, as I go by, the compassionate watchman rubs his tummy and waves me on my frantic way.

It is definitely time to go home.

The second volume of the McClure saga, *McClure: Years of Challenge*, is published by CANEC in 1979. Eventually Penguin Canada will publish both volumes in paperback.

I am under the impression that I have completed the McClure saga, but how wrong I am. Early in 1981 Bob McClure tells me he is going to China as a resource person for a tour group organized by Christian Tours and Travel, out of Toronto. This will be Bob's first return to China since December of 1948, and the tour is headed into the interior, along the Yellow River, where he had indeed worked. Bob is eighty years old, still fit, still enthusiastic, and keen to revisit what is virtually his native land. And Amy is going with him.

This return of McClure must be documented.

I talk the CBC into undertaking the documentation.

The CBC finds the budget within the framework of its religious department's flagship TV series, *Man Alive*. I get the distinct impression that although the executive producer of *Man Alive* has been ordered to incorporate the project into her schedule and into her budget she is not happy about it, but the only major roadblock is raised by the Chinese, who say "no" to a film crew equipped with "professional" equipment, meaning 35mm or 16mm gear. Apparently the subtext is that China, its own professional facilities being somewhat limited, would not like to be asked to supply any emergency support services, because they might prove inadequate, thereby causing China to lose face. But China has no objection to the use of "amateur" 8mm gear by members of a tour group. By making this concession, China unwittingly opens the door to a unique CBC film unit.

I have already worked on two bushel-basket productions for Bob Clark, a peripatetic CBC documentary producer who has a habit of wandering off into the world's hinterlands. Bob and his cameramen have tracked Vietnamese boat people to temporary refuge on tiny islands in the South China Sea, and followed salt caravans across the Sahara to Timbuktu.* He comes back from such projects with thousands of feet of film, sometimes using 16mm, sometimes experimenting with highly portable 8mm, but he always has the footage transferred to videotape. Bob and I screen the material together, and then I, as writer, work out a framework, write an editing script, and eventually write the finished commentary. And so, in 1981, this China "tour" group surrounding Bob and Amy McClure is augmented by producer Bob Clark, cameraman Ian Matheson, soundman Paul Belanger, and me as writer/interviewer.

---

* *My People Are Dying* (1979) and *Sixteen Days to Timbuktu* (1980), respectively.

None of this crew, however, is from the CBC's Toronto production centre. I have a feeling that the executive producer considers us to be as substandard as is our 8mm equipment.

What a great project it is — but ultimately how frustrating.

It is May 1981, and not only am I in mainland China, but I am here on the Great Wall, with Bob and Amy McClure. At the moment, the camera is elsewhere and the other tourists are spread out along this most amazing structure, taking their own pictures, doing their own thing. Dr. McClure stops to ask a question of a Chinese sightseer. The usual happens. McClure is gradually surrounded by an entire gaggle of Chinese, mostly middle-aged or older. There is animated conversation.

He turns to me. "They want to know how come a Big Nose has the accent of a Honan boy."

He tells them it's because he was raised from infancy in Honan. I expect he doesn't say he learned Chinese in the goatyard rather than in the mission house, but it's possible they can tell. Anyway, the conversation continues with two-way questions and answers. Often the Chinese questioners look puzzled and shake their heads as though not understanding. I wonder if McClure's language is deteriorating, but when we eventually move away and continue our stroll I find that it is not.

He explains, "It's amazing. They have absolutely no historical memory. Everything before the communist takeover, before 1949, is a blank. It didn't exist."

He is a little depressed — and he has no need to tell me why. It means these people have no knowledge whatsoever of the enormous effort put into China over a period of almost a hundred years by missionaries, many of them Canadian, who taught literacy and medicine, who established schools and universities, many of whom opposed colonialism, as did Bob, and who in a very real sense laid some of the educational groundwork that made the communist revolution and modern China possible. Whether this communal amnesia is a result of brainwashing, fear, bad memory, or poor education, we have no way of knowing. I do know that too many Canadians suffer from a similar affliction concerning our own history. In our case, the cause is simple apathy, poor education, and a competing indoctrination by our enormous southern neighbour.

We are touring a hospital in a community that borders the Yellow River, which flows from deep in the heartland of China. This hospital would not normally be on a tour itinerary, but the Chinese are complying with a request from a foreign visitor bearing the honoured title of *Tai fu*, "Doctor," and whose Chinese name is Loa Ming Yuan, "Far Shining Brilliance" — in other words, Dr. Robert McClure. I can't speak for other members of the party, but I know that both the *Tai fu* and I come bearing our personal prejudices. McClure has told me that he has little use for some of the quainter aspects of Chinese medicine, such as "cupping" and incense burning. In his experience these would frequently result in an infection, and its victims would come, as a last resort, to the mission doctor, often too late to be helped. As for me, acupuncture, judging from what I have read and heard, is in the same realm of medical idiocy.

We are told that this hospital offers both traditional Chinese medicine and western medicine. When patients are admitted they can opt for one or the other. It becomes apparent that the system is more flexible than it sounds. We view two operations in progress in reasonably modern operating rooms but where the only anaesthetic being used is acupuncture. One operation is for a goitre. The patient is awake, with her throat slit, but looks totally unperturbed. I am sufficiently impressed that years later when an injury "freezes" my right shoulder I will gratefully accept relief and the restoration of movement by means of two highly effective acupuncture treatments from an Ontario M.D. who has been broad-minded enough not to share my early prejudices.

We see patients who show the bruising and swelling effects of cupping treatments and observe a reclining patient who has burning incense sticks precariously poised on his abdomen. These don't impress McClure *Tai fu*, but I am intrigued when he begins to talk in Mandarin to a post-operative patient and then enters into an energetic discussion with the Chinese doctor who is our guide. Bob returns to the patient as though for verification and, judging from the latter's tone and smile and nodding head, appears to be getting positive corroboration. I wonder what esoteric ailment has been so successfully treated with the knife as to be of such interest to surgeon McClure.

"This chap," Bob tells me, "has just had hemorrhoids removed."

"Piles? What's so unusual about that?"

"Ah, but we're still quite barbaric about it. The aftermath can be very uncomfortable. Very painful. In the west, doctors are almost callous about hemorrhoids. But this chap — they've got him corked with a plug made from medicinal herbs. It deadens the pain and it heals, and it's natural. This is the kind of thing we in the west should be paying attention to. There's a lot they can teach us."

We are in the lobby of a large, austere mausoleum of a hotel. McClure, at the cashier's wicket exchanging some dollars, becomes convinced he's being short-changed. The air begins to ring with the sound of Bob's strident Mandarin. An ashen-faced interpreter hurries to him and says, "Dr. McClure, we don't use those words any more."

It is early morning, deep in the heartland of China in the city of Xian. This is the city where Chinese archaeologists are busily unearthing an entire army of life-sized terra cotta figures created and buried more than 2,000 years ago by order of an emperor, whose predecessors would have buried a real army to accompany their deceased ruler into the hereafter. McClure and I are enjoying an early morning stroll, unencumbered by film crew or by other tour companions.

There is a park in the centre of the city, basically an open space covered with patchy grass and clean hard earth. There is nothing particularly elaborate here in the way of gardens, shrubs, or even trees. But it is one of the loveliest parks I have seen, and the adornment is all human. The entire area is alive with people performing their early morning exercises. There is no leader, no Master. Each person is doing his or her own thing in his or her own space, lost in deep concentration, but each person seems to know instinctively how much territory is required by his or her neighbour. The park is ornamented with all the swaying, pacing, gently moving, elegant, measured, elaborate movements of Tai Chi.

McClure and I move off along a side street. We are close to the city centre, but are now walking into an area of narrow dirt streets bordered with homes one could easily call squalid. Children are playing on the streets. They don't see many foreigners in this neighbourhood and are shyly interested in our presence. Bob speaks to one of them and again the magic happens. He is surrounded, this time by youngsters, all talking to the Big Nose with the Honan accent. I notice he appears to be scanning the little group, intently, as though inspecting each individual. He speaks to me while doing so.

"Observe these kids. There's not a running nose, an infected eye, or a dripping ear in the lot. I haven't seen one since we arrived."

The statement is made with both amazement and admiration. Bob McClure, who during the first half of the twentieth century witnessed much of the violence and many of the barbarities that were part of China's chaotic journey through colonialism, war, occupation, and revolution, and who has waged endless personal medical warfare against poverty-induced disease, has finally seen a sight that, to his trained medical eye, indicates an unequivocal advance — healthy children. He describes himself as experiencing "Rip Van Winkle time."

The tour is completed, the congenial tourists disperse, and the film crew returns to Ottawa, only to find the CBC in the midst of a strike that delays access to videotape equipment and eventually cuts editing time in half. There is the added complication of interference from the executive producer in Toronto, who seems to mistrust the abilities of both the producer and the writer in remote Ottawa. Eventually she rewrites the narration, the night before it is to be recorded by host Roy Bonisteel, without ever having seen a single frame of footage. This is a violation both of professionalism and of my ACTRA contract. I am sorely tempted to grieve it to the Association, a procedure that is both messy and unpleasant, but that helps maintain ethics and professionalism in a rather amorphous business. I decide life is too short. I make a note to myself describing the executive producer as "a beautiful, intelligent, sophisticated ass," which is probably unfair to her and unworthy of me. On the other hand, I do withdraw my writing credit from the two programs, and Bob Clark and Paul Belanger withdraw their credits. I forget to withdraw my credit as interviewer, and will always feel badly about that. In the course of a lengthy film/TV career this is the only time when I have felt that a producer has been high-handed, to the detriment of a production. What's more, the unethical action comes from the top of the CBC's spiritually oriented "religious" programming department. Ah well, life has always been paradoxical.

The technical delays that push completion of the China project from late spring to early autumn create a nightmare for Bob Clark, but actually ease summer scheduling for me. Which is fortunate. *The Devil* has come back into my life.

30

THE THIRD COMING
OF THE DEVIL

DENNIS SWEETING HAS SUGGESTED that I write a stage version of *The Devil's Petition*. This is the story of the hanging that was averted when Rev. John Ryerson carried out his prayer filibuster on the scaffold while Dr. Rolph rode to York for a reprieve.

A stage version? It's already had a TV version and a radio version!

The Devil's Petition had been well received when it was broadcast on TV in 1960, but I knew it had problems.* When a story's climax hangs on a multi-hour prayer there are bound to be problems. Then a decade or so later Ron Hartman, who had played the TV lead and was now directing and acting in radio, had asked me to do an adaptation of *The Devil's Petition* for CBC radio. Radio is much kinder to problems of time and space, and I had written in a balladeer as a narrator. Herb Helbig wrote the music. The radio version had worked well enough to capture the prestigious Nellie at the ACTRA Awards in 1974.* My peers told me that winning an award in Canada was a sure way of ending one's career. That's nonsense, of course, but even so *The Devil's Petition* had been the beginning and end of my radio career.

But now, early in the 1980s, here is Dennis Sweeting asking for a stage adaptation!

Okay. Why not?

I change everything, radically. The play becomes a presentation by a group of young strolling players who find themselves having to improvise a bit of Canadiana. I keep the balladeer and add more verse. When I structure the play for the ebb and flow of the open stage, which I still love, it becomes much less formal. The open stage gives a writer the

---

*   The writing and production of the television version was described briefly in Chapter 20.

**   See Chapter 23.

opportunity to conjure up a wilderness without having to recreate it physically, as in a scene where the Balladeer and the Settlers worry about the doctor's horseback journey through Upper Canada's great pine forest:

> BALLADEER: Out there beneath the great pines so thick the sun never shines on the ground below.
> CROWD: We know, we know!
> BALLADEER: Trees so tall their tops are lost in the dark winds.
> CROWD: Oh, yes, that's right!
> BALLADEER: Trees so old they collapse from sheer age crushing travellers under the weight and the roar.
> CROWD: That's right!
> BALLADEER: Swamps so vast that lost travellers go in young and come out old and demented.
> CROWD: That's right!
> BALLADEER: Ravines so wide and deep —
> CROWD: How deep? How deep?
> BALLADEER: — even echoes get lost and come out ten years later.
> CROWD: Oh, that's deep!
> BALLADEER: Mosquitoes so big they sling hammocks for sleep.
> CROWD: Big!
> BALLADEER: Black flies so big they kill horses for meat.
> CROWD: That big?
> BALLADEER: And pitch horse shoes to see who gets to wear the harness.
> CROWD: Now that's big!
> BALLADEER: Oh where out there in that great green hell is Dr. Rolph?

The colossal prayer scene is no longer a problem, because Ryerson's supplication to the Almighty is structured like an old-time Methodist revival meeting, with the assembled crowd interjecting songs. It begins with snatches of authentic, dour, soul-searching hymns, when it appears the victim must die —

> Happy soul thy days are ended,
> All thy mourning days below;
> Go by angel guards attended,
> To the sight of Jesus, go!

— then it gradually escalates into full-throated triumphant gospel songs as Dr. Rolph and his jubilant stage horse arrive with the reprieve.

The snatches of prayer, once almost a dramatic liability, now become a useful and justifiable cry for release from nineteenth-century Canadian "justice":

> O Lord, keep us from the gallows, the stocks, the whipping posts, the tread mills and all such black instruments.... I see infants cast into prisons with their offending mothers, the sane locked up with the insane, the debtor with the murderer. Spare us! ... I see the blind and the infirm and the sick in prisons reeking of filth and disease where even the strong in body die....

The prayer is interspersed not only with escalating song but also with dialogue. Around the foot of the scaffold the less devout members of the ad hoc congregation make book as to how long the parson can last, and, thanks to theatre's marvellous stylistic conventions, the players freeze at intervals to permit the balladeer to condense time itself:

> He's prayed for reprieve by the Governor's hand,
> He's prayed for all sinners, the saved and the damned,
> He's prayed for the rider, the people, the land!
> How he has prayed!
> He's prayed for the crops, for the peas and the hops,
> For the birds of the air and for children who swear,
> For those who get frisky from drinking of whiskey,
> For girls who like candy, young studs who get randy,
> For all kinds of evil, both new and primeval —
> How he has prayed!

And the balladeer, of course, has the final say:

> May the Doctor ride and the Parson pray,
> May the hand of the hangman willingly stay,
> And may Law with Love forever be
> The golden chains of our Liberty.

The play goes on the boards in July 1981, while the McClure programs for cbc's *Man Alive* are in chaotic hiatus. The actors and the audience seem to enjoy the play, but the only review is in the *Lindsay Daily*

Post. It's under the byline of a female stringer, but theatre friends tell me her boyfriend wrote it. Whoever the writer is, he or she has problems with actors stepping out of character to address the audience in rhyme, and seems to think a troop of contemporary roving actors who "improvise" a story set in the 1800s should not be wearing sneakers. Courteous Dennis Sweeting's only comment is, "The reviewer has obviously never heard of Bertolt Brecht."

As for me, I know *The Devil's Petition* has finally found its correct form. It's made available by *Playwrights Canada*, and for many years, whenever the topic of capital punishment appears on the political horizon, or a Canadiana heritage celebration is in the offing, I will send out scripts to numerous artistic directors. With the notable exception of James Douglas at Barrie's Gryphon Theatre, who seems genuinely apologetic that he can't stage it, most will never reply.

In the meantime, after *The Devil* has come and gone and the two *Man Alive* programs have struggled through adversity to completion, Hilda and I make another lifestyle decision.

We decide that times are changing. The culture is changing. For me, as with McClure, it is "Rip Van Winkle time." Hilda and I both wake up and decide it's time to put a dream into effect. David and Janet are married and in Toronto, where he has his feet on the first rung of the corporate ladder, Ian is studying film at York University, and Rob is training as a professional "hard hat" commercial diver, but has his eyes on Science at the University of Guelph. Our nest is empty. We abandon town life and move out into God's country, lake country, the land of rock, trees, peace, beauty, and loons. We establish ourselves as year-round residents on the shore of beautiful Balsam Lake, a half-hour drive north of Lindsay. In order to do so we buy a place that symbolizes what real estate agents mean by "in need of Tender Loving Care."

31

DO-IT-YOURSELF

THE PROPERTY WE BUY has been subdivided from land that used to belong to a large commercial summer lodge known as Cedar Villa. A derelict dance hall on the lakeshore completely blocks the view to the southwest. Hilda assesses it as a monstrous white elephant. A small cottage partway up the lot blocks more of the view. The house, on the highest ground, is not a homemaker's dream. Hilda's initial reaction is Lancashire direct: "There's nothing there a bulldozer can't fix."

But she relents. "You know, the house has potential. Tear out those two downstairs bedrooms that block the view of the lake, rip out the two bathrooms between them, do something about that sagging ceiling in the living room, rebuild the bay window so you don't see daylight under the window sill, improve the insulation, change all the windows, rebuild the kitchen, and straighten the roof. Yes, I think it's really got potential."

"The labour would cost a fortune!"

"Won't cost anything. You've been wanting to give yourself a sabbatical. You like carpentry. Now's the time. Besides," she says in that logical way that only illogical females can master, "it's got a full basement. Poured concrete. You like basements."

"The fireplace has got lung cancer."

"Underneath all that soot," she says, "is beautiful red granite. You see," she explains, "we can live in the cottage while you fix the house. First thing to do is to take out those two downstairs bedrooms."

"Those two bedrooms are holding the place up."

"Well they're not doing a very good job of it. Then we'll get rid of that mess on the waterfront."

The mess on the waterfront happens to be the old Cedar Villa dance hall. It's a structure about 150 feet long by 65 feet wide. It contains a boathouse with nine wet slips. Over the boathouse is the derelict dance hall, with a floor that would make a sailor seasick. Beyond the dance hall there are twelve guest rooms hanging over the lake. Thanks to a nasty ice breakup a few years ago, the rooms on the lower level no longer have floors. I say they have potential as a boaters' cathouse, but am ignored. On the second level, at the shore end, there's a reception room larger than our former Lindsay backyard. We've seen entire cottage lots that were smaller than this one derelict building. The first time David and Rob walk into this decaying disaster I loiter outside to let them form their own opinion, but I hear it, loud and clear, voiced with a certain tone of awe: "Holy shit!"

As soon as we take possession of the dream home I phone a good friend in nearby Coboconk. "Who's a real good freelance carpenter in your area? I'm going to need some help holding a place up."

"Times are bad," he says, "but the guys aren't that desperate."

"No, no, I mean beams — big beams. And posts."

"Oh. Well in that case, call Gerry."

So I phone Gerry and make an appointment. Right on schedule Gerry turns up. He's of medium height and well built. I figure he can handle a beam or two by himself. I take him on a tour of the house to show him my sagging floors and drooping ceilings.

"Look, it doesn't have to be straight but it's got to be strong."

He merely nods. Disturbingly quiet guy, this.

"This wall," I say, "I want to tear it out, so we'll need a thirty-foot support beam here. And a fifteen-footer across to the fireplace. Can you do it?"

He eyes the whole thing in a quietly sad way.

"I'll help," I offer, by way of inducement.

He eyes me balefully. "I have a helper. Hire me, hire my helper. Al and I work together."

"How much will it cost?"

"Who knows? I never quote on a job like this. Never know what you find. We work hard. You pay by the hour." He walks over to the fireplace and glares at the wall above it. "I suggest you open that. Nice to know if anything's behind it."

"Oh sure. I'll do all the demolition. I just want you to do the ceiling beams."

We go into the basement, where the main support beam has rolled slightly under the weight of an off-centre support wall above it.

"No problem," says Gerry.

I'm having second thoughts. "Do I go with this guy," I wonder, "or get somebody in who'll give me a quote?"

I've spent a good chunk of my life among the small-town and rural folk of the Ottawa Valley, and right now, in Victoria County, I'm getting some familiar vibes from Gerry. Those vibes tell me he thinks I'm an idiot, and that assures me that he isn't.

"Okay," I say. "How soon can you do it?"

"Two weeks."

"Fine. In the meantime, I can strip the place down. I'll get that bearing wall on the main floor down to the studs."

I do just that. I tear out the two bathrooms and the two bedrooms, all occupying prime space on the lake side of the main floor. When I strip the bearing wall down to the bare studs, I find one squirrel's nest amazingly entrenched almost in the dead centre of the house. I burrow into the wall above the fireplace and into the bay window. In a moment of exasperation I put my fist through the header above the bay window and find there is no header. But there, and above the fireplace, are the only spots of rot in the entire place. And the whole building is sheathed on the inside of the studs with one-inch, full-dimension hemlock planks! Hemlock's difficult to find these days. It's theoretically a soft-wood, but it's hard as a rock. You can bend spikes trying to penetrate hemlock. Farmers like to use it for horse stalls, because an irate stallion may try to kick the hell out of it, but good luck to him!

In one area I penetrate past the inner sheathing and the studs to the outer wall. It, too, is sheathed, under the clapboard, with hemlock. I'm beginning to feel some confidence in this structure.

Brother Doug drops in and prowls the premises. He seems unimpressed with its aesthetics, but with an engineer's appraising eye he inspects the poured concrete basement walls and the sturdy hemlock boards. "It's sure not going to fall down."

By the time I have the main floor gutted, Gerry turns up to say he and Al can't take on the job.

"We've joined up with a contractor," he apologizes.

I'm appalled. I've turned our dream home into a ruin so it can be resurrected, and the guy with the wand is reneging. However, he looks unhappy.

"I'll ask Fraser to talk to you."

"Who's Fraser?"

"The contractor."

Fraser turns up. He's a short, sandy-haired guy wearing high-heeled boots and a cowboy hat. His resumé says he's recently been building mushrooms for the Muppets.

I'm feeling hostile. "I didn't count on a contractor in the middle of this."

"I know," he says, pleasantly.

"You do?"

"Sure. Gerry told me. You booked him. That still holds. I'll give you a maximum quote. Four days to install the beams, straighten the cellar beam, and level the floors."

"What's that mean?"

"It means if we take six days you pay for four."

"How long do you think it'll take?"

"Two days. If it does, that's all you'll pay."

How can I lose? We shake on it and dispense with a written contract. This is rural Canada.

Gerry and Al turn up on schedule. Saws buzz and hammers ring. The cellar beam is levelled with shims. Support posts are dropped through the main floor directly onto the basement beam so that the floor can float around them. New beams go up across the living room. Jacks strain. The old house creaks and screeches. The ceiling rises almost to its original position. Visual strength and internal solidity miraculously re-appear.

It takes two days.

As the men leave, Gerry says, "Take down the old support studs on the weekend."

"Why the weekend?"

"So if the beams don't hold there's nobody here but you."

I take their advice, but the beams hold.

I am billed for the two days, and as the summer goes by Fraser wanders in every so often, offers encouragement and free advice, and ambles on his way. Al and Gerry do the same. My Ottawa Valley instincts have not betrayed me. The building inspector wanders in on one of his unobtrusive visits and watches me hoisting a header into place where I've knocked a hole in an outer wall to make way for a patio door. This house is "balloon" framed; you open outer walls with care. He watches until I become nervous.

"Is this okay?" I pant, sweating the timber into place on its jack studs.

"Well-l-l — let's just say if we need a bridge built I'll give you a call. You're way over code. You're doing fine."

It's mid-April and Ian phones from Thompson, Manitoba. Last summer he took off after his second year studying film at York University and went hardrock mining up north. Been at it ever since. He started out wielding a shovel on an underground muck pile, then became a handyman's helper. He graduated from that and now not only has his blasting papers but is a qualified scoop tram operator, as well as a certified jackleg drill operator. He's captain of his shift's first aid team, which has just won some kind of competition. But now he's looking at a new challenge.

"Hi, Dad. I'm coming home."

"I thought you'd be up there until fall semester?"

"Yes, but David's told me all about this Balsam Lake folly. I want to get in on the act. Okay?"

It turns into the best summer, possibly the best year, a man could have. Ian stays all summer. Rob comes whenever his university studies and his commercial diving assignments permit. David and Janet come on weekends. David's first job is to climb into the attic and shovel up bat droppings. Hilda and Janet take over the job of stripping old wallpaper from the upstairs walls. Hilda slips on wet wallpaper and falls, cracking a wrist bone, but keeps on going. Downstairs I make the error of building a new wall without consulting with Hilda, and consequently have the experience of quickly removing it. We all muck in and turn the proverbial sow's ear into — well, we like it, anyway.

The support from the family in all this is intriguing. It's only in recollection that I will try to analyse it. It is as though right from the early days the boys sense there is something intriguing about the way their parents earn a living — albeit often a thin one — without being tied to the monthly goal of a company pay cheque. Money, the medium that converts effort into food and shelter, has always been tied to something more nebulous than the mutual dependence of employee and employer. It baffles me, now as then. It seems to me they approve of our unstructured life.

The dance hall is a long-term project. Even the summer neighbours get involved. Material from the dance hall is up for grabs to anyone who is willing to do the work to acquire it. A neighbour and his teenage sons add a nice sunroom to their cottage. When winter comes and the lake freezes, David, Ian, and Rob turn up for a weekend, along with a friend, Danny, who spent the summer as a lumberjack. So now I have David, an all-round handyman, Ian, a hardrock miner, Rob, a commercial diver, and Danny, a lumberjack, all eyeing the enormous spread of roof on this dance hall monstrosity. The shingles alone are a problem. We don't want them and their nails in the water. That's why they're being removed in the winter. The boys do the high-level work while I shovel shingles and nails off the ice. The gigantic roof comes off in a weekend.

Our next-door neighbour, Ferne Alexander, joins the performance. She and Hilda get their jollies chainsawing walls. There's a big, empty, derelict cement septic tank that used to serve the dance hall system. We use it as a winter firepit, and dance hall debris is turned to ashes. Two thousand years from now some archaeologist is going to unearth that vast cement box full of old bolts, hinges, nails, and glass shards, and make some highly creative deductions about burial rituals and sacred artifacts.

This is good therapy for me. For most of 1982 I've been unable to write so much as a letter. I have been totally, unreservedly happy as a do-it-yourself renovator, but as for writing, my brain has been as blank as an unlit screen. The legendary Writer's Block, something I have never believed in, has proven to be absolutely real. Partly because of this affliction, I've turned down a commission to write the biography of a former commissioner of the RCMP. But apparently the prescription for full recovery from The Block involves a hammer, a saw, and some old buildings beside a beautiful lake.

I take on some modest assignments in 1983, and by the spring of 1984 am loaded for bear. Almost on cue, the phone rings. It is Cam Graham, but he's not calling on CBC business. He's relaying an SOS from the National Capital Commission in Ottawa.

32

SOUND-AND-LIGHT

I'VE HAD SOME STRANGE ASSIGNMENTS, but this one takes the biscuit. I'm here in Ottawa thanks to the call from Cam Graham, but he had simply been responding to a request from the National Capital Commission for some hurry-up advice, which he gave and they accepted. Namely, me.

Seems the Commission, the NCC, which oversees most of the federally owned parkland in and around Ottawa, has been planning a sound-and-light show on Parliament Hill for this coming summer. Sound-and-Light, or *son et lumière* as the cultural elite prefer to call it, is very big in Europe, but so far not in Canada. I've seen it twice before, once here in 1967 on the back end of the Parliament Buildings, using the Library as the setting, and once in 1978 at David's Tower in Old Jerusalem. Other than that it's a new ball game for me, but here I am being asked to write the script for this new offering.

It was nice of Cam to recommend me, but I'm soon wondering whether he's just fed me to the bicultural wolves. There's more going on here than meets the eye, or ever will meet the eye. This show has been in the works for more than two years. A director has already been hired and he is Pierre Arnaud, from France. M'sieur Arnaud has an impressive list of *son et lumière* credits, including castles in France, temples in Egypt, and, yes, David's Tower in Jerusalem. A technical company from Quebec City that also has *son et lumière* experience is already assembling the elements of an elaborate outdoor theatre on the grounds in front of the Centre Block of the Parliament Buildings. There is theatrical lighting that consists, I am told, of 640 special lights — and a sound system designed to surround an audience with full range audio — and a computerized nerve centre to control both music and lights — and portable bleachers designed to fold up so that they can be trundled onto the lawn just before twilight and rolled away again before midnight. In fact, everything is designed to vanish during the day. This is a theatrical exercise that requires its own landscape architect and consulting engineer. The project is running on a budget of more than two million dollars. Not only that, but apparently it is being done without a script! Wait, I'm wrong. They had a script, but it has just been thrown out.

I find this somewhat disconcerting. I am told it was an excellent script, but, having been envisioned through Québécois eyes, it failed to celebrate Canada adequately. Others suggest it was simply not sufficiently story-driven. Whatever the reason, I, an anglophone writer, am now being abruptly inserted into the midst of a project for which most of the creative people are francophones. The man who has made the decision is the firm-handed Director General of the NCC, Ian Dewar. Having spent a good part of my life observing the internal political warfare associated with bilingualism and biculturalism in Ottawa, I find myself admiring the Director General's guts, and experiencing considerable apprehension for the safety of my own.

It seems to me a few things must be clarified in negotiations, but I soon find that for once I'm in a strong position, because opening night is alarmingly close. It is already late February and the show is scheduled for the upcoming tourist season. We agree I am not doing a rewrite, I am starting from scratch. The mandate is for a show that gives an impression of Canadian history. How I shape it and what I tell is up to me — subject, of course, to approval. But it can't be more than twenty-five minutes long.

The NCC hires a researcher to help me, because I won't have time to wander around archives. The CBC, although not officially involved, donates an empty office, a phone, and a typewriter at the CBO-TV studios. For hotel living quarters I request, and get, a room that has a view of Parliament Hill. This is like a playwright being lodged in a theatre with a view of his stage.

There's only one problem. How many French-Canadian toes are being stepped on here? How many Québécois egos are being dented? This worries me, but not for long. The NCC staff most intimately connected with the project are French-Canadian. They expedite everything with courteous equanimity. The producer, Yvon Sanche, from Quebec City, is friendly, encouraging, and co-operative. The only one who seems appalled is the foreign import, the director Pierre Arnaud, and I can't say I blame him.

M'sieur Arnaud, an older man than me, is an *artiste* who works in the abstract. He paints with light and music. When I have completed a first rough draft, we meet in my hotel room. After telling me what an excellent script I am writing, this Gallic gentleman proceeds to explain, charmingly, why it is all wrong for *son et lumière*. M'sieur Arnaud and I are poles apart. He wants to paint a musical sunset, whereas my mandate is to tell a story.

I'm a documentary storyteller dealing with certain events of history. I'm making use of dramatic dialogue, poetry, song, sound effects, and music, and am trying to draw upon my film background to suggest a creative use of lights, but I know that M'sieur Arnaud is frustrated by my approach. The biggest bell in the Peace Tower, "Bourdon," is to be my principal narrator. The bell will have a voice more articulate than its magnificent brass tone. The Precambrian Rock of the Hill will talk. Even the Forest Primeval (enacted by the shrubbery) and the great River will talk. Their disembodied voices are to be accompanied by others, such as those of Sir John A. Macdonald, Queen Victoria, and assorted malcontents. I know this is a far cry from the esoteric sublimity of the David's Tower *son et lumière* in Old Jerusalem. But I also know that show bored me to distraction.

M'sieur Arnaud deals with his frustration most professionally. It's not easy for a director to have a writer imposed upon him, nor is it easy for the writer. But there is no rancour here, and we both try to adapt. I have no doubt that if we had more time to indulge in mutual education the end result might be improved, but the deadline is rushing at us.

The first rough draft establishes structure and a sense of narration and dialogue. I take it for granted that my approach has to be approved by Ian Dewar, but now I find that he is reporting on this project to one of Prime Minister Trudeau's cabinet ministers, the Secretary of State, the Honourable Serge Joyal. I am requested to read my rough draft to the Secretary of State. Writers don't like showing rough drafts to anyone, let alone reading them aloud. This is a new one for me. I go along with it, but the damned process escalates. Every so often during the next couple of weeks Ian Dewar calls me to say we've got a reading. Soon I get the feeling that when the Honourable Serge is bored he calls Tom over at Finance, Dick at Citizenship, and Harry at Public Works and says, "Come on up and hear Munroe read his script." I'm not an actor, but I like reading and I must be getting fairly good at it, because eventually I'm getting applause. But it's an exercise that digs holes in a tight schedule.

I am into the final detailed polishing with one day to go to script deadline when Ian Dewar calls me into his office and says, apologetically, that we have one more reading to do. I dig in my heels. "No way. My time now is better spent polishing. It's all been approved."

The Director General is patient. "You don't understand. When a cabinet minister says 'jump,' we jump."

"No, no, Ian. *You* don't understand. I'm freelance. You're a civil servant. When the minister says 'jump,' *you* jump."

He sits a moment, looking so sadly introspective that I do believe he accepts my position. I relent. We go for the reading.

The final script goes off in two directions, to Toronto and to Montreal. Even while I was working on the final polish I had met René Dionne, a personable young French Canadian playwright and translator who was preparing to write the French adaptation (also under great time pressure). A composer, Jean Cloutier, is now working on the music score. In Toronto my English language script goes into the hands of a senior CBC radio drama producer, Fred Diehl, who is about to retire after a distinguished career. Fred assembles a cast whose credits read like a who's who of Canadian actors.* We all come together in a large studio in "the Kremlin," CBC's old radio building on Jarvis Street. I'm not at all sure that the CBC's involvement in any of this is legal, but I ask no questions. Time does not allow for the niceties. The cast, bless them, seem to like the script. Several of the veterans tell me I should be writing for radio. I refrain from telling them that I received a "Nellie" for radio drama ten years ago and have never since been able to penetrate the medium. But I do give Fred Diehl a copy of my stage sequel to *The Merchant of Venice*, and just before he retires he passes it on into the maws of CBC's radio drama bureaucracy.

The final recording, the "mix" that blends all the ingredients of dialogue, narration, sound effects, and music is masterminded by Pierre Arnaud in Europe.

Our *son et lumière* opens on schedule for the tourist season of 1984. On this, the opening night, the weather is good, the bleachers trundle out and unfold as ordained, the lights bathe, caress, stroke, pinpoint, flood, and generally illuminate the beautiful old buildings while the dialogue, sound effects, and music waft over the audience. The first presentation is in English, then the audience changes and the show is repeated in French. The order alternates night by night — equal advantages, equal inconveniences. In my opinion everyone has done an amazing job of pulling all the pieces together. My only real aesthetic disagreement has to do with pacing. I'd like the show to have more drive, to move more

---

*   Robert Christie, Warren Davis, Moya Fenwick, Angela Fusco, Thomas Harvey, Jack Mather, Judith McGilligan, Sheila Moore, Earl Pennington, Frank Perry, Sandy Webster.

quickly. M'sieur Arnaud has taken a genteel, restrained, dignified approach to the pacing. I don't know how we ever got the country built. There is a transcontinental railroad-building vocal chant that should pound along like the pistons of a 100-mph Royal Hudson, but instead it meanders as though it's strolling beside a stream. How did we ever make it across the Canadian Shield! When more time should be taken on a musical chant that makes use of political riding names — Nipigon, Algoma, Kamouraska, Assiniboia, Okanagan-Similkameen, and so on — it is truncated for lack of time. However, lethargy makes for a long life. The show runs, in the summers, from 1984 to 1993.

This first night, there is a reception in the Centre Block. A senator says to me, "I like the way the voice of the Rock lists the various American attempts to conquer us and then — you know — reacts sarcastically to the myth of the 'undefended border'." He laughs. "You must have gone to Queen's."

"Yes."

"And took Canadian history from Arthur Lower?"

"Yes."

"Thought so."

Later there is a peculiar sidebar to the whole experience. I get a rejection notice from the CBC saying that my *Shylock's Treasure* is not suitable for the fifteen-minute drama slots in its radio talk program, *This Country in the Morning*. I absolutely agree! I wonder what route it has followed! I also receive a note from the federal government saying that my application for employment has been turned down. I can't imagine what wires got crossed in that exercise, but it's an interesting experience to be rejected for an unknown job for which I never applied. The rejection comes on letterhead from the office of the "Minister Responsible for the Status of Disabled Persons," and is signed on behalf of my favourite one-man audience, the Honourable Serge Joyal, who must be wearing a supplementary hat.

I think of my involvement with the National Capital's sound-and-light show as a kind of big Do-It-Yourself experience. The trouble with really big DIYs is that you only get to do them once. I don't suppose I'll ever write another *son et lumière*, just as I will never get to tear down another dance hall. But when this year of 1984 is little more than half gone I find myself involved in an even stranger learning exercise — one in which I step, for an entire year, out of my freelance shoes.

33

CAVALIER
TREATMENT

SOMETIME DURING THE SUMMER of 1984 I actually apply for a staff job as a newspaper editor.

(Two decades later, I can no longer recall what motivated me. I may have felt I was getting too old for documentary ramblings. It may have occurred to me that stage success was eluding me. I don't even recall whether the job was advertised. I do remember it was Hilda who alerted me to it, and that her alert had a certain sense of recommendation attached to it. A local newspaper, the *Lindsay Daily Post*, had lost its editor in the spring, apparently as the result of an ill-conceived April Fool's Day "news" item, and was now looking for a replacement. I applied, was interviewed by the board, and must have been able to give more reasons for wanting the job than I can now imagine, because I was hired. I think I may have had some fool idea about being able to make a modest living while at the same time being of service to the community.)

It is a beautiful summer day at Stoney Lake, and I announce to Doug and Jean and some other family members, and to Don Jack, who is visiting, and to Hilda, who already knows, that I am to be the editor of the *Lindsay Daily Post*. There is surprise, which is justified, because writers usually seek journalistic experience near the beginning of their careers and build upon it. Entry level is more likely to be as copy boy than as editor. But the family all seem to be pleased. Even Don congratulates me. I don't know it at the time, but I should be hearing laughter and receiving condolences.

I take over my new job on the morning of September 4, 1984.

A venerable paper, the *Post* is also a genuine community paper, having been in the hands of one local family from 1895, when it was established, until recently, when the last owner died and the family became extinct. It is now in the hands of a board of trustees. Historically, the

Lindsay Daily Post is a Liberal paper, although during the rule of Ontario's Conservative premier, Leslie Frost, the paper supported him. And why not? Les Frost was a Lindsay man, and he said his instincts for good government came from what he heard in Lindsay barbershops. He may have been correct. I remember Mike Pearson telling the CBC cameras that he had encountered more wisdom around the farm tables of Algoma than he ever heard around the board tables of the United Nations. No doubt the farm tables of Algoma and the barbershop chairs of Lindsay have a lot in common.

The current board of five trustees — four men and one woman — are nice people, but they do tend to be conservative, both large- and small-c. I have never yet belonged to a political party. My first federal vote was cast for the CCF, in a Quebec riding. I have also voted Progressive Conservative and Liberal and NDP. I suppose emotionally and intellectually, if one may use that term with respect to politics, I am a small-l liberal, possibly a Pearsonian Liberal — a dying breed. Eventually, in later years, when I am no longer writing for either public affairs TV or a newspaper, I will join the NDP in a more or less desperate move to find a political home with some vestige of integrity and principle. But not yet.

Brian Mulroney and the Progressive Conservatives come to federal power on September 4, the very day I become editor. I realize that the new breed of Tories and I are not friends, and that I am probably on a modest collision course with the board of trustees. However, my first transgression is not political. It comes in my first editorial, where I refer to certain local citizens (unnamed) as "knuckleheads." I am told this is not acceptable language. Even though I humbly acknowledge my mistake, I am instructed to submit a draft of each editorial to George, the assistant manager, who will approve it before it goes to the composing room. George's principal job is oversight of the printing department, whose big presses rumble away in the basement. I am assured he is well qualified to look over my shoulder, because he is an excellent speller. I absorb the somewhat humiliating experience of having to submit my draft editorial every morning to the printer for approval, but, in George's favour, I must say he never challenges anything. It's quite possible he, too, does not like the drill.

George is, of course, also concerned with the business of business — making money. We clash over that almost immediately. The routine is that the reporters come in about 7:00 A.M. and complete their reports of the previous day's happenings. I come in around 7:30, and their articles soon begin crossing my desk for approval, alteration, or polishing before going on to typesetting (as yet, no computerization in this establishment). Having seen the news, I write the headlines and sketch a suggestion for the arrangement of the front page. By mid-morning I am in the composing room with Wayne, the chief compositor, who assembles the front page. I enjoy this. The composing room staff are a cheerful, laidback bunch. Wayne follows my suggestions when he thinks they will work, and when he thinks they won't, he doesn't. But on my first morning I find him putting advertisements on the editorial page.

"No, no," I say. "No ads on the editorial page. Only the editorial, opinion, letters, comment."

"Oh-h-h," says Wayne, looking dubious, "they're not going to like that."

"Never mind. My problem." I am attempting to sound as though I know what it's all about. I have the impression that Wayne approves, but has his own problems.

"I've got to ask George."

"No asking. If you must, report. But it's done."

I lock horns with George. The editorial page is a lucrative place for ads. He calls me an arrogant SOB, but ads are kept off the editorial page. This is more of a breakthrough than it appears. Until recently, this newspaper has devoted its entire front page to classified ads, a quaint tradition that violated one of the Ontario Community Newspaper Association's criteria for a community newspaper, namely that it must have a "newsworthy" front page. But then this paper doesn't qualify under the rules as a "community" newspaper, because it publishes more than three times a week. So much for definitions. Besides, this paper can confuse and confound any definition. There used to be a *Saturday Post*, which was printed on Friday and delivered on Friday simultaneously with the Friday paper. This *Saturday* aberration was finally laid to rest by labelling the Friday *Daily* as "The Weekend Edition." Charming confusion is part of the essence of a community newspaper, but in this case it has been overdone. When I come on board there is the *Thursday Post*, not to be confused with the *Daily*, which, being daily, is also published Thursday. The *Thursday Post* is, in fact, the Wednesday *Daily* with a name change (it is even dated Wednesday), but with an additional wraparound of material gleaned from the *Daily* during the previous five publishing days. We bury the *Thursday* special and concentrate on a genuine weekly called *Post Vision*, which the locals dub "Hindsight." (The rival weekly, *Lindsay This Week*, is referred to as "Lindsay Last Week," which it is.)

I am, theoretically, the editor of *Post Vision*, but I manage to have Penny Barton, a senior reporter, named associate editor, and Penny really takes it over. We take turns writing the weekly Vision editorial. Penny, the most experienced of the reporters, is for me a very quiet advisor, guide, and mentor. I wouldn't be surviving this experience were it not for Penny's quiet tutoring. For the record, I receive nothing but friendly wholehearted support from all the other reporters — Mike Puffer, Jerry Grozelle, Alan Hirst, David Selby, Martha Perkins, Guy Skipworth, and Ralph Robinson.

This newspaper has personality, and that personality was not created overnight. Much of it can be directly attributed to the late forceful and often eccentric publisher and owner, Leroy "Roy" Percival Wilson. I never met Mr. Wilson, but the old-timers on staff are full of stories. A veteran in the composing room maintains that Roy made his fortune (and he did make a fortune) by ruthlessly suppressing wages. He is sardonic about the fact that because of Wilson's generous bequest to the town, to be used for the purchase of parklands, Lindsayites are now canonizing Roy in death. There is some truth to this.

But often reminiscing gets around to the fact that Roy Wilson was a man of principle, who considered gambling a sin and was willing to turn his back on major advertisers who wanted to advertise cash register lotteries. On one occasion some of this "sinful" advertising got into the *Daily* accidentally, and a senior member of the firm found himself at the town dump, burning and burying an entire issue. Mr. Wilson disliked the Thomson Newspaper chain, and one day he discovered that his newsprint was being delivered from Abitibi in Thomson trucks. An ultimatum immediately went out to Abitibi to find alternative transportation for the *Post*'s raw stock or the *Post* would find an alternative supplier. In years to come, a threat of that kind will probably become a violation of somebody's rights, but apparently Abitibi complied. (Ironically, the trustees will eventually sell the *Post* to the Thomson chain.)

The old building the Post occupies has a certain deteriorating charm. I am told the archives are in the upper floor, the third floor, the attic. I venture up to investigate and certainly find pile upon pile of newspapers dating back into the nineteenth century. But this is no traditional attic. It's an abandoned Masonic Temple. Substantial walls support a vaulted ceiling and are decorated with painted pillars and symbols. The atmosphere is appropriately mystical.

One day George finds me in the basement talking to the press operators, hoping to learn a tiny bit about the printers' craft. He is not happy.

I find him several days in a row in my area telling my reporters how to function. I am not happy. We both circle the wagons.

Eventually a teletype machine is installed in a corner of my small office, two feet from my left shoulder. It makes a lot of noise and spews out endless reams of material from the Canadian Press. I am supposed to winnow "filler" out of this monster to plug gaps in the inside pages of the papers. I want it out of there. I also want an editorial assistant, one of whose duties would be to sort through all this stuff. George thinks I'm being unreasonable, and I throw an entire armful of filler at him. I am sure he, too, finds these times trying. I get my assistant. She is Karen Parks, and she is experienced, tough, and efficient.

I really like the reporters. They are all young, and their experience is varied. (In later years only two remain in the newspaper business.* In retrospect I regret that because of my own lack of newspaper experience I felt so insecure I never gave this gang the opportunity to play creatively with this newspaper.)

A great deal of my energy is consumed by the writing of a daily editorial. I've not been restricted by office hours since 1957, and now I find myself not only in an office routine but meeting a daily deadline for a column! I take it all seriously. According to Hilda, too seriously.

She chides me, saying, "You're not writing editorials, you're writing mini-essays! Relax."

I cannot relax. Eventually it begins to fray my nerves. I don't know how professional columnists manage it, day in, day out, for years.

I devoutly hope that my nerves aren't what's affecting Hilda. She develops ventricular fibrillation of the heart. But the doctors get her onto medication that apparently sorts out the rhythm, and she appears to be okay. She is reading Will and Ariel Durant's *The Age of Napoleon*. The plus side of the newspaper job is that although I'm away during the day, I'm not far away, and at the end of every day and on weekends I am a true homebody.

The paper is "put to bed" each day before noon and is on the streets by one o'clock. By then, I like to go for a stroll up the main street and chat with the merchants. In general the citizenry is understanding and

---

* Martha Perkins edits *The Haliburton Echo*, a truly fine community newspaper. Gerry Grozelle edits *The Minden Times*. Both papers are still locally owned into the twenty-first century; they are among a dying breed.

supportive. In the afternoon I worry about administrative items and try to see that the reporters discover some purpose in life. But mostly I worry about the damned editorial. It usually gets written at home, late in the evening.

There's a recurring problem with this community paper. Lindsay has a population of about 17,000, and gossip is enjoyed here as much as anywhere else. Petty crime makes for juicy gossip. Naturally, one of our reporters is assigned to the police and courthouse beat, but I soon run into the delicate problem that being charged with a crime is as good as being convicted, and in a town where so many people know each other the automatic assumption of guilt is an unfair penalty. I undergo considerable angst trying to decide whether or not to name citizens who have been charged, but not, as yet, tried.

A parallel problem presents itself. I find myself faced by supplicants pleading for mercy, imploring me not to print an account of their, or a relative's, transgressions. "It's going to break my dear old mother's heart, and her on her sickbed," runs the plea.

I build a barrier to these pleas by attempting to turn them aside before they are verbalized. As soon as I realize where the conversation is headed, I interrupt.

"Excuse me, but I think there is something you should understand. Whatever it is you might be worrying about — well, it's quite possible it may not have been covered by a reporter, or even if it has it might already have been eliminated for lack of space. But if you are going to ask me not to publish it, then I will have no choice but to print. Otherwise I can be accused of showing favouritism. As editor I have to protect my own integrity and that of the paper. I do hope you understand."

Most folk, who are not as dumb as the elite like to imagine, ponder the problem then back off, hoping that luck will prevail. One young fellow, though, about to plead for himself, listens to my speech then surges recklessly ahead with his pitch. He stops in mid-flight, but too late. He looks thoughtful. "I think," he says, "I've just cut my own throat."

Sometimes I hear an appeal that should be printed in the paper in bold block letters, complete with names. One such comes by phone from a lady who wants me to suppress an account of her traffic accident. "I'm a victim," she complains. "I was just backing up, and the fool man just sat there, didn't blow his horn or anything, and let me back right into him!"

The selling of advertising has nothing to do with me, and the manager of the advertising department is scrupulously careful never to suggest that it does. However, one day he ambles into my office looking a little perturbed, and says he merely wants to alert me to a problem with the Kavaliers.

Lindsay has an excellent drum and bugle band called "The Kawartha Kavaliers." The band's numerous awards attest to the fact that their eye-catching black and gold uniforms and rakish, gold-plumed cavalier hats are backed up with good musicianship. They have been around since 1957, and I'm not only well aware of them, I'm a fan. Why, just yesterday I ran a front-page news item concerning the fact that the local realtor, who has been their business shepherd for some time, is resigning his Kavalier post. But that, apparently, is the problem. My headline announced "Kavaliers Lose Kingpin," and the kingpin has just now phoned the advertising department in high dudgeon, protesting that "kingpin" is a mafia term. He has withdrawn all his real estate advertising, a not-inconsiderable account.

I break my non-involvement rule and stroll over to the realtor's office for a friendly chat concerning the interchangeability of words like kingpin and linchpin, both of which denote absolutely indispensable mechanical items. The conflict soon dissolves in laughter, and advertising is restored. The ex-kingpin eventually goes on to become a federal Liberal Member of Parliament.

The Kawartha Kavaliers are invited to Disneyland to strut their stuff. They acquit themselves in fine fashion, but while they are en route home reporter David Selby is informed by a phone call from a well-entrenched agent (a board member's daughter, who is soon to marry Selby) that on the occasion of the momentous march through Disneyland the PA system announced the band as the "Janetville Kavaliers." Janetville is a tiny hamlet to the south of Lindsay, and this confusion tickles my rather questionable funnybone. I run a large headline welcoming home the "Janetville Kavaliers."*

The paper no sooner hits the streets than a large and very irate male citizen is in my alarmingly small office loudly and angrily berating me for trying to undermine the marching band, one of the town's finest institutions. So virulent and so loud is his opinion of me and of the paper that a cluster of healthy young male reporters gathers outside my door in case non-journalistic services might be required. It is nice to have protection.

There is an unexpected advantage to being the editor of a town's daily newspaper. Until now, work has always taken me out of my community. Now work draws me in. I am invited to speak to various

---

* "'Janetville' Kavaliers Return to Lindsay," *The Lindsay Daily Post*, 17 January 1985.

organizations such as service clubs, church groups, and the local Canadian Club. This is not a totally new experience, but it is, at first, somewhat nerve-racking. I am not a natural platform speaker. My brain works more nimbly through my fingers than through my mouth. I always make careful preparations — not just notes, but a full script. It's amazing how much time is required to prepare for a brief, inconsequential, supposedly informal after-dinner talk. Gradually, however, I come to enjoy these public sessions.

I've been in the *Post* saddle for almost a year when there is an Ontario provincial election and Premier Frank Miller, who has just succeeded Bill Davis, comes a-campaigning to Lindsay. A Progressive Conservative public barbecue is held in a downtown park. Before the formal proceedings get underway we are briefly entertained with some totally unauthorized mime presented by a scruffy-looking but not unhandsome individual. We don't know it at the time but he will turn out to be the leader of a rural commune and in the news for bigamy, mutilation, murder, and other assorted peccadilloes — not the most auspicious advance act for a campaigning premier of any persuasion, but not totally out of character for the counties of Victoria and Haliburton.

I, of course, maintain my perspective and listen with due attention and respect to the premier's pitch, and the following day describe it, editorially, as "a blue bucket of bull." This does not win me any friends among local Conservatives, nor does it warm the cockles of the board members' hearts. Soon after the election I am informed by the Chairman of the Board of Trustees that they are going to set up a committee to guide my editorial opinions. The chairman is a very pleasant, friendly lawyer whom I happen to like and respect. There is no animosity here and never has been. But politics in Victoria-Haliburton is serious stuff. However, his announcement poses problems for me. I write a letter to the Board.

> I am writing as a follow up to our meeting of Thursday, May 9th, at which time Mr. McQuarrie explained, in most moderate terms, the concern felt by the Board over some of my editorials at the time of the election. If I understood correctly, the Board perceived a "bias" in some of those editorials. If bias means that the editorials did not all lean toward the Conservative Party as it was at that time performing then of course there is no need to debate the statement, although I am not certain that I would have been said to be biased if the editorials had leaned the other way.

However, the important point to be made is that, as far as I know, an editorial can only do one or two things. It presents opinion and/or background.

Editorials that do nothing but present background would surely repel readers, which is not a newspaper's intention. Opinion is an essential ingredient in editorials and opinion must be presented with some candour and vigour. I am sure that the Board does not disagree with this.

It was suggested, however, that the Board should form an editorial committee to guide the editor's opinion in the event of another election or a debate on such sensitive issues as separate school funding.

I have given a great deal of thought to this proposal and must acknowledge that the Board has every right to institute such a committee and to guide opinion expressed in the newspaper in any way the members so desire. The other side of the coin, however, is that I, as a professional writer at this stage of my career, can decide not to permit anyone to either dictate or censor my opinion. To do so would be tantamount to committing creative and personality suicide.

It seems to me that this discussion, that was raised so casually, has opened a chasm that is almost impossible to bridge because, indeed, both sides are correct. It is possible, however, that the Board is correct only in relation to the scope of its authority and quite incorrect if it considers the health of the newspaper.

You might be interested in a recently published statement by Peter Desbarats, Dean of Western's Graduate School of Journalism. "If, the day before an election, the editor ... wants to condemn the whole municipal council as certified lunatics, in my view that is his established, undeniable right, and it is extremely dangerous to tamper with it in any way."

As I told you several months ago I have not been entirely comfortable with this job. One of the things that has kept me able to muster enthusiasm, not to mention energy, has been what I thought was the unqualified support of the Board. I find it discouraging to think that that support is no longer there. However, I cannot afford to regain that support by sacrificing independence of mind. At the same time I cannot function as an editorialist and have my political "bias" either corrected or guided.

The obvious solution to this problem would seem to be for me to remove myself from it. I have therefore decided that I will not seek a renewal of my contract after September 1st, 1985. I will, of course, continue to be supportive of all the *Post*'s endeavours during the next three months and will take my cue from you as to when this termination will be made public.

The day I leave, the reporters give me a present. It is a T-shirt with a sentence on the front in large bold black lettering that says, "Go ahead, ask me not to print something." I am touched.

At Balsam Lake, Hilda throws a party. She says it is my "Freedom Party." This notion is nailed down by our beloved neighbours, Ferne Alexander, Jean Boyd, and Nancy and Jeanette Burns. They, too, give me a T-shirt. Emblazoned across the back are the words, "Freedom From the Press."

It is not the end of my newspaper career. After only a brief hiatus, I am writing a weekly column for the rival community newspaper, *Lindsay This Week*, privately owned at this time by its publisher, Gordon Brooks. This is a totally different exercise than overseeing reporters and feeding editorials to a daily. This is not time-consuming, and it has no restrictions other than a gentleman's agreement to abide by good taste and the laws of libel, an agreement that holds even when LTW is eventually swallowed by Torstar. My nerves and peace of mind both improve immeasurably with the restoration of full freelance status. The column keeps me and, I hope, my readers entertained for more than six years. I find it stimulating to have an ongoing creative challenge with loose parameters.

I call the column *Down Paradox Lane*, a grab bag of a title that permits me to explore the absurdities of just about anything. I am able to chronicle an on-going battle with garbage-gobbling coons and bird-feeder-raiding squirrels. I decry the stupidity of weekend boaters who spend thousands on expensive watercraft but will not shell out for a navigation chart, and then complain when they strike submerged rocks. In 1986 I am blessed by the Ontario Community Newspaper Association with the Bell Canada Award for "Best Column, General Interest." The Bell representative tells me I am the first freelance writer to win it. (I remember the award with pleasure but have no recollection of what item was entered. I doubt that it was one of my political rants.) Writing this column is good fun. Hilda observes that I enjoy the soapbox.

It is my intention, by and large, to keep *Paradox Lane* lighthearted, but I do use humour to vent anger. Sometimes the anger excludes humour; this is particularly so as I watch Prime Minister Brian Mulroney and his Tories grease the skids to help Canada slide into the American abyss. At the beginning, Mulroney is not actively advocating the "Free Trade" that he swore, when running for leadership, eternally to oppose. But the signs are all there.

In April 1987 the American president, Ronald Reagan, visits Ottawa and addresses the House of Commons. I have no quarrel with Reagan. He is not my president, thank God, but our own parliamentarians make me want to throw up.

> The leader of the most powerful nation in the world stood smiling-ly in our parliament and said his country would certainly talk with ours about Arctic sovereignty and Arctic defence and "other inter-ests". The other interests presumably referred to oil rigs and super-tankers and other Arctic commerce that can not only destroy our Inuit brothers but can also destroy global ecology. Our M.P.s applauded vigorously....
>
> He talked with great passion and sincerity about free trade and its importance to our standard of living.... [T]here was a prolonged ovation from our M.P.s and my mind wandered history from the American Revolution to the War of 1812 to the Fenian Raids to Pres-ident Teddy Roosevelt's aggressive cry of "Fifty-Four Forty or Fight". The Americans can't beat us, I said to myself while watching our obsequious M.P.s, but they can buy us....
>
> I would expect polite, respectful applause from Canada's M.P.s for an American president but standing ovations in a house devoted to debate, for a totally propagandistic speech immune from rebut-tal, were immeasurably humiliating....

By the first week of January 1988 I am still steamed up, and I take lib-erties with the title of a well-known Canadian history text written by my old Queen's professor, Arthur Lower. His book was *From Colony to Nation*; my rant is "From Nation to Colony."* What has me steamed is the call for "open investment" and a "level playing field":

> Open Investment entrenches empire and the Level Playing Field ensures its continuity. Once it's established, any change to that so-called Level Playing Field brings a reflex protective reaction from the controlling country.

------

*   "Down Paradox Lane," *Lindsay This Week*, 5 January 1988.

Any nationalist movement that attempts to keep profits at home is a threat to a mercantile empire. It is no accident that the United States has consistently opposed ANY regime, anywhere, that impedes American business interests....

In the economic union of our new colonialism Canada will have lost her ability to sway in creative tension between the productivity of the right and the humanism of the left. She will be committed to the Neo-Conservative Right....

A people that is docilely willing to be stripped of such future options is a people devoid of both pride and honour.

I cannot forgive or forget what I called "the president's fatuous promise of active non-action" with regard to acid rain and other environmental problems. Our own government, busily supporting the "Free Trade" that was anathema to it before attaining power, is equally dedicated to environmental non-action and is equally skilled at talking about the need to acquire all the facts before doing anything. I find that lightening up and resorting to satirical verse is one way to maintain sanity in an increasingly illogical world. "Earth Day" is celebrated in doggerel in "The Good Ship,"* which describes the fate of a ship that develops a hole up forward because of an acid leak, but whose captain insists on a full study of the situation:

As news from the bow got worser and worser
A report from the stern came in from the purser.
"I'm happy to say we ride higher and higher,
The air is much clearer the nearer the sky we are.
I really don't see why all the suspense —
My ledgers are dry and the view is immense."

"You see?" said the Captain to quavering Mate,
"The more we learn the safer our fate.
A loss at the bow but a rise at the rear
All averages out, we've nothing to fear.
We've heard from a man who floats loans and debentures,
And mortgages, bonds and similar ventures.
The least we can do is have faith in his skill.
Your mariner's instincts are worth less than nil."

---

*   "Down Paradox Lane," *Lindsay This Week*, 25 April 1988.

An hour or so later the ship was at rest,
Her keel on the bottom her flag at the crest,
And up where the mast is so skinny it wiggles
The Captain was sending out semaphore signals:
"She's steady and level, I'm certain at last
She's no longer leaking, the danger is past.
She's firm as a rock, remarkably stable,
I'll bring her on in as soon as I'm able
Because, I assure you, I'm ready to act —
I've studied the case and a fact is a fact."

In this year of the great Free Trade debate government propaganda moves into high gear, firmly backed by the coffers of Canada's major corporations, the majority of which are American owned.

But other trails are converging. Thanks to an Ontario provincial program, I recently spent time as Writer in Residence at the Lindsay Public Library, and later teamed up with its adventurous Chief Librarian, Moti Tahiliani, and with Bob Mark, a community-oriented Lindsay businessman. We have already taken a crack at the publishing business, under the name "Tri-M," with a book by a young historian (one of my former reporters), Dr. Ralph Robinson, that examines the history of public education in Victoria County. We have followed with *Waltz for a Pagan Drum*, a novel of mine that has too confusing a pre-publication history to relate here.

Now, as the 1988 election approaches, some of my columns are pulled together in a small book and published by Tri-M under the title of one item, *Nation to Colony*. Pierre Berton, himself an outspoken opponent of the Mulroney version of Free Trade, writes a brief forward that is disarmingly direct: "I suggest the reader accept these mini-essays as what they are — passionately prejudiced. However, since the prejudice is for a humane, compassionate, egalitarian and evolving Canada that is greatly in peril, then the passion can only be applauded." Larry Zolf, the CBC's curmudgeonly, humorous, brilliant philosopher-critic, gets into the act and writes a one-liner for the back cover blurb. "Munroe Scott," he says, "is one of Canada's best writers." Then, already teetering on the brink of perjury, he plunges forward over the edge: "Anything Munroe says merits attention, so please pay attention to this book."

My contribution to the Free Trade battle is remarkably insignificant, but, like so many others in the arts community, I have at least carried arms. High-profile authors such as Pierre Berton and Margaret Atwood and playwright Rick Salutin are bloodied to the elbows, but all to no avail. The Multory corporate-backed juggernaut rolls onward. ("Multory" is my *Paradox Lane* term. I refuse to call the Mulroney government either "Tory" or "Conservative" out of respect for a fine old party with an honourable past.) Parliament is overwhelmed, the balky Senate is stacked at the last minute with enough Multory votes to win the day, Free Trade becomes the law of the land, and Corporate Rights begin to trump Human Rights. Eventually, the Jean Chrétien Liberals destroy the Multories by promising, among other things, to amend Free Trade, and, of course, once in power do no such thing. By then, fortunately for my blood pressure, I am no longer writing *Down Paradox Lane*.

There are those who say the column is stopped because I write a tongue-in-cheek item disparaging children, and I do receive some flak from readers who take this ridiculous life too seriously. But not so. I stop the column when the newspaper, now chain-owned, indulging in the "rationalizing," "downsizing," and "cutbacking" that becomes the mantra of the 1990s, decides to cut back my fee. In reply, I cut the column. As for the Tri-M venture, it has died in infancy, strangled by the arcane problems of Distribution.

Writing a weekly column and tiptoeing into publishing has been good fun, almost relaxing, but it has been only an ornamental thread running through the fabric of a larger tapestry. I have continued to do bushel-basket documentary assignments with CBC's Bob Clark,* and Dr. Bob McClure and his saga have come back into my life. I have returned to theatre.

---

*   Land of the Mountain Elephant, 1982; The Spirit People, 1986; The Killing Zone, 1988 (Bob shot the first two in Thailand, the third in Thailand and the jungles of Cambodia).

34

THE AGE OF AQUARIUS

IT SEEMS THAT I HAVE just barely achieved "Freedom From the Press" when my study phone rings. The caller introduces himself as Stephen Newman, the production manager of Theatre Aquarius, in Hamilton, Ontario. Aquarius is a solid professional company that is in many senses a true "regional" theatre, but one that has the nerve and the chutzpah to work within the cultural shadow of Toronto.

"I've been reading your book, *McClure: The China Years*. It's a really interesting book."

"Well, thank you."

"I've shown it to the Artistic Director here, Peter Mandia. We're both wondering whether you've thought of doing anything with it for the theatre."

I open a desk drawer, withdraw a folder, and open it, mainly to make certain I'm awake and not dreaming.

"Yes, I have. As a matter of fact, I have a rough draft of a full-length script right here in my hand."

And I have, too. It's only a first draft and it's not very good, but it demonstrates intent and enthusiasm. Above all, it demonstrates that I've already been seriously pondering the idea. And even a rough script makes a good launching pad. Talk about serendipity! Talk about luck! Talk about angels in heaven!

The upshot is that Theatre Aquarius commissions me to write a stage play based on Bob McClure's China adventures.

I soon realize how fortunate I am. Peter Mandia and Stephen Newman are the two principal founding spirits of this rather remarkable theatre company and they have chosen to shepherd my play through production themselves.

The three of us give a lot of thought to the problems of size. I've been thinking of a small cast, playing multiple roles. An alternative is to go for a large cast and elaborate scenery — the story is, after all, of epic proportions. Yet another alternative is to go for a single actor interpreting multiple characters on a basically "open" stage and to let the audience put its imagination to work. For various reasons, not the least of which is budgetary, we opt for the single-actor approach. We also opt for a one-word title. We call it *McClure*.

I have a contract that makes the choice of actor subject to my approval, but this is a no-brainer. Peter and Stephen know their stuff, and a young actor by the name of Wayne Best is chosen for our McClure. It is the happiest of choices. Wayne is experienced and intelligent. He can also be highly physical, a useful attribute in portraying a man who has been called a "muscular Christian." Wayne is one of those actors of medium build who seem to expand in stature the minute they walk on stage. It's a phenomenon I can't explain. It's as though the actor is destined for the stage, and draws sustenance from the very boards. Sometimes the same actor is diminished by film or tv.

Working on this play with Wayne, Peter, and Stephen is one of the most creatively happy experiences of my career.

The experience is enhanced by the fact that Hilda, recovering from back surgery performed by our favourite neurosurgeon, is able to accompany me. While I write she can relax in our downtown hotel, which is attached to an enclosed mall, an excellent walking track during harsh February weather. She is reading Marion Meade's *Eleanor of Aquitaine*.

There are numerous creative people involved here, whose contributions are upfront while they themselves are self-effacing. One is the set designer, Jonathan Porter, a towering man with a towering talent. Totally in tune with the open stage concept, he gives Wayne a savagely raked playing space that slopes downward like the vast, dry, sun-baked mud banks of China's Yellow River. On one side there is a large figure that can be interpreted as anything from a warlord to a Chinese god. There is also a fragment of a stone wall.

The one-actor storytelling format proves to be highly appropriate, because the real McClure is an accomplished raconteur. The virtually open stage is a natural. The actor's principal prop is a stationary bicycle, which he rides to indicate scene transitions. The stone wall fragment can be sat upon in a clinic waiting room, hidden behind during an air raid, or stood upon to view a student riot.

Peter Mandia decides he wants to underline, when suitable, with offstage music. He commissions a Hamilton composer, Elma Miller, who writes a score for a solo cello as mercurial as the principal character. I cannot listen to it without being moved.

The rehearsal studios are in an old school on the edge of downtown Hamilton. The play itself is presented in the theatre space next to the Grand Hall in Hamilton Place. Bob and Amy McClure are with us for opening night, along with their old China friends (and my mentors), Bruce and Marnie Copland.*

I have some apprehension as to how Bob will react to being portrayed on the stage, but he greets the play with the enthusiasm with which he greets all of life, eventually confessing, "I didn't think I was that aggressive." Then he adds, "But my family tell me, 'That's you, Dad'."

Our play is invited to the Guelph Spring Festival — an invitation that is, to us, as prestigious as receiving an award. It is taken to Toronto and presented in the nave of venerable Bloor Street United Church, from which Bob McClure first departed as a missionary-in-search-of-adventure way back in 1923. The Lieutenant Governor, Lincoln Alexander, is here, along with a uniformed aide. The aide does his stuff and seats His Excellency and other VIPs according to some arcane protocol. Just as the house lights begin to dim, Bob suddenly rearranges the seating, moving both himself and the Lieutenant Governor. No vice-regal protocol is going to keep Bob McClure from sitting beside Amy.

We Aquarians are chuffed by the Guelph and Bloor Street United experiences. They prove that the play is portable. It's roadworthy. It can tour. Not only that, it has had good reviews.

Arnold Edinborough, writing in the *Financial Post*, finds the play "humorous, witty and startlingly dramatic." He lists such characters as "a dotty English doctor, a forbidding warlord, an austere Mao Tse-tung, a drunken Norman Bethune, and a wildly funny Scottish university registrar," then goes on to pay a glowing and oh-so-well-deserved tribute to the one and only actor. "All are played, with consummate skill, by Wayne Best. This is, almost beyond belief, a one-man show. Best carries on dialogue with a variety of people merely by shifting his head, varying his voice or changing his stance. His rage is awesome, his sudden deflations pitiable. He plays on the audience as skilfully as a violinist plays on his strings." I emphatically agree. Wayne is the answer to a playwright's prayer.

---

* *McClure* ran in the Studio Theatre, Hamilton Place, from 5 March to 29 March 1986. It was published by Simon & Pierre in 1988.

The play is booked for a tour. But it goes without Wayne. At almost the last minute Wayne gets the proverbial "career opportunity." This is not uncommon in the acting world, and few artistic directors in Canada would invoke contract and stand in the way of what could be a career break for an actor. Wayne's break eventually leads to his becoming a Stratford Festival stalwart. But right now, Peter and Stephen do some fast re-grouping, re-casting, and rehearsing. It is a *fait accompli* before I even learn there is a problem. My right of approval is violated, but time is too short for the niceties. Stephen Black, the new actor, a little younger than Wayne and not quite as experienced, is almost too handsome for the rugged McClure, but he is a brave thespian, willing to hurl himself into the breach and soldier on. His soldiering takes him on a national tour, coast to coast. I catch the play a couple of times while it is still in Ontario and send a few cautionary notes to Aquarius having to do with pace and diction.

It is Saturday, March 4, 1989, and Hilda and I are in Ottawa attending the play in the National Arts Centre. It's not in the Theatre, that most beautiful space, but in the Studio, that most flexible of venues. The last time we were here in the Studio was when we took Rob to see *The Tempest*, which set me off on the abortive quest to interest actor John Neville in *Wu-feng*. But here we are again. It's the final night of the final leg of the national tour. Outside, freezing rain is falling.

A few days later, somewhat sadly, I write a letter to Stephen Newman at Theatre Aquarius:

> Hilda and I were planning to nip down to Ottawa for NAC opening night but I caught the flu and we had to cancel. However, we did make it for closing night last Saturday. Really good audience, in spite of a day of sleet. In my opinion, the show is deteriorating.... Ottawa reviewers were not complimentary and it's to their credit.
>
> I know, of course, that it's a desperately difficult life for a young actor touring a one-man show. So easy to get tired, or careless, or to drop into bad habits, and I believe he's been in and out of the flu. I wonder if he's getting any guidance. Anyway, it's come and gone to the NAC and I doubt it did any of us any professional good. (Some very knowledgeable friends told me they don't consider they've seen the real play.)

My concern has nothing to do with characterization or interpretation, but with the two most vulnerable aspects of any play — pace and diction. Both can be severely damaged by weariness. Touring, particularly with a one-actor play, must be one of theatre's most tiring experiences. But it's these vagaries of live theatre that make it simultaneously daunting and exciting. No two performances are ever the same. No two productions are ever alike.

I find it a sad irony, however, that it is this touring production that is preserved on videotape, not to run as a whole, but to be used for supportive clips in a Berkeley Studio film about Bob McClure.

Dennis Sweeting mounts *McClure* for the Kawartha Summer Theatre. He casts long, lean Robert Haley, who puts a gangling, rural-rooted imprint on his chief character, which makes his McClure totally different from Wayne's more tightly wound interpretation, and very effective. A production is mounted in the Maritimes. Bob McClure is invited to attend, and does. I am not in the loop on that, and have no idea who played McClure. David and Dorothy Gardner mount the play for Ontario's old Red Barn Theatre and cast Max McLaughlin, whose interpretation is again different, and to my mind virtually on a par with Wayne's.

Bob and Amy attend the Red Barn production. I find Bob outwardly cheerful but inwardly seething. He's angry with the medical establishment in general and with his own doctors in particular. He's not been feeling well lately and has been under a doctor's care; however, he had already diagnosed himself, and has just had his diagnosis confirmed. He has pancreatic cancer. What's burning Bob is that his own doctors seem to have been reluctant to tell him, as though he were some kind of weak-minded jellyfish! He is riled by their attempt to shelter him from the knowledge that his own death is imminent, he who has seen so much of it, in all four corners of the globe. Hilda and I find Bob's anger, voiced in private, almost humorous. It is vintage McClure. It is only weeks before I am visiting him in hospital. His anger has gone; he is weak, but still cheerful, and still full of optimism for mankind. I see no deterioration of personality. A few days later he dies, just short of his ninety-first birthday. Amy follows him two years later. Good lives, well lived; what more can one say?

While the McClure play is on the boards I find *Paradox Lane* a useful soapbox from which to answer a question that has been bothering me.

> I'm being hit these days by a persistent question — "How come we've only heard about Bethune?" ...

When young people put the question to me there is often more than amazement in their tone. There is a sense of accusation that makes me, as a Canadian, acutely uncomfortable.

Why, indeed?

Why have we as a nation learned to idolize Bethune, who was in China for 21 months, while we know nothing at all about a whole host of Canadians who devoted their lives to China?

McClure's own father went to China in 1888. He not only founded a hospital but taught an entire generation of Chinese doctors. He translated medical texts into Chinese and laid foundations in pathology that Chinese doctors are building upon to this day. Dr. William McClure? Who's he?

And what Canadian ever heard of Dr. James Menzies, Dr. Percy Leslie, Drs. Gordon and Ernest Struthers, Dr. Mary Grant Atak, Dr. Helen Craw Mitchell? The list can go on and on and on.

Bob McClure is a writer's dream because he enjoyed adventure. The Age of the Warlords, the Second Revolution, the Sino-Japanese War, the Civil War, the rise of Communism, all provided a gung-ho surgeon with enough adventure for a lifetime.

But Dr. Richard Brown, a Canadian Anglican, was no slouch when it came to adventure. Battle-field surgery or night time ventures through Japanese lines, it was all breakfast and dinner to Dick Brown. He even worked for several months in the Shansi caves with Bethune. Ever hear of Dick Brown?

Here in Canada, Bethune made an enormous contribution to thoracic surgery and to the treatment of TB. In Spain he made an indelible mark in the area of battlefield blood transfusions. Every time we go to a mobile blood clinic we are indebted to Bethune.

But we idolize him for his 21 months in China!

Those months were heroic, and he died of them, but in the epic story of Canadian doctors in China they were a mere blip in a paragraph.

We've established a shrine to Bethune and have already, through TV and film, invested huge sums in perpetuating his mythology. A Canadian film crew is in China this very minute busily continuing the strange exercise.

I expect the film will show Bethune, in 1939, laying the foundations for Chairman Mao's much vaunted system of rural medicine based upon the "barefoot doctors". It was a system that McClure (and at least one other doctor) had going back in the mid thirties while Mao was still on the Long Trek, but history means nothing to us.

I've still not answered the question the young people put to me with that look of combined surprise and accusation.

The only honest answer I can give is appallingly embarrassing, and it comes in two parts.

First: Bethune was a card carrying communist and as such was taken to Mao's bosom. In later years his story was seized upon by the Chinese government, for propaganda reasons, as an example of the communist international brotherhood. The Chinese sold the mythology to us and for diplomatic reasons we bought it. The Bethune shrine at Gravenhurst was established, after Chinese urging, by our Department of External Affairs!

Second: We Canadians are an insecure people who still have to be told by others what is good, or admirable, or heroic and who, by and large, have surrendered our own values and judgement. We have even given others the mandate to create our heroes. We are victims of self inflicted amnesia, dedicated to the betrayal of our past.

How can I unload all that onto an eager but innocent questioner?*

For the record, any reservations I have about the idolizing of Bethune have nothing to do with his being a communist. Anyone who knows the history of the rise of the industrial west must have sympathy with the philosophy of communism, if not the practice. Anyone who knows the history of China during the nineteenth and the first half of the twentieth century knows that unfettered capitalism created Chinese communism as surely as infection creates gangrene.

---

*   "Down Paradox Lane," *Lindsay This Week*, 7 July 1987.

THE FINAL DECADE:
PART ONE

WHAT A STRANGE DECADE this is shaping up to be, this final one of the twentieth century. It gets underway with the Gulf War and is a roller coaster from there on, both nationally and privately.

Hilda and I are thinking of selling the Balsam Lake establishment, partly to realize on our investment but mainly to ease the workload of general maintenance. We actually sign with an agent and I drive a stake into the ground to hold a For Sale sign. We are saved from this precipitate folly by a plunging economy. Nothing sells, anywhere. Canada is in a depression. The politicians and economists take a long time to admit to the fact, but there's not a lay person in the nation who isn't totally aware of it right from the beginning. For a freelance it's a good decade in which to turn sixty-five and qualify for a share of our proverbial social safety net. Besides, surely it's about time to step aside, back off, slow down, smell the coffee, and listen to the call of the loon. Here, on the shores of an idyllic Kawartha lake, Hilda and I are beautifully situated to do so. And the Balsam Lake establishment is turning into a family Mecca. David and Janet Chapman have been married for more than a decade and now Ian brings Marnie Myers into the family and Rob brings Krista Boline. Hilda and I have acquired three lovely daughters!

It's not that I'm not working. Late in 1988 I began research in the University of Toronto Medical Library on a project that seems to be ongoing. And as this final decade begins I find myself in Ottawa doing research in the Parliament Buildings. Both projects are for books and both are highly speculative. I also plunge into another full-length stage play. Equally speculative. There's something about all this that's even more bizarrely chaotic than usual.

The play is a two-character mystery whose main character is somewhat outrageously based on the late film pioneer, my old employer,

Budge Crawley. The parliamentary research is for a book about our Parliamentary Sculptor and her masterworks. The "medical" research is for a book about flatulence.

The flatulence book is the first to come to fruition, if one may use that term. It's really the result of a joke, or a challenge — I'm not sure which.

Don Jack was visiting. He and Nancy had recently moved to England to be near their daughters, who were now settled there, but Don, a staunch Canadian, returned here for a visit at every opportunity. He and Hilda and I were sitting at table one day when a gastrointestinal event occurred; one of us fellows came up with an esoteric bit of pertinent information, which was immediately topped by the other guy with an even more erudite fart fact. The conversation escalated for a few moments, then dissolved in laughter, with Don saying, "You know, somewhere in all that there's a book."

"Yes," said I, in sudden hearty agreement and inspiration, "and we're at my table, in my house, so it's my book!"

"It's all yours." Don probably thought I was joking. No way.

Writing the book is an exercise in relaxation. I can't say the same for the research. In quest of the innermost truth I waft my way into publications whose titles are as eclectic as is my subject. There is *Medical Clinics of North America*, *The Annual Review of Medicine*, *The Australian Family Physician*, *The New England Journal of Medicine*, *The Twelve Caesars*, by Gaius Suetonius Tranquillus, St. Augustine's *The City of God*, *The Merck Manual of Diagnosis and Therapy*, *Miss Manners' Guide to Excruciatingly Correct Behavior*, *The American Journal of Gastroenterology*, Chaucer's *Canterbury Tales*, *The Complete Essays of Montaigne*, and so on and so forth, including, for heaven's sake, a thing called *Frog Raising for Pleasure and Profit and Other Bizarre Books*, the latter reference coming to me from Don in a spirit of either collegial co-operation or mischief. Son Rob gets into the act — indeed, aren't we all — with some scholarly advice from his chiropractic realm. (He's progressed from diving to science to chiropractic. I can barely keep up.) Ian contributes contemporary nomenclature and pithy sayings gleaned from the technical crews who enrich the air in modern movie studios. David passes on practical advice culled from the executive suite of Canada's (and North America's) largest non-profit cemetery company.

There is one problem in writing a book like this. Well, of course, there are numerous problems, but a major one is the choice of a title. A title should be honest and yet contain a touch of elegance. Indeed, for this project, being elegant throughout is a major objective. A poetical quotation for a title would be nice, but where to find one? Chaucer's "thunder-clap" is a bit too aggressive, nor is it instantly evocative. I create the solution. I write three stanzas of poesy, a fancy term for doggerel. Stanzas two and three I tear up. The remaining stanza can now be called a "fragment," which gives it the cachet of literary archaeology:

> Oh, vulgar wind that blows where'er it pleases;
> That fans the stools of wise men, fools,
> And kings as rich as Croesus;
> That pipes its way with merry note
> Through prelate, parson, priest and pope,
> And rests but never ceases.

This "fragment" contributes the title, *Oh, Vulgar Wind*, which in the interests of clarity is accompanied by a subtitle, *A Sympathetic Overview of the Common Fart*.

The writing goes easily and quickly. With a full manuscript in hand I embark on a quest for a publisher. My first approach is to Penguin Canada, who issued the McClure biography in paperback. Initially, an associate editor and the managing editor (both women) react with enthusiasm and attempt to move quickly. Soon, however, I am told that the *Wind* can't fly because the sales people say it can't be pigeonholed.

Several other major publishers give the impression that the *Wind* is beneath them, which, if they would only pause to think, it is.

I send the manuscript off to a large firm in the States that specializes in medical books, and after a decent interval of a few days follow up with a phone call to the editor. He greets me cheerfully and says he has passed the manuscript on to an associate. "She has it right now," he says. "Every so often we have to pick her up off the floor."

Eventually the American company declines, explaining that the plunging economy is forcing it to refrain from speculative ventures. However, unlike Canadian firms (apart from Penguin) it is morally supportive and encouraging.

I am beginning to notice an intriguing fact. The readers most susceptible to *Wind*, most likely to be tickled by it, to understand it, and to embrace it, are women. And, indeed, the publisher who eventually shows serious interest is a woman, Dr. Thelma Barer-Stein.

Thelma has a small Toronto publishing company called Culture Concepts. She has an abiding interest in things dietary (she did her Ph.D. on the subject). Thelma submits the manuscript to scrutiny by several dietary and medical consultants — a useful and supportive exercise.

Oh, Vulgar Wind is eventually produced (in a typographical sense) by Culture Concepts, and very handsomely released (again, typographically speaking). A medical reviewer actually uses the term "elegant," thereby inflating my ego. Toronto's *Globe and Mail* selects it as an "Editor's Choice," then tempers my pride by describing it as "a breath of fetid air." But who am I to complain about the use of double entendres, puns, and other verbal tools? I find myself giving a reading to an elite group of connoisseurs, comprised of members of the medical staff of Toronto's venerable St. Joseph's Hospital. They are brought together for this hour of literary introspection by the head of the Department of Gastroenterology.

In true authorial fashion I surreptitiously visit Toronto bookstores to see how distribution is going. In *The World's Biggest Bookstore* (and at this time it may be) I can't find my masterpiece. I inquire, identifying myself as the author. They tell me they don't know how to classify my opus. Does it go on the Humour shelf? Or Health? Or Psychiatry? But they've found a solution. They lead me to the checkout counter, and there, right beside the cash register, is a rack displaying my child. I find that the same solution is applied in several other city stores. Literary success has arrived! I had never expected to find the author's much-sought-after prize, the universal subject, located between the stomach and the sphincter.

When, in 1998, Thelma sells the Culture Concept list to another publisher, *Oh, Vulgar Wind* is left behind. Remaindered. Out of print. Gone, as it were, with the wind. So much for universality.*

In the meantime, while I am searching for an outlet for *Wind*, I am also immersed in the life and times of Eleanor Milne, Canada's Parliamentary Sculptor.

I first became acquainted with Eleanor Milne in the late 1980s, when cbc producer Bob Clark had a great idea for a tv documentary series, which he intended to call *Temples of Glory*. He planned to take his cameras to Angkor Wat in Kampuchea, Santiago de Compostela in Spain, the Palenque complex in Mexico, Divrigi in Turkey, the Kailasa Temple in the western mountains of India, the Temple of Amon-Ra at Karnak in Egypt, Wells Cathedral in England, and the *tomb* of Ch'in Shih Huang Ti in central China.

Bob wanted to explore all these places and ask the same questions: what were the artists' mandates? how did they achieve them? what effect did their work have on their societies? As host for this proposed

---

*   *Oh, Vulgar Wind* was reissued in 2005 by Practica, http://www.vulgarwind.com

series Bob was intending to use Eleanor Milne, who, since 1962, had been Canada's official Parliamentary Sculptor. As Bob's chosen writer I got to meet Eleanor Milne. I found a tall, personable, friendly woman with a vast knowledge of things artistic. She and her Parliament Hill team of carvers had already carved a Frieze of History into the stone parapet of the balcony that surrounds the foyer to the House of Commons. (My earlier observation of her in action there, late one night in 1970, is described in chapter 22.) They had also carved an interpretation of the British North America Act into twelve great stones that protrude from the walls of the House itself. In addition, she had designed and helped build the magnificent stained-glass windows that adorn and illuminate the House of Commons. In doing this, she had made extravagant and glorious use of Canada's provincial wildflowers. Canadian history and Canada's Constitution in stone, and Canada's flowers in glass, all at the heart of Canadian governance, the House of Commons — what a set of masterworks for an artist to have achieved!

When Bob's *Temples of Glory* project fails to get financed I'm not really surprised. The CBC seems unimpressed by the man's abilities. I suspect that as the result of international sales his documentaries have earned the Corporation as much if not more per dollar invested than have those of any other producer, but little of the money earned gets ploughed back into his budgets, which are consistently reduced. His office space shrinks. Eventually he is assigned a small windowless office, where, undaunted, he continues to plan and expedite documentary forays abroad.*

But I have met Eleanor Milne. Here, I believe, is a worthy subject for a biography. Eleanor co-operates, and, beginning late in 1990 and continuing through the following year, I do extensive interviews with her and with others.

This promises to be a time-consuming project. I make early contact with major Canadian publishers in hopes of a pre-publication contract that might provide some money up front. Freelance writers don't mind speculating, but there comes a time when it's also nice to eat. At this moment, the *Wind*, although written, is also speculative, and still very much up in the air.

Our publishers amaze me. In general, their reaction to the idea of a Milne biography is absolute indifference. They say that no one outside of Ottawa has ever heard of Eleanor Milne. This might well be true. Her

---

*   Bob Clark died of cancer in 1999.

and her team's creative efforts have been carried out, year after year, at night. She's not been a regular on TV interviews. She's not been controversial. She has merely been spending her life enhancing the interior of Canada's symbolic heart, the beautiful Gothic building at the centre of Parliament Hill.

The people at the University of Ottawa Press are an exception. They, of course, happen to know what I am talking about. But they are not in the biography business. They do, however, authorize some modest funding from their portion of the Ontario Arts Council's Writers' Reserve. The OAC complies promptly. A submission to the Canada Council is turned down, but I am pushing on.

A major publisher tells me, orally, "There is no national hook." I am beating my head on a wall.

I do know, of course, that biography is a special realm, more or less monopolized by academics, university professors, preferably those in possession of Ph.D.s. I don't possess a Ph.D., and my only prior venture into this biographical terrain is with the two volumes of McClure. Once more I'm beginning to wander, aimlessly, in unfamiliar, even hostile territory. It's quite possible I have ventured too far.

I discuss the topic with Don Jack, who is here again. This is a sadder visit, because Nancy has died, but Don is soldiering on. All the residents of our little Balsam Lake enclave enjoy a visit from Don. He is, as always, kind, eccentric, talented, colour-blind, and warmly humorous. However, he gives serious consideration to my current frustrations and tells me to confine the Milne saga to a magazine article. I refuse to take his advice.

Then, one day I am sitting on the stone bench that surrounds the Eternal Flame at the foot of Parliament Hill. I am somewhat dejected. A class of high school students rendezvous at the Flame. It's obvious from their conversation that they have just toured the Hill.

I speak to two of the girls. "You've just been through the main building?"

"Yes."

"Did you see the Frieze of History?"

"Where?"

"The foyer — just outside the House of Commons."

"Well ... yes ... we were through there. I guess so."

"And in the House — the windows? The Constitution stones?"

"Yeah. But it was sort of fast."

"Did you know a woman designed, carved, helped create all that?"

"No!"

Suddenly they looked intrigued.

"Here, did you see these?" I have some rudimentary photos in my briefcase. I bring them out. "Here's John Cabot's ship. See how it is being held back by fish? That's the sculptor's way of symbolizing business and nature coming into eternal conflict in North America."

First thing I know I have a group of students around me, showing interest, asking questions about the carvings and about Eleanor Milne.

The penny drops. I'm not going to write a standard biography. I have a story to tell, an epic tale, an almost mythical yarn, about a sculptor's career-long struggle to depict history and, in doing so, to help create a country. No country can survive, I tell myself, without a national mythology. This whole Gothic building, including Eleanor Milne's masterworks, is surely an attempt, conscious or unconscious, to create and preserve a positive national mythology.

It's a yarn worth telling, so I settle in to spin it for elastic minds of any age and to hell with the publishers. It becomes "a tale told beside a campfire."

Eleanor is not pleased, and in a letter she accuses me of betrayal. I don't blame her. I have veered sharply away from my initial goal of factual biography. Now I, too, am creating mythology. But as an artist, she should understand. I'm still attempting to fashion a portrait. If she were sitting for Dali or Whistler would she expect the same outcome from both? Obviously not. But I do sympathize.

The manuscript takes form under the working title, *The Woman Who Carved Canada*, but I soon realize it's as much about Canada as it is about the artist and her associates. It becomes *The Carving of Canada*, and its sub-title is *A Tale of Parliamentary Gothic*. But now, as we approach the mid-1990s, I see no sign of its ever being published.

In the midst of all this, while I am writing about our country's history and its governing institutions and their depiction in stone and glass, I find myself involved in a real-life attempt to influence history.

Canada is in the midst of the Charlottetown Accord debate and is asking us all to vote either "Yes" or "No" in a referendum on October 26, 1992.

In the years since my ill-considered attempt to be a newspaper editor I have continued to do a considerable amount of public speaking in the counties of Victoria and Haliburton. Even as an editorialist I was urging reform of our electoral system. In addition, fallout from the Spicer Commission on Canadian Unity has me deeply involved as one of the founding members of an informal local group calling itself "The

Citizen's Open Circle." We are, among other things, deeply interested in the device of a Community Parliament, an idea that is being pushed by Vaughn Lyon, a political science professor at Trent University. Its purpose is to advise and monitor local M.P.s in order to remind them it is the electorate they represent first and foremost, not the party. I am more and more convinced our democracy is becoming seriously frayed.

What really tears my shirt now are certain aspects of the Charlottetown Accord that are ostensibly intended to give special recognition to the Province of Quebec and to First Nations. What I see is a handover of power to governments, not to people, and I say so on the public platform:

> It's one thing for people to have an innate desire and a will to preserve their values. It's quite another thing to hand their governments a constitutional tool for perpetual manipulation. That is what this Accord does.

As for the First Nations governments, initially I am inclined to endorse their "Inherent Right of Self-Government." However, I see traps built into the sections concerning these undefined governments:

> Listen to the powers we are planning on giving to these governments — not to people, to governments. These ethnic politicians will be given the authority to safeguard and develop not only "languages" and "cultures", but "traditions", "identities", and "the integrity of their societies". The politicians of these ethnic governments that nobody knows how they will work will have access to the Notwithstanding clause that overrides the Charter of Rights. So here, too, ethnic-driven *government* is being given the constitutional power, nay, command, to control its people along ethnic lines!

I'm a firm believer that constitutions, whether established by precedent or enshrined in writing, are vital instruments of governance and, quite correctly, should be difficult to alter. A good constitution defines how the people entrust power to government, but, equally important, it establishes the tools with which they protect themselves from the misuse of that very power:

> History shows that social evolution takes peoples along undreamed of and amazingly creative paths. These proposed amendments fly in

the face of social evolution by ordering ethnically-driven governments, whether Aboriginal or Quebecois, to "preserve", "safeguard",
"maintain", "control" — the words are not mine, these are the
words of this Accord. It is littered with such words and they all apply
to government control of people, never to people control of government.

I have a deep dislike for referendums. The subject is invariably too
complicated for a simple "yes" or "no." If we see even one fundamental
flaw, how can we vote "yes"?
Nationally, the Accord is voted down.

Every so often Hilda tells me I should enter politics, to me a most worthy and most thankless calling, but I've never felt the slightest urge.
With notes, I can give the illusion of being articulate on my feet, but I'm
not. Hilda has already joined the NDP. She campaigned door-to-door in
the provincial 1990 election. I eventually follow her example and also
join the NDP, even though I am developing a somewhat jaundiced view
of political parties in general. In fact I am developing a rather perverse
theory that all institutions, whether political, business, or religious, tend
to be demonic; they are founded with commendable human-oriented
goals but gradually undergo a subversion of intention, and eventually
their overwhelming priority becomes their own survival. How else can
one explain how a company that lays off thousands of employees can
give its CEO a million dollar bonus for good work? Indeed, there's a
speech in *Wu-feng* in which Governor Wu says it all:

> We men at least create our gods in our own image and ignore them
> at will, but companies we hallucinate into a reality more real than
> ourselves. Long after we are dead our companies will be left to
> assess our demise as profit or loss, mechanically counting the total
> on an abacus made from the ivory of our own bones.

Fortunately for my state of mind, theatre comes back into my life.
There's that full-length two-act play I've been writing. This one is for
two actors, one man and one woman, the first playing a retired businessman and the second a young oral historian. It's a mystery called *Corpus Delectable*, and it deals with corporate betrayal. Peter Mandia decides
to produce it. Not only that, he says he will direct it himself. For me it is
still the Age of Aquarius; I am overjoyed.

Hamilton's Theatre Aquarius has undergone a remarkable metamorphosis in the few years since it produced *McClure*. Peter and his colleague, Stephen Newman, have realized a long-standing dream. Their theatre company is now housed in its own building, a beautiful architecturally designed plant that houses a 750-seat proscenium arch theatre, a flexible studio space, and generous backstage facilities for dressing rooms, wardrobe, carpentry — all the things that are required for live theatre, one of the most labour-intensive of enterprises. Again, I am excited, gratified, and enthusiastic at the prospect of working with the Aquarius team.

October 8, 1994, is a dark day. Peter Mandia dies.

A remarkable full-house memorial event is held in the Theatre. Hamiltonians are here in droves, but it also looks as though half the Canadian theatrical community is on hand. I realize that although, for the most part, Torontonians and their theatre critics tend to be unaware of cultural developments in saucy Hamilton, it's obvious that stage people from all across the country hold Peter, and Aquarius, close to their hearts. It's also obvious that the old adage, "The play must go on," seems to be as strong now as ever; within a few short months I am presented with a practical demonstration of it.

My play is scheduled to hit the boards in the main theatre toward the end of February 1995. The male character is a cantankerous retired pioneer film producer, and he may be planning a murder. The female character is a young, attractive oral historian who may be an assassin. I have taken the outrageous liberty of basing my aging male character on Budge Crawley. It's no coincidence that my character, also named Frank, had two wives, simultaneously, and took them both to the Oscars, also simultaneously, nor that he still has a deep love of country and of the wilderness, and a warm affection for Aboriginals, nor that although retired he is still hoping to create a cinematic masterpiece based on a love story between a Canada goose and a wild duck, nor that he is mischievous, a con man, and a patriot.

The production of this opus turns out to be a drama in itself. After the play has completed its run, I write a letter to Don Jack that tells it all:

> I had my little creative burst during most of February when *Corpus Delectable* was in rehearsal at Theatre Aquarius. Fortunately the rewriting was more in the nature of polishing than in any major restructuring so was quite fun.
>
> But what a production! Only two characters, M & F, and the male supposed to be in his seventies. (You'll remember I said he

was outrageously based on Budge.) A guy in his sixties was cast who'd been away from big theatrical parts for quite a few years. A good actor.... In November, Peter Mandia, who was going to direct, died of a heart attack and Aquarius brought a freelance director on board (Robert Rooney — excellent director). Robert cast the female part and we had a one day workshop before Christmas and everything looked good. Then the actress got one of those "career opportunity" offers for a film and dropped out. So in January Rooney was hunting for a female lead at a time when most schedules were booked. He finally cast a friend, Mary Long. Mary, it turned out, is Budge's daughter-in-law! (Married to Sandy Crawley.) Mary would also be playing a heavy part in a Tarragon* production every evening for at least the first two weeks of our rehearsal period.

As it turned out, Mary was absolutely terrific. A quick study, very professional, very patient, and an excellent actress. With anyone else I think the production would have foundered.... During the last week, Mary, exhausted, was getting sick so two on-stage rehearsals, badly needed by Aron, were cancelled and Rooney banished Mary to her bed.

Dress rehearsal in that theatre is in front of a pay-what-you-can audience and there were a couple of hundred in attendance. Dress rehearsal was the first time the director and I had ever seen the second act (2 acts) run all the way through without interruption. The next two preview nights went pretty well and by opening night it was more or less intact except for pacing and the occasional garbled key oration.

Hilda and I went home and returned in 10 days time for a "Talkback-night" in which the audience is invited to remain after and quiz the actors, director, writer, etc. But that morning Aron had a temperature of 104 and was confined to his bed! No understudies. What to do? Mary to the rescue. She threw her husband into the breach. Sandy had been helping her learn her lines so was familiar with the part, but of course would have to carry the book. He's President of ACTRA so had to cancel a trip but turned up in time for one 2 1/2 hour blocking rehearsal that was completed in his dressing room. The curtain rose (actually, no curtain) a half hour late and Sandy did a quite remarkable job.

*   A Toronto theatre.

So now the principal character was being played by Budge's son! Sandy had to carry the flag for the next night and then Aron was back on duty for the rest of the run. We saw it again closing night and Hilda confessed it wasn't until then that she realized I had a really good play. No wonder.

The publicity people tried to get mileage out of the Crawley coincidences but the Toronto media ignored it all, totally. We got one lukewarm Hamilton review from opening night and one enthusiastic *Stoney Creek News* review, so I don't expect much of a life for *Corpus Delectable*. Ah well, an experience and a few shekels in the bank.

We're halfway through this final decade of the twentieth century. It's October 1995 and everything goes on hold as Hilda goes on life support.

36

THE FINAL DECADE:
PART TWO

HILDA IS DIAGNOSED as having a severe blockage in at least three major arteries and is admitted to Toronto's St. Michael's Hospital for triple by-pass surgery.

Ian is detailed by his brothers to keep me off the walls during the operation, so we take a walking tour of downtown Toronto. We return to find David and Rob on hand to join us in greeting their mother when she comes round. We are told she has in fact undergone a quadruple by-pass and, in the quaint way surgeons have of declaring a procedure a success so long as the patient leaves the operating room alive, her doctors tell us the operation has been successful, but that her condition has been complicated by a heart attack suffered just after she reached the Intensive Care Unit.

Hilda is several days in Intensive Care, followed by additional time in Coronary Care and the surgical ward. During these days the boys and I watch as the intravenous attachments gradually dwindle from twelve to zero, and our amazing wife and mother recovers her spirits and her equilibrium. She and I both chuckle with sardonic amusement over the verbal wire-walking performed by the cardiologist when he makes his final assessment. "There was a moderate amount of damage. It's not small. It's not the largest ..."

Neither of us chuckles over the strange paradox that the savage chest wound heals almost overnight with little discomfort, while the comparatively superficial wounds in her leg, from which veins have been purloined, seem to take ages to heal.

At the end of it all we have nothing but respect for the professionalism and the kindness of the staff. And we have not had to worry about the horrendous financial burden of illness — the cost of the surgery, the Intensive Care Unit, the Cardiac Care Unit, the myriad I.V.s, the monitors, the nurses, the specialists, the medications. That worry has been lifted from us by our fellow Canadians, who have made the cost of health care a co-operative burden, shouldered by all and therefore, by and large, onerous to none. What kind of civilized society, I often asked myself, would expect its citizens to go through such medical stress and then traumatize them at the end with bankruptcy?

We have survived a major crisis and are devoutly relieved. And there is a positive side to this trauma. It has put me in a frame of mind to contemplate retirement. After all, I'm sixty-eight years old and, because I'm freelance, we have to consult no one but ourselves. We can draw on our own savings and on the Canada Pension Plan, federal Old Age Security, ACTRA Fraternal Retirement Savings — bless the union that is not a union — and hope for at least a trickle of royalty payments via Public Lending Rights, CanCopy,* and elsewhere.

It's most definitely a time to scale back, recuperate, and relax.

Hilda is doing well — going to heart rehab classes in Lindsay, paying full attention to medication and prescribed diets, and in good spirits in spite of other accumulating ailments. She is reading Robert Massie's *Dreadnought*, and telling me I'd enjoy it. The book is almost as large as the battleships it features.

I've always been the lawn keeper, the carpenter, and the general handyman. Now I have to take more interest in flower gardening, which until now has been Hilda's exclusive preserve. This is a problem, because I have always disliked gardening, and have carefully cultivated protective ignorance. Now I find that if I work on a square yard at a time and follow basic instructions ("Pull those and not those") I can almost tell the difference between grass and a tulip. And I'm reinforcing the knowledge that it's pleasurable to do something I dislike for someone I love.

We've been married since 1951. Where have the years gone? And what kind Fate ordained that I should walk into Woolworth's way back in 1948 and meet my Lancashire lass? I've felt fortunate ever since. I've even attempted to express my good fortune in words. Oh, not out loud. There are things a fellow wants to voice to his love, but really can't. Fancy spoken words are okay for *Cyrano* (Hilda loves that play) but would sound silly coming from me. It's always safer to type a note.

---

*   "CanCopy" later became Access Copyright. Both it and Public Lending Right Commission are federally established organizations designed to compensate creators for copying and for library use.

> In darkness when the thermostat is low
> And winter winds pile up the sheltering snow
> And we in bed lie snuggled face to face
> I fear Eternity itself will end.
> It's all too brief a time to spend
> In your embrace.

Balsam Lake is an ideal haven. I like to slide out in the canoe early in the morning before the west wind rises. If the wind does rise, my Hobie catamaran is still sailing and still friendly, although I am losing my enthusiasm for tumultuous hull-flying; I no longer relish the thought of either a sudden immersion or the ensuing struggle to clamber up on an overturned float and turn myself into a human gin pole in order to right it again. The little beast threw me once when I was running before a good wind; it buried both bows simultaneously, causing a somersault that fired me off the trampoline like a rock out of a catapult. On my way through the rigging I hit the mast and wound up in emergency having my thigh X-rayed for a possible fracture. Some of this close-to-the edge stuff is not as enticing as it used to be. I must be getting older.

If visitors are here we take our old, somewhat eccentric powerboat and do a shoreline cruise of this lovely lake, sometimes wandering up the Gull River to Coboconk, then back downstream, out around Indian Point, and across to the edge of the Provincial Park, then farther south to where the Trent-Severn canal exits toward Lake Simcoe on its way downhill, ultimately to Georgian Bay. It's pleasant on a cool summer evening to cruise a mile or so into this man-made canal, wondering at its borders, which are composed of great ridges of shale that were dug out a hundred years ago by hand and by horse bucket. On a summer's day one can encounter the sweltering heat of hell in here between the confining banks, and one can't help admiring the workmen who endured it. On the lake again, we can cruise onward to the end of West Bay and the wildlife preserve, then loop back around Long Point and down into South Bay, at the mouth of which the gulls like to congregate in the evening, clustered together like a great white raft of floating feathers. Eventually we come back to our own eastern side, slide under the highway bridge at Rosedale, and burble down to the set of locks that starts the system off on its long descent in the other direction, to Trenton, the Bay of Quinte, and, if one is adventurous, the world. Then it's home to old Cedar Villa, which we were going to re-christen "Singing Cedars," but that was before a psychotic neighbour cut the singing cedars down and then moved away (praise the Lord) to somewhere in the Far East, where, one hopes, the locals have developed a tolerance for eccentricity. We have circumnavigated the lake and in doing so have been past Ball Island, Snake Island, Grand Island, Dellemere Island, and Cherry Island. We have avoided unmarked underwater hazards like Grand Rock and the reef I refer to as "the Roman road," because it looks like the remains of one. Beside the main channel there's a shoal that is marked with a large mustard-coloured billboard whose prominent lettering proclaims "Isle Submergée," which, when one comes close enough to read the smaller print, translates as "Submerged Island." Ian and I discovered this one day when sailing the Hobie in half a gale and were almost lured to destruction by the peculiar sign with the French inscription. French, however, is quite appropriate. The first white man to sail these waters was Samuel de Champlain.

As for writing, Krisztina, my agent, is still assiduously attempting to rouse some publishing interest in the manuscript about Eleanor Milne's masterworks on Parliament Hill, but to no avail. I do, however, have a temporary resurgence of enthusiasm and decide that a better portfolio of pictures will enhance the sales pitch, and will be required anyway if a publisher is ever found.

I renew contact with Parliament Hill, and the Speaker of the House of Commons grants permission for a photo session. Ian volunteers his time, equipment, and talent as my photographer and we spend an interesting long weekend taking pictures in the foyer of the House and in the House itself. The staff, whether commissionaires, guides, or maintenance men, once they know we are authorized and understand our project, go out of their way to be helpful. I never meet anyone who works in the building who is not proud of it to the point of adoration.

But the whole project is still speculative. The new pictures, however, do elicit a little more reaction. Now a publisher is more likely to say, "Oh, yes, there might be a coffee table book here. Lots of pictures. Not much text."

Damn it all, I'm a writer. Pictures are fine but there are things to say in a text. Things that have to do with an artist's struggle to achieve and a people's struggle to survive. It's one thing to display a picture of a carving of a well-muscled human being, wreathed in foliage and holding a massive chain that is attached to a cage from which doves are being released, and to have a printed caption saying it represents Freedom to Choose. But I want to be able to go beyond the picture and explain that here the sculptor is saying it requires muscle to protect this freedom and Freedom to Choose is a terrible freedom indeed because a people can choose to lose it, and without it all will be lost. Moreover, I want to say that around us in this beautiful building the "all" is interpreted, in stone and in glass, and that it is artists who interpret, and even create, the essence of a country. But I am beginning to despair. I feel this book will never be published and I know I am becoming weary. Hilda is encouraging me to admit to both.

There is surely more satisfaction to be gained now in shoving off in the canoe, or going sailing, or mowing the lawn, or simply enjoying the warm companionship of our small enclave of extraordinarily fine neighbours, and frequent visits from our incredible sons, our three lovely daughters-in-law, and our four blossoming grandchildren.

The second millennium is winding down and life is good.

37

INTO EXILE

IT IS JANUARY 19, 1999. I wake up adrift in Nowhere. I rise from my bed and open the window drapes. I have no idea where I am! I walk through the house. I know this is my house and that I live here. I know that I have not lived here very long. About two months, I believe. I also know that I have moved here without Hilda. And I know why. But where am I?

The furniture, the paintings, the books — all are familiar. Correspondence, addressed to me and lying on the kitchen table, makes absolutely no sense. I look outside again. Nothing out there is familiar. No matter what window I look from, nothing has an identity. I can see across a few neighbouring yards, and then there's a border of trees. Beyond those trees — what? Water? A town? Space? The neighbours, if those few houses are inhabited, are nameless, faceless, disembodied, non-existent. I might as well be on an island on a cloud. I have absolutely no idea where I am.

Slowly this unknown world dissolves into a recognizable reality. There is a city out there. A modest, pretty city on the shores of the Otonabee River. It is Peterborough, Ontario.

I phone a doctor and make an appointment. His diagnosis is simple and he tells me not to worry. "Delayed emotional trauma," he says. "Everybody reacts differently. You'll be all right."

Can he be correct? Can it have taken almost three months for me to "react"? Possibly. Two nights before the awakening in Nowhere I did, I now remember, cry myself to sleep. That's only the second time in three months.

But I clearly remember the early morning of October 21, 1998. I am lying beside Hilda, my wife, my lover, my friend, my companion for forty-seven years. No, for fifty years, because we loved from the moment we met. I reach out to take her hand, knowing she will wake just enough to curl into my arms for another hour of slumber.

Her hand is cold. Inert.

I leap out of bed and stand, staring away into semi-darkness. I shout, "No! No! Wake up!" It is myself I am attempting to awaken. I seize my own arm and squeeze it savagely. I am dreaming a nightmare. I must wake up.

But I am awake.

Hilda is not. Never again will she be awake. She has passed into death, quietly, peacefully, with no sudden surge of fearful awareness.

I stumble from the room and phone Ferne, our next-door neighbour and dear friend.

"Hilda is dead!" This is not a time for the banal "passed on."

"I'll be right over." And she is.

I go onto automatic pilot. I have no recollection of time passing. Ferne makes the initial mandatory phone calls. It seems as though the ambulance men, and the coroner, and a policewoman, and a man from a funeral home, are here almost instantly. They perform their professional duties with enormous kindness. I phone David and ask him to phone his brothers. Family materializes as though by magic. Even Rob is here by late afternoon, all the way from Minneapolis. The boys and their wives assign themselves duties. In retrospect I feel ashamed. I act as though Hilda's death is *my* loss. It is equally theirs. Automatic pilot is not prone to sensitivity.

I have been told there is no healing force equal to that of the love of family and friends, and the day of the funeral I am surrounded by three sons, three daughters-in-law, four grandchildren, big brother Doug, four sisters-in-law, a brother-in-law, numerous nieces and nephews and first cousins, and three neighbours who are like my own sisters. David MacDonald joins us from Ottawa as our minister. We have been friends ever since the time long ago when I observed the second coming of Jacques Cartier. His calm presence is a balm for all of us.

This extended family gathers privately on a late morning at Beaverton's Auld Kirk* Cemetery, where my beloved Hilda's ashes are interred beside those of previous generations of Scotts. It is fitting that this is in the pioneer section. She immigrated from England while still a teenager and grew to love this country with a passion. We leave her resting where she expressed a desire to be and proceed to a simple memorial service in Queen Street United Church, where she and I had sung in the choir, had courted, and were married. As for me, and family, and

---

*   It is still the "Auld Kirk" to old-timers, but the "Old Stone Church" to others.

friends, embraced by each other, there is obviously nowhere to go but onward.

Onward?

Where is Onward? What is Onward?

Hilda has gone.

Gone? Where?

The sudden extinction of a loved and loving sentient being, so entwined with my own being, forces me into introspection.

Some religions tell me I will see Hilda again, in the Hereafter.

Christianity implies that personality survives.

But do I believe in that survival? For that matter, are "personality," "self," and "soul" all one and the same? This is beyond me and I suspect it is beyond most of us.

Personality can be altered by chemicals, distorted by disease, destroyed by drugs. In this technical age we have to wonder whether the human brain is an organic computer. Fearfully and wonderfully made, to be sure, but whither personality when the neurons no longer function?

I do not believe in the resurrection of the physical body. To me, that makes no sense whatsoever. I am too simple-minded to be able to abandon logic. Theologians like to talk about a "spiritual body" and they may think they know what they mean, but I don't know. The Apostle Paul may have known what he meant, but I have never been sure Paul wasn't a little mad. A touch of madness can be an asset when making proclamations about the Hereafter.

For many months it is a rare night that I do not dream of Hilda. But there is nothing ghostly about this. No visitations from the next world. It means she is firmly entrenched in my memory, in my neurons. I miss her deeply, but not as much, strangely, in the mundane surroundings of a new house as when suddenly confronted by the magnificent colours of an autumn maple; when cresting a rise and seeing a lush Ganaraska-like valley spread before me; when hearing a breathtakingly clear soprano voice singing the Bell Song from *Lakmé*. These are the moments when I turn to speak to her, or simply reach to squeeze her hand, to say, voicelessly, "Yes, I also see, hear, feel the beauty." These are the moments on the edge of the void.

But is it a void?

Is there a God?

Surely I should know, by now, near the end of my life's journey, whether or not I believe in God!

What I do know is that we did not make ourselves.

In memory I talk to Hindus in Trinidad, Animists in Angola and Sarawak, Muslims in Gaza and Java, Jews in Jerusalem, Hindus in India and Bali, Buddhists and Taoists in Taiwan and Thailand and China, and Christians interwoven with the others. All of them predicate their beliefs on the one fundamental rock. We did not make ourselves.

"I am fearfully and wonderfully made," says the poet in the King James version of Psalm 139, and he speaks truth to me. "Marvellous are thy works; and *that* my soul knoweth right well."

There, surely, is the nub of the whole thing.

I suspect I couldn't pass any orthodox test that would qualify me as a Christian, but I do believe that we are an intrinsic part of Nature and that happiness lies in embracing the world and its inhabitants, not in exploiting either it or them, and that to pursue happiness itself as though it were a commodity is a folly of the first order. For a massive portion of our North American society to be indoctrinated with the belief that material consumption is the route to happiness, and for that pursuit of happiness to be consecrated as a constitutional directive, is surely the most dangerous combination of ideas ever to afflict the human animal.

But enough.

I have learned something in terms of human relationship that I never fully understood before. Hilda was more than a homemaker. She was, indeed, my home. In all my wandering assignments, when the job was done, the research completed, I would head for home like an arrow to its target. If there was an earlier plane, I'd catch it. If there was a chance for a relaxing stopover in Hawaii, I'd forgo it. If I rendezvoused with her in Holland, or England, or at her sister Anne's, or in Manotick, or Lindsay, or Balsam Lake, when I came to her side, to her loving embrace, I was indeed "home." And I know now that I will never truly be home again. I am in permanent exile.

But surely I have known that this time would come? She knew. Just a few days before that terrible October 21st she suddenly said, "I'm so glad you have a nice house in Peterborough."

We had been packing, having sold and purchased, but were not due to move for another month. We were to "take possession" in November. But, "*You* have a nice house," she said.

I laughed. Hilda smiled. She knew. I denied.

Yet I did know. Deep inside.

There was the day, ages ago now, that I broke a plate. It was a lovely plate, delicately hand-painted by a local artist, commissioned by our three sons, their beloved wives, and myself, bearing all our initials on the back, along with the dedication to her, the date, and the artist's signature. Hilda loved hand-painted china, and this piece was unique. It sat on a little stand on an old piece of Canadiana furniture in the bay window of the Balsam Lake living room.

I accidentally upset the stand and the delicate plate shattered on the hardwood floor. There were neighbours present, but I wept. Hilda was calm, but I wept. Our friends must have wondered. But I had a sudden feeling of how tenuous life is, how fragile her life was, how transient is beauty, love, and existence. A plate broke and I wept, more then than I do now. It was a down payment on grief.

I don't console myself with pious platitudes about joining Hilda in a Heaven. I do console myself with the thought that whatever loving creative force made her, it also unmade her, gently, carefully, swiftly, thereby saving her from what was promising to be a very debilitating, painful decline into old age. This was the rare and wonderful Good Death, unkind only to those who are left.

And now, as I have already said, for me and the family, embraced by each other, there is obviously nowhere to go but onward. Life is a strange adventure. I must see what it offers next.

38

EPILOGUE

I PROTECT MY SANITY and recover my equilibrium by throwing myself into the completion of writing projects that have not only been pushed aside but that I had decided to abandon. First, I polish the text for *The Carving of Canada*, create a mock-up using Ian's photos, and resume the search for a publisher. It is published by Penumbra Press in late 1999 and, as a result, the Association of Canadian Clubs sends me on speaking engagements in Quebec, Vancouver Island, and many points in between. I complete *The Liberators*, a light-hearted novel about pioneer politics and post-rebellion skulduggery in the Upper Canada of 1838 that has been on my mind for more than thirty years. In 2001 it, too, is published by Penumbra Press. Finally, this current project, these "re-collections" (also encouraged by a reckless Penumbra), have proven to be the most time-consuming, puzzling, complex, and arduous endeavour of my career, and it's a relief to complete them, however imperfectly. Now, perhaps, I may indulge an interest in genealogy, and chronicle the family history in such a way that my grandchildren can gain a sense of their own roots. I might even write another play. Why not a sequel to *Wu-feng*? You see, with Governor Wu gone — after all, they had killed him and then enshrined him, so there was — oh well … never mind … we'll see. In the meantime, the ranks of the old-timers are thinning. Even talented, cheerful, supportive Don Jack is gone.* Eventually it will be time to sign off with the universal and inevitable filmscript ending: Fade to Black.

But wait — in my parallel existence in the theatre, life is an Open Stage, and there is No Curtain. And besides, there's always an updraft.

---

*   Donald Lamont Jack, 1924-2003. RIP

LEGEND TO PHOTO MONTAGE

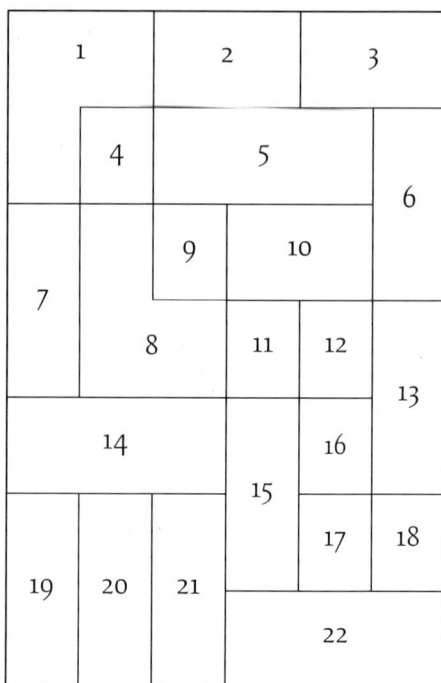

1	2	3
4	5	6
7 (9, 10, 8)	11, 12	13
14	15, 16	17, 18
19, 20, 21	22	

1 The wedding, 1951 (l to r) the author, Hilda, Anne and Bob Smith, and the bride's mother.

2 Dr. "Bob" McClure at the Great Wall of China, 1981

3 Daniel, the carver, Rankin Inlet

4 Hellen Scott, the author's mother

5 Village dance, Angola

6 Rev. David MacDonald, P.E.I., 1964

7 In Holland, 1959

8 The Rt. Hon. John G. Diefenbaker, Barbados, 1974

9 Rev. W.J. Scott, the author's father

10 The author and Hobie Cat

11 Douglass Scott, 1942

12 Taoist Scholar, rosewood

13 The portable survey tower, Northern Ontario, 1949

14 The author with Native guide, Fort Prince of Wales, N.W.T., 1960

15 Principal lady, Balinese coming-of-age ceremony

16 Donald Scott, 1942

17 Eskimo Hunter, soapstone, by Daniel, Rankin Inlet, N.W.T.

18 The author, 1942

19 The author and his brothers, 1932 (l to r) Munroe, Donald, Douglass

20 Forestry, 1949

21 Python slayer, Angola

22 Ian with Palestinian youths, Gaza City beach, 1978

LEGEND TO PHOTO MONTAGE

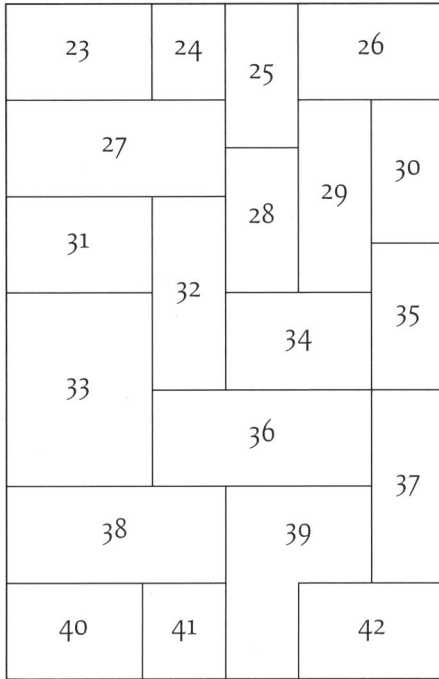

23	24	25	26
27		28	29	30
31	32			
33		34	35
		36	37
38		39	
40	41	42	

23 The author with Ian Fleming (r), Jamaica, 1964

24 Ted De Wit, Holland

25 A mother and child, Angola

26 Aftermath of the author's interview with Bajan lawyers, 1963

27 Hilda and Munroe with sons (clockwise) Ian, David, Rob, 1967

28 Donald Jack, author, playwright, filmwriter

29 The "Nellie" for "Best Writer, Dramatic mode, Radio," 1974

30 John Munro, Diefenbaker historian, 1974

31 Cameron Graham, Executive Producer; Paul Peguenat, cameraman (r), Jamaica, 1964

32 Goddess of Mercy, ivory

33 Bob Clark , Executive Producer, China, 1981

34 John Foster, cameraman; Douglas Bradley, soundman, 1963

35 Rev. Anson Moorhouse, Executive Producer, Berkeley Studio, United Church of Canada

36 Hilda and Munroe with family (l to r) David, Rob, Ian, Janet (Chapman), 1978

37 Courtship, 1950

38 Indonesian women

39 The Taj Mahal

40 Corn-pounders, Angola

41 Buddhist Butcher God, enamel on wood

42 Munroe and Hilda, 1997

Type set in Cartier and printed on Rolland Opaque Vellum, Natural

PRESS

ARCHIVES
of
CANADIAN ARTS
CULTURE & HERITAGE
www.penumbrapress.com